THE EX-FACTOR

THE EX-FACTOR

THE COMPLETE
DO-IT-YOURSELF
POST-DIVORCE
HANDBOOK

Bernard Clair and Anthony Daniele

DONALD I. FINE, INC.   NEW YORK

Library of Congress Catalogue Card Number: 86-80056
ISBN: 0-917657-71-3
Manufactured in the United States of America
10 9 8 7 6 5 4 3 2

This book is printed on acid free paper. The paper in this book meets the
guidelines for permanence and durability of the Committee on
Production Guidelines for Book Longevity of the Council on Library
Resources.

ACKNOWLEDGMENTS

Writing a book of this scope while simultaneously carrying on an active law practice is no easy task. In fact, it would have been virtually impossible were it not for the support, enthusiasm and tireless efforts of our staff, a few of whom must be mentioned by name: Gail Mendelson, Venessia Davidson and Cathy Hartmann.

Special appreciation is due to Nancy Deming, Esq., for some last minute but valuable input, and we cannot forget to specifically thank our talented literary, editorial and publishing team of Richard Pine, Deborah Wilburn and Donald Fine.

To our wives, Jeanne Clair and Barbara Daniele, we offer our keen appreciation not only for their patience and endurance, but for their insightful suggestions as well.

Finally, we must thank those clients, past and present, whose experiences form the backbone of this book. Of course, their identities must remain confidential, but without them we could not have provided the numerous real-life examples that illustrate the legal principles that apply to post-divorce situations.

CONTENTS

We have tried in this book to cover every important post-divorce problem and give the reader essential advice on how to deal with it. Naturally we do not expect that our advice will apply to every case or individual since the practice of law has always been more art than science. Nevertheless, we believe that the principles described in this book will provide ample guidance to intelligently face and ultimately solve most legal issues that arise after the marital breakup.

Throughout this book we give numerous examples of actual situations to illustrate our points. Although names are used, they are made up, and any resemblance to real persons is unintentional and purely coincidental. As attorneys, we are obligated to safeguard our clients' confidences and identities, as well as those of other litigants, but this does not mean that we cannot use the underlying facts in our examples, which we have done from time to time. There is one exception. Whenever we discuss a reported, or published, court decision, we are free to use real names, so we have.

INTRODUCTION

WE COULD START with statistics and tell you that almost half of those entitled to spousal maintenance or child support do not receive full payment as required by the divorce judgment or support order. Indeed, a whopping 24 percent receive no payment at all. That translates to a full 1 million women in 1983 who were forced to foot the bill for child rearing entirely alone, receiving not one penny from their ex-husbands.

Or we could start with a discussion of the psychological pain experienced by fathers who are denied proper visitation with their children after the divorce. Is there any worse torment than being shut out of your children's lives? Particularly when you are one of those fathers who represent the *other* 50 percent who have continued to meet their financial obligations?

But cold statistics and a rehash of emotional woes do not provide any real solace or practical assistance. And this is why we have written this book. We state at the outset that we have a distinct point of view: we do not believe that people must remain helpless victims, totally powerless to enforce their hard-earned legal rights. As practicing attorneys in the field of matrimonial and family law, we have seen far too many cases where the divorce represents only the first chapter in a continuing epic of broken promises and unrealized expectations.

If you have a right to receive weekly maintenance and child support, then you are entitled to expect it. Not weeks or months late. Not in partial amounts. And not when your "ex" whimsically decides to pay it. This book will show you how to enforce or adjust your rightful money awards.

If you are a father who has earned the right to visit your child on a "broad and liberal" basis, then you too are entitled to expect more than snatched hours doled out as your former spouse sees fit. Weekend visitation awarded by the court means just that. Not a few hours every other Sunday morning so that your daughter's mother can sleep late. And not a Saturday cooped up in your ex's apartment as she finds excuse after excuse to "supervise" those precious times with your child.

This book speaks to all of you who remain locked into inaction and helplessness because of lack of knowledge, fear of lawyers or the legal system, anxiety over the anticipated expense, or even because of inexplicable, irrational, but quite common, embarrassment about the problem. Many of you may feel worn down. The divorce took over one year to finalize and you just don't have the strength to start all over again because of two missed child support payments. Maybe your problem will just go away by itself. Maybe the check really *is* in the mail.

We understand your plight, and we want to help. In fact, if you have picked up this book and read this far, you are already way ahead of the game, simply because you have demonstrated the desire to take control over a situation that seems pretty hopeless. We intend to disperse those self-defeating feelings and provide you with the necessary information and wherewithal to enforce your rights. There are simple procedures that can insure compliance with child support orders. There are ways to obtain more quality time with your child. The time is now. Even Congress has lost patience with post-divorce shenanigans. So have the state courts. And judges have become stricter when it comes to enforcing prior court awards. Jail is no longer a dirty word.

This book is divided into two parts. The first chapters deal with issues affecting your money. The second part addresses the problems wrought by child-related issues. You or someone close to you needs this book if the answer is "yes" to any of the following questions:

- Are your child support and alimony (or maintenance, as it is now called in most states) payments chronically late?
- Did the original judicial decree fail to anticipate your present need for financial help to send your child to college?
- Has your "ex" missed three or more payments during the last year, or unilaterally reduced the original court-ordered amounts?
- Do you need an increase (or decrease) in the original award on account of unforeseen expenses or unexpected reversals?
- Is there a future obligation which you believe will be ignored?
- On the other side of the coin, is there a future obligation which, through no fault of your own, you cannot perform?
- Are you or your child entitled to third-party payments, such as private school tuition or medical coverage, which have not been forthcoming?
- Are your visitation rights being thwarted or do they need to be enlarged or otherwise modified?
- Are you a grandparent who has been prevented from maintaining meaningful contact with your grandchildren since the divorce?
- Is your "ex" refusing to comply with her agreement to consult you about major child-rearing decisions, such as education, religion or health?
- Are you thinking about moving out of state with the children against their father's wishes or in direct contravention of the divorce judgment?
- Are you contemplating a request that the original custody arrangement be changed or modified?
- Are you living through the hell of a child snatching or considering such extreme action yourself?

Post-divorce problems are not insurmountable. While it is true that many lawyers are generally reluctant to involve themselves with enforcement-related problems, there are many practical steps that may be taken without an attorney, steps that will successfully enforce, reduce or modify your original award or legal obligations.

We will show you how to take these steps and will guide you through all of the procedures that have been recently created to combat the very problems that you are currently facing. We will discuss real cases, with real people (names changed, of course), in order to illustrate the advice that we give. You will learn that you are not alone, that your problem is not unique. But most importantly, you will learn how to help yourself.

—Bernard Clair
Anthony Daniele
New York, New York
April 1986

YOUR MONEY

PART 1

YOUR MONEY

CHAPTER ONE

Where's My Check?

LET'S START WITH the usual situation.

John and Mary were married for 9 years. Within two months of their tenth anniversary, they both became acquainted with the member of our species called the divorce lawyer. Actually, this particular couple obtained their divorce a lot easier than most.

On her part, Mary was horrified at the thought of having the case go all the way to trial. She heard that approximately 90 percent of divorce controversies are settled out of court, and she wanted to be sure that she was included within that majority. Mary was also motivated by a keen desire to maintain cordial relations with her husband throughout the dissolution process. She understood that John would not lose his status as father to their 5-year-old daughter, Amy, just because he was divorcing his wife. Mary wanted to protect the parent–child relationship, and she knew that a bitterly fought divorce trial would increase the chances of a tragic unraveling of the ties between father and daughter.

Mary's lawyer advised her that she was entitled to receive child support from John. The attorney also figured that a judge would probably allow her to receive spousal maintenance, as well, for approximately 3 years— the time it was estimated that it would take for Mary to reenter the job market in a meaningful fashion. She was told to prepare a budget of present and future expenses that she and their daughter could expect to incur. Mary remembers facetiously telling her lawyer that she didn't have a crystal ball at home, but she would do her best.

Meanwhile, John's lawyer told him that if he expected a negotiated settlement, he would have to provide the other side with full financial disclosure. All past tax returns, bank accounts and other data would have to be forwarded. John was advised that a court would tell him to turn over this information anyway, so he might as well do it voluntarily in order to show his good faith and maximize the possibilities of reaching an out-of-court settlement. John did as he was told; he had no desire to play craps with a judge either. He had heard all kinds of horror stories at the office about husbands and fathers who had been left seemingly penniless by unfeeling and insensitive judges. And he, too, wanted to be fair. He knew that it would take a while for Mary to become economically self-sufficient, and he was aware that his daughter would need his financial help. So he cooperated during the discovery phases of the case and took pains to maintain open communication with his wife and child.

The time eventually came when the parties and their lawyers began serious settlement discussions. Both sides were armed with as much financial data as possible, and using their best efforts to estimate their own expenses and future needs, John and Mary reached an agreement on the issues of spousal maintenance and child support.

John agreed to pay $120 per week for child support until Amy was of age. Mary would also be entitled to $150 per week as spousal maintenance for 3 years after the divorce became final. In addition, it was agreed that John would provide a blanket medical insurance package for the benefit of his daughter and would share any unreimbursed medical expenses as they might arise. Mary had been particularly pleased by her husband's agreement to pay for the child's dental expenses as well.

Times change. Don't we know it.

For the first 11 months after the divorce, the support was dutifully paid. Actually, if Mary were totally honest about it, she would report that by the fifth month after the divorce John's weekly payments were increasingly late in coming. While the agreement and court order called for maintenance and child support to be received on the first Monday of each week, more often than not, Mary would get the checks on Wednesday or Thursday. In fact, there were two times when John missed an entire payment. Mary never made a fuss about it, hoping that it was a fluke and nothing to worry about. But by the eleventh month it was pretty obvious that John did not intend to continue to honor his written agreement and the court judgment.

At this point, we are not concerned with John's reasons for violating the agreement. Maybe he has a good excuse; maybe he doesn't. But families are not fed on excuses or good intentions. At least that's what Mary keeps telling herself when she picks up the telephone to call her ex. No luck, and for the next 7 days all she succeeds in doing is speaking to John's answering machine.

About ready to take off from work and pay John a personal visit, Mary decides to telephone one more time—only to discover that the line has been disconnected. Eventually she finds that John has relocated to another county about 220 miles away. Actually it didn't take much detective work; John called about three and a half weeks later to speak with Amy. Of course Mary answered the phone, and after a heated exchange she was able to get her former husband to begrudgingly disclose his new address.

"Yes, I'm working, but I don't think it's a good idea for me to give you my number at the office," reports John through the static of 220 miles of telephone wire. "I've been through a rough time, but as soon as I recoup some of my moving expenses, I'll try to get myself square with you girls again."

All Mary can think about are the weeks she spent with calculator in hand, trying to work out a fair and reasonable budget she believed John could afford to maintain. Indeed, it took only three months after the divorce to see that she had underestimated Amy's needs. How could she have been so naive to have thought that food prices and rent would remain relatively stable? Her anger and frustration rising, she ends her conversation with John and contemplates her next move.

But where does she begin? Who does she turn to? With $1,500 in the bank, a lawyer seems out of the question. Mary's job just about covers her most basic expenses; John's financial support was the difference between survival and decent living.

With any number of variations on this theme, the basic elements of this story illustrate the most common problems that must be resolved. When a former spouse takes it upon himself to openly violate a court order, you are in the area of post-divorce enforcement. This neutral-sounding term for the hell that results from noncompliance of support orders is what this part of the book is all about. The key here is enforcement. How do you get him to pay? And how fast? As one advertisement says: "How do you spell r-e-l-i-e-f?"

WHERE DOES IT BEGIN?

You are not alone. With a national estimate of somewhere between 4 and 5 billion dollars in unpaid support monies to be collected, you can be sure that your problem is not unique. For the most part, support enforcement problems, particularly when children are at stake, are handled through local family and domestic courts, each state having its own system.

Virtually every state, however, has a particular division *within* its court system that deals exclusively with divorce and post-divorce issues such as support and custody. For example, in California, the Superior Court has a special Family Division. Some states, like New York and Delaware, have specialized courts called Family Courts. In Virginia the custody and support problems are handled by the Domestic Relations Court; in Utah it is called the Juvenile Court. Whether the place is called the Family Division of Superior Court or even the Probate Court's Division of Child Welfare, as in some counties in South Carolina, the point to be made is that the court system remains accessible to your particular problem. In fact, the problem has grown to such dimensions that most states have an entire court system devoted to it.

If you turn to the appendix at the back of this book, you will find a state-by-state listing of those courts or divisions within the court system that are devoted to post-divorce problems, including support, custody, visitation and the like. Because this chapter is devoted to money problems, we will focus our discussion on economic issues.

In addition to the underlying court system, each state has local and statewide support enforcement agencies to assist you with *child* support collection. Moreover, if your original divorce judgment or support order permits you to receive both child support *and* spousal maintenance, then these agencies will also offer much needed assistance. As will be discussed in the next chapter, support agencies offer a way to obtain help without the necessity of even going into court. Some of these agencies have names like Division of Child Support Activities (Alabama), Office of Child Support Enforcement (Florida), or Child Support Program Management Branch (Sacramento, California). In our appendix we have provided you with a state-by-state listing of the names, addresses and telephone numbers of the child support enforcement service agencies located in your jurisdiction. If you have trouble getting through to your local agency, you should try to contact the *regional* office in charge of overseeing the local agency office. Consequently, our appendix also contains a listing of these regional offices, and although they deal primarily with supervising the State efforts, these Federal offices will offer much needed information to insure that you are on the right track.

With post-divorce enforcement problems looming ever larger in this country, it is no coincidence that the Federal Child Support Enforcement program was reformed by 1984 legislation called the Child Support Enforcement Amendments. Basically, the new law requires all states to tighten up their support collection methods and abilities. This applies to agencies as well as Family Court enforcement procedures. It is estimated that by the end of 1986 every state will have a system of support collection agencies in place, just waiting to help dependent spouses receive the money to which they and their children are entitled. At the same time, Family Courts throughout the country will offer a much wider and more effective range of enforcement devices to collect support arrears. In fact, most already do.

In short, and as will be seen in later chapters, when it comes to child support, states are saying "We don't mess around." For example, the Child Support Enforcement Amendments Act of 1984 permits both the Internal Revenue Service and the child support agencies mentioned in our appendix to literally intercept tax refunds on their way to fathers (or mothers) who owe the other person court-ordered child support payments. The Act also requires states to impose mandatory wage withholding if violation of a court order continues for more than one month.

We will discuss the triggering mechanisms of specific enforcement devices in subsequent chapters, but for now it is important to emphasize that these mechanisms are in place in virtually every state, just waiting for the knowledgeable person to take advantage of them. Let's now take a brief look at the enforcement devices which are available.

THE ENFORCEMENT ARSENAL

Wage Deduction

One of the most heartening legal trends is the ease with which *wage deduction orders* may be obtained. A wage deduction order goes by many names. Some states call it "salary garnishment," while others call it "payroll or salary deduction." Whatever name it goes by, a wage deduction order requires an employer to make the support payments directly to the wife or mother, or to a local support collection unit. Federal legislation requires that states permit a wage deduction order to be put into effect when the one who is supposed to pay doesn't do so for more than 30 days or misses 3 consecutive payments.

Thomas discovered a few months ago just how neat and effective this enforcement tool is. Having been divorced for 8 years and remarried with another child from the second marriage, Thomas believed a second home in the country was more important than his first wife. The original court order obligated him to pay her support for 8 years. "I'm just not going to pay her for the eighth year," he coolly announced to a co-worker. "No way will she be able to take me to court on her salary. And what judge in his right mind is going to penalize a man for having paid all these years? Hell, I read that most guys don't even bother paying after year one. I'm in the clear."

Wrong, Thomas. His former wife was awarded a wage deduction order which was forwarded directly by the clerk of the court to Thomas's supervisor. The order stated that from that point forward, Thomas's weekly paycheck was to be reduced by the amount of his court-ordered monetary obligation. The employer was given the address of Thomas's ex-wife and was directed to cut a separate check and mail it directly to her each week. Additionally, his employer was advised to make additional deductions so those two months of arrears were repaid in full over the remaining ten months of the wage deduction order's life.

As you will learn later, most states apply a rather wide definition to the word "employer." You can now "garnish" money that comes not only from your ex's salary, but from his worker's compensation checks, disability benefits, unemployment insurance benefits and federal social security income. In a recent case, we represented a mother of two children who was seeking enforcement of a child support order from their father who had "suddenly" announced his total disability and loss of employment. Our client's ex was getting his money from somewhere, and it was a simple matter to ascertain that his employer had maintained a nice disability package for him. When these monies began to be paid on a monthly basis, an immediate wage deduction order was forwarded, resulting in child support payments being mailed directly to our client from the insurance company.

We deal with the nuts and bolts of how to obtain a wage deduction order to enforce spousal maintenance orders in Chapter 5. For the most part, the procedure varies little from state to state. However, as we caution you throughout this book, it is always best to first check with the Family Division of your County court or the regional or local office of the Child Support Enforcement Agency to discover any local procedural quirks. Happily, a lawyer is not even needed most times. Court clerks and personnel from the various enforcement agencies are trained to assist you in obtaining the wage deduction without hiring an attorney.

Tax Refund Intercept

A recently created enforcement device is the ability of a dependent spouse to intercept her ex's federal or state tax refund check. In some cases you may be entitled to such interception on a yearly basis without reapplying. In other situations the tax intercept method is a one shot deal, a means of getting you the arrears that may be owed. The beauty of this device is that it disregards state boundaries. If you live in Ohio and your former husband lives in Rhode Island, the taxing authorities in his home state will be put on notice of the tax intercept and you will be entitled to receive his refund. As will be discussed in the next chapter, the procedure used to get federal refund checks is even easier.

The Attachment

So you say he's now got a nice home, while you still live in the original marital two-bedroom apartment. Perhaps he owns a car or a piece of undeveloped real estate. Didn't your ex always fancy himself the brilliant investor? The idea behind the attachment enforcement device is to iden-tify property and then tie it up with legal strings. Sometimes this method is called a *property lien*.

Assuming your ex owes you back child support or maintenance, you may be able to prevent him from selling or transferring the property until the support debt is paid. As we will explain in Chapter 5, the levy does not in itself result in the immediate sale of the property so that you can collect the money. While getting the attachment is no big deal, the selling process which comes later is filled with procedural complexities and bureaucratic quagmires. However, if you persevere, a sale will result and you will get the money as a credit against the support arrears.

On a more practical and important note, however, the placement of an attachment on his property is often enough to make him realize his mis-taken ways. What good is having property if you can't sell it? What buyer in his right mind will purchase your ex's home when the most basic title search identifies the existence of a support dispute? Most individuals faced with a property attachment will do their utmost to have it removed. The good news is that the only way to release the property is to pay the underlying debt.

Restraining Orders

Restraining orders are very similar to the attachment device. These no-tices are keyed specifically into his bank accounts. Cars, real estate and other properties are one thing. A bank account is another, and the law recognizes that should you be fortunate enough to locate one, you should have access to it when it comes to the preservation of you and your family.

Here's an interesting case:

Janet was owed approximately $2,500 in support payments. She got a restraining order, and it was delivered to a local branch of the bank in which she believed her former husband maintained a bank account. Her homework was impeccable—and the results even better than she could imagine. Sure enough, her former husband had a total of approximately $7,000 in his checking and savings.

As is the usual custom, the bank froze $5,000, double the amount due. Although Janet did get her $2,500, that's not the end of her story. The bank restrained his accounts, and in accordance with most states' laws, it also put a restraint on a little-used safe deposit box which had also been leased in his name.

As it turns out, Janet's ex had recently done a shady deal which netted him $15,000 in cash. And we all know what "smart" businessmen do with unreported cash income. Well, Mr. Support Violator was so afraid that the restraining order would reveal the existence of these funds to the IRS that he simply admitted the whole thing to her and agreed to split his earnings in half. After scooping up the $2,500 in arrears, Janet gladly accepted. Of course, because the IRS might be reading this book, we advise with tongue firmly in cheek that Janet report *her* half on that year's tax returns.

The Money Judgment

Child support, maintenance—whatever he owes, it is still money. And when someone does not pay money he has agreed to pay or, for that matter, the court has ordered him to pay, the other person may sue for the amount in question.

The law treats child support or maintenance arrears just as if they were any other debt. If you can prove the amount owed, and the person who was supposed to pay has no defense, you will win. That is, you get a document that says you are entitled to receive the amount of money owed. Usually, you also get interest on the amount and other disbursements, such as the fee involved in filing the judgment in the county where you won it.

Once you have the judgment, it is as enforceable as any money judgment, but most importantly, it can be triggered and put into effect many years after its filing. For example, in New York State a person can enforce a money judgment up to 20 years after first obtaining it. We will talk later about how money judgments are enforced, but the point to be made here is that every state recognizes that it may take many years to get the money back if there are no assets or funds available when it's first ordered. Once a money judgment is filed, it remains a part of the court records for a long time. Many a client with enough patience has been able to enforce a money judgment years after it was first obtained, waiting in the wings until their ex's fortunes have changed for the better. Then they act, the judgment as effective as if it were just ordered yesterday.

Contempt/Civil Arrest

When all else fails, or when the other enforcement devices are inappropriate to your situation, the bottom line remains punishment. Of course, before anyone is going to lock your former spouse up for failing to pay his child support or maintenance, it will have to be amply demonstrated that you have made all other efforts to get your just due.

But every state still has a civil arrest statute on its books. In order to put him away, a court must first find him in contempt. This simple phrase includes a lot. When a person fails to obey a court order, he is in technical contempt. Our society does not encourage people to flout an order of the court. In Chapter 5 we will explain how the procedure may be utilized in appropriate circumstances.

Usually, civil arrest will only occur when a contempt order has also been violated. When a person is judged in contempt for failure to obey a support order, the judge generally permits the individual to "purge" himself from such status. In most instances, the payment of the amount owed, together with a lot of other economic penalties such as lawyers' fees and the like, will dissipate the threat of jail. Generally, the contempt order will allow the person a set time period—the average is 60 days—to pay up, or he will face a similar period in the slammer. It is amazing how many people will find the economic means to satisfy a support order when the heavy steel bars of a jail cell loom on the horizon.

Although we emphasize that arrest remains an option of last resort, some recent studies have shown that, when combined with an efficient overall collection system, arrest is a useful technique to gain compliance of post-divorce support orders. The arrest method is used with excellent results in the state of Michigan, where judges routinely order jail sentences each year for thousands of parents who repeatedly violate post-divorce orders.

The awakening interest in arrest as an effective deterrent of nonpayment has resulted in "blitz days" in some other states. For instance, a couple of summers ago in Prince George's County, Maryland, deputy sheriffs knocked on hundreds of doors and arrested 86 people who had failed to comply with court-ordered child support awards. And in a county in California, more than 200 delinquent child support payers were arrested in one month.

* * *

Our goal in this first chapter has been to introduce you to the assortment of enforcement devices that exist for one purpose: to offer you a means of getting what is rightfully yours. As we go on, we will offer a more in-depth discussion, showing you the do's and don'ts of support collection. But for now, we expect you to be breathing a bit easier. After all, you have just learned that you have first-strike capability. And if you must resort to warfare, it's good to know that you have an effective arsenal behind you. All *is* fair in love, war and support enforcement!

CHAPTER TWO

Bypassing Court

TO TAKE ADVANTAGE of two of the most effective enforcement devices, you don't even have to go to court. We are referring to the support collection weapons known as a wage deduction order and the tax refund intercept. Think about that for a moment. No judges. No trial. Just you and your local support collection agency. And this chapter tells you just what to do.

First, you must know some of the ground rules. *Most importantly, you can only bypass court if the money that is owed you is either child support or child support combined with a maintenance award.* If you are in a situation where your original judgment or support order relates only to spousal maintenance (alimony), then you will not be able to utilize the services of your state child-support agencies. Of course, you can still get enforcement of your support order by starting a proceeding in Family Court, which we describe in Chapter 3.

We recognize that for those of you with maintenance awards, enforcement remains of paramount importance. You may rightly question why the agencies have distinguished between your maintenance and your neighbor's child support payments. Actually, there is no clear-cut or simple answer. We can only point to the traditional concern that states have afforded to children. They truly are a national resource, and on a priority system, they come first when it comes to post-divorce collection. Also there is the purely practical matter of the capacity of the state agencies to handle the additional cases that would be represented by individuals seeking only to enforce their maintenance orders. As it is, the existence of your state agency is the result of fairly recent legislative action. The idea is not to supplant the Family Court system; rather the agencies we're discussing in this chapter have been created to offer a much needed boost. And when you seek to enforce child support or combined orders of child support/maintenance, the agency is a potent weapon.

In order to really take advantage of the child support agency located nearest to you, it helps to understand the genesis of the entire system. It all started around 1975 when Congress passed the Child Support Enforcement Act. This Act created the mechanism—not to mention some of the money—for states to administer child-support agencies. Under the umbrella of the Department of Health and Human Services, Congress was empowered to:

- establish standards for state programs for locating absent parents, establishing paternity and obtaining child support and maintenance;
- provide guidance and create minimum organizational and staffing require-

25

ments for the state agencies that would be carrying out the enforcement programs;
- assist the states in establishing adequate reporting procedures and document maintenance;
- provide technical assistance to the states in order to help them establish "effective systems for collecting child and spousal support and establishing paternity";
- in general, oversee and encourage a national cooperative effort to increase the effectiveness of a spouse's ability to enforce support orders.

We discussed in Chapter 1 how various states call the agencies by different names, but for the most part their origins remain rooted in the 1975 legislative action. Most experts concede, however, that until fairly recently there were some real problems in the initial stages.

To begin with, the services of most of these support collection offices were limited to individuals who were receiving public assistance. Thus, if you were not a welfare recipient, you could not avail yourself of the agencies. In every instance, you were forced to take your claim to Family Court or a similar division.

There were also problems with getting states to adopt the federal guidelines that were supposed to make it easier to collect child support. In 1975, states were more interested in staying one decimal point behind the inflation rate. An entire agency system, even with the assistance of the federal government, seemed less significant than keeping the cities out of bankruptcy. But this book is about change, and public perception goes through a metamorphosis just as surely as divorced families do.

By 1983, more and more politicians were feeling the nation's pulse, and the signal was coming through loud and clear. It could not be denied any longer: we were all involved in a national disgrace. When approximately 50 percent of the mothers entitled to child support are receiving less than the amount ordered by the court, and when there remains billions of dollars in child support yet to be collected, you cannot shut your eyes to the problem any longer. To their credit, many politicians swung into action. They began to pressure their various states to increase the effectiveness of the support agency programs that had been in existence for some time but were largely forgotten.

The distinction between dependent mothers who receive public assistance and those who do not was also increasingly called into question. Why shouldn't the support collection program be expanded to include non-welfare recipients? Doesn't the scourge of uncollected child support cut across economic lines? And at bottom line, don't children have the same right to expect financial assistance whether they are economically disadvantaged or from a middle class home? The answers to these questions became more and more obvious. And from 1983 forward, a heartening emphasis began to be placed upon the collection of child support, regardless of economic status. Along with this emphasis came a renewed nationwide commitment to strengthen the state agency system and to make it not only more accessible but more effective as well.

As noted in our first chapter, Congress passed an all-encompassing amendment to the original legislation in 1984. This amendment required states to tighten up their enforcement procedures. Wage deduction orders and the tax intercept method of collecting support arrears were made mandatory in appropriate situations. The states were directed to open the collection units to *all* dependent spouses who were behind the eight ball because of non-receipt of child support or child support/ maintenance. No distinction was to be made between people receiving public assistance and those who were not. A greater budget was provided, and with a general feeling that recalcitrant fathers had been getting away with violating court orders long enough, states began to wake up to their responsibilities in a remarkable display of public concern. As one federal support collection agency director recently noted, "The 1984 amendment represents one of the largest and most serious joint efforts between the executive branch of our government and the judiciary ever seen."

Remember, you are dealing with a joint effort between national and state governments. This is in and of itself unique enough to warrant not only a portion of a chapter, but an entire book! But enough of legislative history, let's get down to basics. What is the wage deduction order and how can you put it to use?

THE WAGE DEDUCTION ORDER

The first weapon in the agency's arsenal is the wage deduction order. Remember, you can still obtain a wage deduction order from Family Court, for example, in those situations where you are dealing only with alimony or when you have decided to utilize the court system as opposed to the statewide collection agency. We assume, however, that like most people, you do not relish the thought of going into court if you can avoid it. And the ever-increasingly powerful child support collection agencies provide a critical and effective secondary approach.

The Wage Deduction Order is a legal document that can be issued by child-support collection agencies for the purpose of garnishing your ex's salary if child support payments are in arrears. It is called by many names, including *wage execution, execution of income* or *employer deduction notice,* to name a few. In this book, we consistently refer to it as a *wage deduction order,* the name most commonly used. Your ex is the first person to receive a copy of the order. He then has a certain amount of time—usually between 2 and 3 weeks—to wake up and respond. He either begins paying or notifies the agency that there has been an error, giving the specific reasons for his contention that a mistake has been made. If he ignores the order, his employer receives an official notice that, commencing immediately, each paycheck must be reduced by the amount of court-ordered support. Sometimes the employer is given a grace period to comply, depending on the frequency of paychecks.

The order contains certain standard information, including the court in which the support order in question was originally obtained, the amount so ordered, the child-support arrears presently due and the nature of the particular default. The wage deduction order also contains your name and address. How else can you be paid? In some situations, the employer may be directed to pay the deducted child support into court or directly to the agency. This is becoming the preferred procedure.

LOCATING AN EX-SPOUSE AND OTHER SERVICES PROVIDED

Before getting down to the nitty gritty of processing your claim, let us review briefly the services that are provided by state child support collection agencies. One important area of assistance is helping to find an absent parent. Obviously, before any enforcement device works, you must have some knowledge of the whereabouts of the person who is obligated to pay. We will discuss the parent locator services in Chapter 6.

The agencies also assist in establishing fatherhood, or *paternity* as it is legally termed. Paternity proceedings are beyond the scope of this book, although we know of several instances where the couple started dating again after the divorce—and in one of these situations the woman did become pregnant—but obvious space limitations require us to stay within the mainstream of post-divorce issues.

The support agencies are also involved in establishing support orders in the first instance. These situations occur when the parties are separated but still married and the economically stronger partner stops supporting his family. Not everyone presses the divorce trigger at that point; many go into Family Court to obtain the necessary support order which is effective even though the parties remain married. Again, our book is devoted to post-divorce issues; we assume that you already have a final support order in place. But it is nice to know that the state collection agencies will be there at the dependent spouse's side when an initial support award is needed.

The important aspect of support collection agencies—at least for the purposes of this book—remains just that: *enforcement.* This aspect of the agency system seeks to insure that support orders, once obtained, are not violated and that, if they are, you get a fair opportunity to collect that which is due. Initially an agency may try to get your ex to meet his court-ordered obligation on a voluntary basis. They may send out a registered letter or mailgram threatening to impose harsher enforcement should payment not be forthcoming. But assuming your ex remains hopelessly recalcitrant, and keeping in mind that the order in question revolves around child support, a state enforcement office has a lot of clout.

WHERE TO GO

First you must locate the nearest office of child support enforcement in your state. Most states have locations in each county, but your state may have a different setup. In the appendix, we have provided you with a listing of the various regional offices; they will be able to point you in the right direction. For example, Region II includes the states of New York and New Jersey, as well as the territories of Puerto Rico and the Virgin

Islands. Region VI encompasses the states of Arkansas, Louisiana, New Mexico, Oklahoma and Texas. By telephoning the regional office, an individual living in Cayuga, New York can learn that a state child support collection office is located just across the way in Auburn. The appendix also includes a state-by-state listing of the State Child Support Enforcement Offices, and they too will be able to identify the nearest agency in your county. This has become a far-reaching program; there is even a child support enforcement unit in Guam!

Once you have determined where to go, we suggest that you take a moment to telephone a few days before your intended visit. We have found that an initial contact, somebody whose name you can use when you get there, is well worth the telephone call, even though you may initially experience the frustration of endless busy signals or being put on hold for interminable periods of time. Eventually you will get through to somebody who is knowledgeable; at the very least, you will be given a room number and other pertinent information to ease the process somewhat.

We also recommend that you review your original court order before you visit the agency. The following case illustrates the importance of this:

Jennifer's daughter was 17 and had just started her freshman year at a fine out-of-state university. Her former husband had always been up-to-date in his child support payments, so it greatly surprised Jennifer when she did not receive either the October or November payment.

Cursing under her breath, she headed straight for her child support enforcement office. She told the caseworker that the bum had suddenly stopped paying "just when our daughter needs it the most. How can I expect her to remain in college without my ex's continued contributions?"

The caseworker calmly asked for a copy of the divorce decree that Jennifer had obtained about 9 years before. As in many situations, the divorce judgment made specific reference to a prior stipulation of agreement that had been specifically incorporated into the decree.

"May I see a copy of the stipulation to which your judgment refers?" asked the caseworker. With a private smile, Jennifer turned a copy of the document over. She was always prepared and knew how to handle these "bureaucrat types." But what the hell was taking her so long? Why didn't the caseworker just get on with it? "I can't wait to see his face when his wages are garnished," thought Jennifer.

"Madam, you say that your former husband has missed two months in a row?"

"Exactly. The worthless bastard."

"Have you spoken to your daughter about the situation?" the caseworker asked.

"No. Why should I? We have never spoken about money matters. As it is, my daughter has enough pressure having just entered her freshman year in college. What kind of question is that? I'm the mother, and I have always received the child support."

"Well, I see from reading the stipulation that your former husband was supposed to begin paying his child support directly to your daughter once she entered college. And the court order specifically incorporated that understanding. Why don't you come back when you have a little more specific information," the caseworker suggested, already calling off the next name on her two page list.

Of course, you have already guessed the ending. Jennifer telephoned her daughter at college and asked her whether she had received her father's "spending allowance." As it turned out, not only had she received the "missing" child support, but Jennifer's ex had given their daughter an additional $500 to help her get settled in her new environment.

When Can I Use the Wage Deduction Order?

Under the Child Support Enforcement Amendment of 1984, all states *must* impose automatic mandatory wage withholding whenever the past due amount equals one month's support. Thus, even in situations where a person makes partial payments, as soon as the missing amounts add up to a month's support, a wage deduction can be made. Alternatively, the wage deduction order may be imposed when the person owing the support misses three payments in a row.

In the days when wage deduction orders could only be issued by a court, a person was forced to prove his or her entitlement to a wage deduction order by way of formal proceeding. As lawyers, we would describe the old procedure as having placed the burden of proof upon the one seeking collection. Now, the situation is largely reversed. There is a legal presumption that you are entitled to have a wage deduction order imposed on your former spouse when he misses either three payments in a row or one month's worth of child support, whichever comes first. In essence, the agencies have been empowered to "shoot first and ask questions later." The idea is to strike hard and fast; any mistakes or overzealousness in collection can be remedied at a later time.

How Do I Apply for A Wage Deduction Order?

The support collection agency will require you to complete a standardized form, the first of several. This is known as the Application for Child Support Services and contains the basic information that will be required to start the ball rolling. A copy of this application follows so that you can familiarize yourself with it before you visit the agency. When you sign the document, you will be *affirming* the truth of the information contained in the application, so be sure that the data is accurate and truthful.

Also be prepared to provide the following information or documentation on subsequent forms:

- Full name, home address and telephone number of former spouse, if available
- His social security number
- Name and address of employer and, if possible, the actual name of his immediate superior or other supervising contact
- The court order or divorce judgment and any written stipulation or agreement that affects your right to receive child support or child support/maintenance

DSS-2521 (REV. 7/82)

APPLICATION FOR
CHILD SUPPORT SERVICES

NEW YORK STATE   DEPARTMENT OF SOCIAL SERVICES

FOR AGENCY USE ONLY		
NAME OF REFERRING OFFICIAL		TELEPHONE NO.
UNIT	DATE OF REFERRAL	APPLICATION TYPE ☐ Original ☐ Supplemental

A — Applicant/Petitioner

NAME (Last, First, M.I.)	RELATIONSHIP TO CHILDREN	SOC. SEC. NO.	DATE OF BIRTH

ADDRESS - Legal Residence (Street, City, State, Zip)

TELEPHONE NUMBER (Incl. Area Code) (N/P = No Phone) — HOME / BUSINESS

SUPPORT COLLECTION UNIT APPLICATION ONLY ▷ I have applied for or am in receipt of ☐ HR ☐ ADC — I have not applied for nor am I in receipt of HR/ADC

B — Absent Parent/Respondent

NAME (Last, First, M.I.)	RELATIONSHIP TO APPLICANT	SOC. SEC. NO.	DATE OF BIRTH

ADDRESS - Legal Residence (Street, City, State, Zip) Current or Last Known

TELEPHONE NUMBER (Incl. Area Code) (N/P = No Phone) — HOME / BUSINESS

EMPLOYER'S NAME/ADDRESS (Current or Last Known)

PLACE OF BIRTH	MOTHER'S MAIDEN NAME	FATHER'S FULL NAME	DATE OF DESERTION

C — Child, Subject of Application

NAME (Last, First, M.I.)	DATE OF BIRTH	NAME (Last, First, M.I.)	DATE OF BIRTH

D — Services Requested Applicant/Petitioner

☐ FILE SEARCH (Location)
☐ PATERNITY ESTABLISHMENT
☐ SUPPORT ESTABLISHMENT (Includes Medical Support)
☐ SUPPORT COLLECTION (Includes Medical Support)
☐ *FIELD INVESTIGATION (Location)
☐ *LEGAL REPRESENTATION
☐ SUPPORT ENFORCEMENT (Includes Medical Support)
☐ COLLECTION OF CHILD SUPPORT BY IRS

DATE OF COURT ORDER | DOCKET NO.

COURT

* Right to Recovery MUST Be Signed in the presence of a IV-D Unit Staff Member, and Notarized to Be Eligible for Field Investigation or Legal Services.

E — Affirmation

AFFIRMATION - I hereby apply pursuant to Social Services Law § 111-g and 111-h for child support services under Title IV-D of the Social Security Act as amended. I subscribe and affirm under penalty of perjury that this application is made for the sole purpose(s) of obtaining assistance in establishing paternity and/or obtaining child support from an individual who is (or may be) legally responsible for the support of dependent children; and that statements made in this application or accompanying document have been examined by me and to the best of my knowledge and belief are true and correct.

SIGNATURE   X _____   DATE _____

FOR AGENCY USE ONLY						
HR	SSI	MA	CW	COURT ORDERED	FS	GENERAL PUBLIC
APPROVED		APPLICATION REVIEW			DENIED	

REASON FOR REJECTION OF APPLICATION

DSS REPRESENTATIVE   X _____   DATE _____

NOTE TO APPLICANT: On the back of this form, please write additional information which might be helpful in efforts to locate or secure/enforce support from the absent parent.

- All information concerning your former spouse's income. Is he receiving a salary on a weekly or monthly basis? Remember, a wage deduction order applies with equal validity to nonsalaried income such as worker's compensation, disability benefits, unemployment insurance, social security payments and pension or retirement benefits. If your spouse's income falls into any of these categories, be prepared to offer as much specific information as possible.

And don't forget the basics:

- Proof of your own identity
- Proof of your relationship to the child, by way of birth record, income tax forms, and church, synagogue or school records
- Documents concerning any previous efforts to obtain child support, such as prior court petitions or orders

When you arrive at the agency, you will speak with a caseworker. You will be given various applications to complete that incorporate the information that we have just itemized in the checklist above. Once the application is completed·and the information provided to the caseworker is found acceptable, the ball is in their court. The support collection unit will do the rest.

The first thing they do is communicate with your ex. Some agencies prefer an informal contact in the initial stage. If the support arrears have not yet accumulated to monstrous proportions and you are not in truly desperate financial straits, the caseworker may opt to try for voluntary compliance before pressing the formal wage deduction order button. This usually takes the form of a registered letter to your ex. This correspondence, although in most instances a form letter, is processed on official, state agency letterhead and usually reads something like this:

October 16, 1986

Mr. John Downs
123 Gary Street
Anywhere, Wisconsin 08584
            RE: *Child Support Delinquency*

Dear Mr. Downs:

Under this state's Support Enforcement Act of 1985, our agency has the specific authorization to withhold your income if you are behind in your child support payments. This withholding is called a wage deduction order and requires your employer or any other source which provides you income to withhold from your income the amount of support you are under court order to pay, plus an additional amount to pay past-due support.

We have been advised that you have failed to make three full child support payments on the date when they became due, and under such circumstances a wage deduction order is mandated. This wage assignment may be imposed directly from this office; your former spouse is not required to go back to court. We intend to immediately begin processing your former spouse's right to obtain a wage deduction order to insure her receipt of court-ordered support. The purpose of this letter, however, is to afford you the opportunity to voluntarily pay to this office the arrears you owe so as to avoid the imposition of automatic wage deduction.

To this end we shall forebear from any further steps to effectuate formal wage deduction for a period of ten (10) days from the date of this correspondence. We trust that you will see to your legal obligations immediately, and your cooperation in this regard is appreciated.

Sincerely,

David Harris
Director, Child Support
Collection Unit

Please be aware that there will be times when a former spouse will get the letter and—miracle of miracles—actually pay the support due. In this case, a common problem arises when your ex pays the amount directly to you, even though the letter requested the agency's receipt of moneys due. The support collection unit will have no way of knowing if its letter was successful without your taking a moment to call and advise the agency of your good fortune. Otherwise the agency will be likely to continue its efforts on your behalf. Avoid confusion and keep in close touch with your support collection unit.

Conversely, do not be reticent to telephone the agency after the time period has expired without your having received a dime. The agency system, particularly as it relates to wage deduction orders, is relatively new. There remain many kinks to be worked out. It is not uncommon for a caseworker to be so overburdened as to simply forget to follow up on the letter asking for voluntary payment. Even computers make mistakes. Although you can correctly assume that the process to impose the order will automatically occur after no voluntary payments have been received within the time specified, it does not hurt to telephone just to make sure.

Although we advise telephoning the agency directly when you have additional information they may want or when you need an answer to a question, we should tell you that some urban offices require that all communications be either in person or in writing. These offices are so busy that a telephone call is almost useless. In addition, state and federal law restricts the type of information that can be released to an individual without proper identification. An overburdened caseworker will find it difficult, if not impossible, to adequately identify a caller on the telephone. In order to protect all interested parties, certain local agencies will strictly adhere to the communication-by-writing rule.

* * *

Okay, let's say that you are not one of the fortunate few whose ex has seen the light after receiving a letter from the agency. What happens next?

If your former spouse ignores the letter requesting voluntary compliance, he can expect another contact. But this time, he receives the formal wage deduction order. It is important for you to understand that it is your ex who first receives notice of the wage deduction order, not his employer. Under all state laws, the spouse must receive formal warning before the agency forwards the order to the employer. Formal notice simply means that the agency delivers a copy of the actual wage deduction order to him. The order includes a short instruction that upon receipt, your ex has a certain period of time to question the validity of the imposition of a wage deduction order. Has there been a mistake? Is he really current in his payments? Is this just another computer glitch? Is he still working for the targeted employer?

The time usually provided to a former spouse to make a claim that a mistake has been made is rather short. Most states give him about 2 weeks to take some affirmative action. As we said previously, should the agency receive no response, then the final phase of the wage deduction order is put into motion: delivery of the notice directly to the employer for immediate imposition. And woe unto the employer who ignores the order.

It was the year when Robert's printing business was enjoying its first real financial success. He had been at it for a long time, but things were finally looking up. In fact, Robert had just moved his operation to larger quarters; the five new guys he had hired were working out just fine, too. During this expansion, Bill had been promoted to supervisor. He'd been with the business almost from its inception, starting as an apprentice typesetter and gradually working his way up through the ranks. Robert considered him a valued employee and more importantly, a good friend.

About 3 weeks into the new year, Robert received a certified letter from the county support collection agency. It directed him to deduct $75 per week from Bill's paycheck. The notice looked pretty official and made it clear that the money to be deducted was the amount Bill was supposed to be paying as child support to his ex-wife. Robert immediately summoned Bill to his office and presented him with the wage deduction order. "Do you know anything about this?"

"Yeah, Rob. I got the same thing a couple of weeks ago. It's my old lady again. It's the same old thing. She just doesn't want to understand that I'm remarried and have to make another life for myself."

"Look, Billy. I don't want to get in the middle of this thing. But this notification looks pretty official to me. They're directing me to deduct $75 from your paycheck."

"So what? This is just another threat. She probably got a lawyer with an 'in' at some do-gooder welfare office or something," said Bill. "You're right, pal. Don't get involved, let me handle it. Anyway, it's my responsibility, you have enough problems of your own."

Against his better instincts, Robert acquiesced. And when no follow-up notification or order was received, he began to feel a lot better. By the next week, he had put the entire matter out of his mind.

About two months later, Robert was visited by the deputy sheriff who handed him a summons and complaint. With total disbelief, he began reading the document. The first thing that caught his eye was the caption:

X----------------------------X

Catherine Malle,
                    PETITIONER,   *Verified Complaint*
                    -against-   Docket No.: 82936-85
Robert Deegan and Presto Printing Corp.,
                    RESPONDENTS.

X----------------------------X

"That's Billy's ex-wife," he muttered. "What the hell is she suing me for?"

To make a somewhat lengthy story shorter, Robert's realization that he was being sued by his employee's former spouse was totally correct. The lawsuit demanded judgment against him for the amount of child support that he should have been deducting from the date the original notice required. A sentence in the complaint indicated that the amount would continue to increase up to the time of trial. In addition, Catherine was demanding that the court require Robert to pay her for the filing fees and other costs she had incurred in commencing a suit against him.

After Robert finished his telephone conversation with his own attorney, he felt even worse. Any wild hopes that it was all a mistake had been completely dashed. Robert had been advised that the 1984 amendments to the Child Support Enforcement Act specified that employers must be held liable for their failure to comply with a wage deduction order. While the lawyer went on to explain that the federal legislation left the extent of such liability to the individual states to determine, he was quick to explain that "our state, like most, permits an individual to collect attorney's fees in these circumstances."

"You mean I have to pay Billy's ex-wife for the pleasure of her taking me to court?"

"Nothing I can do about it, Mr. Deegan. The law is the law. You should have immediately complied with the wage deduction order."

"But I was only . . ."

"Listen, Mr. Deegan. I don't doubt that you had good reasons to do what you did. But ignorance of the law has never been a defense, and our state is really cracking down on child support violators."

"But it's Billy's responsibility, not mine."

The lawyer, with practiced patience, continued. "No argument on that score, except you forget one thing. The responsibility became yours once you were notified by the agency to deduct your employee's wages."

"She's got me, doesn't she," Robert said.

"Let me put it this way," countered his lawyer. "I think that now will be the best time for me to call Catherine and tell her we intend to pay the arrears and to immediately effectuate the wage deduction order. Maybe I can talk her down a few bucks on her costs; we'll see."

* * *

Robert learned the hard way. A wage deduction order cannot be ignored. And if it is, the federal legislation has given the states wide latitude in fashioning suitable relief. Most have opted for direct lawsuits to be brought against the violating employer. If you are forced to sue your ex's employer, your jurisdiction will more than likely permit you to collect attorneys' fees, as well. This is great incentive for a lawyer to become involved with post-divorce litigation. If he or she knows that the employer will have to pay the fee or some portion of it, then the lawyer will generally be more willing to enter the fray.

The point to remember is that a wage deduction order remains an effective enforcement weapon in the war against child support violators. Indeed, according to an associate director of the Human Resources Division of the General Accounting Office, child support officials feel the withholding of support payments from wages is "the most effective collection technique for cases involving employed absent parents." This official then cited a General Accounting Office study which showed that the percentage of support payments made when a wage deduction order was utilized was a full 14 percent higher than when the device was not used. Therefore, each state has given their support collection agency system an immense amount of power to obtain wage deductions for needy spouses.

What If Your Ex Contests the Wage Deduction Order?

If your ex contests the withholding on the grounds that a mistake of fact exists, the law requires that the child support agency "determine the merits of the objection" within 45 days, at which point they are obligated to notify your ex-spouse of their decision. If, indeed, a mistake has been made, the story ends there. Most times, the agency will require further information from the objecting spouse so that the determination can be made in an environment of full disclosure. As is apparent, some unfortunate delay is built into the system if your ex makes formal objection to the wage deduction order. But in most cases it remains a relatively simple exercise for the agency to determine, on a factual basis, whether or not the former spouse's objections have any merit. Either there *has* been compliance under the support order or there has not. There is little room for error.

What to Do if You Receive Notice of a Wage Deduction Order

For those of you who might be at the receiving end, we offer some important advice. Remember, if you receive a copy of the payroll deduction order, do not—repeat do not—ignore it. It will not go away by itself.

Read it over carefully. Assuming that you are in default of support payments, determine if the amount claimed to be owed is accurate. Perhaps you are in default but not to the extent indicated. If you really have not been paying, then don't bother reading on; our advice is geared to those of you who have a legitimate question about your former spouse's right to obtain an automatic deduction from your salary. Move fast. At this juncture, your employer has no idea of the potential problem. Get all of your records of payment together for the period that your ex claims you have been defaulting in child support payments. Canceled checks are obviously the best proof, but receipts of any kind will suffice. Now look closely at the order. Do you see the index number in the upper right hand corner? That number is your file identification. Any contact with the support agency should contain not only your name, but your case number as well.

Next, get on the telephone. Your first step is to immediately contact the agency which issued the order. During this first conversation, you will identify yourself by the name which appears on the order. Then tell the person the case number. With this information, you will generally be put through directly to the caseworker who dealt with your former spouse in determining that a wage deduction order was, indeed, warranted. Do not give vent to your frustration and anger—in other words, keep your cool.

Explain your situation succinctly and without undue emotion. Tell the caseworker that a mistake has been made and give him or her the reasons why. Explain that you have documentation that demonstrates that you have been making the necessary court-ordered payments.

We emphasize that no matter how well this first telephone conversation goes, it is *not* enough. The law requires that your objection be submitted *in writing* to the agency. The real purpose of your initial contact is to learn the procedure that your local agency follows in dealing with objections to prematurely issued wage deduction orders. There may be a standardized form that the agency wishes you to complete. In this case, do not wait for them to send it to you; take the time to visit the agency personally and get the form yourself. Remember, you are working against the clock, and like all automatic processes, if you miss the boat in the first instance, you will always be swimming against the tide.

Whether the agency has a particular form or not, the information required remains the same in every state. Namely, you will be required to submit your reason, in writing, for your contention that an error has been made. We know of some cases where the dependent spouse has attempted to use the wage deduction order as a form of harassment. If you are actually up-to-date in your support payments, then say so in no uncertain terms. Whatever the reasons for the mistake, be prepared to attach copies of any documentation that supports your position.

And please do not forget to make a copy of your written objections for your own files. Again, you are dealing with bureaucracy—effective, yes—but still a bureaucracy. Things get lost. And do yourself a favor—either hand deliver your written statement directly to the agency, getting a stamped receipt on your personal copy, or forward it by registered mail, return receipt requested. You never want to put yourself in the position of having to defend the claim that you did not respond in time. Try to anticipate anything that can go wrong and act accordingly. We usually advise the objecting party to follow up the registered letter with a copy forwarded by regular mail. Again, we would rather you take redundant steps in order to fully protect your rights. While we are absolutely in favor of wage deduction orders being imposed when appropriate, we fully understand the potential for error or even abuse. Don't be a victim if it isn't necessary.

Finally, it is important for you to know that an employer cannot penalize you for having had a wage deduction order imposed. The law is clear that no retaliatory action can be taken by your boss. While a wage deduction order is not necessarily the best evidence of your fiscal responsibilities, and while the employer's compliance with a wage deduction order is often a pain in the neck, your job is safe. No disciplinary action may be taken against you. Should you suspect that your employment has been terminated for this reason alone, contact the appropriate support collection unit. They have the specific authorization to fine your employer for any actions that violate the rules of the game. In addition, it is our opinion that you will have a terrific lawsuit against your employer for wrongful discharge, especially if you have a written employment contract. A consultation with an attorney with knowledge of your state's labor and anti-discrimination laws should be helpful if you find yourself in this unfortunate situation.

The Power of Wage Withholding

Before leaving the subject of the wage deduction order, some other interesting observations should be made. For example, the federal legislation makes it clear that once salary withholding is effectuated, it must be given priority over any other attempts to impose wage withholding.

It must also be noted that there are certain limitations on the amount which is to be deducted. Each state has established its own rules and regulations, but in virtually every jurisdiction the total deducted amount cannot exceed 65 percent of your ex's net income. Your caseworker will be in the best position to explain the technical limitations that control this.

So what are you waiting for? The wage deduction order represents one of the most effective devices to collect unpaid child support. A support collection office is waiting to help. Believe us when we say that they are willing to meet you even more than half way. With a little preparation and organized thinking, you can begin getting your child support on a consistent basis as long as your ex continues to receive income. And should he think that he has invented the wheel by quitting his job, you just start the process all over again when he resurfaces. When he finds out how easy it is for you to obtain relief and just how exposed his salary checks are, he will resign himself to his fate and won't be so quick to evade his responsibilities. And your children come out the ultimate winners, having received the economic boost to which they remain entitled.

THE TAX INTERCEPT

Brad had stopped paying child support a long time ago. If he sat down and took a moment to figure his arrears, he would have been shocked to learn that it totaled approximately $9,000. He had never planned to stop paying, it just sort of happened when he landed his out-of-state job. It wasn't that he didn't feel a sense of responsibility, it was just easier to let things slide. Anyway, the extra money helped in his relocation; it just became easier and easier to forget the monthly payments after awhile.

Brad is employed in a job that pays him a salary of approximately $30,000 per year. Not bad for a streetwise kid, he likes to think. And once he stopped making the support payments, it was just a natural thing to lose contact with his family altogether. At this point, he is sure that they don't even know where he lives. And if his former wife ever discovered his present salary . . .

He is totally correct. His former wife and two children do not know his present whereabouts or how much he makes. They know he moved to Rhode Island; when he first got there he was temporarily staying in a motel and wrote his daughter a short note. Sharon often thinks about the irony of having "lost" her former husband in such a small state.

After chalking the entire thing up to experience, Sharon has her eyes on the future, not the past. She is a modern woman; there are no recriminations at her end. But in the evenings when the children are asleep, she can't stop the bitter sense of loss from surfacing. Unlike Brad, she knows to the penny how much is owed.

One day, she overhears two women talking on the bus. They are referring to a good experience that one has had with something called the child support collection office. She hears only snatches of conversation, but her instincts and curiosity are aroused. She vows to do some preliminary research, and before the week is out she has made an appointment with a caseworker.

Because she has no idea where Brad lives or works, the payroll deduction mechanism appears to be ineffectual. "Do you know his social security number?" asks the caseworker. It just so happens that she has a copy of an old joint tax return. His social security number is printed underneath his name.

Using the parent locator services available to it, the agency is able to trace Brad's address in Rhode Island. Of course, no system is perfect, and the information obtained by the agency does not reveal his employment status or where he works. The caseworker suggests the tax intercept method of collection, explaining that the agency has the right to notify her ex of their intent to take his tax refund, if any, in reduction of child support arrears owed. This device applies with equal validity to federal and state tax refunds.

The procedure begins in the same way regardless of which refund check is targeted. As in the case of the wage deduction order, Brad must receive advance notice of the potential diversion of refund monies to the agency. As you have probably guessed, Brad has the opportunity to voice his objection upon receipt of such notice. Not too surprisingly, he ignores it. "She's halfway across the country," he figures.

Having received no written objection to the notice, the caseworker starts phase two. She formally notifies the Department of the Treasury with the necessary information, which we will be highlighting in a moment. With notice of the intercept, the Treasury contacts the regional Internal Revenue Service. Should Brad be entitled to a tax refund, it will be flagged and rerouted to Sharon via the support collection agency.

Because Brad is living out of state, the caseworker must obtain Rhode Island's cooperation in getting his *state* tax refunds, if any. After a telephone call and follow-up memorandum, the child support enforcement agency in Brad's county swings into action. With the necessary documentation forwarded from the originating state, the agency in Rhode Island notifies the state taxing authorities of the potential tax intercept. Brad's name goes into the computer.

And for all this, Brad's former wife has done nothing except pay a $25 fee to the agency. Several months later, the agency notifies her that Rhode Island has just forwarded the tax refund check that was to be received by Brad. Five weeks later, the same thing happens with the federal tax refund. Not only did Sharon receive a total of approximately $1,500 in much needed child support, but the caseworker reported that Rhode Island would continue to cooperate insofar as future refunds were concerned until all arrears were paid.

What Do You Need?

To take advantage of this recent enforcement creation, in virtually every instance, you will need to provide your support agency with the following information in order to intercept your ex's state tax refund:

- A sworn affidavit that your order of support is final and that it is no longer subject to further pending judicial review. This sworn affidavit must also contain a specific statement that there remains a definite sum outstanding and uncollected. Take heart; many agencies have reduced the affidavit requirements to a simple form and will assist you in filling in the necessary data.

- Your ex's full name, last known address and social security number will also be necessary. A date of birth helps a lot as well.
- Some state agencies require that the sworn statement be supplemented by the presentation of an actual money judgment for the amount owed. We explain how you can obtain a formal money judgment in a later chapter. For now, it is enough to know that many states have simplified procedures to make it easier for you to get the judgment that forms the basis for much enforcement relief.
- Many states also require that the accumulated amount of arrears be in a sum greater than $1,000.

In order to obtain your ex's *federal* refund check, as opposed to his state tax reimbursement, the data required is basically the same. The following federal guidelines have been established:

- The support obligation must have been established under a court order or an order of an administrative process established under state law.
- The amount of past-due support must not be less than $500.
- You must be registered with your support agency, and they must be attempting to enforce your order through other appropriate methods besides federal tax intercepts.
- The support must be owed to, or on behalf of, a minor child (spousal support may not be submitted).
- The state agency must verify the accuracy of the arrears, have a copy of the order and any modifications, and have a copy of the payment record or an affidavit signed by you that attests to the amount of support owed.
- The agency must check its own records to determine if any other arrears have been declared.
- The agency must verify the accuracy of your former spouse's name and social security number.
- Most importantly, your agency must have, or be able to determine through parent locator services, your ex's current address.

As we saw in the wage deduction order situation, your former spouse must receive written advance notice of the intent to divert the tax refund check. Regardless of the targeted money—be it a state or federal refund —your former spouse must receive notification of the following:

- That he has the right to contest the determination that past-due support is owed or that the amount of arrears is what is claimed.
- That he may avail himself of an administrative review, such review to occur in either your state or his, depending on his choice.
- The notice must contain the specific procedure and time frame for contacting the agency in order to trigger the administrative review where your former spouse will be contesting the tax intercept.
- The notification must emphasize that in the case of a joint return filed by your ex and his new spouse, the Internal Revenue Service will be notifying your ex's new spouse regarding the steps to take in order to protect the share of the refund which may be payable to that spouse.

This is what the notification will look like when the support collection agency has begun to effectuate a federal income tax refund intercept:

```
FEDERAL TAX REFUND OFFSET PROGRAM
CHILD SUPPORT ENFORCEMENT UNIT            CONTACT:
DEPT. OF HEALTH AND SOCIAL SERVICES       PHONE:


OCTOBER 15, 20001



                    MR AND/OR MRS
```

THE AGENCY IDENTIFIED ABOVE HAS DETERMINED THAT YOU OWE PAST-DUE
CHILD AND/OR SPOUSAL SUPPORT. OUR RECORDS SHOW THAT YOU OWE AT
LEAST THE AMOUNT SHOWN BELOW, AND THIS AMOUNT WILL BE REFERRED TO
THE INTERNAL REVENUE SERVICE (IRS) FOR COLLECTION. ANY FEDERAL
INCOME TAX REFUND TO WHICH YOU MAY BE ENTITLED MAY BE RETAINED IN
FULL OR PARTIAL SATISFACTION OF THIS OBLIGATION.

YOU HAVE A RIGHT TO CONTEST OUR DETERMINATION THAT THIS AMOUNT OF
PAST-DUE SUPPORT IS OWED. YOU MAY REQUEST AN ADMINISTRATIVE
REVIEW BY CONTACTING US NO LATER THAN NOVEMBER 25, 1985 AT THE
ADDRESS OR PHONE NUMBER LISTED ABOVE. IF YOUR SUPPORT ORDER WAS
NOT ISSUED IN OUR STATE, YOU HAVE THE RIGHT TO REQUEST THAT AN
ADMINISTRATIVE REVIEW BE CONDUCTED IN THE STATE WHICH ISSUED THE
ORDER. WE WILL CONTACT THAT STATE WITHIN 10 DAYS AFTER WE RECEIVE
YOUR REQUEST, AND YOU WILL BE NOTIFIED OF THE TIME AND PLACE OF
YOUR ADMINISTRATIVE REVIEW BY THE STATE WHICH ISSUED THE ORDER.
ALL REQUESTS FOR ADMINISTRATIVE REVIEW MUST BE MADE BY CONTACTING
THE AGENCY IDENTIFIED ABOVE.

TAXPAYERS WHO FILE JOINT RETURNS WILL BE NOTIFIED BY THE IRS AT
THE TIME OF OFFSET REGARDING THE STEPS TO TAKE TO PROTECT THE
SHARE OF THE REFUND WHICH MAY BE PAYABLE TO THE SPOUSE WHO DOES
NOT OWE SUPPORT.

SSN   CASE NUMBER   LOCAL ID   PAST DUE AMOUNT CLAIMED

As with the wage deduction order, a person receiving advance notice of an anticipated tax intercept should not ignore it. It is simply foolish to think that it will go away by itself. Speak up and take the required administrative steps if a legitimate error has been made. If the notice goes unanswered or you fail to convince the agency that a mistake has been made after having been afforded the opportunity to do so, then you can expect to receive a notification directly from the Internal Revenue Service that looks like the example on the following page.

Tax intercept, or *offset* as it is also called, is an effective enforcement tool. Much of the procedure is fully automated; once you provide your caseworker with the necessary data, the agency takes care of virtually all the procedure from that point forward. The information required is really quite basic. This is the form that many agencies have adopted, and as you can readily see, it calls for very little in the way of detailed information.

A couple of points you may want to note regarding this form are that, first off, the State can hold a tax intercept for up to six months if your ex filed a joint return. This is to allow them the necessary time to process out the portion of the return that may be applicable to the earnings and income of your ex's new spouse. You may also be confused about the reference to a "child support debt" in No. 8. This simply refers to individuals who have been receiving support by way of public assistance or welfare, as it is usually called. Technically, the monies paid to welfare

If you have any questions refer to this

```
Date of This Notice:
Social Security Number:
Document Locator Number:
Form          Tax Year Ended:
Call:
or
Write:  Chief Taxpayer Assistance Section
        Internal Revenue Service Center
        If you write, be sure to attach this notice
```

OVERPAID TAX APPLIED TO PAST-DUE OBLIGATION

UNDER AUTHORITY OF SECTION 6402(c) OF THE INTERNAL REVENUE CODE, WE HAVE KEPT ALL OR PART OF YOUR OVERPAYMENT OF TAX TO FULLY OR PARTIALLY SATISFY A PAST-DUE OBLIGATION. IT WILL BE PAID TO THE AGENCY NAMED BELOW.

IF YOU HAVE ANY QUESTIONS ABOUT THIS OBLIGATION OR BELIEVE THE AMOUNT IS IN ERROR, YOU MUST CONTACT THAT AGENCY .

IF THIS WAS A JOINT RETURN, THE SPOUSE WHO IS NOT LIABLE FOR THE PAST-DUE OBLIGATION (THE INJURED SPOUSE) MAY OBJECT TO HAVING HIS OR HER SHARE OF THE OVERPAYMENT APPLIED AGAINST THE OTHER SPOUSE'S OBLIGATION. IF SO, A FORM 1040X, AMENDED U.S. INDIVIDUAL INCOME TAX RETURN SHOULD BE FILED INDICATING "INJURED SPOUSE". (TO QUALIFY AS AN INJURED SPOUSE, YOU MUST HAVE HAD INCOME THAT WAS REPORTED ON THE JOINT RETURN). YOU MUST FILE THE FORM 1040X USING THE "MARRIED FILING JOINT RETURN" STATUS AND SHOULD SHOW THE SAME SOCIAL SECURITY NUMBERS OF BOTH SPOUSES IN THE SAME ORDER AS THEY APPEAR ON THE ORIGINAL TAX RETURN. IT SHOULD CLEARLY INDICATE HOW ANY INCOME, ITEMIZED DEDUCTIONS, EXEMPTIONS, CREDITS AND TAX PAYMENTS AS ORIGINALLY CLAIMED SHOULD BE DIVIDED BETWEEN THE TWO SPOUSES, YOU MUST FURNISH THIS INFORMATION BEFORE ANY ADJUSTMENT CAN BE MADE. THE INJURED SPOUSE, AT LEAST, MUST SIGN THE RETURN.

THE SERVICE CENTER WILL FIGURE THE DIVISION OF THE TAX LIABILITY AND REFUND. IN COMMUNITY PROPERTY STATES, THE JOINT OVERPAYMENT MUST BE DIVIDED ACCORDING TO THE STATE LAWS.

IF YOU HAVE ANY QUESTIONS ABOUT YOUR JOINT OVERPAYMENT, YOU MAY CALL OR WRITE US – SEE THE INFORMATION IN THE UPPER RIGHT CORNER. TO MAKE SURE THAT IRS EMPLOYEES GIVE COURTEOUS RESPONSES AND CORRECT INFORMATION TO THE TAXPAYERS, A SECOND EMPLOYEE SOMETIMES LISTENS IN ON TELEPHONE CALLS.

TAX STATEMENT

```
YOUR OVERPAID TAX ON RETURN.....................$$$$$$$$$$$$$
AMOUNT OF OVERPAID TAX APPLIED TO THE AGENCY......$$$$$$$$$$$$$

AMOUNT TO BE APPLIED TO OTHER OBLIGATIONS,
REFUNDED,OR APPLIED TO YOUR ESTIMATED TAX ........$$$$$$$$$$$$$
```

(IF YOU ARE DUE A REFUND FROM THE INTERNAL REVENUE SERVICE, YOUR CHECK WILL BE MAILED TO YOU IN 6 TO 8 WEEKS. ANY INTEREST DUE YOU WILL BE ADDED).

NAME OF AGENCY

```
      DEPT. OF SOCIAL SERVICES
      DIV. OF INCOME AND SUPPORT
      CHILD SUPPORT ENFORCEMENT
      1575 CHERRY STREET
      TIMBUKTU, CO 99999
CONTACT:
PHONE:
```

recipients remain a State debt, and consequently any support received by a person on welfare from other sources (such as a tax intercept) must be reported and possibly paid back to the welfare authorities.

* * *

You have now had a guided tour of the support collection agency system, and we cannot overemphasize the real beauty of the process: no court!

The range and effectiveness of state child support collection offices is constantly improving. A lot of the procedure is new; expect some confusion and possible error. But after reading this chapter, you will be in a position to take real advantage of this relatively recent cooperative effort between the state and federal governments. With each passing

Non-AFDC Federal Tax Refund Offset Information Form

Custodial Parent's Name_____   SSN_____

   Address _____   Home Phone_____

   Employer _____   Work Phone _____

Absent Parent's Full Name _____   SSN _____

   Address _____   Home Phone_____

   Employer _____   Work Phone _____

   Employer's Address _____

Children's Name (1) _____   DOB _____
           (2) _____   DOB _____
           (3) _____   DOB _____
           (4) _____   DOB _____
I have received public assistance in the past.   YES _____ NO _____
When? _____   Where? _____
                                        STATE

Date of Support Order _____
State Issuing Support Order _____   County or Court_____
Support Amount $_____   per _____
Date of last payment _____
Current Amount of Arrears $ _____   from _____ to _____

Conditions for Submittal

1) There is a valid court or administrative order for child support.
2) The absent parent must have a child support arrearage of at least $500.00.
3) The absent parent's social security number has been verified.
4) A fee of $25.00 may be charged for each case submitted for offset.
5) There is no guarantee that monies will be collected on my behalf.
6) If an offset is made on my behalf, the State has the authority to hold the refund (if it involves a joint return) six months before sending the collection to me.
7) If the order for child support was not entered in this State, the State must have a copy of the order, any modifications, and a copy of the support payment record or a signed affidavit from me before the case can be submitted for offset.
8) I understand that if I have received public assistance in the past that any child support debt owed to the State may be satisfied first.
9) I understand that I am personally liable for the return of any amounts received by me which were paid erroneously, including any amounts which must be returned due to the filing of an amended return by the absent parent's spouse.

I swear or affirm that the information provided in this form is true and correct to the best of my knowledge.

_____   _____
Signature   Date

_____   _____
Signature   Date

year, more people will discover this hidden national treasure. The time to act is now. The programs are in place; the caseworkers are still able to offer a personal touch. Get moving. You have no reason to delay.

CHAPTER THREE

Enforcing Support Orders, Phase 1: Starting the Ball Rolling

No MATTER HOW effective the federally mandated support enforcement regulations turn out to be, there will be instances where they will not be enough, or simply inappropriate, and you will have to initiate a court proceeding on your own. For example, if Charles is self-employed and has no tax refunds due him, all the payroll deduction orders and tax intercepts in the world are not going to put a single cent in your pocket. No, you will need something like a money judgment before your local sheriff hauls away his BMW and auctions it off for the arrears Charles owes you.

On the other hand, you may not even be eligible to utilize the support agency collection system. If all you are owed is maintenance payments, the child support collection agencies cannot help you. That doesn't mean, however, that you won't be able to obtain enforcement relief, such as a payroll deduction order. It means only that such enforcement will have to originate in the Family Court.

WHAT IS FAMILY COURT?

Court is a word that instills fear in the heartiest of souls. It is natural to be afraid of court or to fear the unknown. That is why so many cases settle out of court, which is just as well from a practical point of view. Can you imagine the court system if the majority of divorcing couples could not settle their own differences? Talk about backlog!

At any rate, we understand your resistance to court, which has to be compounded tenfold if you are among the unfortunate minority whose divorce went to trial. To contemplate the possibility of a court appearance *after* the divorce is enough to keep even Rambo up past his bedtime. We have news for you. The simple truth of the matter is that there is court, and then there is *court*. In other words, a divorce trial is the proverbial horse of a different color when compared to a post-divorce hearing to collect support or obtain a money judgment. The latter is a whole lot easier.

Most of you, having escaped the court process during the divorce process, have no sense of comparison. But take our word for it. Every state has created a simplified system by which you can prove your right to receive court ordered spousal maintenance or child support without experiencing a nervous breakdown.

44

Family Court should not be considered a major obstacle. Remember, this is the name we have chosen to use in the book; where you live it may be called something else. In most of the situations concerning support collection, an attorney is not even needed. That's right, as a general rule you need not dip into savings or hock your jewelry to hire a lawyer. Remember, we are practicing attorneys, and although we are happy to take on new business, we consistently turn clients away in situations when post-divorce support is at issue. We turn these clients away not out of callousness, but for the simple reason that they do not need us. And after we finish advising them of their rights and the Family Court procedure —as we will do here—they succeed as admirably as if they had been represented by high-priced legal talent.

This chapter will show you how to begin a support enforcement proceeding in your local court. Of course, the particular procedures vary, not only from state to state, but sometimes from county to county. Nevertheless, one common thread runs through all these courts—they are designed to be used without attorneys, being as close to a "people's court" as anything in our judicial system. This is not to say that some do not use attorneys in these courts; some do. In fact, many Family Courts provide *free* legal assistance to individuals below a prescribed income level; if you think that you may qualify, the answer is no further away than your nearest telephone. The point we wish to make is that lawyers are not necessary in these courts. You do not have to be a closet Perry Mason. Court personnel, usually called caseworkers, assist litigants in preparing all the necessary legal papers. The proceedings are considerably less formal than regular court. Hearings are often conducted before hearing officers, instead of before judges. Hearing officers are individuals, usually lawyers (not surprisingly) who are appointed by the court to hear and rule on support cases, leaving the judges free to decide paternity and custody cases. The hearings themselves are conducted in small officelike rooms, with the parties and the hearing officer usually sitting at the same table.

There are three distinct stages in an enforcement proceeding. The first is the *intake session,* in which you meet with a caseworker who assists you in drawing up the necessary initiating papers. You may also have to appear before a judge to swear to their contents. This begins the proceeding, and it leads to your former spouse receiving some form of notice that invites his attendance, so to speak, at a designated time and place. The second stage is the *hearing,* where you establish your case and your ex gets a chance to refute the charge that he owes you a dime. The result is a decision, hopefully in your favor, which may find your former spouse in arrears for x number of dollars. The last stage is *enforcement,* which can range anywhere from a money judgment to civil arrest, depending upon the circumstances of your case, your ex's stubbornness and your persistence. This and the the next few chapters will take you through the whole process.

Since we will be taking you to court, you should become familiar with some of the terms.

As you will be the person initiating the proceeding, you will more than likely be called the *petitioner*—or claimant or plaintiff, depending on where you live. The person against whom you are bringing the proceeding is called the *respondent*, or defendant. The proceeding is commenced by the filing (or in some states the serving, that is delivering) of a *petition*, or complaint. The end result of the proceeding is an *order* or *judgment*, the legal document that entitles you to use the arsenal of enforcement devices that the law places at your disposal.

So let's get down to it. Step right up for your guided tour into the legal procedural system we call Family Court.

PACKING FOR THE TRIP

We assume that you have taken the first step as outlined in the first chapter and learned the whereabouts of your county's Family Court. Remember, it goes by different names in various parts of the country, so don't be surprised if you are directed to the nearest Probate Court, which is usually synonymous with estate proceedings. As odd as it may seem, many post-divorce problems are heard in Probate Courts throughout the United States. In the appendix you will find the name that is used in your particular jurisdiction.

Before we actually get to court, some other preliminary preparation must be done. To begin with, we assume that you know the whereabouts of your former spouse. In Chapter 6, we will deal with parent locator services and the particular issues that are raised when you don't know where your ex lives. We are also assuming that you are actually owed the support that you claim. It is obviously important that before you start any Family Court proceeding you compute the support arrears that are owed. This will be the first question that is asked of you when you get inside, so you might as well play it straight and be prepared. What do we mean by playing it straight? Make sure that you have your figures right and that you have credited your former spouse with all the payments that he has made, even if they have been cash and—you presume—will be difficult for him to prove. As for being prepared, we strongly suggest that first you take the time to write out *neatly* a brief summary of what you are owed and what you have received during the applicable period. While not necessary, this small step will speed things up for you considerably. Just put yourself for a moment in the shoes of an overburdened caseworker who must process hundreds of cases just like yours each week, and you will see how helpful this piece of paper can be.

Your summary sheet should look something like this:

AMOUNT OWED BY PAUL COLLINS

Divorce Decree (Superior Court, Orange County) 11/3/82

Maintenance	$125/wk
Child Support	75/wk
TOTAL:	$200/wk

Payments received from Paul Collins from 1/1/85:

1/11	$200	4/22	250
1/23	175	5/14	75
1/29	200	5/21	75
2/12	150	5/29	75
2/27	200	6/11	75
3/12	350	8/8	225
3/29	110	9/9	35
		TOTAL:	$2195

Amount due Sharon Collins:

Weekly maint/child supp.		No. of weeks (through 10/7/85)	TOTAL OWED
$200.00	X	40 =	$8,000

Amount of arrears:

Due SC	$ 8,000
Pd by PC	−2,195
TOTAL ARREARS:	$ 5,805

The next thing that you will need to bring with you are the vital statistics and important documents pertaining to the support obligation and your former spouse. We recommend once again that you write or print the information neatly on a separate sheet of paper. Here is a basic checklist of materials and documents that you should bring with you to Family Court when commencing a collection proceeding.

- Name and address of the parent obligated to pay
- His (or her) social security number, if you have it
- The name and address of his or her present or most recent employer
- Any information in your possession pertaining to his or her income or assets, such as tax returns, bank statements, paystubs or the like
- Your children's birth or baptismal certificates
- A copy of your support order
- Your actual divorce decree or financial agreement
- Copies of any relevant documentation indicating payments, such as checks, deposit slips, savings passbooks
- Your home or office telephone number, or the telephone number of anyone who will be able to contact you within one or two hours on any given day

Of course, not all of the items found in our checklist are applicable to every situation. If you have a support order or divorce decree, you will probably not have a written support agreement. While it is helpful to have financial information concerning your ex, most people are not so lucky. The point remains: if you are able to, bring as much of the information listed above as is appropriate to your situation.

Any petition for support collection must be directed to somebody. Hence, the Family Court will need the name and address of your former spouse. Because your ex will be getting formal notice of your collection proceeding, it will be helpful if you can tell the caseworker his office address as well. What do we mean by "formal notice"? The Constitution requires that a party receive proper notice of any legal proceedings brought against him. This is what is meant by *due process.* The actual requirements vary from state to state, but are actually unimportant for our purposes; your Family Court will know what is necessary to serve the notice. Depending upon where you live, the formal notice will be a *Notice of Petition,* a *Citation* or a *Summons,* and will direct the named recipient to appear in court at a particular time and date. It will probably be accompanied by a *Petition* or *Complaint* setting forth the facts upon which the claim is based. Regardless of the name it goes by, the idea is that the formal notice is something more than a telephone call.

Each state also has specific requirements dealing with how the person must receive the formal notice. Although some require personal delivery, many states allow for the papers to be sent by certified mail, sometimes regular mail. Again, this is something you need not be concerned with; the court personnel will see that the proper method is used.

All right, back to the tour. For now, we will consider the issues of child support and spousal maintenance together. Some jurisdictions distinguish between the two, but the vast majority of Family Courts provide the individual with the same procedure whether you are enforcing a child support or a maintenance obligation, or both.

Having completed your homework, you are ready to make the trip to Family Court. It is important to make yourself presentable. Many people figure that they will immediately receive sympathy points if they dress in their worst clothes. After all, the bastard hasn't paid for 2 and a half months; my wardrobe is totally shot! Let's get one thing clear. You are looking for money, not sympathy. The law is already on your side and the support collection system is just waiting for you to push the right button. All you want is that which the court has already ordered must be paid.

It is much more important to be taken seriously, so we advise that you dress the part. Remember, you will be dealing with the court system. And whether your particular court building is a modern glass highrise or a wooden walkup, it is part of the court system, which is to say "traditional." Dress up, not down. Dress conservatively, not in the latest styles. What is at stake here is your economic lifeline, and it will be necessary for you to relate one-on-one with a caseworker who might be having a bad day. Don't give him or her the chance to give you a hard time.

Secondly, go to the courthouse prepared. By reading on, you should be in a position to anticipate the questions that you will be asked. Rehearse your answers and have the necessary documentation at your fingertips.

Myra Townsend did not bother. All she knew was that Craig was 3 months delinquent in payments, their son Sandy needed braces and her expected raise had not come through. She called in sick on Tuesday morning and headed downtown to the Family Division of the Superior Court with a certified copy of her divorce decree. A court officer directed her to the appropriate section on the second floor. There she was directed to Intake B, where she completed a short form at the reception desk and handed it to a clerk.

A young caseworker called out Myra's name some 30 minutes later. She led her around the counter to a small cubicle formed by bright green movable partitions. The caseworker identified herself as Miss Tomassino and asked Myra to take a seat. She explained that it would be necessary for her to obtain certain information before Myra could proceed against her ex-spouse. Myra got as far as names and addresses.

"Mrs. Townsend, how much did you say your ex-husband is supposed to be paying you each week?" Miss Tomassino asked.

"It's right here in the decree." Myra turned to the second page and handed it to Miss Tomassino. "There it is—$155 per week for maintenance and $100 for child support. At first, Craig wanted to pay me $125, combined. I don't think he wanted to be that cheap, but his lawyer took that position. My lawyer really pressed for more money and threatened to take the case to trial, which would have killed me. My friend Gloria went through a trial, and she nearly got her head handed to her. Probably because she was seeing her tennis instructor, and the judge hated—"

"Mrs. Townsend, I am sure that your past experiences are interesting, but please stick to the arrears. I have at least ten cases waiting after yours."

"Oh sure. Why don't you just ask your questions then."

Miss Tomassino took the decree from Myra. "How many payments has Mr. Townsend missed?"

"Well, let's see. It's been about three months."

"Do you know the date of the last payment?"

Myra paused. "Not exactly. I believe it was the weekend of Jodi's wedding."

"Who's Jodi?"

"Oh, she's Mary's oldest daughter. They had a wonderful reception down by the Shore Club. Some of us thought she would never get married. She had been living with this veterinarian for the last five or six years."

"When was the wedding?"

"Uh, I believe it was the second Sunday in March. I'm not really sure. I can check with Mary."

Miss Tomassino explained that they needed the exact date. She asked Myra if she had any other way of remembering. Finally she let Myra use her phone to call Mary, who told her that the wedding was on March 24th.

"No, I'm sure that he stopped paying before then," Myra said as she hung up the phone. "I just wish I could remember."

"Well, maybe I can help. How did Mr. Townsend pay you before?"

"He was always a day or two late."

"No, I mean was it by cash or check?"

"Check. Always by check."

"Did you deposit these checks?"

Myra nodded.

"Do you have a record of these deposits?" Miss Tomassino asked. "You know, like deposit slips or a checkbook. Something like that."

"Sure I do, but I don't have them with me now." Myra leaned forward and grabbed the calendar on the desk. "Look, let's make it the 10th. I think that's right."

Miss Tomassino explained to Myra that she could not guess, that she had to swear to the exact date. Sensing an impasse, Myra finally told the caseworker to use the date Mary had given her. Miss Tomassino told her that she hated to see her lose a few weeks of payments, but it was up to her whether she wanted to go home to check her records and come back a second time. Myra said that the few hundred dollar's difference was not worth the trouble.

"Okay, we'll use the 24th. Now we just have to figure the amount of the arrears. You haven't done the arithmetic by any chance, have you?" Myra shook her head. "Okay, I'll look for a calculator and be right back."

Myra waited almost ten minutes. Miss Tomassino returned with a half-drunk coffee container and a small calculator. Meanwhile Myra had done the arithmetic on the back of her copy of the divorce decree. Either way, they both came up with eleven-weeks worth of arrears, $2,805. Miss Tomassino next asked if Mr. Townsend should be credited with any payments during that time.

"Well, he paid Dr. Stafford $150. I know this because I had an appointment with him two weeks ago, and his receptionist, what's her name—I can't recall—anyway, she told me that Craig was in the other night and had paid my last bill. And that was about time too. I think that bill was outstanding for at least two months."

"Is Mr. Townsend required to pay your medical bills?"

"You bet he is, honey. I had a pretty damn good lawyer for this divorce. Cost me enough, that's for sure. Besides, Craig gets most of it back from insurance."

Miss Tomassino told Myra that the medical payments were irrelevant to the support arrears, and that she was just interested in knowing if her former husband had made any payments directly to her during the last 11 weeks. Myra said that he had not, and that he had told her that she would have to take him to court. Miss Tomassino began to complete a printed form.

"You know, Miss Tomassino, before you write this down, maybe I should tell you that Craig did give Sandy an envelope for me last Sunday. When I opened it, there were five $100 dollar bills inside."

"Don't you think you should have mentioned that to me? Obviously that reduces his arrears." Miss Tomassino reached into her desk drawer for another form.

"Can't we just claim that he gave the money to Sandy? You know, a gift, or something." The caseworker looked up and stared. "Okay, I just thought that . . ."

"Mrs. Townsend, we are going to be preparing court papers for you.

You're going to sign them under oath. You have to tell the truth."

When Myra next told the caseworker that she had forgotten to bring her ex's employment data, the interview was quickly brought to a close with Miss Tomassino curtly telling Myra to make another appointment when she was "better prepared." She explained that there were still ten people waiting for her, and they all had to be processed before lunch.

THE INTAKE INTERVIEW

Every collection proceeding starts with the intake interview, such as the one just described. When you arrive at the courthouse, ask the first court officer you see to direct you to the support collection unit. There you will be met by a caseworker whose job is to obtain the necessary information from you that will trigger the support collection proceeding. This caseworker is called by various names: investigator, enforcement worker, collection specialist, probation officer, child support worker. We will use the term *caseworker* to describe the person who conducts the interview and assists you in filing your support petition.

This process is rather simple. The caseworker will immediately ascertain whether or not you have a legitimate right to collect support arrears. This means that as a preliminary step you will be called upon to prove your entitlement based upon a prior existing court order for support.

We hasten to mention that in some states, the "proof" problem has been virtually done away with In these states, such as Pennsylvania and Michigan, all court-ordered support is automatically paid directly into court by the obligated spouse. Thereafter, the court forwards the check to the dependent party. As is obvious, this method insures a nice computer printout of payments received or owed at the time of the interview. If you are in a situation where your ex has been making payments to the court, it is a safe bet that a computer profile can be easily obtained. We suggest that you telephone 2 days in advance of the time that you have set aside to visit Family Court and ask that you be provided with a computer printout of your ex's arrears status. In this way you will have something tangible with which to check your own computations of the amount owed. Most importantly, you will be able to provide the caseworker with actual proof of your claim at the time of the interview.

Unfortunately, most states have not yet adopted the automatic "pay into court" method, although many are introducing it as part of the recent federally mandated child support enforcement overhaul that we discussed in the last chapter. If your state does not provide this service, the caseworker must first assure himself of the viability of your support claim. For example he or she will ask to see a copy of the divorce decree or support order that gives rise to your support rights.

The next thing you will be asked is how much you believe you are owed and how you calculated this amount. This is where the summary sheet proves so effective. Armed with this ready and presentable information, you will assure yourself of the caseworker's cooperation and assistance, an incalculable advantage at this stage.

The caseworker will also ask you questions about your former spouse. Again, the information that you have compiled by using the checklist on page 47 will enable you to provide the necessary answers. We cannot overemphasize how important it is to give the caseworker all the accurate and relevant facts. It is this information that will be used to prepare the necessary court papers and assures that your ex will get prompt formal notice of your support enforcement proceeding. And the information must be accurate and truthful. Do not try to make your claim better than it is. Do not lie about not receiving payments, assuming there have been any. Do not claim anything to which you are not legally entitled. All the relevant facts that you tell the caseworker will be incorporated in the petition, which you are required to sign and swear to. If you lie you will have committed perjury, which is a crime, albeit rarely prosecuted in civil cases; but on a more practical level you may inadvertently destroy your own case. Should you have to attend a hearing, your misstatements can end up ruining your credibility as a witness, giving a judge or hearing officer the right to disregard all or part of your testimony. Many a litigant has been his or her own worst enemy. In the words of a colleague of ours, "My case would be really good if it weren't for my client."

Whatever you tell the caseworker should be relevant to the case. Of course, no one is going to expect you to know the precise elements that make up a claim for enforcement. This is what the caseworker is there for. However, you should try to restrict yourself to discussing those facts that have to do with support. Going off on a tangent to talk about your son's poor grades, or the reasons why you and your ex got a divorce, is a waste of time. Moreover, you may find yourself quickly losing the caseworker's interest and attention. Your detour may just get him thinking about his upcoming vacation. Avoid doing what Myra did.

Don't be surprised if, once the caseworker gets all the necessary information, he or she picks up a telephone and speaks directly to your ex, either asking him right then and there about the support payments or inviting him to come in to discuss it informally. Some states require this voluntary or probationary step before your proceeding can begin. Under certain circumstances, you can ask to skip this preliminary step—*waive probation* is the jargon—especially if you can show that there have been several recent attempts to work out the situation that proved completely unavailing. However, if you think there is a chance that a call or letter from the court is all your former spouse will need to reform his wayward habits, then probation is a recommended, and time saving, step. It is always far better to enforce your rights expeditiously than to wait for the wheels of justice to grind out the necessary relief.

To complete our tour, we will assume that probation was waived or it did not work; in any case, you are ready to prepare the petition. Actually, in many states the caseworker prepares this document, using the information that you have provided, but even if you have to do it yourself, you will find that the necessary form is fairly simple to complete.

All support enforcement petitions (or complaints) have essentially the same information—just the name and the form may change. Regardless of the jurisdiction, a petition sets forth the basic, necessary facts, such as:

- the identity and addresses of the parties;
- the date of the support order;
- the name of the court that issued the order;
- the amount of the support order, breaking it down to maintenance and child support;
- if the original support order has been modified, the manner, date and description of such modification;
- the amount presently owed (the arrears); and
- whether any other steps have been taken to enforce the support order.

After the petition is completed, you will swear to the truth of its contents. It is then filed with the court, which will issue either a summons or notice ordering your ex to appear in court on a certain date. The way your ex receives the summons or notice depends on local law. Some courts automatically mail it, others require that you have someone deliver it personally to him. Whatever the rules, you will find out from the caseworker or court clerk.

Naturally you will also be showing up in court on the appointed date, and you will have to be ready then to try your case. However, do not be dismayed if your ex, or his lawyer, manages to wheedle one or more adjournments (postponements), and your hearing does not take place right away. The court's case docket may also be overcrowded, which means that some delay is inevitable. We will be talking about how to prepare for the hearing in the following chapter. See you in court.

IF YOU DON'T HAVE A SUPPORT ORDER: HOW TO GET ONE

So far, our discussion has assumed that you have a valid support order or judgment. After all, this book is concerned with post-divorce situations. Your divorce decree by necessity should contain the relevant support provisions, and if so, you will not need a separate support order to proceed with enforcement. We have seen a few cases, however, where the support provisions were omitted, usually where someone prepared his or her own divorce papers. The maintenance and child support obligations were previously specified in a separation agreement or other such document. The decree makes no mention of them and, instead, incorporates the terms of the agreement by reference. While the divorce is perfectly valid, the decree is insufficient for enforcement purposes, and a separate support order will be required.

It may also be possible that some readers are not yet divorced, yet the separation has been so long that they now think of their estranged spouses as ex's. Some may be legally separated, with support rights spelled out in a *separation agreement,* which, although a legal document, is alone not enough to begin enforcement—at least in Family Court. Others may have no agreement at all. Without shifting the intended emphasis of our book, two recent cases should give you an idea of what to do, if you find yourself in any of these situations.

Rachel Syms had been separated from her husband for 3 years. All they had was a separation agreement, according to which George was obliged to pay her $750 monthly for maintenance and another $500 for child support. Everything was fine for the first 2 and a half years. While not in the running for any timeliness awards, George managed to make all the payments, rarely with complaint. Then Stanley, their only son, joined the Marines in February, which under the agreement constituted an "emancipation event" that would automatically terminate child support. George immediately reminded Rachel that he no longer had to pay child support, and she agreed. So far so good. A month later, however, George decided that he was going to enlarge the scope of the emancipation clause.

Notwithstanding that Rachel's maintenance had some 7 years to run, George felt he should no longer have to contribute to her support. She was still young and healthy enough to get a real paying job, instead of just doing freelance graphic design work. When Rachel demanded her check, George told her to take him to court. She did just that. Using the same approach that we have just outlined, Rachel brought a support proceeding against her husband. She could have brought a divorce action instead, but she was in no rush for a divorce, and, more importantly, she did not have any money to retain an attorney. And it was money that she wanted at the moment. The court papers were prepared and served on George, who refused to give up. He even hired a lawyer.

After a short hearing, the court decided on the spot that George was still obligated under the separation agreement to continue the maintenance payments. A support order to that effect—that is, $750 per month, until death or remarriage—was entered. Best yet, Rachel used the hearing to show George's history of chronic lateness. Based upon such evidence, the judge also directed that George's employer deduct the maintenance payments from his paycheck and send them directly to Rachel. Perhaps contributing to this ruling was the judge's pique over George's misguided attempt to avoid his maintenance obligation altogether.

If you find yourself in a similar predicament, you should do the same thing as Rachel did. If your spouse has been delinquent in making payments under a separation agreement, you may also be entitled to an enforcement order as well. In other words, you can ask the court to convert the terms of the separation agreement into an effective support order and also to give it some teeth by way of an enforcement order, such as a payroll deduction or a security deposit. There is nothing that prevents you from combining both requests in a single application. Stella Perkins' problem, however, was just a bit more complex.

Stella had been separated for several years. However, she and Michael never had a formal agreement. He had been voluntarily paying her $500 or $600 a month, which was enough to supplement Stella's earnings as a medical receptionist. Then Michael met Ruth, and her two children, cat and dog. The voluntary payments became sporadic and then stopped altogether. Stella went to court. Unfortunately, she had nothing to establish the support obligation. All Michael's payments had been by cash or money order. The caseworker told her that even if she had copies of checks, the voluntary payments would not automatically mean that she was entitled to receive them; they would just show that Michael was able to pay that much each month. Stella's cause was not lost, however, just more difficult. She had to prove at the hearing the two essential elements upon which a court may order spousal support—her actual monetary needs and her husband's ability to pay. The hearing, adjourned three times, spread over the course of 3 months. The decision came down about 4 weeks later. Stella was awarded $450 monthly for 3 more years. At least Stella now has an order to enforce her rights, should Michael forget about his now legally mandated obligation.

INITIATING OUT-OF-STATE PROCEEDINGS

Susan Jackson was fed up and out of luck. The divorce was almost 5 years ago, yet she still was not through with Joel. Twice she had to drag him into court to get support payments for their three children. She considered herself a veteran, willing to bet that she knew the inside/out of the local Family Court better than most matrimonial lawyers. The last time she went to court she was able to obtain a payroll deduction order, and since then the payments had been coming from Texas Instruments, Joel's employer, as regularly as a monthly subscription to Good Housekeeping magazine. Besides, the checks never bounced. Susan was proud that she had made the system work for her. She was not left a helpless victim of child support delinquency, like the multitudes of women that one reads about every time one of the news-magazines decides to do a piece on child support as the national problem of the week.

Then Joel threw her a curve. He quit his job in the accounting department of Texas Instruments and went to work for Caterpillar Tractor, in a different state and some 1,200 miles away. He had not told her or the kids. The first word she got was a copy of a notice that Texas Instruments had sent the Family Court informing it that Joel was no longer in their employ and that they would no longer be remitting Susan's support checks. The shock was not unlike receiving notice of being fired, which, with ghoulish coincidence, Susan was 2 weeks later. Susan did not feel desperate until she left her supervisor's office that Friday afternoon. Mr. Stills explained that the plant was cutting back because of imports from the Far East and that they had to reduce the payroll. Under the union contract, the layoffs had to go by reverse seniority, notwithstanding that Susan was one of the best drillpress operators in the company.

Thomas, her oldest son, spoke to his father a few evenings later and found out his new address. Susan's initial excitement faded in the sudden realization that she could not afford to travel to Joel's new town and spend the necessary time to initiate and prosecute an enforcement proceeding, to say nothing of who would watch the children while she was gone. Her cousin Melvin, an estate attorney, had told her several weeks ago that her payroll deduction order was worthless out of state and that she would have to travel to wherever her ex moved to begin a new action.

Even assuming she could manage to scrape together a few dollars to make the trip, Susan felt that she knew absolutely nothing about the court system where Joel now lived. She figured it had to be similar—after all, this is one country—but she had no way of really knowing. She decided to drop in first thing Monday morning on Mrs. Wilkes, the caseworker at the Family Court who had always been so helpful to her before. Throughout the years she and Susan had managed to strike up a decent acquaintance, and Susan was confident that she could obtain the necessary information about the other court system.

Susan met with Mrs. Wilkes at 10:30. She could not believe how crowded the intake section had become since the last time she was there. Mrs. Wilkes was delighted to see Susan, and after hearing the full story, she did not appear to be too seriously concerned with her plight. She reached into the file cabinet behind her and pulled out several familiar-looking forms.

"I don't believe that you have forms for Iowa. You're absolutely amazing, Mrs. Wilkes."

"Who said anything about Iowa forms? These are ours." Mrs. Wilkes put them down on the desk in front of Susan. "You've seen them before, Sue."

"Yes, but like I explained, Joel lives in Iowa now. That's where I have to go to do something, right?"

"What are you talking about, dear? We'll handle this from here, that is unless you want to make the trip because you think you're going to do a better job out there yourself."

"What are *you* talking about, Mrs. Wilkes? My cousin Melvin said I have to go there and start all over."

"Who's your cousin Melvin?"

"He's a lawyer—does estate work at Adams and Gibbs."

Mrs. Wilkes laughed, "I suggest that Melvin stick to his area of expertise, young lady, and keep out of mine. Either that or learn about URESA."

"Who's Uresa?"

"Not who! It stands for Uniform Reciprocal Enforcement of Support Act. Every state's got it. We do and Iowa does."

"What's it for?" Susan was able to maintain her businesslike demeanor, even though she felt like jumping up and down on this nice elderly woman's desk.

"Basically, it provides nationwide enforcement without someone like you having to leave town to get it. You start an enforcement proceeding here, like usual, and we prepare a neat little package of papers and ship them to the corresponding court where your ex-husband lives. They handle everything over there."

"Oh, I see. They file a petition and serve it on Joel." Susan watched Mrs. Wilkes begin to fill out one of the forms. Her enthusiasm began to wane when she realized that Joel would probably fight it, as he did all the other proceedings. "But won't I still have to go there and appear at the hearing? Also, do you think I should get a local lawyer? Maybe my aunt can lend me the money."

"Don't be silly. Everything is taken care of by the Iowa court. Under URESA the local court has to appoint a lawyer to handle your case free of charge." Mrs. Wilkes smiled at Susan. "Although from what I've heard about what a tiger you are in the hearing room, maybe you're better off trying your own case." Both woman laughed.

"No, that's okay. I'll let this URESA do the talking."

Mrs. Wilkes prepared the petition, which was then read before Judge Tyler. Susan was sworn in and testified that the facts set forth in the petition were true to the best of her knowledge. Several stamps and official-looking seals were affixed to the petition. Susan was told she could leave. Mrs. Wilkes said that she would make sure that the papers went by express mail first thing the next day.

Susan had been through enough court campaigns to know that justice is not instant. Thus she was hardly surprised that two months passed before she heard anything. Mrs. Wilkes telephoned her with the good news. The Iowa court had ordered a payroll deduction, large enough to wipe out the arrears in 3 months. In addition, it made Joel post a $2,500 bond to secure future payments, just in case he left Caterpillar without warning. Susan received formal notice a few days later. Two weeks after that the first check came.

* * *

The Uniform Reciprocal Enforcement of Support Act (URESA) is a uniform law that has been adopted by every state across the country, as well as the territories of Guam, Puerto Rico and the Virgin Islands. Although there is no federal law for support enforcement, the uniform act comes as close as possible to providing an effective nationwide method of enforcing support payments. Each state enacts its own separate legislation that conforms with the model uniform code. Indeed, in most instances the language is practically verbatim. If you are beginning to think that URESA is set up somewhat like the activating state legislation under the Child Support Enforcement Amendments of 1984, which we discussed in Chapter 2, you're right.

URESA gives courts broad jurisdiction over the parties, and it permits enforcement proceedings to cross county and state lines as easily as a long distance phone call. The petitioner commences the proceeding in the Family Court, or equivalent, of her home state, which is called the *initiating* state. The place where the nonpaying former spouse lives is called the *responding* state. The procedure is virtually identical to the one discussed earlier. A verified (sworn) petition is filed, containing the following information:

1. The name, age, residence and circumstances of the petitioner
2. The name, age, residence and circumstances of the respondent
3. A statement that the petitioner is entitled to support from the respondent, identifying the divorce decree or support order that is being enforced
4. A demand that the respondent be made to pay such support

If your former spouse lives in the same state but in a different county, the petition is forwarded to the court in his county for further proceedings consistent with your state's law. If he lives in a different state, however, to move the proceedings along in that state the judge in your Family

Court will certify that a verified petition has been filed in his court under URESA; that a summons had been issued for your ex, the respondent, in your state (the initiating state) and he couldn't be located; that the respondent is believed to be residing in the state the papers are being forwarded to (the responding state) and that, in his opinion, the respondent should be compelled to answer the petition and be dealt with accordingly. The judge's certificate is then sent to the appropriate court in the responding state, along with certified copies of the summons and petition, a copy of the initiating state's version of URESA and several certified copies of your divorce decree or support order, including all modifications.

Upon receipt of the requisite papers from the court in the initiating state, a judge in the Family Court in the county of the state where your ex lives will fix a time and place for a hearing on the petition and at the same time issue a summons for your former spouse to appear. Should this judge subsequently discover that your ex lives in a different county in the responding state, the papers will be forwarded to the proper court in that county, and notification of the transfer will be sent to the initiating court, giving you a way to keep track of matters. In the meantime, if child support is involved, one or more copies of the divorce decree or support order will be filed in a Registry of Foreign (and Out-of-State) Child Support Orders, if the responding state maintains such a system. There are certain technical advantages to the latter that permit more expeditious treatment of your claim, but these are beyond the scope of this book.

Now here comes the best part. A *petitioner's representative* is assigned to your case. He or she is a county attorney, state attorney, corporation counsel or any other designated public officer authorized to institute and maintain a URESA action. The petitioner's representative will appear on your behalf at every stage of the proceeding—at no charge to you!

It is unnecessary for you or your witnesses to appear personally at the hearing in the responding state. The petitioner's representative is there for you. If your ex contests the petition and files a verified denial of any of its material statements, the judge will temporarily stay (suspend) the hearing and transmit to the initiating state court's judge a transcript of his denials. You are then notified by your judge to appear before him with your witnesses to provide the necessary evidence in support of your petition. (We discuss how to conduct a hearing in the next chapter.)

After considering your proof, your judge makes a recommendation, which he sends to the responding state's court, along with a certified transcript of your testimony and other evidence. That court then reschedules the hearing and gives your ex a "reasonable opportunity" to appear and reply to your evidence. Once again "due process" rears its fair-minded head, providing your ex with the right to cross-examine you and your witnesses by preparing written questions called *interrogatories,* to which you and your witnesses, if any, must supply sworn answers. Also, he is given the right to take your and your witnesses' depositions. A *deposition* is an informal procedure whereby a person appears and answers questions under oath. A stenographer records the testimony, just like in court, but no judge is present. Fair being fair, you are given the same right to cross-examine your ex and his witnesses by interrogatories or deposition. The court reviews the typed transcripts of the depositions and the interrogatory answers, which are considered equally with any "live" testimony.

After the hearing is over, the court in the responding state issues a decision, which may take several weeks, depending upon that particular judge's caseload. If the judge finds that the evidence supports your petition, he will issue an order directing your ex to pay support. A certified copy of the order is also transmitted to the initiating state's court, and it is made part of its official record. The judge also has the power to place your former spouse on probation and to direct that he furnish a cash deposit or surety bond as security for future payments. Moreover, the order can direct that your ex make payments directly to the support collection unit and that he report personally to the unit periodically and remain under its supervision. Usually payments to the support collection unit are sent directly to your court, which then turns them over to you.

This procedure may strike you as somewhat cumbersome and time-consuming, but it provides important assistance in situations where you cannot afford to travel to another state and perhaps retain a local attorney to enforce your rights. Often it is not the cost of the trip—especially with today's competitive, deregulated airline fares—rather, it is the expense of staying long enough to see the proceeding through to the end. It is important to realize that all court matters have built-in delays. A respondent is given a certain amount of time to appear and, if requested, find an attorney. Conflicting commitments and congested court calendars often translate into adjournments and postponements. Your stay may end up stretched to more than a month or two, ordinarily too much time to spend away from home.

URESA is not perfect, but it has filled an important gap in support enforcement. It may be all that you will need.

CHAPTER FOUR

Enforcing Support Orders, Phase 2: Trying Your Case

YOU HAVE a date—with the court—as well as a time and room number. Everything has gone fine so far. Intake was a snap. The Family Court judge had a few questions when it came time to swear out the petition, but they were no problem. The date is fixed, the summons issued. You have a copy in your wallet. You have looked at it at least 7 times in the last 2 days: you, the petitioner, versus that rat, the respondent. Each time your eye has been drawn to the date typed in the appropriate blank. That is it, your big debut.

Opening day jitters are expected. You will still have them even after you have read this chapter and done everything that we suggest. However, while we may not be able to completely alleviate your anxiety, we hope to give you enough information and helpful hints so that you can prepare and conduct a successful support enforcement hearing. Our goal is not so much to make you a full-fledged trial attorney as it is to assure that you are prepared to try your case to a successful conclusion. Nevertheless, a short legal primer course is in order.

BASIC TRAINING

Elements of the Claim

Whatever name is attached to your proceeding, it is, in simplest terms, a claim. You have come into court and claimed that your ex owes you money. You expect that he will show up and deny it. This means that you will have to prove your claim. That is how the system works.

It is not sufficient merely to make a claim against someone and expect to receive payment, unless the other party virtually collapses from the shock of receiving court papers, which happens sometimes but not often enough to count on it. These papers may cause your former spouse a sleepless night or two, but sadly they do not often result in a perceptible change of well-ingrained habits, such as failing to pay support. Most likely he will continue to play hardball, figuring you will not have the nerve to see this thing through. If he has the money, he will surely hire an attorney to try to scare you away. His lawyer may be comforting to him, but should really make no difference if you have done the necessary preparation for the hearing. *This is what will get your money.* So get ready.

Since you are the petitioner, you must prove the essential elements of your case, which in support enforcement proceedings are:

1. The right to support
2. The identity of the person from whom you are to receive the support
3. The amount and frequency of the support payments
4. Nonpayment

We will discuss how to establish each of these separately. Taken altogether, they constitute your *prima facie* ("at first sight" in Latin) case, which is a lawyer's way of saying that all of the necessary factual and legal elements of the case are present.

Cross-Petition

Do not be surprised if your ex responds to notification of your enforcement proceeding with a cross-claim or cross-petition for a *downward modification* of his support obligation. This is a common knee-jerk reaction, especially if he has a lawyer representing him. The idea is to give him a bargaining chip with which to negotiate a settlement. He agrees to drop his cross-petition, providing you allow the arrears to be cut in half. His lawyer tries to scare you into accepting half of a loaf by threatening to close down the bakery. Sometimes the reasons behind the maneuver, however, are legitimate. Your ex may have been laid off, or his expenses unexpectedly increased because of an illness. Your income may have doubled since the divorce. These are factors that a court will consider.

Divorce decrees and support orders are not final. Either spouse can ordinarily apply later for an upward or downward modification, which will be granted upon a showing of substantially changed circumstances. We discuss modification—and the grounds for it—in Chapter 7. For now, you just need to keep two things in mind. *First, a court will modify support obligations upon proof of substantial, changed circumstances. Second, former spouses often make a claim for a modification in an enforcement proceeding purely for tactical reasons.* If your ex makes this move, you can reach a fairly accurate conclusion about whether his ploy is real or a bluff by reading Chapter 7, which explains those instances where downward modifications have been allowed. If it appears he has decent grounds, you may wish to discuss settlement and avoid chancing a reduction of your maintenance and child support payments. However, do not be scared away too quickly. Courts are generally reluctant to modify support when they encounter such a request as part of an enforcement proceeding. A cross-petition for downward modification is customarily saddled with the inescapable conclusion that it was brought solely for untoward leverage, and that if the party had a real grievance, he would have petitioned the court long before his ex-wife had to drag him in for nonpayment.

In essence, a petition for enforcement and a cross-petition for a downward modification are two separate proceedings that will be tried and decided together in the same proceeding. You will find yourself both prosecuting your claim and defending yourself against your ex's. We will soon be discussing certain basic legal concepts such as burden of proof and evidence. Naturally our discussion will be keyed into your role as a petitioner. However, should your ex serve a cross-petition, you then have dual roles; although the labels do not change, your ex becomes the "petitioner" on his claim for modification and you become the "respondent." Whatever we will be saying about your role as a petitioner will thus apply equally to your ex on his claim.

Compromise and Settlement

In the preceding section, we mentioned for the first time considering the possibility of a settlement. Perhaps we should have done so even earlier, because our overtaxed legal system operates on the premise that most disputes will be settled. This includes support controversies.

Indeed it is quite common for a judge or other court personnel to first attempt to reach a settlement between the parties before the hearing is scheduled. Often the differences can be worked out, especially if each side is willing to compromise somewhat. Phil Hector owed Marsha $2,000 in arrears. Marsha had served her petition and prepared her case. She was all set to go. The hearing had already been postponed twice.

Judge Splain was not quite so ready. He explained to Marsha that all the available hearing officers were booked through next week. He also said he could not see why this problem could not be worked out. The four of them—Marsha, Phil, his lawyer and the judge—sat around a small conference table and discussed the problem. Marsha was desperate for money; Phil was strapped. However, he did expect a small tax refund by next month, and his raise was overdue. Judge Splain and Phil's lawyer went back and forth on different proposals. Finally, Phil and Marsha agreed on one. Phil would pay Marsha $500 by Friday, and he would resume his weekly $150 child support payments in 10 days. The payments would also include an extra $100 until the balance of the arrears was paid off. Meanwhile, Judge Splain would retain jurisdiction of the case; if Phil missed one payment, Marsha was to call his chambers and the case would be scheduled for a hearing within 3 days. Part of Marsha was disappointed that she could not show off her newly practiced trial skills; a greater part was relieved it was over.

Do not permit your anger with your former spouse to close you to the possibility of settlement. However, the settlement must be fair. You should not be forced to give up your rightly owed support, no matter who tries to intimidate you—your ex, his lawyer or even the judge. Yes, the judge. Do not be surprised if he is the one putting on the greatest pressure. After all, he is aware of the case backlog, and if he can settle a case and avoid tying up another judge or a hearing officer for a whole day, he has helped the system as well as the parties. In addition to good wishes, he also has the persuasive cloak of authority, impartiality and reason, which makes him someone who is very difficult to turn down. For all his power, though, he cannot force you to settle. You are entitled to your day in court and can rightly insist upon it.

Several years ago we were representing a client whose arm the judge was figuratively twisting in order to persuade him to accept a small settlement. The judge told him that his case was weak and that he hated seeing anyone leave his court without a dime. Finally, the client said that he wished to go to trial. The judge asked why.

"Because I'm right, your Honor," he answered.

"Sir, I'm sure that your counsel has explained to you that sometimes there is a big difference between what is morally right and what is legally right." The judge puffed on his cigar.

"Well then, your Honor, I would like to go to trial to find out just how big that difference is."

The judge was speechless for a moment. "All right, I'll send you out to a hearing officer this afternoon."

After 5 days of trial, the parties agreed to a settlement that was 7 times the size of the judge's recommended offer.

As we mentioned before, if your ex has cross-petitioned for a downward modification, you may want to weigh carefully the merits of his claim and consider a reasonable settlement offer. Again, do not let this tactic fool or scare you. Do not even pause to contemplate a compromise reducing the amount of money owed or the level of support unless there are some damn good grounds for modification. As you will see in Chapter 7, just any old change of circumstances is insufficient. The change must be substantial. Moreover, it cannot be a change that he has voluntarily imposed upon himself. A trip around the world may have left him $15,000 in debt, but that will not be a factor that the court will consider.

If you do accept a settlement offer, make sure that as part of it your ex withdraws his cross-petition and expressly waives (gives up) his right to seek a future modification either within a certain number of years or upon the same reasons alleged in his cross-petition. If you are not careful to do this, you may find that you have reduced your claim and that he later comes after you for a downward modification.

LAW SCHOOL CONDENSED

Before we turn to the specifics of preparing and prosecuting (or trying) an enforcement case, it is necessary for you to become familiar with some legal terms that we will be using in this chapter.

(A) Burden of Proof

You have the burden of proof, which essentially is the burden of persuasion. Since this is a civil proceeding, the burden is relatively easy. You may have heard the expression in movies or television of proving a case beyond a reasonable doubt, but that only applies to criminal cases. Although you may find your ex's recalcitrance to be criminal, your case is not. Like any ordinary civil case, you have the burden of proving your claim by a *preponderance* of the credible evidence. This means that more of the evidence has to support your side than his. However, just a little more is sufficient—51 to 49 percent, if you like numbers; majority wins, if you prefer slogans.

Preponderance of evidence is an elusive judicial concept; judges know what it is when they see it, but few can describe it. Neither can we. However, you should not get too concerned over this. The important thing to remember is that you, not your former spouse, have the burden of proof. You must prove the essential elements of your case. If the evidence is a draw, he wins. If the evidence favors him, he wins. Equally balanced evidence, or evidence that leaves the court with such doubt that it is unable to decide the case, results in a losing decision for you.

Ordinarily, the burden of proof in support enforcement cases is relatively simple. After all is said and done, there really is not too much to the case. You have a right to receive child support and maintenance payments, and you have not been getting them. Simple. All you have to do is make sure that your evidence establishes this, and we will cover later how to do this.

The burden of proof can sometimes change in the middle of the case. If your ex asserts what is called an *affirmative defense,* such as payment, the burden of proof shifts onto his shoulders with regard to the defense. In other words, if he defends himself by claiming that he has been making payments to you all along, he has the burden of persuading the court that these payments were made. If he asserts that there has been a modification of the original decree, reducing or eliminating his obligations, or that the decree is defective and unenforceable, again he has to convince the court. Finally, if he brings a cross-petition for a downward modification, he has the burden of proof.

(B) Evidence

Even though enforcement hearings are informal, the technical rules of evidence apply. Since you are trying your own case, the judge or hearing officer will probably bend over backwards to assure that you are not frustrated by complicated evidentiary rules. Nonetheless, a certain degree of familiarity cannot hurt.

Evidence, to quote an old case includes "all the means by which any alleged matter of fact, the truth of which is submitted to investigation, is established or disproved." *Proof* is the conclusion that is reached after considering the evidence. Put another way, you prove your case by presenting evidence. The judge or hearing officer rules on what is admissible evidence and what is not, what goes in and what does not. He is the referee who makes the call. Sometimes the judge will make a ruling on his own, but usually it is prompted by an objection by the other party or his attorney. If the objection is *sustained,* the question is improper; if it is *overruled,* the witness must answer.

Evidence may be testimonial, given by witnesses under oath, or documentary, in written form, such as divorce decrees or bank deposit slips. A court is allowed to permit the introduction of all evidence that is relevant, material and competent to the case. Relevant evidence is anything that has a reasonable tendency to prove a fact. It is something that makes the existence of a particular fact more likely than it would be without such evidence. To give you a specific example, the fact that you have maintained a record of bank deposits is relevant to whether certain payments were not made by your ex. A conclusion of nonpayment is much more likely with such evidence. "Material" means that the evidence has something to do with a fact that is at issue. Evidence that your ex prefers the color red is immaterial in a support proceeding. The question of what evidence gets into the hearing, that is, what is competent and admissible, is up to the judge, who acts as the referee and makes the calls whenever necessary. Any evidence is admissible as long as it is not barred by some *exclusionary rule.*

An exclusionary rule is one which keeps out otherwise relevant and material evidence. They are very complex and well beyond the scope of this book. However, you are probably already familiar with the most common and important one—the rule against *hearsay.* A precise definition of hearsay is difficult to come by. To put it as simply as possible, in your situation hearsay is a statement made out of court by someone other than your ex that is offered to prove the truth of the facts made in such statement. Say that again? We wish we could make it clearer, but this is a concept that usually drives law students crazy. Perhaps a few illustrations are worth more than the thousand words we would otherwise need to explain this.

LAWYER 1: Did the respondent (your ex) take any vacations this past year?

WITNESS: Edward Smith told me that Charles was in Aruba this past winter.

LAWYER 2: Objection.

COURT: Sustained. You can't prove that the respondent went on a vacation by a statement made outside of court by a friend of yours. That's hearsay.

LAWYER 1: To your knowledge, did the respondent make any major purchases this year?

WITNESS: I called Jennifer Stans, and she told me that Charles had bought a new Cadillac.

LAWYER 2: Objection.

COURT: Sustained. Again, that's hearsay. You can't prove that he bought a new car that way.

LAWYER 1: Did the respondent lose his job?

WITNESS: Well I don't really know for sure, but I have a letter here from his mother, and she says that in February he was still . . .

LAWYER 2: Objection.

COURT: Sustained. A letter, or any writing for that matter, made out of court is hearsay and inadmissible. Next question.

LAWYER 1: Did you ever receive a letter from the respondent's mother stating that her son was still working in February?

LAWYER 2: Objection.

LAWYER 1: Your Honor, I am only asking this to show that Mrs. Hawthorne wrote the letter, which she has denied in her testimony. The purpose of my question is to impeach her credibility. I am not asking it to prove the truth of the statements she made in the letter.

COURT: I understand, Counsellor. Objection overruled. I will consider the answer only so far as it relates to whether Mrs. Hawthorne wrote a letter stating this, not whether such information is true or not. You may answer the question.

WITNESS: Yes. I did receive a letter from my former mother-in-law that said that Charles was still working in February.

Confused? Don't feel too bad. Every judge or hearing officer has a slightly different idea of what constitutes hearsay. Moreover, because all enforcement hearings are conducted without a jury, the court will usually be more liberal in permitting otherwise tainted, hearsay testimony than it would be were a jury present, the idea being that the court knows what evidence is competent for consideration and will ignore evidence that is not. However, since you will have no idea how strict your particular judge or hearing officer is going to be, you have to be prepared to deal with this important evidentiary rule.

You should also know that judges will usually not explain the reason for their evidentiary rulings, although you can always ask them. However, do not do it too often; most judges will quickly become impatient with your attempt to turn the hearing into a seminar on trial advocacy, although they will permit a party trying his own case considerably more leeway than they would an attorney, who is expected to know the rules.

Now that you have a sense of what hearsay is, you have to deal with the exceptions to the hearsay rule. There are several, but we will keep it simple and discuss only one, which is the most common and applicable exception. An *admission* is an act or statement of a party that can be used as evidence against him at trial. In other words, it is something either you, the petitioner, or your ex, the respondent, said or did outside of court that is generally inconsistent with the position taken at the hearing. For example, you are claiming that you did not receive any support from June through September. Your ex calls as a witness Mrs. Applebaum, your neighbor, who testifies that you told her in August that he had given you $500 in cash. Granted, your statement was made out of court and is being introduced for its truth, making it hearsay, but it is also inconsistent with your position at the hearing. Thus it is an admission that is permitted under this exception to the hearsay rule.

Admissions can also be in the form of conduct that is inconsistent with the party's position at trial. You are claiming near poverty because of your ex's nonpayment, yet your ex is able to produce witnesses who have seen you shopping for a mink coat. The judge is permitted to infer from such circumstantial evidence that your finances are not so dire.

Whenever an admission is used against a party, he or she is allowed the opportunity to explain it. Thus you could take the stand and explain that you told Mrs. Applebaum that you were still getting support payments because she is a nosy busybody and you didn't want her knowing about your problems, and that you were trying on mink coats in Neiman-Marcus because you were so depressed over your situation that you decided to have a little harmless fun.

* * *

Evidentiary rules are complex and take up volumes in law libraries. Our purpose here is to familiarize you with the essential basics, so if the hearing officer mentions "hearsay" or "admissions," you will have some idea of what he or she is talking about. The best advice we can give you is this: if you have any doubt, ask your question or make your objection. The worst that can happen is that an objection to your question will be sustained or your objection overruled. Better to try than to miss an opportunity to score a point because you are uncertain about a fine point of evidence.

(C) Order of Hearing

Enforcement hearings are informal—to a certain extent. They usually are conducted in small officelike rooms by a hearing officer. The parties, and attorneys if any, sit at the same table, across from the hearing officer or examiner. Even in situations where a judge is present, while the courtroom will lend a certain degree of formality, the proceedings remain low key. Regardless of the locale, however, there are still ordinary conventions that must be observed. For simplicity and consistency, we will assume for the balance of this chapter that your hearing will be before a judge, even though it's more than likely it will be a hearing officer or examiner. Nevertheless, it is a good idea to keep in mind that the person is like a judge and therefore entitled to respect and deference. Although hearing officers are for the most part attorneys, just like us, we always refer to them as "your Honor" during hearings, finding that this degree of respect helps maintain proper decorum and assure reciprocal respect from the officer.

Since as petitioner you have the burden of proof, you get to go first. If you wish, you can ask permission to make an opening statement, a brief introduction of your case and what you intend to prove. Many lawyers do not bother with it because there is no jury to impress. Others, including ourselves, feel a short introduction is helpful in setting the stage for the hearing. Your ex, the respondent, also has the right to make an opening statement, which he will likely do if you have made one. We will talk a little more about opening statements later in this chapter.

You then present your case. Hearings, like trials, are normally interrogative, not narrative. In other words, lawyers ask questions and witnesses give answers; a witness does not take the stand and give a speech. Your hearing will be different, since you are representing yourself. Asking yourself questions would be cumbersome, at the very least. Under such circumstances you are permitted to offer your testimony in narrative form, that is, tell your story, subject to the respondent's right to object to any inadmissible portions. Like any witness, you will be sworn in and be expected to tell the truth under penalty of perjury. Finally, do not be surprised if the judge interrupts you frequently to ask his own questions. This even happens in situations where you have your own attorney and is particularly common when a party is representing himself.

There is a certain order of examination that will be observed throughout the hearing. Assume for the moment that you call a witness on your behalf. You begin by questioning your witness. This is called *direct examination*. All the relevant evidence this witness can offer should be elicited by your questions during this examination. After you have concluded your questioning, your ex, or his attorney, then asks the witness questions about matters that were raised in the direct examination. This is called *cross-examination*, a term you have surely heard before. Its purpose is primarily to undermine the witness's testimony, either by catching him with inconsistent statements, by exposing a faulty or suspect memory or by attacking his credibility. Strictly speaking, except for questions pertaining to the witness's credibility, cross-examination must be confined to facts that he testified to during the direct examination. However, you will find that many judges give considerable leeway and permit questions that are unrelated to the direct examination. This is especially so in support cases where there is no jury present.

If your ex's lawyer caused some damage during his cross-examination of your witness, you have the right to *re-direct examination*, where you can ask your witness questions about matters that were brought up in the cross-examination. The primary purpose of a re-direct is to rehabilitate your witness's testimony or to offer explanations that were not provided during the cross-examination. The latter happens frequently. An experienced attorney will often direct a witness to answer a question "yes" or "no." Many questions do not lend themselves to such a response, but nonetheless the person asking the question is entitled to demand a one-word answer. Your witness may have been forced to testify this way, where a more complete answer would have provided a sufficient explanation consistent with the thrust of your case. You then are allowed to ask the witness for this explanation as part of your re-direct examination. Before you do, however, be certain that the full explanation helps your case; otherwise you will have only succeeded in pushing the knife in a bit further.

The respondent's attorney is permitted a *re-cross examination* if you have conducted a re-direct. The scope of inquiry is severely limited: he can only probe matters raised in the re-direct. Thus, if your witness gave the explanation that you requested, your adversary could ask him questions about it with the hope of obtaining a concession or inconsistency that will help his side.

This concludes the examination of the first witness. You then call your other witnesses, in each instance the process being repeated. Keep in mind that the different examinations are serial. If your adversary does not cross-examine the witness, you obviously cannot re-direct; if you do not re-direct, he cannot re-cross. After all your witnesses have testified, you rest—your case, not yourself. The respondent then presents his case. The procedure is the same; only the roles are different. Your adversary will conduct a direct examination of his witness. You will cross-examine them, although you should not feel compelled to. Sometimes it is best to leave an adverse witness's testimony alone. After the cross-examination, your adversary may re-direct if he wants, and you may re-cross. And so it goes until he rests and his case is concluded.

Should your ex or his witnesses raise matters that were not touched upon, or for that matter fully explored, during the presentation of your case, you will ordinarily be allowed to call *rebuttal* witnesses who can offer testimony that contradicts evidence presented during the respondent's case. For example, your ex takes the stand on his own behalf and states that he has been unemployed for the last 6 months and has no income. You then call a rebuttal witness who testifies that the respondent cuts his lawn each week for $35 cash and that he knows at least five other people in the neighborhood for whom he does similar work.

Once both sides rest, the court will allow them to make summations or concluding arguments. The idea here is to sum up the important facts—marshal the evidence, in the words of our profession—and argue that the court mandate a finding in your favor. The respondent does his summation first. You not only get the first word, but the last as well, and close the hearing with your summation. The judge may issue a decision right then and there or reserve decision, depending upon the complexity of the case.

(D) Winning the Case

Before we discuss how to prepare for your hearing, let us highlight the cardinal rules that you must bear in mind as you prepare and follow if you expect to win:

1. *Be prepared!*
2. *Never say in your opening statement that you are going to prove something that you cannot.* Many a good opposing lawyer later makes mincemeat out of such promises in his summation.
3. *Get the witness's entire story out during the direct examination.* Do not try to save something for re-direct, because your adversary may purposefully stay away from the subject during his cross-examination and thereby preclude you from exploring the matter on re-direct.
4. *Never ask a question to which you do not know the answer.* Surprises are fun, but not in court.
5. *Listen carefully to the cross-examination.* Although you should take notes, the most important thing to do is to pay attention. Be prepared to object.
6. *Don't be afraid to ask a question* because you are unsure whether it is proper under the rules of evidence.
7. *Don't be afraid to object to a question,* even if you have no idea what the grounds for the objection are. If it sounds like it shouldn't be asked, object.
8. *Control the witnesses,* especially during cross-examination. Do not let a witness say more than you want him to.
9. *Keep cool, polite and respectful,* especially to the judge. Do not start an argument with your ex or his lawyer.
10. *Never ask that one question too many.* Every trial attorney regrets asking that one last question that either opened a Pandora's box or destroyed the case. Try to remember the defendant who was representing himself in a robbery case where he was accused of purse-snatching. He had been doing fabulously and was just about finishing his cross-examination of

the complainant. However, he could not resist that one last question: "Madam, did you really get a good look at my face when I grabbed your pocketbook?" Two to five years, with parole.

The hardest part of trying a case is maintaining the proper perspective. An inexperienced attorney, like a novice boxer, frequently expects to come up with the big punch that knocks out his opponent, and he quickly becomes frustrated when things do not turn out that way. He begins to press, leads with his chin and soon finds himself on the canvas. An experienced trial lawyer, on the other hand, knows that testimony rarely comes out the way one would like. Questions are difficult to frame. The adversary's objections are distracting; the judge's rulings confusing. He bides his time, methodically jabbing away, looking for a small opening, striking a few quick blows and backing away before the opponent hits back, hoping to score points with the judge instead of flattening his opponent.

If you keep this in mind, you should have no trouble remembering most of our rules, which, by the way, are the same we give to our new lawyers before their first trial. Finally, we caution you not to expect any preferential treatment simply because you are representing yourself. The judge may bend some evidentiary rules and try to help you through the hearing, sometimes even suggesting questions, but he will nevertheless retain his impartiality. You will win or lose your case on the basis of the evidence that you present, not on your performance. Consequently, your case must be thoroughly prepared if you expect to win. We will now discuss the steps you must take to prepare and try your own case successfully.

PREPARATION

Any experienced, successful trial lawyer will unhesitatingly state that preparation is the key to winning cases. It matters little how eloquent his words, how dramatic his oratory, how relaxed his demeanor, how reflexively quick his responses, if the case has not been properly prepared. Bluff and bluster can get one only so far, no matter how convincing it may be. It is evidence that proves the case, and evidence comes only from preparation.

When it comes to preparation, there is really no such thing as overdoing it. Far better is evidence that is ready but not used, than evidence that is needed but not ready. You must set yourself up for every possible contingency, reducing the possibility of your standing fumbling before the judge, trying to think of your next question. This especially holds for someone like you, who has never conducted a hearing and may very well be appearing in a courtroom for the first time, traffic citations excluded. What you lack in experience, you can make up for with preparation. Preparation can give you the "unfair advantage," the edge you may need to win the case, even if your ex is represented by the combined forces of F. Lee Bailey and Marvin Mitchelson.

A support enforcement hearing differs from a trial only to the extent that it is simpler. The issues are less complex, in most instances boiling down to two: the respondent's obligation to pay support and his failure to do so—obligation and nonpayment. Since all you need to produce is evidence of these two, preparation is relatively simple. Read on to learn how this basic evidence is produced. Still, there are times where you will require more extensive preparation. On one hand, you may wish to go further in your proceeding. Your court may permit you at the same time to ask for a payroll deduction order, in which case you will need evidence of your former spouse's employment and salary. Or you may be seeking to attach certain property, such as the upstate 24-acre lot he owns, for which you will need documentary proof of your ex's ownership. On the other hand, your ex may have cross-petitioned for a downward modification, and you will have to prepare your defense.

Regardless of the issues involved in your case, you will need to prepare your evidence, your witnesses and yourself. Each step is equally important, and the time and care that you devote to them will pay dividends in results. You may lack experience, but if you do the necessary work to get your case ready, you will be successful. It is as simple as that.

Preparing Your Evidence

This section is concerned with the documentary evidence that you will—or may—use in the hearing. The testimonial evidence of your witnesses will be treated in the following section.

As you may recall, evidence may be documentary, that is in writing. Indeed there are instances where no other form of evidence will do, a concept that is called the *best evidence rule.* For example, there is no better evidence of your divorce decree than a certified copy of it. You can talk about it until you are blue in the face, yet your words will not carry the same weight as the document itself. Without getting overly complex, evidentiary rules actually prohibit establishing your ex's support obligations by testimony; rather, you must introduce the best available evidence—a certified copy of the decree, judgment or order upon which you base your claim for support. A *certified copy* is a photocopy or other suitable reproduction that a court clerk or other authorized person attests is a true and accurate copy of the original. This is usually done by affixing an official multicolored stamp or raised seal, or other official looking markings. Certified copies are used when the original document cannot be obtained. Your divorce decree is part of the official records of the court that granted it, and it cannot be removed from the files. Therefore you must make a photocopy of it and have it certified by a clerk, for which there is usually a nominal charge. The certified copy is as good as the original for all purposes. If you did not bother to certify the copy, you would need the testimony of the court clerk that it is an accurate copy, a needless complexity that can easily be avoided by paying a few dollars for the certification.

Although a certified copy of the underlying support order is the most important documentary evidence that you will produce at the hearing, there are nonetheless other items that are also required, depending upon the scope of the hearing. These may conveniently be categorized as documents (a) in your own possession; (b) in your former spouse's possession; and (c) in the possession of third parties, that is, individuals or companies who are not part of the proceedings, such as employers, banks, credit card companies and the like.

Obviously, documents in your own possession are the easiest to come by, theoretically at least. All you have to do is get your act together. What do you need? Remember, there are two parts to your proof: obligation and nonpayment. The certified copy of the divorce decree neatly takes care of the first. The second takes a bit more work.

Strictly speaking, testifying under oath that your ex has failed to make certain payments is in itself proof of nonpayment. You are not required to go to great lengths to prove a negative, which nonpayment is, for it is often impossible to prove that something did not happen. Moreover, we have already seen that payment is an affirmative defense, which your former spouse has the burden of proving. Nevertheless, you will want to buttress your testimony of nonpayment with documentary evidence.

The first evidence that you should use are your own records. If you had made a habit of depositing the weekly support checks in either your savings or checking account, gather the records that are representative of the periods for which you were and were not receiving support. These will take the form of savings passbooks or statements, checking account statements and deposit slips. These items are admissible because they are records maintained by the bank in its ordinary course of business, another exception to the hearsay rule. They are as good as having someone from the bank present at the hearing to testify what monies you deposited in your account. If the payments were in cash and not deposited into a bank account, even though you may have kept a written diary or record of payments, you will not be able to introduce that at the hearing because it is a personal memorandum and does not qualify as a record kept in the ordinary course of business. However, as we will see, you will still be able to refer to the diary during your testimony for the limited purpose of refreshing your recollection, which may be all you need it for anyway.

The second type of evidence you may want to use is that which you can obtain from your ex. This encompasses such things as *his* checking and savings account records, canceled checks, deposit slips, as well as payroll stubs and tax returns. Obviously the best proof of payment that he can produce is a canceled check to your order, which you have endorsed. If you demand such records and he cannot produce them, the fair inference that a court is allowed to draw is that he did not pay you. Again, if payments were made in cash, the degree of proof becomes considerably more difficult for both you and him. But since he has the burden of proof, it is really his problem. Nevertheless, you can use documentary proof to rebut claimed cash payments.

We have already mentioned using your own bank account statements to do this. For example, if you are alleging that the payments stopped in February, what better corroborating evidence can you introduce than your combined checking and savings account statement that shows the $150 weekly deposits abruptly ceasing that month. You may also be able to use your ex's documents. Assume that he has a weekly take-home pay of $325 and has testified that he has been paying you the $150 each week religiously. Furthermore, he has testified that he has no other source of income. An examination of his bank records, however, reveals that he has been depositing and writing checks from his account to the tune of $200 to $300 a week since February. There is no way he can accommodate your payments within his budget, and thus the conclusion is that he is lying. Score one for your side. Admittedly, this illustration is somewhat simple, but then in our travels we have seen former spouses do some simple-minded things. The point is that if you do not have the documents you will never have a chance of catching him in a lie.

The simplest way of obtaining your ex's documents would be by asking for them, but be prepared for severe shock should he say yes. If for some reason he is willing to voluntarily provide them, your request should cover a specific time period and describe what documents you are looking for. Don't ask him to give you everything he has, as you may turn his cooperation into defiance in no time flat. Most likely, your ex will not give you a single piece of paper unless he has to. This is where a subpoena comes in very handy, an effective device that we will be talking about shortly.

There will be times when your ex is unable to supply the necessary documents. You may recall that when you were married he always threw away bank statements and credit card bills after a few months, and you expect that old habits die hard. Or perhaps he denies he has them and you know he is lying; but you are not entitled to a search warrant to prove it. There may also be materials that he could not possibly have, such as payroll records. In any of these situations you may obtain whatever you need directly from the third party, be it your ex's boss, bank, credit card company, new car dealer, or anyone else you choose. All banks, for example, maintain microfilm records of canceled checks and statements, which you can get for the hearing. However, keep two things in mind. First, there will likely be a reproduction charge, the amount of which depends on the extent of the material you are requesting. Second, the bank may need several weeks to compile the information and comply with your request. Therefore be ready to spend a few dollars and wait several weeks for the information.

The way you go about obtaining documents from your former spouse or a third-party is by using a judicial *subpoena duces tecum,* a legal paper that commands the named recipient to bring specified documents to court on the hearing date. It would be great if the subpoena directed the recipient to mail the documents to you so that you would have a chance to review them before the hearing. Unfortunately, it does not work that way; the only compulsion is to produce the papers at the courthouse. If your spouse or any other recipient disobeys the order, he may be held in contempt of court, resulting in a possible fine or imprisonment, or both. A typical subpoena duces tecum looks something like this:

SUPERIOR COURT: FAMILY DIVISION
MARLBOROUGH COUNTY

· ·

CAROL STEVENS,   Docket No. 55570
                        PETITIONER,
                    -vs.-

EDWARD STEVENS,   **JUDICIAL SUBPOENA
                                                    DUCES TECUM**
                        RESPONDENT.

· ·

          THE PEOPLE OF THE STATE OF SOMEWHERE

TO: EDWARD STEVENS
       4 Orchid Lane R.R.2
       Greenpond, Somewhere

       WE COMMAND YOU, That all business and excuses be laid aside, and
that you appear and attend before the HON. JOHN NEWHOUSE at the Superior
Court, Family Division, in courtroom 316, at 120 Main Street, Bigtown, at 10:00
AM on May 12, 1986 and that you bring with you and produce at the aforesaid
time and place the following documents now in your custody:

       1. All checking account statements, checkbook stubs or registers and can-
celed checks for accounts in your name, whether singly or jointly with any other
person, for the last three years.
       2. All savings account passbooks and statements for accounts in your
name, whether singly or jointly with any other person, for the last three years.
       3. All statements, bills and invoices for any credit cards issued in your
name, whether singly or jointly with any other person, for the last three years.

       NOTICE: FAILURE TO COMPLY WITH THIS SUBPOENA IS PUNISH-
ABLE AS A CONTEMPT OF COURT AND SHALL MAKE YOU LIABLE TO
THE PERSON ON WHOSE BEHALF IT WAS ISSUED FOR ALL DAMAGES
SUSTAINED BY YOUR FAILURE TO COMPLY.

       WITNESS, Hon. John Newhouse, one of the judges of said Court, on April
28, 1986.

     The actual form of the subpoena varies slightly from state to state. The
easiest way to prepare one is to get a preprinted blank form directly from
the court or a stationery store that sells legal and business forms. It is not
necessary that the information be typed; you can print it *neatly*. The court
clerk will tell you if you have filled it out correctly. However, he will
not offer you any advice as to the type of documents you should be requesting, which you will have to come up with on your own, with
our help.
     In addition to the items that are specified in the sample above, depend-
ing on whom you are sending your subpoena to, you may also want to ask
for some of the following:

1. All contracts for the rental or lease of safe deposit boxes in respondent's name, singly or jointly with any other person. (USE TO DETERMINE LIVING EXPENSES/SALARY)
2. All records concerning securities, bonds, warrants and indentures owned by respondent singly or jointly with any other person for the last __ years. (USE TO DETERMINE INCOME)
3. All copies of respondent's federal, (state), and (city) income tax returns for the last __ years. (USE TO DETERMINE INCOME)
4. All records and writings relating to respondent's employment for the last __ years that indicates the following information: wages (including IRS W-2 forms); salaries; bonuses; commissions; advance drawings; stock options; sickness and disability payments; salary increases; payroll deductions; credit union accounts; pension plans and funds; and any other benefits that are, were or may be paid or available to respondent. (USE IF HE IS EMPLOYED)
5. All records and writings relating to fees, charges and other remuneration received by respondent during the last __ years, including IRS #1099 forms. (USE IF HE IS SELF-EMPLOYED)
6. All checkbooks, ledger books, cash receipt journals, accounts receivable and payable records kept or maintained by respondent (or anyone under his supervision) relating to any business in which respondent has an interest. (USE IF HE IS SELF-EMPLOYED)
7. All credit card and loan applications, including financial statements, used by respondent in the last __ years to obtain loans or credit. (USE TO DETERMINE INCOME/EXPENSES)
8. All deeds, mortgages, contracts of sale, options, leases and records of transfer (including closing statements) of any real property in respondent's name, either singly or jointly with any other person, for the last __ years. (USE TO DETERMINE ASSETS)
9. All records relating to the transfer, by sale, gift or otherwise, of any personal property owned by respondent, the value of which exceeds $500, within the last __ years. (USE TO DETERMINE INCOME)
10. All records relating to the purchase of any personal property by respondent, the value of which exceeds $500, within the last __ years. (USE TO DETERMINE ASSETS/EXPENDABLE SALARY)
11. All certificates of title, or registration records, for any automobiles, trucks, vans, recreation vehicles, motorcycles, trailers, boats or the like registered in respondent's name, either singly or jointly with any other person, for the last __ years. (USE TO DETERMINE ASSETS/EXPENDABLE SALARY)
12. All records relating to retirement plans, pension plans, IRA accounts or Keogh plans in which respondent has a vested or unvested interest. (USE TO DETERMINE SAVINGS/FUTURE INCOME)

This list should handle most situations, although it cannot cover every possibility. We recommend that you tailor your subpoena to the circumstances of your individual case. In other words, you should have a fair idea of what kinds of assets and records your former spouse may have, and those are the types of things to go after. If he is a salaried employee, there is little point looking for partnership records. On the other hand, if he is working for himself, do not waste too much time trying to get documents pertaining to employment and fringe benefits. Keep in mind the intended purpose of the subpoena, which is to help you prosecute your enforcement proceeding. If you can show that he has money in the bank, or in the stock market, you easily deprive him of any feeble excuse for nonpayment. The same goes if you can offer the court his credit card records that reveal frequent trips to Atlantic City or Las Vegas.

The goal is not to produce reams of paper, but documents that have some bearing upon your ex's financial situation. Even if your ex is *not* seeking a downward modification, you still want documents relating to his income and assets—bank accounts, stock, property, etc.—to demonstrate that his conduct was willful and inexcusable. If he is looking for modification, these records are even more important to prepare for your defense. The more financial information you have about him, the better off you will be. It is as simple as that.

Subpoenas are issued by attorneys or the court, and they are served upon the person or company either by personal delivery or by certified mail. The rules vary in each state, but many jurisdictions permit a court clerk to sign and issue your subpoena as an agent for the court. Visit the Family Court and you will be advised as to the correct method to employ. Be sure to ask.

One problem with a subpoena duces tecum is that it is normally returnable the same day as the hearing, which means that the "target" does not have to produce beforehand the material you request. This can make it difficult, for your time to review the documents and prepare questions will be severely limited. The problem is somewhat less with third-party subpoenas, because you can usually make informal arrangements with a bank or employer for it to furnish the information at an earlier date. They are only too happy not to have someone appear in court. You certainly cannot expect to have the same cooperation from your ex, although if he has an attorney you may at least be able to discuss it. If you cannot arrange for the documents before the hearing and are deluged with a voluminous amount of information, you should make an oral application to the judge, explaining the situation and requesting a slight adjournment of the hearing, which will give you sufficient time to review the documents. The worst that will happen is that your request may be denied, but that is rare.

A similar concern is a situation where you have subpoenaed your ex's records, and he shows up for the hearing only to say that he doesn't have a single thing for you. What do you do? You do what any experienced trial attorney does: ask for a short adjournment to permit you time to obtain the records directly from his bank, employer or whatever. If your ex or his lawyer tries to complain that the delay is prejudicial, point out to the judge that he never once telephoned you beforehand to tell you that he did not have the documents so that you could have made other arrangements in time. We safely predict that the judge will take your side and grant the adjournment.

Once you have the documents that you intend to introduce as evidence in the hearing, the next step is to organize them in such a way so that you can quickly retrieve and use them effectively. Do not tie them into one big bundle and shove them into a plastic shopping bag, or even a briefcase for that matter. One sure sign of an inexperienced trial attorney is his inability to handle documents at trial. Many a novice has lifted his attaché case up in search of a particular paper and ended up spilling everything out onto the floor, or he has frenziedly fumbled over the counsel table looking for a copy of a canceled check, wasting precious court time and consuming limited judicial patience. We suggest that you separate the information in some manner that makes sense to you—there is no hard and fast rule—and clip, staple, file or rubber band it together. Whichever way you do it, the information has to be readily retrievable.

Before we leave the subject of documentary evidence, some brief mention must be made about how it is used in the hearing. Like any evidence, it must be *introduced* to the court at the appropriate time. However, you neither announce that you are calling the respondent's checkbook as your next witness, nor dump the bundle of bank statements on the judge's bench. There is instead a rather standardized procedure that varies only slightly between jurisdictions. Each document that is introduced into evidence must first be identified and marked as an *exhibit*. This is done by showing it to the witness and asking him if he has ever seen the document before and, if so, to identify it. Once it is identified, you then ask the court if it may be introduced as evidence, in as detailed a manner as allows for complete identification. "Your Honor, I move to introduce the statement dated October 20, 1984, from Central Bank addressed to respondent and referring to account number 28-10678 as petitioner's Exhibit 1." Or, "Your Honor, I would like the Central Bank checking account statement of October 20, 1984 regarding respondent's account number 28-10678 to be marked as petitioner's Exhibit 1."

The judge will direct you to show the proposed exhibit to your ex (or his lawyer) and ask him if he has any objections. If he does not, it is admitted into evidence. If he has an objection, he states it for the record, and the court then rules on the admissibility just as it would any other evidentiary question.

Preparation of Witnesses

The next thing that you must consider in preparing for your hearing is who your witnesses are going to be. The flip side of this coin is figuring out the witnesses that your ex is likely to call on his behalf. Before you take out your local telephone directory, you should first consider whether in fact you need any witnesses besides yourself and your ex. Let's face it; the two of you are the principal players, and anyone else will only have a supporting role. However, since much of your case may turn on simply who the judge believes—you or him—any time you can bring in a third party who can testify about some conversation or transaction between you can be particularly helpful. For example, if your ex is going to claim that he always paid you $200 in cash each week, and you have a friend who was present on several occasions when he said that he did not have the money to pay you, certainly her testimony is important. The same would go for anyone that your ex knows, and who is willing to testify that he was heard saying that he had missed making your payments.

The determination of who you will use as a witness comes down to what you believe they can contribute to your case. Certainly, it would be a waste of time to bring in a friend or relative who can only testify as to what a good mother you are. This has absolutely nothing to do with nonpayment.

Nor can you plan to use someone who can only offer hearsay statements
—"Oh, Mr. Solbowski told me several times that the respondent was
making money off the books." Nor could your witness testify as to anything *you said* about your former spouse's delinquency—these self-serving
statements are not admissions and thus not an exception to the hearsay
prohibition. Remember, the only admissions that you can get into evidence are those made by the other side, so anytime anyone heard your
ex say something adverse to or inconsistent with his interests or position
in the case, that person is someone you should consider as a potential
witness. Also it is not necessary for the person to have heard the statement
in *your* presence; in fact it is very likely that your ex would only make such
a statement in your absence. When you come down to it, there is no hard
and fast rule in choosing witnesses. It is easy to say that they must have
some impact, and a favorable one, on your case. However, the impact
need not be large. Often the best way to build a successful case is in small
increments.

You should also consider the people that your ex may call on his side.
If possible, you should try to meet or speak with them to find out what
their testimony will be. Many times these people will be your ex's friends
who will not be particularly disposed to discussing their testimony with
you. There is little you can do about it. On the other hand, there may be
some neutral witnesses who will not mind discussing their testimony with
you. For example, your ex may be planning on calling the payroll manager
at the plant where he works to testify that his overtime has been eliminated. This person presumably would not have too much difficulty telling
you the same thing over the telephone. There is nothing like getting a
preview of the other side's case, and the effort is truly worthwhile.

Once you have figured out who your witnesses are going to be, the next
thing to do is to prepare them. A good attorney makes sure that his
witnesses are thoroughly prepared. Surprises are to be avoided. Since you
will be your own star witness, your job is considerably easier.

If you are planning to call other witnesses, you will have to get them
ready, a two-step process. First comes the interview, where you attempt
to ascertain all this person's knowledge of the subject about which he or
she will be testifying. Be sure not to ask and listen about only the good
parts, those facts that are helpful to your case. You better know the
downside as well, whatever information this person can supply that is
detrimental to your side and could come out in cross-examination. You
may, as a result of the interview, conclude that a particular person should
not be called as a witness because the chances of an inadvertent, adverse
revelation may be too dangerous, or you may just conclude that the
person cannot offer anything of substance, even though she is your very
best friend and has been forever requesting to testify against him.

The second step is the rehearsal. Just like in a play, you and your
witness should read your lines. Ask your questions and let the witness
answer. Besides, you surely need the practice. Impress upon the witness
that he must answer what is asked and not volunteer anything more,
especially during cross-examination. (Don't forget this rule when you are
on the stand!) You may feel a little foolish conducting a direct examina-

tion across the kitchen table, but take our word that the time is well spent. Trial advocacy, like anything else, is a learned skill. There is no such thing as a born lawyer. The more you practice, the better you get.

After you have gone through the direct questioning to your satisfaction —you may have to repeat it one or more times—switch sides and start cross-examining your witness, trying your best to shake him up, confuse him and discredit his testimony. Once again, the rehearsal helps you both. The witness is ready for the rigors of cross-examination, and you have sharpened your cross-examining skills.

There may be certain witnesses whom you wish to call but cannot expect to prepare—the ones who are on your ex's side. Nevertheless, their testimony may be helpful. For instance, your ex is claiming poverty, yet you notice that his new wife is strolling about in a fur coat. Maybe the judge would like to hear from her about how she got the coat and who paid for it. Or, you have discovered that he has been installing a new kitchen for a neighbor, from whom you would like to know how much he is getting paid. Since it is unlikely that any of these people would be willing to appear voluntarily to testify on your behalf, you will require a way of obtaining their cooperation. It exists, and it is called a *subpoena*. The formal name is *subpoena ad testificandum*, but nobody save for Latin scholars ever calls it that. Nor will we.

We have already seen the subpoena duces tecum, which is used to secure the production of written documents. The subpoena is used to obtain the testimony of a witness. It subjects a witness to the court's jurisdiction (power) and requires the witness to give certain information "under penalty," the literal translation of subpoena. If the person disobeys it, he can be found guilty of contempt of court. If there are witnesses whose attendance you need to assure, you can request the necessary subpoenas from the court clerk. Sometimes there is a nominal fee that must accompany the subpoena; the clerk will instruct you.

Preparing Yourself

You have two people to prepare: petitioner-the-witness, and petitioner-the-attorney. You have the two major roles in your production—director and star—so you better get ready.

The witness side of you can be prepared just like any other witness, except you can skip the interview. The rehearsal is still necessary. If you can get hold of one, use a tape recorder and listen to yourself. Otherwise, use a friend. Your testimony will be narrative, not question and answer, yet you should do as much as possible to present it as if someone were questioning you. This does not mean that you should ask yourself rhetorical questions. Rather, the testimony should be logically organized, touching serially upon the basic elements of your *prima facie* case:

1. The right to support
2. The identity of the person from whom you are to receive the support
3. The amount of frequency of the support payments
4. Nonpayment

Your testimony should therefore relate that you are divorced pursuant to a decree, giving date and court, that the respondent is the person sitting there in court (point), that the respondent is obliged to pay you x dollars per week/month for maintenance and/or child support, and that the respondent has missed the following payments (describe). That is your case, in a nutshell.

The attorney side of your role is more difficult, but do not lose heart. We will take you through a hearing in the following section in order to give you an idea of how it is done. While it is natural to develop your own style of trying a case, we recommend that you avoid becoming too creative. There will be no jury to impress, no multimillion-dollar verdicts to sweeten the pot, so stay away from the dramatics. Present your case in as simple and straightforward a manner as you can. Let your evidence, not your theatricality, impress the judge.

There are a variety of ways to try a case and even more ways to prepare for it. We will give you, however, only one method, the same we give to any new attorney. It is the KISS method: Keep it Safe and Simple. We have already shown you how to get your documents and your witnesses ready. Only you, the lawyer, remain.

We anticipate that many of our colleagues will criticize us for the following advice, but we are going to stick by our guns nonetheless. *Do not* write out your questions for your witnesses. We strongly believe that canned questions are counter-productive. The examination soon becomes stilted. The examiner fails to ride with the testimony *as it develops.* She does not ask that vital follow-up question on direct examination, or go for the jugular on cross-examination if the opportunity presents itself. She is more concerned with following the script than reacting to events and the flow of the case. We call it trying a case with blinders, and it rarely works.

Rather than write questions, outline your case and each witness's testimony. Take a large, yellow legal pad and sketch out the order of your case, identifying who you are going to call and the key facts they will relate. Then take a separate page, or pages, and outline the questions that you intend to ask each witness—yours and his. As for the latter, you probably have *some* idea of who your ex is going to call on his behalf, and you should prepare a brief outline of questions you may wish to ask them on cross-examination. Print everything, neatly and in large letters so you can read it even when standing. An outline for the examination of the helpful neighbor could look like this:

Sheila Barrow (direct examination)

> Relationship
> > – with petitioner
> > > – describe
> > > – how long
> > – with respondent
> > > – describe
> > > – how long
>
> Familiarity with situation
> > – how

— what she knows
— who told her

Respondent's statements
— where did it happen
— when
— where was he
— where were you
— what he said
— whom he said it to
— who else was present

While preparing your case, the newspaper reporter's credo is helpful to keep in mind: GET THE WHO, WHAT, WHEN, WHERE AND WHY! And get them from each witness. Always put the testimony in a time and place. Do not ask what was said, before you ask when and where it was said. Paint a clear picture with the witness' words. Do not leave it to the court or your adversary to supply the missing details.

You should also keep in mind that you can call your ex as your own witness. In fact, we strongly suggest it. By so doing, you may take him by surprise and get a chance to lock in his testimony before his lawyer has a chance to get his side of the story out in the more carefully nurturing environment of friendly direct examination. By this we mean that your ex will not have the chance to tell his story according to the script that he and his lawyer had previously rehearsed, and instead you get to score points for your side first. Moreover, your ex may display certain behavior during your examination, such as hostility or evasiveness, that will turn the judge off right from the start so by the time he takes the stand for his side, he may have lost whatever credibility he had going into the hearing.

It is important that you plan the direct examination of your ex as carefully as any other witness. Let him state under oath exactly what payments he claims to have made to you and the children. Ask him how much money he is making, and how much he is spending. In effect, you will be putting him to his proof before he has a chance to react. Through your questioning you can orchestrate the way you want his story to develop, then leave it to him and his attorney to try to pick up the pieces later. Of course, you must be prepared to risk the possibility that the entire thing may backfire and that the testimony you elicit may prove more helpful to his case than yours. But how much of a risk is it, really? His testimony would have come out anyway, when he or his lawyer presented his case, and so you had little to lose in exchange for the chance to force and manipulate his evidence in a way that might help your case.

Once you have finished your case and "rested," your ex has the opportunity to present his witnesses. He or his lawyer will conduct the direct examination, and you will have the chance to cross-examine. Although we have suggested that you make a brief outline of the questions that you may wish to ask his witnesses, practically speaking the outline that you will actually use is the one that you sketch out during his witness' testimony. While this is going on, you should take *very brief* notes of the testimony, from which you should check off, star or circle (whatever you prefer) those areas that you wish to address on cross-examination. Although you may have properly anticipated what the witness was going to say and may have a neat outline to use, there is an equal chance that the actual testimony is entirely different from this, and that you will have to rely more upon the notes that you make during the witness' direct testimony. You may not be comfortable flying by the seat of your pants, but there is no better effective way to deal with cross-examination. It is more important for your questions to be related to the witness' testimony than to be carefully crafted. There will be times, however, that you may want to ask the witness questions that go beyond his or her direct examination. Technically, you are not permitted to do so, as cross-examination must confine itself to the direct. Practically speaking, many judges will give you some leeway in this regard, even if there is a strenuous objection from the other side. This is where the outline that you previously prepared comes in handy, if there are areas that you in your preparation felt should be explored.

When it comes to cross-examination, every trial attorney has to make important decisions as to whether to use it. Although you may have a right to cross-examination, this does not mean that cross-examination is the right thing in every instance. Often you do yourself more harm than good if you do little more than have the witness repeat testimony that has already been provided. As you are new in the game, we strongly advise that you use cross-examination gingerly, especially of other witnesses besides your ex. With him, you likely know more about his affairs and his manner of doing things. Thus you stand a good chance of catching him in some inconsistencies and mitigating the credibility of his previous testimony. Your chances of doing this with others are significantly less, and unless you think you have a particular angle, you may be better served by limiting your cross-examination to very few questions, or perhaps asking no questions at all. Remember, cardinal rule: No. 10—*never ask the one question too many*—applies *most* of all to cross-examination. We suggest that if you have any legitimate doubts about whether to proceed, don't. However, if you have some questions to ask but are afraid to do so because you are nervous or don't think they are well worded, these are no excuses and you should ask your questions as best you can.

THE HEARING

Come along with us once again for a guided tour of the court. This time we'll take a look at what a hearing is like. We will be going to Hearing Room 17 on the fourth floor. Elizabeth Hartley, who has a dogeared, multicolor underlined copy of this book in her briefcase, is about to begin her enforcement hearing. She is seated at the right side of the table, facing the hearing officer, Referee Sidney Lewis. Her former husband, Peter, is seated at Elizabeth's far left. Between them is his attorney, Allen Cramwell. Except for us and a court officer, no one else is in the room.

Since the proceedings are less formal than regular court, there is no court stenographer to record the testimony. Rather, there is a tape recorder that is operated by the court officer. Should either side wish to appeal the referee's decision, he or she would first have to pay for a typed transcript of the recording. This can be a considerable expense, especially if the hearing is lengthy. As it turns out, there will be an appeal, and we will be able to obtain an official transcript. You do not have to worry about remembering every word, because we will be reproducing parts of the hearing transcript for you. All right, the hearing is about to begin; listen carefully.

FAMILY COURT OF THE STATE OF THE ART
COUNTY OF BOUNTY

· X

ELIZABETH HARTLEY,
               PETITIONER,
         -against-   Docket #3985/85
PETER HARTLEY,   **SUPPORT HEARING**
               RESPONDENT.

· X

April 8, 1986

B E F O R E :
    Referee Sidney Lewis

A P P E A R A N C E S :
    Elizabeth Hartley, Petitioner *Pro Se*
    78 Maplewood Drive
    Crestwood, Art

    Allen Cramwell, Attorney for Respondent
    1010 Central Avenue
    Riverbend, Art

REFEREE LEWIS: Good morning, ladies and gentlemen, are we ready to begin?

ELIZABETH HARTLEY: Yes, your Honor, petitioner is ready.

ALLEN CRAMWELL: Ready for the respondent, Judge.

REFEREE LEWIS: Fine. Are there any opening remarks? If so, please keep them brief.

MS. HARTLEY: Thank you. Your Honor, this case involves one thing, and one thing alone: my former husband's failure to pay child support and maintenance. As I will show, the respondent and I were divorced on January 12, 1982. He is required by our divorce judgment to pay me maintenance of $500 each month and child support for our two daughters of $300 each month, for a monthly total of $800.

Starting in November of last year, the respondent stopped paying this amount, save for one or two isolated payments of a few hundred dollars. I have made repeated requests that he make these payments, but he has refused. He left me with no other choice than to bring this proceeding in which I am asking for a payroll deduction order, a money judgment and an order that the respondent post reasonable security for future payments.

I intend to prove to this Court that the respondent owes me and my daughters $3,300, and not a penny less. However, the respondent is trying to cloud the simple issues in this case. He has made a claim against me for a downward modification of his obligations. He claims that there has been a substantial change of circumstances. Well, sir, claiming and proving this are two different things. I do not think that he will be able to, and I also intend to show this Court that his finances have changed—for the better.

We think that Elizabeth should have stopped just before she said she was going to prove that Peter's finances had improved. No use making his burden of proof hers. She is under no obligation to show that his situation is better, although if she has such evidence it will destroy his case. Still it would be better to be quiet about it and spring it on the other side. In any event, little harm was done.

MR. CRAMWELL: Your Honor, my client and I admit that he has sadly missed a number of payments to the petitioner, although we disagree as to the amount. We believe that the proof will show that he owes her considerably less than the sum she claims.

What I also believe the evidence will show is that my client's failure to pay his ex-wife was not maliciously motivated, but instead was caused by an unfortunate chain of events that has caused his personal finances to deteriorate to the point where he can no longer afford to pay the petitioner $800 each month. Moreover, the proof will show that the petitioner's own financial circumstances have improved significantly since the time of the divorce, and that the time is ripe for her to assume a greater share of the burden of the support of the children and herself. Your Honor, after all is said and done, after you have heard the testimony of the parties and their witnesses, and after you have reviewed the evidence, I believe that you will concur with the respondent that there has been a substantial change of circumstances that clearly warrants a downward modification of the support provisions of the divorce decree.

REFEREE LEWIS: Thank you, Mrs. Hartley, and Mr. Cramwell. Please call your first witness, Mrs. Hartley.

MS. HARTLEY: Your Honor, I call myself as petitioner's first witness. (Witness sworn)

MS. HARTLEY: I will try to state the facts as briefly as I can, sir. My husband, I mean the respondent, and I were married for twelve years. We have two children, Tracy and Susan. Tracy is ten now, and Susan will be seven next month. We got divorced in 1982. At this time, I would like to introduce as an exhibit a certified copy of my divorce decree. It is dated January 12, 1982 and it is from the Superior Court of this State, Bounty County.

REFEREE LEWIS: Show it to Mr. Cramwell, please.

MR. CRAMWELL: No objection, your Honor. It appears to be a true copy.

REFEREE LEWIS: It's certified.

MR. CRAMWELL: Yes, I see that.

REFEREE LEWIS: All right, we will mark this as petitioner's Exhibit 1. Proceed, madam.

Ms. HARTLEY: Thank you. Your Honor, I would just like, if I may, to read something from the decree, I mean Exhibit 1. Here it is. On page four, it states, "The defendant shall pay the plaintiff on the first day of each month the sum of $500 as and for her maintenance and support for a period of six years from the date hereof, and further the sum of $300 each month for the support of the minor children of the marriage, to wit: Tracy Hartley and Susan Hartley, until they reach the age of 21 years, or become emancipated, whichever is sooner."

Now, judge, I wish to state that my former husband did pay me that amount for several years, although I can't say that he was always prompt about it. Sometimes I would have to call him and—

MR. CRAMWELL: Objection.

REFEREE LEWIS: Sustained. Mrs. Hartley, please try to confine yourself to the facts in controversy. As I read your petition here, all you're claiming are arrears for about, let's see, for about five months. Let's stick to that period of time, if you will.

Ms. HARTLEY: Yes, sir. I'm sorry.

REFEREE LEWIS: That's alright. Please go on.

Ms. HARTLEY: Starting with the November payment, which was due on the first—

REFEREE LEWIS: What year are we talking about?

Ms. HARTLEY: Oh, yes. 1985. Starting with the payment that was due on November 1st, 1985, Peter has—

REFEREE LEWIS: You mean the respondent, don't you?

Ms. HARTLEY: Yes, the respondent, Peter Hartley.

REFEREE LEWIS: And that's him sitting over to my right?

Ms. HARTLEY: Yes, your Honor.

MR. CRAMWELL: Judge, we're not disputing that the decree requires the respondent to pay $800 a month.

REFEREE LEWIS: Fine. There have been no subsequent modifications, either by agreement or prior court order, have there?

MR. CRAMWELL: No sir. Just a change of circumstances.

REFEREE LEWIS: Yes, you'll get your chance. Go on, Madam.

Ms. HARTLEY: Okay. As I was saying, I never received the November payment. That's this past November. And I didn't get the December check either, which was horrible with the holidays and everything coming.

MR. CRAMWELL: Objection.

REFEREE LEWIS: Overruled.

Ms. HARTLEY: I kept calling the respondent, at least once a week, to ask him where the money was. All he kept giving me were excuses. One after the other.

MR. CRAMWELL: Your Honor, I would ask that the witness not characterize what my client allegedly said, and instead tell us what he said.

REFEREE LEWIS: Yes, tell us what you said to him and what he said to you.

Ms. HARTLEY: Well I'll try as best I can.

REFEREE LEWIS: You don't have to use his exact words, just give your best recollection.

Ms. HARTLEY: Sure. The first time I called him . . . it must have been around the tenth—

REFEREE LEWIS: What month?

Ms. HARTLEY: November. This was all in November. The first time he said that there was a screw-up with his company's payroll and that everything should be straightened out in a few days. That didn't make sense at all, but he insisted it was true. Anyway, a few days later I run into Jane Simpson at Safeway—her husband works with Peter—and I asked her about the payroll. She said—

MR. CRAMWELL: Objection.

REFEREE LEWIS: Sustained. That's hearsay. You can't testify about what someone else said.

Ms. HARTLEY: Yes, I know. I just wanted to show that he was lying.

MR. CRAMWELL: Objection!

REFEREE LEWIS: I know, but you can't do it that way. Let me ask you this, did you ever confront the respondent with what you learned?

Ms. HARTLEY: Sure I did. That evening I called him and told him what Jane had told me. Peter said that she was full of—I'm sorry—shit and that she didn't know what she was talking about. He also said that everything was straightened out and that I would get paid as soon as his payroll check cleared.

A few more days went by, and still no check. So I called Peter again. This time he said, "Look, I'm sorry, but I just had to put a new transmission in the van." I asked him what was more important, his truck or his children. He said he needed his truck for work. I asked him what he was talking about, and he told me he was trying to pick up a few extra bucks for the holidays by doing some carpentry on weekends. He promised I would have the money by Monday.

REFEREE LEWIS: When was it that you spoke to him?

Ms. HARTLEY: Oh, let's see. It must have been around the third week in November. I think it was a Thursday night, because I remember that I was worried about picking up Tracy in time from her ballet lessons. Yeah, I'm pretty sure it was Thursday.

REFEREE LEWIS: Okay, continue.

Ms. HARTLEY: Anyway, Monday comes and goes, and still no payment. So I called Peter at work on Tuesday and asked him what was going on. He said not to worry and that he'd send the money back with the kids after he saw them Wednesday night.

That night, Tracy hands me an envelope.

REFEREE LEWIS: The night you called him, or Wednesday?

Ms. HARTLEY: Wednesday. Wednesday night.

REFEREE LEWIS: Fine.

Ms. HARTLEY: I opened the envelope, and instead of a check, there's $200 in cash. I tried telephoning the respondent, but there was no answer. I spoke to him the following day, however. He said he was really running tight and that he'd get me the other $600 by next week.

REFEREE LEWIS: Did he actually use those words? Did he say $600?

Ms. HARTLEY: Yes, he did, your Honor. This had never happened before, so I figured I'd give him some slack and not bother him for a week. I believed what he was telling me, although I soon learned what a fool I was. A whole week goes by, and no check, no word or anything. At this point I'm not too worried; I have about $1200 in the savings. Still I figured that—

MR. CRAMWELL: Objection.

REFEREE LEWIS: Just tell us what you did, not what you thought.

Ms. HARTLEY: Sure. That following Saturday evening I called Peter and told him I wanted the money. He said, "Look I know I owe you. Believe me I'm trying to work everything out. I'll make it up in next month's check." I asked what the problem was, but he said it was too complicated to get into. It was almost December anyway, so I figured I'd let things slide.

MR. CRAMWELL: Objection. Her figuring is immaterial, your Honor.

REFEREE LEWIS: Sustained. Stick to the facts, Mrs. Hartley.

Ms. HARTLEY: Yes, I'll try. I'm new at this.

REFEREE LEWIS: You're doing fine. Don't worry. But let me help you a little. Did you ever receive the December payment?

Ms. HARTLEY: No.

REFEREE LEWIS: Did you speak to the respondent about it?

Ms. HARTLEY: Yes, sir, I did, several times. I called him on . . . Just a moment. I have it written down in my appointment book. Here it is. I called the respondent on December 6th at 4:30 P.M.

MR. CRAMWELL: Objection. That document is not in evidence. I object to her reading from it.

REFEREE LEWIS: Mrs. Hartley, you can't read from a document that has not been introduced into evidence. However, you may refer to it to refresh your recollection. I believe that is what you were doing. Correct?

Ms. HARTLEY: Yes, that's what I was doing.

REFEREE LEWIS: Objection overruled.

Ms. HARTLEY: When I spoke to Peter on the 6th, I asked him about the December payment. He said he was aware of it. I asked when I could expect it. He told me that he was working on it and if I didn't like it I could go and . . . Can I say it in court?

REFEREE LEWIS: No, it's not necessary; I believe we have the gist of it.

Ms. HARTLEY: I called him again a few days later, on December 10th. I still had gotten nothing. Not a dime. This time Peter was all lovey dovey. He said he was really sorry for blowing his top and not paying us, but he was in a real jam. He asked me if I could hang on for a few more weeks. I said I could, but just barely. He promised that if worse came to worst he would get a bank loan to get me the money. I told him I would try to manage as best I could.

I next saw Peter on Christmas day, when he dropped off the girls. I didn't think it was appropriate—

MR. CRAMWELL: Objection.

REFEREE LEWIS: Sustained.

Ms. HARTLEY: I didn't mention the money, but he did. Peter said that everything was cool—that's his word—and that I could plan on going out on New Year's Eve and celebrating.

I didn't, and good thing too. Needless to say, there was no check on January 1st, or a few days after. Another week went by and I called my, I mean, the respondent at work. That was on January 8th. He said he wanted to meet me for a cup of coffee at the Crossroads Diner to talk things over. I got my neighbor to babysit and ran over to meet him. When I got there he started to give me a big song and dance—

MR. CRAMWELL: Objection.

REFEREE LEWIS: Don't describe. Just say what he said.

Ms. HARTLEY: Okay. He said that he still hadn't gotten the money together, but he wanted to give me a few hundred bucks because he was really concerned about the children. So he reaches in his pocket. Meanwhile I notice that he's wearing a new Rolex, and I ask him about it. He says it's a fake, and I start yelling at him for having a hell of a nerve blowing money on a watch when me and the kids are eating macaroni and cheese. He stands up, starts cursing at me, bangs on the table and throws a few crumpled bills at me before he runs out like a madman.

MR. CRAMWELL: Objection. I move to strike that last phrase.

REFEREE LEWIS: Sustained. I will ignore it.

Elizabeth goes on to testify about a few other conversations with Peter, who, needless to say, never comes through with the money, except for $700 in cash. So far, she has been doing just fine. She has not let Cramwell's objections throw her off stride. She has kept track of what she wanted to say and made sure that she did. And she has always been polite and respectful to the Judge even when he has chided her for going a bit off the subject. What the transcript does not show, of course, are her emotions. At first, Elizabeth was nervous, her speech halting and uncertain. However, as the hearing has progressed, she has become more confident, and at this point she is speaking in fairly normal conversational tones. When she begins questioning her ex, she will become nervous again, but once more she will settle down into the swing of things. Anyway, let's get back to the hearing. Elizabeth is about to testify about her record keeping, which will complete her testimony. Then Cramwell gets his chance to cross-examine her.

Ms. HARTLEY: I would like at this point, your Honor, to explain my record keeping.

REFEREE LEWIS: As it pertains to respondent's payments?

Ms. HARTLEY: Yes, sir.

REFEREE LEWIS: Fine, go ahead.

Ms. HARTLEY: The respondent has always paid me by check, a single check each month of $800. As I testified already, when all this trouble began back in November, he started to give me cash—$700 over the past few months, but that was it.

Peter's checks usually came in the mail around the 10th. I deposited them as soon as I could, usually the very next day, unless it was a Sunday or holiday and the bank was closed.

I have a combined checking and savings account at First Lincoln Savings in Crestwood, which I have had for about the last three years. All Peter's checks were deposited in this account. I never cashed his checks, like in the supermarket or something.

I have a number of bank statements that I would like to introduce as evidence.

REFEREE LEWIS: How many do you have?

Ms. HARTLEY: Uh, let's see.

REFEREE LEWIS: Take your time.

Remember what we said about preparation? Although the Referee is being kind, Elizabeth should have been trying her case, not his patience. By organizing her documents better, she could have avoided this delay. It is a good idea to pre-mark the back of the exhibits in pencil, or use those yellow Post-it notepads that you are beginning to see stuck to everything in creation.

Ms. HARTLEY: Here, there's fifteen altogether.

REFEREE LEWIS: All right, we'll identify them as petitioner's Exhibit 2, let's see, that would be A through O. Can you state for the record what they are?

Ms. HARTLEY: Yes, these are statements from First Lincoln Savings for a checking and savings account in the name of Elizabeth Hartley, account number 108-834562.

MR. CRAMWELL: What dates?

Ms. HARTLEY: Oh, sure. These are in order. It starts from January 21, 1985, and it goes on for each following month up to March 21, 1986.

REFEREE LEWIS: And each one is dated around the 20th of the month?

Ms. HARTLEY: Yes, it looks that way.

REFEREE LEWIS: Fine, so you are introducing as petitioner's Exhibit 2, A through O, statements of the First Lincoln Savings Bank in Crestwood for petitioner's account number 108-834562? Any objections, counselor?

MR. CRAMWELL: May I have a short voir dire, Judge?

REFEREE LEWIS: Certainly.

A *voir dire* is a cross-examination that is confined solely to the proposed evidence. If an attorney is unsure whether he wants to consent to the admission of the documents into evidence, he is given the opportunity of asking the witness questions pertaining to them.

MR. CRAMWELL: Mrs. Hartley, are these statements in connection with an account maintained by you in the First Lincoln bank?

A: Yes.

Q: And are you the only person on that account?

A: Yes.

Q: And you receive these statements from the bank each month and maintain possession of them?

A: Yes, I usually keep them for a few years.

Q: Is this the only checking account that you have had during the period covered by these statements?

A: Yes, it's the only bank account I have.

MR. CRAMWELL: I have no objection, your Honor.

REFEREE LEWIS: Very well. Officer, please mark these statements as petitioner's Exhibit 2, A through O. As soon as he is finished, Mrs. Hartley, you may proceed.

MS. HARTLEY: I would now like to refer to the statements, your Honor.

REFEREE LEWIS: Your mean Exhibit 2?

MS. HARTLEY: Yes, Exhibit 2. As you can see, for each month starting with the first statement, dated January 21, 1985, under the second column, labeled "deposits and credits," there is a deposit of $800.

REFEREE LEWIS: Are there other deposits?

MS. HARTLEY: Yes, sir, those would be my paychecks. The amounts vary depending on how many hours I work for the week.

REFEREE LEWIS: I see. Proceed.

MS. HARTLEY: Then starting with the November statement—

MR. CRAMWELL: What's the date?

MS. HARTLEY: November 20, 1985.

MR. CRAMWELL: Thank you.

MS. HARTLEY: Starting with this statement, the one dated November 20, 1985, there's no record of an $800 deposit, or any deposit for that matter besides my paychecks. And that goes for each of these other statements I have. No sign of any money from the respondent.

MR. CRAMWELL: Objection.

REFEREE LEWIS: Overruled.

MS. HARTLEY: Then if you look at the next statement—the one for the following month—you'll see there again is no record of an $800 deposit through mid-December, the date of the statement. Again the only deposits you can see are my paychecks, and you can always tell them because they're uneven amounts, you know, like this one here for $196.56. That's a paycheck. Over here is a round number, $400, but you can see the code TRF, which means a transfer from my combined savings account into checking.

REFEREE LEWIS: What's the date of that statement?

MS. HARTLEY: December 20, 1985.

REFEREE LEWIS: Thank you. Always give the date of the document so the record can be precise.

MS. HARTLEY: Yes, sir. Okay, going on to the next statement, the one dated January 20, 1986, there's no sign of any $800 deposit. The only even number deposit is on January 15th, and that's for $200. That's the cash that Peter gave me the day before. I had to put it in to cover some checks; I was starting to run pretty low. Over here I have a deposit slip, dated January 15, 1986, that shows a $200 cash deposit into my account.

REFEREE LEWIS: Would you like to offer that into evidence?

Ms. HARTLEY: Yes, I would, as petitioner's Exhibit, uh . . .
REFEREE LEWIS: Three.
Ms. HARTLEY: Thank you. Exhibit 3.
REFEREE LEWIS: Show it to your adversary.
MR. CRAMWELL: No objection, your Honor.
REFEREE LEWIS: Okay. A deposit slip from First Lincoln Savings Bank for account number 108-834562, dated January 15, 1986, is hereby admitted as petitioner's Exhibit 3.
Ms. HARTLEY: Now I would like to go to the next statement, dated February 20, 1986. It doesn't have any $800 deposit, or any other even amount, except for transfers from my savings, and those are always marked TRF. The only deposits are my paychecks, which, like I said, are the uneven amounts.

Elizabeth then went on to the remaining statement, which showed the same thing. Another deposit slip, indicating a $300 cash deposit, was admitted as petitioner's Exhibit 4. She is just about to end her direct testimony.

Ms. HARTLEY: I also would ask this Court to note how low my balances had become. In fact, right here, there's an overdraft of $20.68 on February 11th. Before the respondent had stopped paying me, I normally tried to keep a few hundred dollars in the account. Also, you can see how my savings account balance went down from about $1,200 to zero from November to now, because of all the transfers.
REFEREE LEWIS: I'll review the evidence after the hearing, Mrs. Hartley.
Ms. HARTLEY: Thank you. Well, that about concludes my testimony. There's really nothing more I can add.
REFEREE LEWIS: Cross-examination, counselor?
MR. CRAMWELL: Absolutely, your Honor.

Cross-examination is an art, but like anything else it improves with practice. Its goal is to diminish, if not destroy, the effect of the witness's testimony during the direct examination. The lawyer probes omissions and inconsistencies, focuses on lapses of memory, stresses weaknesses, and attacks with any contradictory evidence in his arsenal. Judging from Elizabeth's testimony, Mr. Cramwell does not have much room to maneuver. Her account was clear, complete, and adequately backed up by documentary evidence. Notwithstanding this, Peter's lawyer will try to do his best. We have a feeling that his attempt will be a demonstration that cross-examination is also the art of making a mountain out of a molehill.

MR. CRAMWELL: Mrs. Hartley, you have testified that your former husband had been paying you your support by a single $800 check each month. Is that correct?
A: Yes.
Q: Fine. Now I would like to show you this check here, which I would like to mark for identification as respondent's Exhibit A. It's a check, dated May 19, 1984, from the account of Peter Hartley,

number 58-238746, with the Nationwide Commercial Bank, and it is drawn to the order of Elizabeth Hartley.

A: Yes, I've seen it before, but that was—

Q: Please, just answer the question. Have you seen that check before?

A: Yes.

Q: Thank you. And is that your signature on the back?

A: Yes.

Q: And did you endorse that check with your signature and deposit it into your checking account at First Lincoln?

A: Yes.

MR. CRAMWELL: At this time, Judge, I would like to introduce this check as respondent's Exhibit A.

REFEREE LEWIS: Any objections, Mrs. Hartley?

MS. HARTLEY: No, but I just want to say that—

REFEREE LEWIS: You'll get your chance to say whatever you want about this document. All I want to know now is whether you wish to dispute that the check is genuine.

MS. HARTLEY: No, it's real.

REFEREE LEWIS: Fine. So we'll allow it into evidence. Go on.

MR. CRAMWELL: Mrs. Hartley, would you please tell the court the amount of that check?

A: $300.

Q: Did you receive any other money from the respondent that month?

A: I believe so.

Q: Now, Mrs. Hartley, do you recall being served with a subpoena from my office a few days ago?

A: Yes.

Q: And did that subpoena direct you to bring certain things here to court today?

A: Yes.

Q: And did you bring them with you?

REFEREE LEWIS: Counselor, ask for the particular document you want.

MR. CRAMWELL: Yes, sir. Mrs. Hartley, do you have your checking account statement, or statements, for the period in or about the date of respondent's Exhibit A?

A: I believe so. Would you like me to look?

MR. CRAMWELL: Yes.

REFEREE LEWIS: Take your time, Mrs. Hartley.

MS. HARTLEY: I think this one is what you want, Mr. Cramwell.

MR. CRAMWELL: Thank you. Just give me a moment, your Honor.

REFEREE LEWIS: Take whatever time you need. I can never figure out my bank statements in less than an hour.

MR. CRAMWELL: Mrs. Hartley, I show you this statement from First Lincoln Savings, dated May 21, 1984, and ask you if you can identify it for the record?

A: Yes, it's my bank statement.

MR. CRAMWELL: I would like, your Honor, to introduce this statement as respondent's Exhibit B.

REFEREE LEWIS: Any objection?

MS. HARTLEY: No.

REFEREE LEWIS: We'll mark it. Hold your questions until the officer marks it. He'll give it back to you.

MR. CRAMWELL: Now, Mrs. Hartley, I show you Exhibit B, and I direct your attention to the deposit entry for May 17, 1984. Do you see it?

A: Yes, I do.

Q: Very good. Now can you tell the Court the amount of that deposit?

A: $750.

Q: And can we presume that part of this amount included the $300 check from the respondent?

A: Yes. I think so.

Q: Can you tell us what the other part of the deposit consisted of? Was it cash or checks?

A: I believe the rest was in cash.

Q: And where did you get this cash?

A: From Peter.

Q: When did he give it to you?

A: The same time as he gave me the check.

Q: How much did he give you?

REFEREE LEWIS: In cash?

MR. CRAMWELL: Yes, in cash.

A: I'm pretty sure it was $500. Peter told me—

MR. CRAMWELL: Thank you, Mrs. Hartley, that's all I wanted to know, how much it was. We don't need the rest. Now, let me ask you: Did you deposit the entire $500?

A: No. If I remember correctly I kept $50 for pocket money, because you can see the deposit was for $750.

MR. CRAMWELL: Yes, I can. Certainly I can. All right, correct me if I am wrong, but you did testify just a few minutes ago on your direct examination that prior to November 1985 Peter paid all his support by check. Yes?

A: Yes, I said that, but I forgot this one—

MR. CRAMWELL: Please, please. Just answer my questions. We can get through this a lot faster. So you stated that all those earlier payments were by check, right?

A: Yes.

Q: And yet this payment in May 1984 was part check, part cash. Correct?

A: Yes.

Q: Now, madam, were there any other payments from the respondent that were in the form of cash?

A: Before November?

Q: Yes, before November.

A: Not that I can recall.

Q: And what about after November 1985?

A: Just the ones I mentioned. There was $700 in cash. That's all.

Q: Are you sure you are not forgetting any others, just like you forgot about this one in May?

A: Yes, I'm sure. It hasn't been that long ago.

Q: How can we be sure you are telling the truth? You conveniently forgot about the $500 you got in May 1984.

A: Because I am telling the truth! Back then, Peter was pretty good with the payments. Yeah, maybe a week or two late, but he always came through. I had no reason to keep track. But after November, I knew something was wrong. He was different. I can't explain how, but he was. You know, if you live with someone for a long time you get to know them pretty well. Anyway, I knew something was going on, so I made up my mind to keep careful records of everything. That's why I have those dates in my diary. Just to make sure I remembered exactly what I got from him.

Attorney Cramwell just broke one of our rules. He asked one question too many. If he did want to probe this further, he should have remembered another rule: control the witness. His questions should have been framed to elicit "yes" or "no" responses, taking away from Elizabeth a chance to explain her omission and to reinforce the accuracy of her record keeping. Of course, Elizabeth would have still had a chance on her redirect to offer the explanation, but she may not have remembered to do so. Frankly, it is virtually impossible to testify and at the same time prepare a re-direct. Thus there was a good chance that Mr. Cramwell could have scored a small point. Instead, rather than leaving it up to his adversary to rehabilitate her testimony on re-direct, he made certain that she got the opportunity during his cross-examination.

Since she is her own attorney, Elizabeth could have asked the Referee for permission to make brief notes of her testimony during cross-examination. Ordinarily witnesses are not allowed to make notes as they are testifying, but Elizabeth is wearing two hats and should take notes. In this way, she would not have overlooked anything important that she may have wanted to bring out in her re-direct testimony.

We are going to spare you the rest of Mr. Cramwell's cross-examination. He was unable to raise a single significant issue of fact. Elizabeth answered the rest of his questions perfectly, and she did not offer anything beyond what he asked. Elizabeth did not call any other witnesses for her case. A mutual friend had been told by Peter that he was behind in his payments, but he was unwilling to testify against him. Elizabeth debated with herself for days whether to serve a subpoena on the friend to compel his testimony, ultimately deciding that she did not need it badly enough to damage their friendship.

Mr. Cramwell began the respondent's case. Not surprisingly, he called Peter Hartley as his first witness. Peter took the stand and testified that he began having trouble coming up with the support payments as early as May, but that he managed to keep current until November, when he claimed the roof caved in. He stated that he was still able to pay Elizabeth at least half of the required amount. Since he was then making a few dollars off the books, all the payments to her since November were in cash. In all, Peter claimed that he had paid his former wife $2,000, not $700. The balance of his testimony pertained to his cross-petition for a downward modification. Since that subject is treated in Chapter 7, we will skip the details for now. Elizabeth then began her cross-examination. You may find a particular portion interesting.

Ms. HARTLEY: Mr. Hartley, you have testified here today that you paid me a total of $2,000 since November, is that not so?

A: That's what I paid. $2,000.

Q: Do you have any receipts?

A: Hell, no. Since when have you and I needed receipts?

Ms. HARTLEY: Please, I'll ask the questions, if you don't mind. I'll ask again, do you have receipts?

A: No.

Q: Do you recall the exact dates you supposedly gave me these payments?

A: Not exactly, no.

Q: Well, let's start with November. What did you pay me that month?

A: I believe I paid $400 each month, starting with November.

Q: Did you make the November payment at one time, or were there several payments?

A: I don't recall. I think I paid it all at once.

Q: When?

A: I don't remember.

Q: Well, was it at the beginning of the month, the middle, or the end?

A: I said I don't remember.

Q: Was anyone else present?

A: No. Just you and me. Do you think I'd pay you in the middle of the street?

Q: Where were we?

A: At the house, your house.

Q: Was it in the daytime, or the evening?

A: Probably nighttime.

Q: Probably?

A: Yeah, probably. I don't remember.

Q: What was I wearing?

A: Oh, this is ridiculous.

REFEREE LEWIS: Answer the question, Mr. Hartley. Don't comment. If your lawyer doesn't like the question, he'll do the objecting, not you.

A: Yes, sir. I don't remember what you were wearing. I couldn't tell you what you wore yesterday.

Ms. HARTLEY: That's because you didn't see me yesterday.

MR. CRAMWELL: Objection.

REFEREE LEWIS: Sustained. Please, Mrs. Hartley, ask questions; don't you comment either.

Ms. HARTLEY: Yes. Mr. Hartley, do you recall my telephoning you in November to demand that you pay me the alimony and child support?

A: Yeah, but after I paid you the 400 bucks, I didn't hear from you.

Q: Why? Did I say forget about the other $400?

A: No.

Q: Then why wouldn't I call—

MR. CRAMWELL: Objection.

REFEREE LEWIS: Sustained. You can't ask the witness why you wouldn't do something.

Ms. HARTLEY: Yes, of course. All right, Mr. Hartley, how much do you claim you paid me in December?

A: The same. $400.

Q: And when was that payment?

MR. CRAMWELL: Objection. She is assuming it was just one payment.

REFEREE LEWIS: Sustained. Ask first if it was one or more payments, Mrs. Hartley.

Ms. HARTLEY: Was that made in one or more payments?

A: I think it was a few different times. Once when I dropped off the kids, I think I gave you about $150. Then there was another $100 a week later. The rest came a few days after that. I'm not sure of the exact dates.

Q: Are you sure of anything?

MR. CRAMWELL: Objection.

REFEREE LEWIS: Sustained.

Ms. HARTLEY: Where were we when you gave me this money?

A: I'm pretty sure at the house, except for that one time at the Crossroads Diner. That's when I gave you the two hundred.

Q: When you gave me the money at the house, or at least claimed you did, were the girls present?

A: No. You know we don't discuss money in front of the kids.

Q: Did you promise me the rest of the money?

A: I said I would do as best I could.

Q: Did you ever tell me that there was a foul-up with the payroll at work?

A: No.

Q: Did you ever say that you needed money for a new transmission?

A: Yeah, I probably did.

Q: Yes or no?

A: Yeah, I did. You know damn well that the truck broke down—

REFEREE LEWIS: Mr. Hartley, keep your tone civil. Go on, Mrs. Hartley.

Ms. HARTLEY: What was I wearing when you gave me the first payment in December?

A: I don't remember.

Q: Was I dressed up for work, or in jeans?

A: I said I don't remember.

Elizabeth has been doing just fine. Like a seasoned boxer, she is taking a few jabs and backing off before she gets tagged with a left hook from the witness. Of course, she has not shaken Peter from his story. He has not begun to break down on the stand and admit that he did not pay her $400 in cash each month. Only Perry Mason gets witnesses to do that. Nevertheless, Elizabeth has methodically chipped away at her former husband's credibility. Because he cannot provide details of events that happened only several months before, it is possible for the referee to conclude that his version is untrue. As it turns out, Elizabeth is about to get a nice break, one that perhaps pertains more to the cross-petition for a downward modification, but one that also adversely affects Peter's credibility.

Ms. HARTLEY: Where did you get the cash from? The cash you supposedly used to pay me $400 each month?
    A: From my hard work. If you had more concern for where the money comes from than spending it . . .
    Q: Who paid you?
    A: One of the people I do work for.
    Q: Who?
    A: I can't be sure. I pick up a few hundred here and there.
    Q: But haven't I had to sit here today and hear how terrible your finances are?
    A: Well, they are. This extra money isn't helping.
    Q: Well, where's all your money going to?
    A: It's all there in my budget, which my lawyer showed you before.
    Q: Who made up that budget?
    A: Me and Mr. Cramwell. We came up with the figures after we went over all my bills together.
    Q: And do you have those bills here today?
    A: No.
    Q: Do you have any documents that would back up your so-called figures.
    A: Not here today.
    Q: But don't you recall getting my subpoena, which requested you bring all such documents?
    A: Yeah, sure I do, but I didn't have anything I could put my hands on.
    Q: Where could these documents possibly be?
    A: I don't know. Around somewhere.
    Q: Do they exist?
    A: Sure they do. I just couldn't find them in time for the hearing.
    Q: Assuming that they do exist, for the moment, isn't it true that they would show expenses less than what you are claiming here today?
    A: No, absolutely not.
Ms. HARTLEY: Your Honor, I would ask that you note that the respondent has failed to produce the documents set forth in this subpoena.
REFEREE LEWIS: Certainly. Why don't we mark this subpoena as petitioner's Exhibit 5. Mr. Hartley, are you testifying that you do not have with you here today any of the documents itemized in this subpoena?

A: No, not with me today. Like I said, I have these things around, but I just couldn't get my hands on them in time. I'm not very good at keeping records, sir.

REFEREE LEWIS: Do you realize that I can hold you in contempt?

MR. CRAMWELL: Your Honor, if I may. My client advises me that he made a diligent search for these records with the utmost intent of complying with petitioner's subpoena, but that he was unable to find any documents that were responsive to the demand. If I may respectfully point out, your Honor, there must be a finding of willfulness before a person can be adjudged guilty of contempt. The respondent has not been willful.

REFEREE LEWIS: We'll put that aside for now. However, I wish the record to reflect that the respondent has failed to produce the items set forth —in detail—in Exhibit 5, and that this Court will not only note such, as requested by the petitioner, but will further draw from such omission all permissible inferences that are adverse to the respondent.

MR. HARTLEY: Excuse me, sir, I mean your Honor, but exactly what does that mean?

REFEREE LEWIS: It means this, Mr. Hartley. I may, under the rules of evidence, fairly infer from your failure to produce these documents that they would actually show, if they were produced, facts adverse to the claims you are making in this proceeding. In other words, I am allowed to assume that your bills, checks and the like show personal expenses that are less than what you claim.

MR. CRAMWELL: But, your Honor, I don't see why—

REFEREE LEWIS: Mr. Cramwell, I do not wish to argue this with you or be lectured on the rules of evidence. That is my ruling, and you have your exception.

MR. CRAMWELL: Yes, sir.

REFEREE LEWIS: Proceed, Mrs. Hartley.

MS. HARTLEY: Thank you.

Peter and his attorney surely made a big mistake by not producing any documents, although we suspect that if we had seen them their reasons would be quite clear. In any event, they are stuck with a very *un*favorable inference, one that alone practically destroys his cross-petition for a downward modification.

Referee Lewis took 2 weeks to render his decision. We thought you may find some excerpts interesting.

After a hearing in which both parties had an opportunity to present evidence, and after considering such evidence and duly deliberating thereon, I find as follows:

The petitioner is entitled under the divorce decree, dated January 12, 1982, to receive from respondent $500 each month as maintenance and $300 each month as child support, for a monthly total of $800. Petitioner alleges that commencing in or about November 1985 respondent has been in arrears of such obligation, having paid just $700, and therefore a sum of $3,300 is due and owing her. Respondent denies these allegations, and he claims that he has paid petitioner $400 monthly in cash, for a total of $2,000.

Further, respondent has made a cross-petition for a downward modification of his support obligation on the grounds of a substantial change of circumstances.

The credible evidence supports a finding that respondent is in arrears of the amount claimed by petitioner, to wit $3,300, and that she therefore is awarded a money judgment for said amount against respondent, together with interest. I do not find respondent's testimony that he paid petitioner $400 each month worthy of belief. There are no documents that corroborate his claim. To the contrary, petitioner has produced evidence in the form of checking account statements and deposit slips that adequately support her testimony. Further, this court notes that the respondent was unable to provide simple details of surrounding facts to events he claims took place, which occurred no more than several months prior to the hearing.

Since this court has found respondent to be in arrears for more than three consecutive payments, as well as for an amount that is equal to (in fact, greater) than one month's support, a payroll deduction order is granted in the amount of $800 monthly, plus another $300 until the arrears are paid (11 months). In addition, this court in its discretion orders respondent to deposit with the support collection unit of this County the sum of $2,700 as and for security for future payments. Should the respondent maintain a continuous record of timely payments in the next eighteen (18) months, he may petition this court at such time for an order releasing said security.

The cross-petition for a downward modification of the child support and maintenance provisions of the aforesaid divorce decree is denied. Respondent has failed to meet his burden of proving a substantial change of circumstances, sufficient to modify a prior decree. He alleges that his financial circumstances have worsened, and yet he failed to support this contention with any documentary evidence, and indeed admitted that he was earning additional cash.

This constitutes the decision and order of the court.

Not bad, Elizabeth. In fact, she did great. She kept in mind our cardinal rules.

1. She adequately PREPARED her case. The subpoena she served on Peter made a big difference. We fault her, though, for not organizing (pre-marking) the bank statements, and note that with just a little more preparation, she would have remembered the odd cash payment that gave her momentary trouble during cross-examination.
2. She confined her OPENING STATEMENT for the most part to the facts she was able to prove. We criticized her, however, for stating that she was going to disprove her ex's claims of deteriorating financial circumstances, although she did practically that with her subpoena.
3. She got her full story out during her own DIRECT EXAMINATION. She did not try to save any surprises.
4. She NEVER ASKED A QUESTION to which she did not know the answer.
5. There was reasonably effective CROSS-EXAMINATION. Elizabeth quickly realized that she was not going to shake Peter from his story so she chipped away at the edges and found a few cracks.
6. She was *NOT* AFRAID TO ASK A QUESTION.
7. We did not show you any of the transcript when Peter's lawyer was questioning him. Had we, you would have seen that Elizabeth was *NOT* AFRAID TO OBJECT to Cramwell's questions.
8. She did a good job of CONTROLLING her witnesses, in this case her ex.

9. She was always COOL, POLITE and RESPECTFUL.
10. Unlike Cramwell, she NEVER DID ASK THE ONE QUESTION TOO MANY.

Cramwell appealed Referee Lewis's decision, but lost. The payroll deduction order that she was awarded was easily put into effect with the assistance of a court clerk. Elizabeth began receiving regular payments directly from Peter's employer. Approximately 7 months later, Peter quit his job and the support stopped coming. After using the $2,700 court security, Elizabeth let a month's worth of support arrears accrue, and she obtained a money judgment. By following the advice we give in our next chapter, she was able to adequately enforce her rights and change the legal judgment into "legal tender."

CHAPTER FIVE

Enforcing Support Orders, Phase 3

ENFORCEMENT DEVICES. TERRIFYING images are conjured up from the dark recesses of the mind. However, this chapter is not about chains, whips, electric cattle prods or thumbscrews. The subject is legal methods of enforcing a support order, or put simply, the way you go about converting a court award or judgment into hard cash.

A support order, or for that matter even a money judgment, is by itself just a piece of paper with no magical qualities. It cannot be cashed at a bank, nor aimed at a former spouse with the threat of firing a laser, life-ending burst. Alone, it is useless. Used in conjunction with one or more of the enforcement devices, it is highly effective. Enforcement is the final step of a judicial process. The hearing was the necessary prelude, yet it is the enforcement that gives the entire thing meaning, not just in your case but for the whole judicial system as well, for if judicial pronouncements cannot be translated into action, our civilized method of redressing wrongs will collapse into a heap of discarded precedents and obsolete principles. Thus exist the enforcement devices that are designed to coerce an individual into compliance, tying up and ultimately taking his property and, in the most extreme instances, his personal freedom.

We have already learned in Chapter 2 of the highly effective extra-judicial methods that have now been made available to all individuals entitled to child support—the payroll deduction order and the tax intercept. Each has several advantages, the most significant of which are avoiding court, on one hand, and having the assistance of a state agency, on the other. As this is a benefit that is there for the taking, your first step should be in the direction of the appropriate agency if you are supposed to receive child support, alone or combined with alimony or maintenance, from your former spouse. Remember, there is a listing in the appendix that supplies the name, address and telephone number of the agency in the state where you live. We have also seen, however, that these measures may have little or no application to your particular circumstances, which brings us to the discussion at hand.

There are a variety of enforcement needs. One person may have obtained a money judgment and wonders about the next step. Another was married to a famous author who has quit paying alimony, and she wants to figure out a way to get her hands on the royalties from his latest best-seller. Someone else no longer has an idea where her former spouse resides, but knows that he owns a small store that he is renting out. One woman was supposed to receive a portion of her former husband's pension, but her letters to his employer have so far gone unanswered. Still another has tried everything to no avail and wonders if there is some sort of debtors' prison for recalcitrant deadbeats like her ex.

For all of these people, there are legal procedures designed to solve their problems. Like anything involving our legal system, they require knowledge, resolve, persistence and patience. Simply knowing what methods are available is not enough. One must have the willingness to employ them and the dedication to see them through to the end. Finally, the results may not happen overnight, and you must be mentally prepared to give the system sufficient time to work.

Before we turn to each of the enforcement devices, we would be remiss if we did not mention that sometimes the mere entry in court of a money judgment or a restraining order on a bank account is in itself sufficient to prompt a former spouse to make a payment. The manner by which your ex receives notice of the entry of the judgment varies from one state to the other. Some courts send a copy of the judgment directly to him; in other instances you must mail a copy to him or his attorney, a procedure that is often called *notice of entry.* In any event, the court clerk will be able to advise you as to the system used in your particular court. If your ex *does* pay off the judgment it is satisfied, and he is entitled to receive from you a signed satisfaction of judgment, which he can file in the court record. Should you be so lucky, the balance of this chapter is not for you.

ENFORCING MONEY JUDGMENTS

The most popular enforcement devices relate to money judgments. Each day, thousands of money judgments are docketed in courts across the country, and a scramble begins to convert them into money. Money judgments, as you are probably aware, are not confined to post-divorce situations. They are found in all types of cases, from the $36 judgment someone gets against a dry cleaner in small claims court, to the $1,500 judgment a consumer loan company gets against a defaulting borrower, to the $250,000 judgment that a former patient gets in a medical malpractice case, to the $10 million class action judgment that a group gets against the manufacturer of an intrauterine contraceptive device. In each instance, the judgment entitles the petitioner or plaintiff, now called the *judgment creditor,* to collect a specified amount from the respondent or defendant, now called the *judgment debtor.* How easily the money can be collected depends upon the cooperation and the liquidity of the judgment debtor. Both concerns are most often alleviated by the presence of insurance; most money judgments are for personal injuries, usually in automobile accidents, and the defendant is covered by insurance. Enforcement ordinarily entails no more than waiting several weeks for the check from the insurance company. Sadly, for our purposes, there is to our knowledge no such thing as spousal support insurance. Even if there were, given the high incidence of nonpayment, the premiums would be outrageous.

Before we get too far into our discussion, we would be failing you if we did not give you an important caveat:

IF YOUR EX HAS NO ASSETS WHATSOEVER, NOR A JOB,
BUSINESS OR OTHER SOURCE OF INCOME, YOU ARE OUT OF
LUCK.

Remember, a judgment is not magic. It cannot produce blood from a
stone. But if your ex has nonexempt property or income, no matter how
cleverly hidden, a little imagination and persistence on your part will pay
off.

Each state gives a judgment creditor a plethora of enforcement devices.
Their selection depends upon the particular circumstances of the case.
Their use can be limited only by the economics of the situation. Obviously, the $36 judgment creditor is not going to expend untold time and
money going after his dry cleaner. Ultimately, one does what is most
practical.

Property Executions

The first concern is to understand how enforcement of a judgment works.
In the simplest terms, a judgment entitles the judgment creditor to have
a county sheriff, or other authorized official such as a marshal, levy on the
property of the judgment debtor. *Levy* means to seize property for the
enforcement of a money judgment. A sheriff does just that; he takes
custody of certain property, after which he sells it at public or private
auction, and the money is turned over to the judgment creditor after
deducting authorized sheriff's fees and expenses, commonly called *pound-
age.* If the property is money, no sale is needed. The sheriff simply goes
to wherever the money is kept—most likely the bank—and directs that the
money be turned over to him, after which the amount needed to satisfy
the judgment is given to you.

The judgment creditor brings the sheriff into the picture by serving a
property warrant or *writ of execution* upon his office. The names may be
different, according to local custom, but essentially they work the same.
For simplicity's sake, we will refer to these documents as *executions.* Generally, there are two types of executions: income and property. The first is
used to attach, or *garnish,* the judgment debtor's wages. This is known as
an income execution, which we will talk about later. The second is used
to seize property, regardless of its form.

A property execution is issued in most cases by the court clerk, although in some states the judgment creditor's attorney is also authorized.
It is addressed to the sheriff of a particular county, and it contains the
following information: (a) the name of the court where the judgment is
docketed; (b) the date and amount of the judgment (specifying how much,
if any, has already been collected); (c) the names and addresses of the
judgment creditor and the judgment debtor; and preferably (d) any information concerning the judgment debtor's assets. You need not worry
about the particular requirements in your state, because fill-in-the-blank
forms are readily available in either your court clerk's office or business
and legal stationers.

There is a wide variety of property interests that are subject to levy.
Property may be tangible—you can feel, see, hear or touch it—or intangi-

ble. An example of the latter would be a debt. It is not something you can take hold of and put in your pocket, yet it is something of value. If someone owes your ex money, that debt can be levied upon, or attached, and the person made to pay the debt directly to you. A property interest may also be future oriented. The judgment debtor may be named as a substantial beneficiary in his aunt's will. Even a lottery ticket has been held to be property subject to levy. There of course may be some problem with your knowing exactly what assets your ex has after having been divorced for several years, but do not despair. There are a variety of post-judgment disclosure devices which we will be discussing as we go along.

Certain property is exempt from levy in many states. Typically the list includes basic household articles that are considered necessities of life. For example, in New York a judgment creditor cannot have a sheriff seize any of the following: stoves and 60 days worth of fuel; family bible and pictures; books (value not exceeding $50); domestic animals and 60 days worth of food; all wearing apparel, household furniture, a refrigerator, one radio, one television set, tableware and cooking utensils; a wedding ring; a watch (value not exceeding $35); tools of trade (value not exceeding $600); property in trust; maintenance and child support payments; security deposits for rent and utilities; wheelchairs, medical and dental prostheses and life-support systems; and seeing-eye dogs. The last two categories, recently added, are indeed a sad commentary upon the humanity level of lawyers typically representing judgment creditors.

While every other form of property interest is subject to enforcement, it pays to keep in mind a very simple principle: the judgment creditor stands in the shoes of the judgment debtor. In other words, you can only acquire whatever rights your ex has in the property. For example, we have already mentioned debts. If John Stans owes your ex $2,000, that debt can be seized by the sheriff. However, if under the terms of the loan, Stans is not required to pay it back for five more years, you cannot compel earlier payment and must await the five years. The same would hold true for an automobile. Your ex owns a 1983 BMW 528e, which you are told is worth approximately $12,000. After the sheriff seizes the car, you discover that the bank, which lent the money for the purchase, has a lien of almost $10,000 on it. You cannot eradicate the bank's rights, and any money the sheriff receives for the car at auction will first have to pay off the bank. Whatever is left first goes toward the sheriff's fees and auction expenses, and the balance to you. In this example, you may be lucky to end up with $1,000. Still it is better than nothing, and your stubborn former spouse ends up walking.

Bank Accounts

For a judgment creditor, the best asset in the world is an intangible—a bank account. Technically, it is a debt, one that is owed by the bank to the depositor. The good part is that the party owing it—the bank—is solvent and will pay it upon demand. It is usually a very simple process to make a judicially compelled withdrawal lead to a handsome deposit in your own account. The bank is like any other person or entity that holds property belonging to a judgment debtor, defined in legal circles as a *garnishee*. The sheriff levies on the money or garnishes the bank account, much in the same manner as a judgment creditor may garnish a judgment debtor's wages. Assuming there is sufficient money on deposit, the sheriff will simply direct the bank to turn over a specified amount to cover the judgment, plus his fees and expenses. The judgment is then satisfied. Note that although the sheriff is entitled to statutory fees that are deducted right off the top of any proceeds he obtains, you do not pay for this; rather, your ex does because more money will be taken from his account to cover these additional expenses. If the amount is less than the judgment, the entire account will be turned over to the sheriff, and a portion of your judgment is satisfied.

Frequently the trick is to find the bank where your ex keeps an account. The easiest place to start is the bank whose name appeared on the checks he used to send you at one time. It is always a good idea, by the way, to jot down this information when you do receive a support check, noting the bank name, branch address and account number, just in case you should need it at a later time. People do change banks, especially those who find themselves at the wrong end of a money judgment. That is when a little detective work comes in handy.

Of course, you have to know how to go about it. Try walking into a bank and asking a teller if your former husband maintains a checking or savings account there, and at best you will receive an icy stare and a curt, "I'm sorry, but we can't give out that sort of information." You can ask to see the manager and still get nowhere. So how is it done? How do you find out? By using a handy little piece of paper called an *information subpoena*, with an attached questionnaire. We have already seen how useful subpoenas are for obtaining all kinds of information about your ex. There is no reason to think that they stop working just because the hearing is over. Only the form is a little different. An information subpoena is especially tailored for post-judgment situations. It directs the recipient, in this case the bank, to provide sworn answers to questions such as the following:

- Do you have any records of an account in which the judgment debtor has an interest, whether in his name or jointly with others, within the past one year?
- As to each account, what is the title, the date opened, the amounts presently on deposit and, if the account was closed, the date it was closed and the last amount on deposit?
- Do you have any records of a safe deposit box in which the judgment debtor has an interest?
- Are you holding any collateral in which the judgment debtor has or may have an interest, and if so, what is a description and approximate value of each item?
- Do you hold any lien, mortgage or any other right against property owned by the judgment debtor, and if so, what is the nature of each such lien, and the description and location of the property upon which such lien is placed?
- Has the judgment debtor given you a financial statement in the past __ years, and, if so, did you attach a copy?

- What is the judgment debtor's social security number and his place of employment?

The questions must be answered within a certain period that varies from state to state. The answers must be given under oath, although there is not too much reason to suspect that a bank would be willing to lie to protect your ex.

Restraining Notices

The information subpoena is usually served on the bank along with another important little enforcement tool, the *restraining notice.* In fact, in many states they are both incorporated in a single form, which you can purchase at a local stationery store that sells legal and business forms. The restraining notice places a freeze on whatever assets of the judgment debtor that are in the possession of the person or company receiving it. What good is it finding out where your ex has his money if he is still free to withdraw it the next day? The restraining notice prevents just that. The money must remain frozen for a specified period, usually 90 days or until it is levied by or turned over to a sheriff or other enforcement officer. This holds true for anything the bank may hold—a checking or savings account, a safe deposit box, stock certificates that are pledged as collateral for a loan and anything else that a bank may have that belongs to the judgment debtor. Note, the freeze only works if your ex has some money on deposit; if he beat you to the punch and closed out his account before the restraining notice was served on the bank, there is nothing to restrain and the notice is null and void. On the other hand, should you hit his bank on the day that he only has $1.35 on deposit, the freeze goes into effect and also locks in any other monies that he may later deposit.

The restraining notice and information subpoena, as a property execution, are issued by a court clerk or attorney for the judgment creditor. If you are uncertain where your ex keeps his money, the recommended method is to blanket the area's banks with them. You never know what a little fishing may turn up. Although there is sometimes a small witness fee that must be paid to the bank for its trouble, it usually does not amount to more than a dollar or two; truly money well spent if your search turns up a nice plump bank account. Also keep in mind that many keep their savings in money market or liquid asset funds maintained by investment and stock brokerage companies, so be sure to include the local offices of Merrill Lynch, Dean Witter, Shearson American Express, etc. on your list. For once, when *you* speak, E. F. Hutton will have to listen.

Although we are talking about restraining notices and information subpoenas in connection with bank and money market accounts, do not think for a moment that their use is restricted to financial institutions. A judgment creditor may serve them on any person or company that may be holding something belonging to the judgment debtor. If you suspect that your ex's buddy Pete is holding his friend's valuable set of antique Lionel trains in the basement, you can serve a set of these papers on Pete, who is legally obligated to answer the questions and make sure the train does not leave the station. If he refuses to answer or disobeys the restraining notice, he can be held in contempt of court and be subject to fine or imprisonment.

It may even be better to take a calculated shot and have the sheriff serve a property execution on Pete; usually the unexpected knock on the front door by someone in uniform is more than enough to trigger an honest response and minimize the chance that Pete will return the property to your ex the very next morning. Moreover, since the property is capable of delivery—we are not, after all, talking about a cow—the sheriff can relieve your ex's friend of his burden and will usually take the train set away in his patrol car right then and there. The drawback to this approach is cost; many sheriff's offices require an up-front payment of fees before they execute on a judgment debtor's property. Of course, you ultimately get this money back, but that is only if the levy was successful and the property brought a sufficient price at auction. Bullets are expensive, and shooting them blindly may bring you to the brink of insolvency a lot quicker than your ex's delinquent payments. We mention this not to ruin your day, but to make a point worth considering.

While there is a variety of enforcement devices, you must choose between them carefully. Your approach should be like a fine surgeon selecting the right scalpel, not like a blustering woodsman grabbing the first axe he finds. Serving restraining notices or information subpoenas *en masse* on banks and stock brokerages is not going to harm you, since it is unlikely that your former spouse will find out about it and, even if he does, it will be too late anyway. Unless there is really something fishy going on, no bank or stock brokerage firm will jeopardize its license by violating the law for a customer's benefit, even if he is as rich and duplicitous as J.R. Ewing.

Friends or relatives, on the other hand, may be a bit willing to stretch the law and cooperate with your ex to avoid the wrath of your judgment. They may require something more coercive, such as a visit by the local sheriff. Even that may not be enough. Friends lie to cover up murders even though there are serious criminal repercussions should they get caught, so do not be too surprised if one shades the truth to protect a few dollars where the penalty is far lighter. However, in some cases you may have no choice. We have seen several instances where a persistent judgment creditor has been able to shake a close friend or relative into compliance.

Automobiles and Other Vehicles

If the efforts to levy on a bank account are unsuccessful, the next usual step is a property execution on the judgment debtor's automobile. We have already seen, however, that this may not pay off as much as one would expect, because most people normally borrow pretty heavily to purchase a car, and the lender will have a substantially sized lien on it that has priority over your rights. Since the value of most automobiles or trucks depreciates rapidly, especially in the first year, it is highly likely that the bank's lien will equal, or even exceed, the price the car may fetch at auction. Another problem that is arising lately with automobiles is that many are being leased in increasing numbers each year. If your ex leases his, you will have to try something else, because the title to the car will be in the name of the leasing company. The sheriff will not be able to seize the car on your behalf.

Many states require that a judgment creditor first search the motor vehicle title records to identify the true owner of an auto or truck and any creditors having a lien on it, before a sheriff may levy against it. This is done simply by completing a form available at the local Motor Vehicle Department office and sometimes paying a small processing fee. Within a few weeks you will receive an official response that must be served on the sheriff along with the property execution. The best way to check your state's requirements is by visiting or calling your county sheriff's property enforcement office.

If you know or find out the name of the bank or financial company that holds the lien on your ex's car, it pays first to find out the amount of the outstanding principal balance of the loan and compare it to the value of the car to see if the execution would be worthwhile before you take any further steps to execute on it. If you have no idea of the car's resale value, there are several ways to find out. Stop by a local dealer who carries the same make, tell him you have a 19-whatever so-and-so and ask him how much he thinks it is worth. Knowing car dealers, they will invariably say that they have to see the car first, which is true in order to properly ascertain a used car's value, but you can still request that they give you a range. All car dealers have little blue, yellow or black books that list average wholesale and retail prices for each year, make and model automobile and truck sold in this country. You are interested in the wholesale price, which is below retail, as auction prices will likely be unless the car is unique or draws particular interest. Another way to ascertain the price is to go to a bookstore or library. There are several publications available to the public that provide this information.

If your research indicates that the car is worth more than the bank's lien, even if it is just a few hundred dollars, we suggest that you go for it. Besides your receiving some much needed funds, your ex will get the message (along with a new pair of shoes) that you are serious. Sometimes you can win twice. We once represented a woman, call her Lina, who had a $4,200 judgment against her ex, who owned a 2-year-old Ford Mustang convertible. After getting the necessary motor vehicle clearance, we served a property execution on the sheriff's office in the county where Lina's ex lived. It took several attempts, but the sheriff seized the car, which we were told was worth at least $7,500. Lina's former husband must have been either in desperate financial straits or out of his mind, because he made no attempt to retrieve his car by paying the sheriff what was owed under the judgment. In any event, the sheriff advertised the auction in a local newspaper and put up a few notices in several local auto repair shops.

The weather the day of the auction was miserable. Heavy sleet pelted the parking lot next to the sheriff's office. Hardly anyone showed up for the auction, although Lina did, as she was curious to see what would happen. The bidding started rather unenthusiastically. Maybe it was not a good day to buy a red convertible. The highest bid was $2,500. We had told Lina that she could bid at the auction also, and she laughed and asked what she would do with the car. Now she stood, drenched but still fighting the wind with her umbrella, straining to hear the next bid.

"Do I hear anyone else. Going once, going twice . . ."

A sudden impulse hit her. "2600," she shouted.

"Okay, I got 26 from the little lady here. Do I hear 2700?" The auction-eer scanned the small crowd.

"Yeah, 2700." A fat man in a gray hooded down jacket held up his hand.

"2700. 2700. Do I hear 28? 2800? Do I hear . . ."

"2800!" Lina clenched her fists, her nails almost piercing her palms through her gloves. She waited to hear the fat man.

"2800. Do I hear 29, 2900 dollars, for this beautiful, sporty little Mus-tang. Come on folks, this is a real beauty. Do I hear 29?" He looked from left to right. "All right, going once, going twice, sold to the lady in blue for 2800 dollars."

Lina could not believe it. Her initial joy turned into terror. What was she doing buying a car when she could not afford new sneakers for her two boys? Where was she going to get the money from? The auctioneer had announced that all that was required today was a check or cash for a 10-percent deposit, but that the balance had to be paid by cash or certified check in 3 days, or the deposit would be forfeited. Almost mum-mified, Lina followed the auctioneer inside the sheriff's office to write out the check. There goes almost 300 buckeroos, she thought.

Lina got lucky. That evening she did what any mature, responsible, self-reliant individual does when the world becomes overwhelming. She called her parents. Five minutes into the conversation, her father made her a business proposal that she could not refuse. He said he would give her the rest of the money for the car, provided she promised to sell it immediately. After paying him back, she could keep the profit for herself. Lina did just that. She decided against running an ad herself in the local paper, because she was still afraid that her ex might hassle her if he happened to come across it. Instead she visited a few new and used car dealers to get some price quotations. The Ford dealer from whom her ex had bought the car sounded the most interested. The used car manager accompanied her to the sheriff's impound area to inspect the car. They haggled over the price for a few minutes, but he eventually agreed to pay her $7,700 for the car—a sweet $4,900 profit for our resourceful judg-ment creditor.

We could hardly believe Lina's good fortune when she told us the story a few days later. Her biggest surprise, however, was finding that her ex still owed her money on the judgment! It worked out this way: Her judgment was for $4,200. The Mustang only brought $2,800 at the auc-tion; the net amount, after deducting sheriff, advertising and auction fees —remember, these are paid by the judgment debtor—came to $2,486.57. Thus $1,713.43 still remained uncollected, which Lina eventually got from a bank account that her ex had opened in the next town. In all, Lina received a total of $6,613.43, or $2,413.43 more than she was technically entitled to.

No one can *expect* to make out as well as Lina, but strange things sometimes happen. This was one. An automobile is an important asset, for many the single most valuable one besides a house or condominium, and it pays to explore utilizing it to satisfy your judgment. On a practical basis, having a sheriff's deputy take possession of his newly waxed pride and joy may be just the right visceral stimulus to make your ex reach for his checkbook and write you out a check for the entire amount of the money judgment.

Other Assets

There are other assets that you, as a judgment creditor, may properly seek to satisfy your judgment. Of course, the possibilities depend on the financial status of your ex. We had another client for whom we had received information from a major commercial bank in response to a subpoena. She had been divorced from Stanley for over 5 years, and she had very little information about his finances. He owed our client $65,000 in back maintenance and child support. We decided to pursue various leads relating to Stanley's manufacturing business. Conveniently and not unexpectedly, he was on the books for only an $18,000 salary. Although he owned 37 percent of the shares in the corporation, he was neither an officer or director, and the payroll records had him down as an assistant production manager. We debated about whether it paid to bring a supplementary proceeding against the corporation to see what that uncovered, but we finally decided to investigate the two banks where the corporation maintained accounts. Information subpoenas and questionnaires went out to them. A week later, we hit paydirt.

One bank disclosed that the corporation had a $750,000 revolving line of credit that was personally guaranteed by all of the shareholders. As part of the guarantee the shareholders had pledged certain assets, listed on a schedule supplied by the bank. The list showed that our client's ex-husband had apparently put up two thoroughbred race horses as security. The bank, of course, had a first lien interest in the horses, but a cooperative bank officer told us off the record that the corporation only had roughly $340,000 outstanding on the credit line and that the financial statement that Stanley had filed with the bank stated that the two horses were worth $1.2 million. He said that he had no objection to our executing on the horses, as long as the bank was covered for the outstanding loan. Our luck continued to hold. The horses were stabled for the season at Belmont Park, only a half hour from our office. A property execution was prepared and served on the sheriff's office in Queens county.

To make a long story short, the sheriff seized the horses—the transportation, insurance and stabling costs were staggering. Once the bank received official notice of the levy, it sent the corporation notice that unless the judgment was satisfied and the collateral released in 5 days, the credit line would be canceled. It did not even take that long. Stanley's fellow shareholders nicely "persuaded" him to write the sheriff a certified check sufficiently large enough to cover our client's judgment and the sheriff's fees and expenses. Stanley delivered the check himself the next day. As we recall, one of the horses finished second in the fourth race that weekend.

Pensions and Deferred Income

Pensions and other forms of deferred income are becoming increasingly fertile grounds for judgment enforcement. A significant portion of a person's net worth can be tied up in a pension plan, an annuity, an Individual Retirement Account (IRA) or a Keogh plan. The trick is how to loosen the knot and get your judgment paid. The greatest obstacle is the laws that are designed to protect pensions from the ravages of hungry creditors. Pension funds are maintained in the name of a corporate trustee, not the individual. Thus the only way that they can be reached is when the pension is obligated to start making payments. Generally this right can only be triggered by the employee according to the terms of the pension plan. The federal Employee Retirement Income Security Act, commonly known as ERISA, makes it difficult for judgment creditors to get their hands on private, corporate pensions. There are similar laws that protect military, railroad and seamen pensions. The scope of these laws is far too broad and complex to permit discussion here. However, some basic principles can readily be distilled.

The way the laws are currently written, neither you, nor any judgment creditor, can compel a judgment debtor to elect for payment of pension funds. Thus, if your former spouse is entitled to receive early payments, but has refused, you cannot compel the trustee of the pension fund to begin the payments. However, once your ex makes his election and begins to receive the benefits, you can levy upon these payments to your heart's or at least the judgment's, content.

Deferred income is different. Technically it is nothing more than a loan by the employee to his company, whereby the company agrees to withhold paying the employee a certain portion of wages or commissions until a later year. The most common situations involve those who work for commissions, although income deferments have lately become popular even with employees who work for straight salaries. Someone who has a great selling year may find it advantageous, tax-wise, to postpone receiving all the commissions at once. In fact, he may spread them over several years. This way he pays taxes on the money in a lower bracket than he would were he to take it all in one year. The company is all too willing to make the arrangement, because it in effect gets an interest-free loan. Whatever the reasons, deferred income is nothing but a debt to your ex, which you can freely attach like any other asset. Even better, the funds are released immediately even though your former spouse may have had different ideas to begin with.

Real Estate

Since a house or a condominium is the most valuable asset owned by many individuals you may be curious why we neglected to make it number one on our hit list. The reason is that most states have statutory homestead exemptions for personal residences and complicated procedures for the judicial sale of real property. Before you even begin to worry about these, however, we caution you to make sure that your ex actually owns the property. You can do this by checking the county clerk's records or by having a title company prepare a record owner abstract for you. There is a small cost for the latter, so be sure to find out the cost involved before you order anything. Also make sure that the property is in your ex's name alone. If he owns it with his new wife, you will find that the value of his interest is diminished appreciably, for the sheriff could only sell his interest, unaffected by his present wife's rights to occupy and use the property. Very few would be willing to spend much for it.

The homestead exemption gives the judgment debtor a certain amount of equity in his house that is exempt from enforcement. Equity is the value of the home, less the amount of any mortgages, liens or other judgments. The amount of equity that is exempt varies in different states, but whatever the amount, it is not subject to judgment enforcement. Your ex's equity may be so small that there is little to gain from forcing the sale. Moreover, you may find that other judgment creditors, who docketed their judgments before you, are automatically entitled to the first pieces of the pie, by which time the homestead exemption will eliminate any possibility of recovery for you. As an example, assume your ex owns a condominium that is worth approximately $80,000. A title search reveals the following, in order of filing: $65,000 mortgage by First Bank, a $2,300 mechanic's lien by Glitter Kitchens, a $1,250 judgment by Sleep-E-Z Financing. Liens and encumbrances equal $68,550; maximum equity equals $11,450. You check further and discover that your state has a $10,000 homestead exemption, which is nearly enough to wipe out any possibility of recovery. In this case, it would be inadvisable for you to proceed. Property seldom commands its true value at judicial sales. People go to these auctions expecting to pick up a bargain. Therefore it is very likely that the sale, especially after deducting all the costs, will not bring in enough to cover the $68,550 in encumbrances, let alone the exemption. All you end up accomplishing is throwing your ex out of his home and helping some of his creditors get paid. We are sure you have better things to do with your time.

Assuming that there is sufficient equity in the property to recommend proceeding against it, there are a number of procedural hurdles to surmount. First, the judicial sale of real property, as opposed to personal property such as automobiles and race horses, involves elaborate notice provisions. Notices usually must be posted in public places, as well as on the sought after premises, and several advertisements must run in local newspapers. Second, the sheriff also must give specific notice to the judgment debtor and anyone else who has a mortgage, lien, judgment or any other interest in the property. The auction, if it takes place, may not occur until 6 or 7 weeks after the public notices are made. Finally, procedural rules normally permit the judgment debtor to obtain from court a protective order or other form of order postponing the sale, in order to provide him with a reasonable opportunity to come up with the money to pay off the judgment. Judges are usually sympathetic to those who may be losing their home to satisfy a judgment, although most judgment creditors are not looking for back child support or maintenance, a situation that will very likely take the edge off any tears your ex may otherwise have been able to elicit from the bench.

Income Executions

The income execution is the single most effective enforcement tool of most judgment creditors. It is widely used by lawyers who represent creditors such as banks, finance companies, department stores, home improvement concerns and the like that characteristically have relatively small judgments of a few hundred or thousand dollars to satisfy. They find this device inexpensive and quite effective. The specific procedure is different in each state, but basically it boils down to several easy steps.

The judgment debtor receives a notice that unless he pays the judgment within so many days, his employer will be notified and his wages will be attached or garnished. If he fails to pay within this time, the employer receives a notice directing him to deduct a percentage or specified amount from each paycheck until the entire judgment is paid. The employer makes the deduction and regularly—usually once a month—sends a check to the sheriff, who deducts a small fee and forwards the balance to the judgment creditor or his attorney. Generally there are a few restrictions. Most states will not permit more than one income execution to be in effect at the same time. If the judgment debtor is a chronic deadbeat, various judgment creditors may have to wait their turn. Some jurisdictions have minimum salary requirements; if the judgment debtor makes less than a certain weekly amount, there can be no income execution. Finally, there is usually a limit to the amount of wages that can be deducted, around 10 or 15 percent of your ex's income in most cases.

An income execution sounds so wonderfully simple that you may wonder why we do not sound more enthusiastic about it. The reason is that you can probably do better. If your money judgment represents three consecutive missed child support and maintenance payments, or a sum equal or greater than a month's worth of support, you are entitled under the new nationwide laws to a payroll deduction order, which can automatically be issued by your local child support enforcement agency. The payroll deduction order has two big advantages over the income execution. First, the limit is higher; you can receive up to *65 percent* of the wages. Second, the payroll deduction order has priority over all other income executions and other deductions, save for tax and social security withholding. Thus, even if you are behind several judgment creditors, you will not be behind the eight ball when it comes to collecting from your ex. We have already explained how to go about getting one of these payroll deductions in Chapter 2. If you skipped it, we suggest you go back.

You may recall from our discussion in Chapter 2 and elsewhere that you cannot use the agency payroll deduction collection system if all you are entitled to is spousal maintenance. The child support enforcement agencies are only authorized to work for those who are supposed to receive child support, alone or combined with maintenance. If you find yourself left off the boat, you have two choices. One, you can make an application to the Family Court for a payroll deduction order. Courts are granting these with increasing frequency nowadays, even if only maintenance is involved. Two, you can take your money judgment and enforce it by beginning an income execution on your ex's wages. We have already discussed how to begin a court proceeding in Chapter 3. If you choose the latter course, your local sheriff's office is the best place to go for advice on how to start the wage deduction in your home state.

Installment Orders

Closely related to income executions are installment orders, which are just what the name implies. The court orders the judgment debtor to pay off the judgment in specific weekly or monthly installments. An installment order, unlike income executions, is generally not limited to any percentage of the judgment debtor's salary, but is instead based upon the court's reasonable estimation of what excess funds he has available over and above the legitimate needs of himself and his family.

Installment orders are not available in all states, and even where they are, the judgment creditor must begin a post-judgment proceeding, which, in most instances, results in a hearing. However, the time and effort spent in pursuing one may be well spent in situations where the judgment debtor is living high on the hog, but lacks assets and seems to have very little visible means of support. The best way to find out whether you are entitled to an installment order is by telephoning, or preferably visiting, a judgment clerk in the court. He or she will also be able to advise you as to the necessary procedures involved in initiating an installment order proceeding.

Susan Geller's ex seemed to do nothing except hang around a small restaurant downtown. Several friends claimed that Blake was running numbers ever since he was laid off at the auto plant, and Susan would not put it past him. However, she had no way of proving it. He, or rather his lawyer, had answered her interrogatories with statements that he was unemployed, that his unemployment benefits had run out, that he had no assets and that he was supporting his new family by running errands. Undaunted, Susan commenced an installment proceeding. In the course of the hearing, for which Susan had subpoenaed Blake's new wife and neighbors, it was established that the family had just bought two new cars worth over $20,000, had spent 2 weeks visiting Disneyworld in Orlando, had refurnished the entire house and had joined a new health club. The judge, after calculating how much Blake had to make to afford this life-style, awarded Susan an installment order of $350 per month, which Blake paid until her judgment was satisfied.

Receivership

In contrast to the income execution, a receivership is perhaps one of the least popular methods to enforce a judgment. It goes by other names in different states, such as attachment, sequestration or trust imposition. However, just because it is not widely used does not mean that at times it cannot be a very effective weapon in a judgment creditor's arsenal.

Receivership involves a court appointing a person, the *receiver*, to take into his possession a judgment debtor's specific assets and to manage or sell them in the most effective way to enforce the judgment. A judgment creditor must commence a post-judgment court proceeding to appoint the receiver. The judgment debtor is given the opportunity to contest the application. Sometimes a hearing is mandated.

A receiver is very effective in situations where the judgment debtor owns income producing property such as an apartment building and efforts to levy the income have been unsuccessful. The receiver in effect becomes the owner of the property for as long as it is necessary to fully enforce the judgment. He collects the rents and pays the bills, deducts a court-fixed portion of the income for his troubles and sends the balance to the judgment creditor until the judgment is satisfied. After it is all over, the receiver gets the court's permission to resign, and the property is returned to the judgment debtor.

Another situation is where a judgment debtor has assets, but they are unlikely to bring a reasonable price in a public judicial sale. For example, Pete owns all the shares in a small corporation that runs a printing business. His former wife has a $25,000 money judgment against him. She cannot have the sheriff levy upon the printing presses, as they are owned by the corporation, not Pete. The only thing Pete owns, besides some beat-up furniture, is the shares in the corporation; everything else is in the corporation's name, even the car he uses. No one can expect the shares to be sold for any decent price at auction, for who would be willing to bid for them without first having a chance to examine the corporation's books and records in order to determine what they might be worth. The solution is to make an application to the court to appoint a receiver who will take possession of the shares and attempt to sell them through newspaper advertisements and other channels more conducive for selling business interests.

Post-Judgment Disclosure

Having a judgment is one thing; doing something with it, if you have absolutely no idea about your ex's assets, is quite another. Every state has procedures that allow a judgment creditor to compel disclosure from a judgment debtor or any third party relating to the identity, value and location of any assets that may be used to satisfy a judgment. We have already seen one—the information subpoena—and there are several others. A regular subpoena may be served upon the judgment debtor or anyone else, along with a *Notice of Deposition* requiring the person to appear at a designated time, date and place in order to give sworn testimony about the judgment debtor's assets. Many states also allow post-judgment interrogatories (written questions) to be served on a judgment debtor, which he will have to answer under oath.

Resourceful use of these devices can lead to effective judgment enforcement. We know of one case where a woman took the deposition of her ex's mother, who admitted that she was giving her "unemployed" son $800 a week. The woman then made an application to the court for an installment order and, on the basis of Mom's testimony, the judge directed the judgment debtor to pay his former wife $200 a week until her $4,200 judgment was satisfied.

Contempt

Contempt is an effective enforcement method, but its use is limited to situations where the judgment debtor openly fails to cooperate with other enforcement devices. In other words, contempt is not in itself an enforcement device: it can only be used in conjunction with one of the methods that we have already discussed. The idea is that a judgment debtor may legitimately be coerced by threats of fine or imprisonment to comply with an outstanding information subpoena, restraining notice, installment payment order or the like. However, a judgment debtor will never be found in contempt if all he has done is failed to satisfy a judgment; There must be a finding that he has clearly disobeyed a court order or a proper notice involving judgment enforcement.

Every state has its own specific procedures for holding a person in contempt, but a common thread runs through them all. A motion or application must be made in writing—not orally—to the court that issued the judgment or that is located where the judgment debtor resides. The facts underlying the application must be set forth concisely in affidavit form. The judgment debtor must receive notice of the proceeding. In most cases, the notice must be served upon him in person and contain specific warnings that if he fails to appear he may be subjected to a fine or imprisonment. While it would be impossible for us to provide the proper form for every state, we can show you one, in this case New York's, that is typical. We caution you, however, that before you start writing anything you consult either a local attorney or a cooperative court clerk for guidance.

An order to show cause for a contempt motion will look something like this:

WARNING:
YOUR FAILURE TO APPEAR IN COURT MAY RESULT IN YOUR IMMEDIATE ARREST AND IMPRISONMENT FOR CONTEMPT OF COURT

At a Special Term, Part 2, held in and for the County of New York, at the courthouse at 60 Centre Street, in the State of New York, on the 5th day of May 1984

PRESENT: *Hon. John Justice*

. . . . X

MARY FELLOWS,

                PLAINTIFF,   **ORDER TO**
          -against-   **SHOW CAUSE**

SIDNEY FELLOWS,   Index # 4286/83

                DEFENDANT.

. . . . X

UPON the annexed affidavit of MARY FELLOWS, sworn to on May 2, 1984, together with exhibits thereto, and upon the judgment and all the other proceedings had herein,

LET THE DEFENDANT SHOW CAUSE, at Special Term, Part 5, at the courthouse at 60 Centre Street in the City of New York, on the 11th day of May 1984, at 9:30 A.M., or as soon thereafter as the parties or counsel may be heard, why an order should not be entered herein against the defendant citing him in contempt of court, on account of his willful refusal to comply with an information subpoena, dated April 12, 1984.

SUFFICIENT CAUSE APPEARING, let personal service of a copy of this order, along with the papers upon which it is made, upon the defendant SIDNEY FELLOWS on or before May 8, 1984 be deemed good and sufficient service.

ENTER,

s/ John Justice, J.S.C.

NOTICE: THE PURPOSE OF THE HEARING IS TO PUNISH YOU, SIDNEY FELLOWS, FOR A CONTEMPT OF COURT, AND THAT SUCH PUNISHMENT MAY CONSIST OF FINE OR IMPRISONMENT, OR BOTH, ACCORDING TO LAW.

Mary Fellow's affidavit, which comes next, would read as follows:

SUPREME COURT OF THE STATE OF NEW YORK
COUNTY OF NEW YORK

. . . . X

MARY FELLOWS,
                        PLAINTIFF,   **SUPPORTING**
           -against-   **AFFIDAVIT**

SIDNEY FELLOWS,
                        Index # 4286/83
                 DEFENDANT.

. . . . X

(State of New York, County of New York) ss.:

MARY FELLOWS, being duly sworn, deposes and says:

1. I am the plaintiff in the above entitled action, and I submit this affidavit in support of my motion to cite defendant for contempt of this court.

2. I previously obtained a money judgment against defendant in the sum of $2,300.00, which was entered with the clerk on or about March 10, 1984. A copy of the judgment is attached as Exhibit A.

3. On April 12, 1984, an information subpoena and questionnaire was personally served upon defendant, requesting various information about his assets. A copy of said documents along with proof of service, is attached as Exhibit B.

4. Defendant has failed to provide the information as requested in the subpoena and questionnaire. In fact, on or about May 1, 1984, he told me that he never was going to answer my questions.

5. Without the information sought from defendant, I will be unable to discover the location and nature of his assets, and thus remain unable to satisfy the judgment I have against him.

6. It is respectfully submitted that defendant's disobedience of the subpoena has been willful, deliberate and motivated to defeat my rights and discourage me from enforcing my remedies. Further, defendant's conduct was calculated to, and actually did, defeat and impair my rights to enforce my judgment against him.

WHEREFORE, plaintiff respectfully requests that this Court grant an order in her favor against defendant, citing him for contempt and punishing him by a fine of no less than ONE THOUSAND ($1,000.00) DOLLARS and/or imprisonment, because of his willful failure to comply with plaintiff's information subpoena, and for such other relief that is just and proper.

s/ _____
MARY FELLOWS

Sworn to before me
this May 2, 1984

s/ _____
NOTARY PUBLIC

Mary's motion would be submitted to the judge for his consideration on May 12th, the return date. Sidney would be allowed to submit his opposing affidavit, setting forth what he hoped would be a sufficient excuse. Several weeks later, the judge would decide the motion except if there were still material facts in controversy, in which case he would order an immediate hearing. Assuming that Sidney was unable to provide a good excuse, the court would find him in contempt but give him an opportunity to *purge* the contempt by paying a fine, perhaps $250, directly to Mary and supplying the answers to the questionnaire within a certain time. Most judges also add that a daily fine of $25 or $50 will come into effect if the contempt is not purged. Finally, if Sidney fails to purge the contempt, Mary will be allowed to make a second motion for his commitment (arrest).

Arrest

Generally speaking, civil arrest is the enforcement device of last resort in regard to money judgment enforcement issues. Most judges hesitate to use it. Debtor prisons were already long abolished by the time the American colonists began shooting at the redcoats, and the trend ever since has been away from incarcerating judgment debtors.

Civil arrest is granted only in extreme circumstances. Courts are for the most part far more comfortable imposing monetary sanctions on a recalcitrant judgment debtor than imposing detention. This especially holds true where it appears that there may be other ways of enforcing a judgment. Let's be honest, judges are always on the lookout for vindictive litigants who are using the enforcement procedures solely to embarrass or harass a former spouse. The point is that before any order of arrest or confinement is issued, a judge has to be fully convinced that there is no practical alternative. Balanced against the judicial concern for fair play, however, is the common knowledge that absolutely nothing in our laws prompts compliance better than a day or two in the pokey.

But while it may be true that arrest is rarely employed when there is just an ordinary money judgment, you, as a creditor holding a judgment for *child or spousal support,* have a decided edge for obtaining such enforcement. Many states have specific laws authorizing arrest where family support is involved. Moreover, there is increasing social and legislative pressure to incarcerate persons who avoid court-ordered support obligations. Arrest is the ultimate enforcement weapon, but it is *your* task to convince the judge to press the button. Once again, you must convincingly demonstrate that there are no other ways open to you to enforce your rights. This will generally require establishing the following:

1. A property execution on the money judgment has been returned unsatisfied by the sheriff
2. The judgment debtor has no assets that can be attached or sequestered
3. A payroll deduction order is unavailable or has been ineffective

The utilization of arrest as an enforcement device may depend on practical considerations outside of your control or the facts of your case. We have seen time and time again that civil arrest is more typically utilized in rural counties, and that it is rarely granted in urban courts. We believe the reason for this disparity is that judges outside of major cities are less exposed to the rank criminal offenders, and thus they are more outraged by Joe Average violating a court order. Chances are also that these judges are more politically conservative and therefore view incarceration as a proper penalty for a civil infraction. In contrast, judges in large cities regularly encounter numbers of serious criminal charges. Overcrowded jails give them no choice other than to let accused muggers, robbers and even rapists walk away free on bail. You can imagine then what their attitude will be toward a judgment debtor. Moreover, most judges in such situations would be very reluctant to lock away someone who is not paying child support along with the muggers, robbers and rapists who have not been set free.

Notwithstanding all the difficulties connected with arrest orders, we strongly suggest you pursue this remedy if you have nothing else to go on. You have absolutely nothing to lose except, perhaps, some time and effort. Besides, you can hope that your ex has not read this book and has no idea how hard it will be for you to get him arrested. The very threat of arrest may then be all you need.

Enforcing Pension Rights

Strictly speaking, what follows has nothing to do with enforcing money judgments, but it is concerned with enforcing important marital rights. Many spouses at the time of their divorce are awarded a share of the other party's, usually the husband's, pension benefits, either a percentage or a fixed amount. However, payment is not immediate. Unless a contemporaneous lump sum payoff is contemplated, a wife awarded a share of a husband's pension must wait until he begins to collect on it. The wait may be as long as 20 or more years, since pension payments are triggered by retirement. In the interim a former wife can be left wondering whether she will ever see her share of the pot of gold at the end of the rainbow. Worse yet, a woman may belatedly discover that her ex withdrew his entire pension and moved to Tahiti, without paying her a cent.

Well, times change. Thanks to recent amendments to the Employee Retirement Income Security Act of 1974 (ERISA) and the Internal Revenue Code by the Retirement Equity Act of 1984 (REA), women or men who are entitled to a portion of their former spouses pension, profit-sharing or stock bonus plan can be fully protected. Under the new laws, these individuals can apply in their local court for a *Qualified Domestic Relations Order (QDRO),* which will bind the pension plan administrator or trustee and compel him to make the requisite payments to them.

The problem prior to the enactment of the 1984 amendments was that, although many divorce decrees and court orders directed that payments were to be made straight from the pension plan, many administrators refused to comply. They took the position that ERISA expressly preempted all state laws pertaining to pension plans and prohibited all transfers of benefits to anyone other than the plan participants. This issue has prompted myriad legal battles between the parties looking for the payments and the pension administrators, some of which resolved in favor of the spouses, some in favor of the administrators. Courts have held that Congress never intended that ERISA deprive a former spouse of marital benefits, while others have interpreted ERISA strictly and held that the direct payments were prohibited by federal law. The only clear-cut result was confusion.

The new law makes certain that pension plan administrators *must* comply with a QDRO, which is defined as any judgment, decree, order or approved property settlement agreement under a state's domestic relations law that provides for child support or maintenance payments or any other marital property rights to an *alternate payee,* who is defined as a spouse, former spouse, child or any other legal dependent of a plan participant. In other words, the person who is supposed to be getting a piece of the pension. The *plan participant,* of course, is the employee who is obliged to share his pension with a current or former spouse.

The plan administrator initially makes the determination if the judgment or order is properly qualified. A QDRO must contain the following information:

- The names and last known mailing addresses of the plan participant and the alternate payee
- The amount or percent of the payment, or the manner by which this amount is to be calculated
- The number of payments or the period they are to last
- The name of each plan to which the judgment or order applies

The administrator has a specific time under federal regulations to determine whether the order meets these qualifications. While this is being considered he must segregate your benefits and hold them in escrow for 18 months. If it is necessary to go to court in order to resolve this issue in your favor, the escrowed monies will be turned over to you, *provided the determination is made within the 18 months.* Otherwise they are released to the plan participant. So move fast, should you be turned down.

The real beauty of a QDRO is that it gives you the right to receive payments directly from the pension plan. No more keeping your fingers crossed hoping your ex sees fit to pay you. Moreover, there are added bonuses. You now have a good deal of flexibility in choosing the form and timing of the payments. Most plans give their participants several payment options: a single lump-sum payment, a greater amount over fewer years, a lesser amount with greater survivor benefits, or an endless variety of options. A QDRO can have the plan administrator paying you your share according to any option offered by the plan, regardless of the way your ex has elected to take his remaining portion. For example, you are supposed to receive one-third of your former husband's pension, which is valuated at $90,000. His plan permits him to receive a single lump sum payment or an annuity policy for that amount, with payments over his lifetime. Your QDRO may now choose either option, the $30,000 at once or lifetime payments, and it does not matter which one your ex selects.

Another advantage under the new law is that the QDRO can require the administrator to pay you your share of the benefits as soon as your ex reaches the plan's minimum retirement age, which is usually 55. It does not matter whether he retires then or when he begins to receive benefits. As long as his age qualifies, you can receive benefits. Furthermore, as an alternate payee, you are also treated as a *beneficiary* within the ERISA requirements. This means that you are typically entitled to receive plan information and have the right to sue the plan administrator for breaches of his fiduciary duties, such as not paying you. The latter right can be important in situations involving a small plan that your ex participates in managing, where he may try to manipulate the benefits in a way that is against your interests.

Many attorneys specializing in matrimonial law are aware of the QDRO requirements, and orders and judgments since 1985 often contain the necessary information to enforce the nonworking spouse's pension rights. Earlier judgments, however, may not qualify, and they will have to be judicially modified before a plan administrator can be legally bound. As we will see more particularly in the following chapters, divorce judgments and decrees are NEVER final. They are always subject to modification upon a substantial change of circumstances, and REA's passage in 1984 surely qualifies as such. The procedure for modifying a judgment to meet the QDRO standards is the same as for increasing the amount of maintenance or child support, only much simpler. In most cases, all you need do is provide the court with the necessary information to be added to your judgment. Of course, all this presupposes that your original judgment awarded you a share of your ex's pension. If not, with extremely limited exceptions, there will be nothing you can do about it.

JUDGMENT DAY

We have tried in this chapter to give you a broad look at the various enforcement devices that you may find useful to protect your rights. Of course, the scope of this book limits the detail that we could provide you, but the basic information is here to help you set the process in motion. Indeed, the methods of enforcing judgments could fill a book, but we still have other things to talk about. Nevertheless, you should now have a good idea of what the various devices are and how they work. Like any fine tool, they may not be easy to use at first, but you will be amazed to discover the ease a little practice can bring to the task. You will also find that court personnel can be extremely helpful. Because you understand the basic procedures, your questions will be much more to the point, and thus seriously entertained. You won't be a typical, anxious and harried former spouse demanding, "What am I going to do?" You'll know.

CHAPTER SIX

Locating an Ex-Spouse

ANY ENFORCEMENT DEVICE that we have been discussing cannot work its magic if your ex is not around. It is impossible to attach his wages when you don't know where he lives or works. While accurate statistics are hard to come by, the number of parents who simply drop out of sight in order to escape financial responsibility is high enough to represent a national disgrace. Even worse are those financially dependent parents or ex-spouses who believe that they are totally without recourse because their ex-mate has pulled a disappearing act.

Well, you are *not* without recourse if you find yourself in this situation. Depending on the circumstances of your case and the reasons for your need to find your ex, there are several avenues of assistance.

If you are seeking to enforce a child support order and do not know the whereabouts of your ex, you can get help from your local support enforcement collection agency. In Chapter 2, we discussed the agency's ability to offer assistance in collecting your support order through automatic wage deduction and tax intercept. Many parents do not realize that the agency also provides parent locator services. These services provide investigation, statewide search and a nationwide process that reviews appropriate files of the Internal Revenue Service, Social Security Administration and Department of Defense. Although a thorough search for a missing parent may take as long as 6 to 8 months, the agency's abilities in this area increase with each passing month. Computers are becoming more sophisticated and inter-departmental cooperation is increasing.

It bears emphasis that the support collection agency's parent locator services are only available when you are seeking enforcement of a child support order. If you are entitled to utilize the agency system discussed in Chapter 2, then you are equally entitled to have them assist you in first finding your ex-spouse. The procedure is relatively simple and painless.

Initially you will be asked to complete an application called *Registration of Absent or Putative Parents*. The term *putative* applies to child support orders that are not part of any divorce decree because the parents never married. Parenthetically, you might be interested to learn that the obligation to support a child exists regardless of whether such child may have been born out of wedlock. It is not the marriage that gives rise to the legal obligation to support, but rather parental status.

We have reproduced below the registration form that you will be required to fill out and sign when you seek to avail yourself of a support collection unit's parent locator services. You will see that the information required is rather basic. The section on the absent parent's background is crucial, particularly his or her date of birth and social security number.

FORM **DSS-2655** (7/76)

REGISTRATION OF ABSENT OR PUTATIVE PARENTS

STATE OF NEW YORK   DEPARTMENT OF SOCIAL SERVICES

NAME OF AGENCY   **USE BALL POINT PEN**   REOPEN | ADD. INFO. | PLS NO. (3-9)

RA | (1-2) | PLS.NO. (3-9) | AGENCY CODE (10-11) | FIELD OFFICE (12-13) | DSS CASE NO. (14-22) | IV-D REGISTRATION NO. (23-31) | IV-D REG. DATE (32-37) Mo. Day Yr. | NO. OF CHILD. (38-39) | PLS RECEIVED DATE (40-45)

REGISTRY TYPE (46)

- 1. Absent Parent (In Wedlock)
- 2. Absent Parent (Out-of-Wedlock)
- 3. Putative Parent

REGISTRY CATEGORY (47-48)

01. ADC	04. HR	07. Out-of-State
02. MA Only	05. Non-Welfare	08. SSI
03. CW	06. Court	09. Food Stamps

COURT DATA (49)

- 1. Support Petition Filed
- 2. Court Order Issued
- 3. Violation Petition Filed
- 4. Voluntary Agreement Signed

ABSENT or PUTATIVE PARENT →   LAST NAME (50-63)   FIRST NAME (64-73)   M.I. (74)   JR, SR, ETC. (75-76)

RB | (1-2) | PLS.NO. (3-9) | DATE OF BIRTH (10-15) Mo. Day Yr. | SOCIAL SECURITY NO. (16-24) | SEX (25) 1. Male 2. Female | RACE (26) 1. White 2. Black 3. Other 4. Unkwn | HEIGHT (27-29) Ft. In. | RELATIONSHIP TO CLIENT (30) 1. Spouse 2. Relative 3. Other | DATE OF (31-36) DESERTION Mo. Day Yr.

FULL LEGAL NAME OF CLIENT/APPLICANT →   LAST NAME (37-50)   FIRST NAME (51-60)   MI (61)   Jr, Sr, Etc. (62-63)

RC | (1-2) | PLS.NO. (3-9) | CLIENT'S SEX (10) 1. Male 2. Female

NO. AND STREET (11-37)

CLIENT/APPLICANT'S MAILING ADDRESS →   CITY OR TOWN (38-55)   STATE (56-57)   ZIP CODE (58-62)

SECTION II - ABSENT OR PUTATIVE PARENT BACKGROUND

ARREST RECORD (63)	MILITARY SERVICE (64) (PAST OR PRESENT)	BRANCH OF SERVICE (65)	MILITARY RETIREMENT (66)	VETERAN BENEFITS (67)
1. Yes 2. No	1. Yes 2. No	1. Army 4. Coast Guard 2. Navy 5. Marines 3. A.F.	1. Yes 2. No	1. Yes 2. No

RD | (1-2) | PLS.NO. (3-9)

MOTHER'S FULL MAIDEN NAME →   LAST NAME (10-23)   FIRST NAME (24-33)   MI (34)   Jr, Sr, Etc. (35-36)

FATHER'S FULL LEGAL NAME →   LAST NAME (37-50)   FIRST NAME (51-60)   MI (61)   Jr, Sr, Etc. (62-63)

RE | (1-2) | PLS.NO. (3-9)

POSSIBLE ALIAS of ABSENT or PUTATIVE PARENT →   LAST NAME (10-23)   FIRST NAME (24-33)   MI (34)   Jr, Sr, Etc. (35-36)

PLACE OF BIRTH CITY OR TOWN (37-54)   State (55-56)   PROBABLE OUT-OF-STATE DESTINATION (IF ANY) CITY OR TOWN (57-74)   State (75-76)

RF | (1-2) | PLS.NO. (3-9)

LAST KNOWN ADDRESS of ABSENT or PUTATIVE PARENT →   NO. AND STREET (10-36)

→ CITY OR TOWN (37-54)   STATE (55-56)   ZIP CODE (57-61)

DATE OF LAST KNOWN ADDRESS (62-67) Mo. Day Yr. | DATE OF LAST KNOWN EMPLOY. (68-73) Mo. Day Yr. | NAME OF LAST KNOWN EMPLOYER

NO. AND STREET ADDRESS   CITY OR TOWN   STATE   ZIP CODE

RG | (1-2) | PLS.NO. (3-9) | NAMES OF DEPENDENT CHILDREN: LAST NAME (10-23) | FIRST NAME (24-33) | MI (34) | DATE OF BIRTH (35-40) Mo. Day Yr. | LAST NAME (41-54) | FIRST NAME (55-64) | MI (65) | DATE OF BIRTH (66-71) Mo. Day Yr.

RH | (1-2) | PLS.NO. (3-9) | LAST NAME (10-23) | FIRST NAME (24-33) | MI (34) | DATE OF BIRTH (35-40) Mo. Day Yr. | LAST NAME (41-54) | FIRST NAME (55-64) | MI (65) | DATE OF BIRTH (66-71) Mo. Day Yr.

RI | (1-2) | PLS.NO. (3-9) | LAST NAME (10-23) | FIRST NAME (24-33) | MI (34) | DATE OF BIRTH (35-40) Mo. Day Yr. | NAME OF PREPARER | DATE

After the application is completed, you will meet with a caseworker. The purpose here is to "flesh out" any other important data that may assist the agency in locating your ex. This interview process will be more productive if you prepare yourself beforehand. This means that you should not limit yourself to the information that appears on the registration form. This is only the basic data that starts the ball rolling.

There are other important clues that you may have that will make all the difference in locating your spouse. Much of this information may be lying around the house, dusty artifacts of your prior marriage. These items are often overlooked, yet the information is crucial:

- Your ex's educational records
- Old bankbooks and checking statements
- Postmarks on envelopes forwarded by your ex
- Name, addresses and telephone numbers of your ex's relatives
- Your ex's expired passport
- And let's not forget the most obvious—any recent photographs of your ex that you may still have in your possession

All of these items greatly assist a support collection unit's efforts to locate your spouse. Incidentally, this same data will be extremely helpful if you are forced to hire a private detective, an option that we will discuss shortly.

After the interview process has been completed, the support unit will enter the appropriate information into their computer. The computer then cross-checks police records; voting registration data; IRS lists; motor vehicle records and other sources of population identification. Most agencies will provide you with periodic reports of their progress, but do not be unduly disheartened if you receive no word for 6 to 7 months. It only means that the agency has nothing to report yet. We suggest that after your interview has been completed, you specifically ask your caseworker for an estimate of how long it may be before the agency has exhausted all possibilities. If you haven't heard after this time, then feel free to telephone. However, as anxious as you may be feeling, the worst thing that you can do is become a pest. Calling your caseworker every other day will not help matters; you have no other choice but to be patient and let the process work itself out.

As indicated, you will not be eligible to use the support collection unit's parent locator services if you are only seeking enforcement of a spousal maintenance award. The agency is also generally unavailable in child-snatching cases. In the latter situation, you may be able to enlist the assistance of your local police and even the FBI. We explain how to go about doing this in Chapter 13. However, when you are trying to locate your ex in order to obtain enforcement of a financial award, the police are, unfortunately, more reticent to become involved.

If, then, you need to find your ex so that your maintenance award can be enforced, you have two basic options. You can *hire* a private detective or *play* private detective. Of course, the two options are not mutually exclusive.

DOING YOUR OWN DETECTIVE WORK

Private detectives will be the first to admit that the work they do can be accomplished by virtually anyone. They merely know the sources of information that unlock the puzzle of locating a missing person. So let us give you a couple of their tricks: it may save you a lot of money later.

Your ex's social security number is one of the major keys to success.

Somewhere around your house is a document with his or her number on it. Start by going through some of your old papers. Have you checked your old joint tax returns? If you do not have copies, all you need do to get one is complete a Form 4506, pay the nominal fee and send the request directly to the IRS. These request forms can be obtained at your local IRS office, from any certified public accountant, or even from many post offices.

Or how about the application that was submitted when the two of you were trying to get your first mortgage? Another source is old financial records and statements; your ex's "tax ID number" is often synonymous with his social security number. The point is that if you do not know your ex's social security number, you can find it easily enough. Once you have the number, a whole universe of possibilities opens.

For example, you probably know that approximately 90 percent of Americans have some kind of basic medical insurance coverage. By far, the majority have a Blue Cross/Blue Shield plan. What you may not have realized is that an individual's insurance identification number is the same as that person's social security number.

Typically, a private detective will begin his search knowing only that an individual resides in a certain state. However, with social security number in hand, the investigator can usually pinpoint the person's exact address by using the information stored within the central subscriber computer system maintained by each state's Blue Cross/Blue Shield office. By using some sort of subterfuge and identifying himself by the appropriate policy identification number (your ex's social security number), the investigator can obtain a specific home or mailing address.

For instance, he may say that he is calling from out of town and needs the exact amount of reimbursement that he received in regard to his last medical or dental claim. When the agent gives him the information, the investigator will offhandedly ask for the exact spelling and address of the particular doctor. The address will key him into state, county and probably even your ex's neighborhood!

Or how about calling Blue Cross/Blue Shield to "doublecheck" if they have "your" (your ex's) most recent mailing address? The company will invariably recite the address in their files. This is a favorite trick of the trade used by many investigators. Just keep a pencil handy and write fast.

Private investigators are also fond of taking your ex's date of birth and making it a potent weapon in the investigatory arsenal. For example, every state registers car owners by name and date of birth. By using a little imagination, you can probably figure out how a private investigator can very often obtain a present or very recent home address directly from the Department of Motor Vehicles. The key remains "imagination."

If you merely sit back and accept the immutability of your ex's disappearance, you will never get any enforcement satisfaction. On the other hand, if you take a little initiative, you may find your efforts greatly rewarded.

We know of one woman who found her ex by canvassing the casinos in Atlantic City. Her ex had always been a big gambler, and she recalled that he always had a credit line at one or two of the largest gambling casinos. By using some charm, acting ability and just plain "chutzpah," she discovered her ex's Delaware address.

THE PRIVATE INVESTIGATOR

When all else fails, there are many professionals who can lend assistance. As with any other service, you must shop around for a good private investigator; certainly you should not hire the first name you come across in the telephone book. Most investigators work on an hourly fee basis. The amount may range anywhere from $35 to $250 per hour.

We recommend that you do your own "investigating" before you hire anyone. When choosing an investigator, the following points will prove helpful:

- Be sure that the investigator specializes in locating missing persons.
- Ask for a recent client list and references.
- Make sure that the investigator is licensed in your state.
- Determine the hourly rate in advance, plus all other expenses for which you may be responsible, such as travel, long distance telephone calls, mailings, etc.
- Request and insist upon a written contract of services and a written cost estimate.
- Make sure that the investigator understands that he is to contact you as soon as he has expended a certain amount of time on your case, let's say ten hours.
- During the first interview, get a clear idea of the procedure that the investigator intends to use in your case. For example, does he think that fieldwork as opposed to telephone inquiries will be needed.
- If you get a good feel for the individual, have him or her agree to personally handle your case. After the initial intake interview, many investigators rely on inexperienced underlings.
- Request and insist on periodic written progress reports. This helps to insure that you don't begin to spend money on futile pursuits.

This chapter is short because there are not many hard answers to the question: Where is my ex? However, we have provided this interlude to emphasize the importance of taking affirmative steps to locate your former spouse, should the need arise. There are agencies with specific parent locator services to assist you. Professionals have been trained to help you put together the "missing" pieces of your puzzle. And *you* are capable of doing a great deal of the legwork on your own. The only certainty is that doing nothing gets you nowhere—fast.

Finding an ex-spouse—whether it be by your own efforts or those of a private investigator—depends on almost equal measures of hard tedious work, science, artistry and just plain smarts. Remember that an individual is rarely successful in burrowing totally underground. Your ex will be sure to surface somewhere. He may change his name, but the all-important social security number and birthdate cannot be so easily modified. Thank heaven for this age of computers, automobile licenses, tax returns and employment/disability benefits. They almost assure that your ex's name is somewhere on someone's silicon chip.

CHAPTER SEVEN

Getting More–or Giving Less

TIMES CHANGE. SIX years ago, Myra believed $55 a week was more than enough for Toby, who was only 2 years old then—long before school, babysitters, day camp, Pro-Keds and GI Joe began. Even though she is working full time, Myra can no longer make ends meet.

When Thomas signed the settlement agreement in 1979, Celeste was, by day, earning about $140 a week as a part-time secretary and, by night, completing an undergraduate degree in marketing. Now she is a regional vice-president in a large paper products company earning $55,000. Thomas wonders about that $100 weekly maintenance he pays which still has almost 4 years to go.

The passage of time can bring about many changes that render an original judicial award or consensual settlement irrelevant. At the time of the divorce, no attorney or judge is equipped with a crystal ball to foresee all the events that may occur in the next several years. While it is debatable whether people change, their circumstances certainly do, for better or worse. Everyone knows this, but rarely can anything be done about it at the time because there are too many contingencies to consider and effectively plan for. Only rarely will the immediate future be somewhat predictable. A wife is in her third year of medical school; it is obvious that spousal maintenance need only extend for a few more years, barring some unforeseen illness, accident or disability, which may happen but is not likely enough to worry about. One can easily come up with an appropriate arrangement, acceptable to all. But this is the exception. Most times all one can do is guess—or at best, realistically estimate—future needs and events. Negotiating good settlements is more art than science. Judges are even at a worse disadvantage. They may have heard endless testimony about actual and projected expenses, but when the time comes to make a decision on maintenance and child support, they often miss the give and take of intense negotiations, which so often reveal facts that are more relevant and much closer to the truth, and which typically lead to fair— but not prophetic—settlements.

Children make the calculations tens of times more difficult. Everyone says that raising them is expensive. Few realize how much more expensive it becomes each year. As children grow older, the prices keep right up with them. Everything gets more costly—clothing, education, doctors, dentists, toys, extracurricular activities, allowances, transportation and vacations, and these are in the normal course of events. Should something unexpected happen, either good or bad, the costs can skyrocket beyond anyone's wildest estimations.

Overlaid on everything is the national and world economy. An oil embargo drives up the prices at the supermarket. A strong dollar contributes to a trade deficit that results in layoffs at the steel mill, that, in turn, forces someone's luncheonette out of business. The increased cost of living and the destructive ravages of inflation by themselves can eat away at a maintenance or child support award that at one time seemed fair and sufficient. Surely no one can forget living with the double-digit inflation of just one presidential administration ago, and who is to say that it cannot happen again?

Fortunately, the law recognizes the problem. No divorce judgement or decree, nor any support settlement or order, is ever final. It is always subject to modification either by the consent of the parties or by the order of the court. The latter approach requires the proper grounds, that is to say the right reasons, which is the subject of this chapter. The same reasons will be necessary for a successfully negotiated change. We will attempt to provide you with an overall review of the situations where courts have allowed either an upward or downward modification of a prior support order, in addition to those where modifications have not been allowed. You should come away with a fairly good idea of whether you have sufficient grounds to seek a modification. Chapter 8 will tell you how you go about negotiating and, if necessary, litigating your request.

THE CHANGED CIRCUMSTANCES DOCTRINE

At the heart of all modifications of prior support orders is the *changed circumstances* doctrine. This rule requires that the person seeking a modification of the order must demonstrate substantially changed circumstances that reasonably mandate the desired change. The change must have taken place between the time of the original order and the application, and it must be relatively permanent and substantial. The change must result in real need and must not have been previously provided for in the prior order or agreement. Moreover, it must not have been something that the person seeking the modification did to evade his responsibilities. Let us take a few examples that illustrate these principles.

1. Time of the change.

Mary Taylor had been diagnosed at age 10 as having a learning disability. Her parents were divorced soon after her 13th birthday. Her mother was awarded custody by the judge, and her father was ordered to pay $100 weekly for child support. Two years later Mary's mother went back to court seeking to get her former husband to pay for special tutoring for Mary. Her father opposed the motion by stating that the original child support award took into account the extra expenses that would be occasioned by Mary's disability. He pointed to the portion of the trial court's written decision that acknowledged that his daughter suffered from a minor learning disability. The judge, while sympathizing with the predicament that Mary and her mother faced, ruled that the condition preceded the original support order and that Mrs. Taylor had failed to convince him that there had been any change of circumstances, such as the disability becoming significantly worse, upon which he could grant her request for an upward modification. Application denied.

2. The change must be permanent.

Arthur Tyler had been paying his wife maintenance and child support for 7 years. Six hundred dollars every month. He was sick and tired of the sizable dent it made in his personal budget, and every once in a while he would call the lawyer who handled his divorce and ask him if there was anything he could do to cut it down a little. Each time the answer was the same: he needed to show substantially changed circumstances. The trouble was that nothing ever changed. Then it happened, his union went out on strike. Although he received union benefits, they came to a little more than half of his take-home pay. Delighted with the "fortunate" turn of events, Arthur called his old lawyer. The receptionist put him on hold. While waiting, he tried to guess how much the guy would charge him to handle the modification. The conversation never got that far.

"Arthur, how are you doing? It's been a while since I last heard from you."

"I'm doing just fine, Mr. Stykes, just fine. As a matter of fact I'm doing great. My union went on strike last week and I'm out of work."

Stykes knew instantly what was coming. "Are you receiving any money, Arthur?"

"Oh, sure. I'm getting about $220 a week from the strike fund."

"Well, that's not too bad."

"No, I'm managing, but you know its about half of what I normally get. Anyway, I know you're busy as hell, so I'll get to the point. You remember I called you a few times and asked you about cutting down the payments to my ex and the kids?"

"Yes, I vaguely recall." Stykes tried to suppress any sound of the smile on his face.

"Yeah, good. You know each time you told me I had to show a big change."

"Substantially changed circumstances."

"Well, I have. Haven't I? My income has been cut in half, so can't we cut Louise's likewise?"

"I doubt it, Arthur. You see, the change must not only be substantial, which this certainly is, but it must also be something that is relatively permanent, which this isn't. I'm sure that you'll be back to work soon, probably sooner than the judge can reach a decision on our motion. Anyway, the point is that this isn't good enough. No way we're going to convince the court that you're going to be out of work for more than a month or two. Maybe if you stay out on strike long enough, your company will go under and you'll be out of a job, which in this town can be a real problem. Then you'll have real good grounds to go on."

"I see what you mean. Thanks for your time, Mr. Stykes."

3. The change must be substantial.

Our friend, Arthur, remained undaunted. The strike lasted for 5 weeks. The union representatives tried to convince the membership that the results were worthwhile, but Arthur could see little beyond some relaxed work rules, a 5-minute longer afternoon break and slightly better dental coverage. Meanwhile, the company announced 3 weeks later that it was eliminating overtime. The union lawyers were unable to prove that the move was in retaliation for the strike. Arthur's biweekly paycheck went down by about $32. Once more, he called Stykes, this time certain that he had the goods. Once more, he was wrong. Stykes told him that the change of circumstances had to be substantial; a $32 reduction every 2 weeks was not.

4. There must be need.

Stacy Bennett was outraged. Since the divorce 5 years ago, Ted's salary had quadrupled. He was now a senior vice-president and earning over $125,000 a year. He and his new wife, who was 6 months pregnant, moved into a beautiful contemporary, cathedral ceilinged, balconied and sky-lighted house on two acres of land in Shaker Heights. Her two daughters spared her no details each time they came home from the alternate week-end visitations. Meanwhile, she and the girls still lived in the 3-bedroom dump that she and Ted had bought 2 years after the wedding, when he was making about 15 grand as a computer programmer. She got the house as part of the settlement, but after all these years she hated it.

Stacy really had no beef with her ex. He was more than generous with the girls. He gave them a liberal allowance and often purchased much of their clothing. Whenever there was an extra expense, such as tennis or ballet lessons, he always gave her a check, no questions asked. No, the thing that bothered Stacy was that the combined maintenance and child support payment had stayed the same since the divorce. Frequently, she would complain to Paula, her closest friend.

"The same lousy $950 check each month, for five years now. And it's never late!"

"So, what are you griping about? Do you know how many women don't get one cent from their ex?"

"I know, and I feel bad about complaining. Yet every time I hear Wendy and Tara bragging about how stupendous Ted's new house is, or how pretty his new wife is, I get crazy. It's just not fair. We struggled together when he was nothing, and now that he's hit it big, me and the girls are left out."

"But doesn't he take good care of the girls? You're always telling me that he's great with them."

"Oh, yeah. He's wonderful. That's what makes it so hard. I really shouldn't complain. I'm meeting my expenses. It's just that I would like something a little extra. You know, even a janitor gets a raise every now and then. Why not me?"

"I see what you mean, but I don't think you should rock the boat."

Paula stood up. "Anyhow, I got to go and pick up Fred from Little League. Catch you later."

Stacy should have taken her friend's advice. Instead, she retained a lawyer virtually fresh out of law school, who made a post-judgment motion for an upward modification. Her young attorney should have first done his homework. The court denied the motion because Stacy had failed to show any increased needs that warranted an upward modification. The judge noted that Stacy's own financial affidavit revealed that her salary and Ted's support payments were enough to cover all her expenses, and that it was undisputed that Ted was incurring the cost of any unexpected or extra childrearing costs. The short decision said it all.

> Motion for upward modification of maintenance and child support is denied. Although defendant admits that his income has increased significantly since the divorce, plaintiff has failed to show any current need for which an increase of the support is necessary. A party must show requisite need before this court may inquire into the supporting party's changed circumstances.

5. The need cannot have been previously contemplated.

David Wachtel thought his lawyer was crazy. When the property settlement was being negotiated, Stan Evert recommended that he give Betty a $50,000 lump sum cash payment in addition to the alimony and child support payments that her lawyer was demanding. Moreover, Evert insisted that David offer to set up a trust with another $50,000 for the benefit of the three children. David reluctantly agreed to go along with the suggestions. Evert had come highly recommended by David's corporate attorneys. Betty's lawyer did not waste a second accepting both proposals.

Eleven years later, Betty hired a big-name law firm to bring on an upward modification motion. Their papers were thorough, documenting to the penny additional expenses incurred by Betty due to the rising cost of living and increased needs of the children. David was sure that he would be hit up for more money by the judge, and he was frankly surprised that Evert did not recommend giving away the farm on this round. David and Betty both attended the oral argument on the motion. Evert was magnificent. He eloquently argued that the large cash payment to Betty was given with the express intention of meeting the higher cost of living, and that the children's trust fund had been created solely to cover the certain eventuality of their greater needs. The decision came down a month later. Betty's motion was denied, as was her lawyer's request for counsel fees. The last David heard, Betty had to dip into the $50,000 nest egg to pay her hotshot lawyer the balance of his $8,500 retainer.

6. The reasons for the change cannot be self-induced.

Barry Dobrell felt it was time to put an end to the maintenance payments. Rather than stop and wait for his ex to drag him into court, Barry figured that he would outsmart the system. He had talked to an attorney friend of his brother's and had the whole thing figured out. He first quit his job and waited until his unemployment benefits ran out. Then he went by himself to family court and filed a petition seeking a downward modification of his support obligations. He was confident that there were no better changed circumstances than being out of work.

Barry's application was set down for a hearing. Stephanie got the same lawyer who had represented her in the divorce to try the case. The lawyer was better than Barry remembered, very effective on cross-examination. Barry was unable to offer satisfactory explanations for his failure to get a new job. The lawyer shredded to pieces his halfhearted excuses and vague recounting of attempts to find work. The judge ruled that Barry had failed to convince the court that the alleged changed circumstances were not, in fact, deviously brought about by him solely to avoid his financial obligations. This was especially apparent by the lack of credible testimony regarding good faith attempts to find new employment. Barry had never anticipated that he would be asked to produce copies of his resume. Motion for downward modification denied; cross-motion for contempt granted. The next day, Barry borrowed $600 from his brother to pay Stephanie the arrears and found a new job.

APPLICATION OF THE DOCTRINE

The changed circumstances doctrine has developed throughout our legal system to the point where courts have tremendous flexibility to modify support orders and agreements. This was not always true. Divorce judgments were never exactly carved in stone, but many jurists historically acted that way when it came time to change them. Older cases stood for the proposition that the change had to be extraordinary and completely unanticipated. Unfortunately, this dinosaur thinking still survives in some states, which will be listed below. Readers in these jurisdictions will have to jump over several additional hurdles. For the vast majority, however, the test is that of substantially changed circumstances, which will be the basis upon which our discussion will proceed.

If you reside in Nebraska or Washington, you will have to establish that the change of circumstances was unanticipated and not contemplated by the parties at the time of the divorce. This means that you are effectively limited to changed circumstances that were honestly unexpected. Illness or disability would surely qualify, as would losing the capacity to earn a decent living. College education or piano lessons for the children probably would not. As you are the one seeking the modification, you will have the burden of convincing the court that the change could not have been anticipated at the time of the divorce. Generally, this is somewhat easier to do with child support than it is with maintenance or alimony because there are many unexpected things that can happen with children.

Readers in Colorado, Missouri, Kentucky and New Hampshire must show that the changed circumstances are extraordinary or that it would be unfair or unconscionable not to grant a modification. Here you have a tremendously more difficult burden to overcome before you can be awarded a modification. Showing that a change was substantial and unforeseen is not good enough. The current laws in these states require that you convince a judge that the changed circumstances are extraordinary or that it would virtually shock the court's conscience to deny the modification. This is a tough burden in all but the most extreme situations, and if the facts in your case fall short of this, you have a steep hill to climb. You must show the court that the changed circumstances have wrought a tremendous hardship upon you and that it would be unfair to deny your application. It can be done, but under such a severe test that motions for upward modifications are denied more often than they are granted.

If you live in any of the six states we mentioned above, you have, at least as of this writing, a much more difficult task than former spouses in other jurisdictions. However, there is a glimmer of hope. These additional barriers are rapidly eroding as the substantially changed circumstances test continues to become universally recognized. For example, had we written this book several years earlier, Florida and Connecticut would have been included in the first category. Perhaps by the time you make your application, your state's courts will have already fallen into line with the rest of the country.

NECESSARY SPECIAL EFFECTS

Now that you have some familiarity with the concept of changed circumstances and how it relates to modification applications, the next important thing you must learn is that, in the case of upward modifications, there also must be a necessary financial need brought on by the change, or, in the case of downward modifications, a noticeable dollar impact—decreased needs or inability to pay.

In other words, a party seeking an upward modification must establish NEED. Just because your ex is making more money is not enough. You must first convince the judge that the cost of maintaining the standard of living contemplated by the original decree or agreement, which *should* have been based upon what is commonly called the pre-separation standard of living, has been increased by the changed circumstances. Only then is the court allowed to inquire into your ex's higher earnings, and then only for the purpose of determining whether he has sufficient excess income to defray the costs brought about by the change. Similarly, grave illness certainly amounts to changed circumstances, but if all costs are being picked up by medical and disability insurance, there is no need for the supporting spouse to contribute anything further. A good way to look at this is to realize that divorce ends the "for better or for worse" nuptial promise. A divorced spouse can no longer share her ex-husband's good fortune, nor can he necessarily be made to share her misfortune, without evidence that his increased assistance is required to preserve the status quo contemplated in the terms of the divorce.

The same principles operate in a motion for downward modification, where it becomes necessary to show the *effect* of the changed circumstances. The supporting spouse cannot simply say that his income has decreased, or that his ex-wife's has increased. Rather, he must prove that the decrease makes it impossible for him to maintain the same level of support and that his former spouse is now in a position to take up the slack, even if she is still not working. Moreover, he must satisfy the court that his changed circumstances were not devious or brought about by subsequent events that he was able to control. For example, subsequent remarriage and the expenses of a new family are generally insufficiently changed circumstances to permit a supporting spouse to lower the payments to his first wife and children. The courts take the position that such a person was well aware of his obligations to his first family at the time he got engaged, and if any family should feel the pinch, it should be the second one.

There is, of course, no precise formula as to what exactly are changed circumstances sufficient to trigger an upward or downward modification. Determinations are made on a case by case basis. As Judge Pashman observed in an important New Jersey case, *Lepis v. Lepis:*

> The frequency with which courts are called upon to make or modify support awards needs no documentation. The lack of uniformity in their approaches and predictability in their decisions is similarly widely recognized. In part, the inability to predict dispositions is responsible for the volume of modification motions.

The goal, as Judge Pashman noted, is to base the supporting spouse's obligation upon the economic standard *during the marriage,* "not bare survival." The needs of the dependent spouse and children require maintaining, if possible, the standard of living to which they had become accustomed prior to the marital breakup. But if, for example, your ex has become substantially wealthier since the break-up the courts, in practice, will be fairly more liberal when it comes to child support, since there is an awareness that children should not be deprived of the fruits of one parent's labors.

> The supporting spouse has a continuing obligation to contribute to the maintenance of the dependent spouse at the standard of living formerly shared. . . . *An increase in support becomes necessary whenever changed circumstances substantially impair the dependent spouse's ability to maintain the standard of living reflected in the original decree or agreement. Conversely, a decrease is called for when circumstances render all or a portion of support received unnecessary for maintaining that standard.*

To sum up, in order to get an upward modification, you have to show that the change of circumstances has reduced your ability to maintain the standard of living that was contemplated in the original divorce decree or settlement. In order to get a downward modification, you must show that a change of circumstances has made some or all of the support you are paying unnecessary for your ex to continue living at that standard. We strongly suggest that you keep these rules in mind throughout the rest of our discussion.

EXAMPLES OF CHANGED CIRCUMSTANCES

After a thorough review of the leading cases throughout the country, we can offer an accurate summary of what events typically amount to changed circumstances sufficient to permit a modification of a prior agreement or decree. Each will be discussed, in no particular order. Do not lose sight that all of these grounds must produce the prerequisite result: *need,* for upward modifications, or *effect,* for downward ones. Without either, the alleged changed circumstances are, in the eyes of the law, really no change at all.

To make it a little easier for you, each category will be coded to indicate whether it concerns (U) upward or (D) downward modification. Also, as we will be using two phrases that commonly appear in all court decisions, let us define them for you. The financially *dependent spouse* is the one receiving the maintenance and child support payments. Most times this is the ex-wife, but of course it does not have to be this way. The *supporting spouse* is the one paying the money; again it usually is, but doesn't have to be, the ex-husband. Because we will be dealing with modifications both up and down, it will simplify matters if we use these terms instead of "you."

1. Increased earnings of supporting spouse (U)

Probably one of the most popular grounds for seeking upward modifications is the supporting spouse's higher earnings. However, this must be coupled with a demonstration of increased needs. Actually, we have the cart before the horse. Before the judge even begins to look at your ex's income tax returns, paycheck stubs or W-2s you must convince the judge that your needs are greater. This is ordinarily not a difficult task, especially if you have children. In most instances, it is possible to show greater need several years after the divorce. Prices always seem to go up, and the children always need (or want) something else.

Once the court is convinced that there has been a substantial change of circumstances, that is, you have legitimate, additional needs—forget the Jacuzzi—it then must determine whether you or your ex have the income or means to contribute to these higher costs. If the judge believes that you can afford the extra expenses, there may be no modification, or at best, the expense will be split between the parties. Only after this first stage of inquiry does the court look to your ex to see if he can afford the increase. A judge not only examines his income, but he closely scrutinizes your ex's expenses in order to determine whether there is a reasonable surplus that may be used for additional support.

Supporting spouses often defend against upward modification motions by inflating expenses. If you are the one bringing a motion to increase support, be prepared for this tactic, which may require that you be ready to prove that your ex's expenses are not as high as he claims. On the other hand, you should not be disheartened to discover that your ex's spending has kept pace with, or even exceeded, his earnings. To some extent this is expected. A person should not be faulted for enjoying the fruits of his labor. If he has found a new job or landed a big promotion, there is nothing evil about buying a boat or a new condo. Still, there are limits, and a judge will not hesitate to impose them if he feels that the extravagances are really at the expense of his lawful dependents. As much as some people abhor the fact, there is no question that divorce and post-divorce proceedings can become intrusive. No court of law would ever question someone's spending habits, except when he is involved in one of these motions. Suddenly a person's entire financial status is laid bare and open to inquiry.

Of course, you can not sit back and hope that the judge puts your ex and his sworn financial statement on the grill. You will have to be the one who probes the alleged expenses, pricking the balloon of overstated and inflated costs. Your job is to expose those alleged expenses that are frivolous, unnecessary or overstated. The thoroughness of your pre-hearing preparation and the resulting effectiveness of your cross-examination, both of which are discussed in the following chapter, will make the winning difference.

A frequent problem arises when the supporting spouse is not earning up to his potential. His income has stayed the same, or even gone down, and yet the dependent spouse feels that he should be using his Ph.D. for more than driving a taxi. Courts are not overly sympathetic with this argument; it is still a free country. Rarely will they focus upon a person's *potential* income. Rather, *actual* income controls nearly all modification decisions. However, there is an exception, and an important one: if the court believes that the supporting spouse is not making what he should be on account of his own calculated acts to avoid his financial responsibilities, it can impose upon him an increased support obligation in situations where he

1. willfully, *i.e.*, without good reason, refuses to seek gainful employment;
2. deliberately fails to apply himself to his business;
3. intentionally depresses his income to an artificial level; or
4. intentionally leaves his employment to go into another business without good reason.

Another issue that commonly enters the picture is the actual or potential earnings of the supporting spouse's new wife. Courts will take her *actual* earnings and include them in the computation of a husband's income so far as as they contribute to or reduce his expenses. In other words, it is fair to assume that a portion of the new wife's salary helps defray rent, food, utilities and other regular living costs, thereby making some more of the ex's income available for his first family. But this is as far as it goes. Never will a court pay the slightest attention to the new wife's earning *potential*, for to do that would impose a burden on her to support her husband's first family, which is improper under our laws.

A recent California case illustrates this. Karolyn Williams took her former husband to court, seeking to increase the monthly support for their two children from $300 to $600. She alleged a substantial change of circumstances, based on the fact that James's net monthly income had gone from $685 to $2,360.50 in 4 short years. However, one of the principal reasons for the change was the salary of his new wife, Christine, who was employed by TRW and earning approximately half of the latter amount. Karolyn was able to show that since the divorce James had acquired numerous assets, including a commercial building and a duplex apartment in Los Angeles, a home in Redondo Beach, two cars and a truck.

Once on the witness stand, James pulled a rabbit out of the hat. He testified to another change of circumstances that had occurred after Karolyn had filed her motion, and just 2 weeks before the hearing. Both he and Christine had voluntarily quit their jobs and moved to Reno, Nevada. He explained that the cost of living in California was too high, and that he and his wife wanted an easier lifestyle. He had sold two assets, his home and the commercial building, which were presumably heavily mortgaged, since he only realized some $23,000 in cash and accepted two purchase money mortgages paying him $600 monthly.

James had found a job in Reno, and he was making about $1,100 net each month. Christine was pregnant and not looking for work. Nevertheless, the trial court ordered James to pay an additional $100. Karolyn appealed, arguing that the trial court (1) failed to consider James's earning ability as opposed to his current financial circumstances and (2) failed to take into account his new wife's earning potential instead of her current unemployed status.

The Court of Appeals agreed with the trial judge, holding that the "amount of child support awarded was not an abuse of discretion in light of the reduction in Mr. Williams's monthly income and Mrs. Williams's failure to establish she needed more money." The court observed that the application of the "ability to earn" standard is limited, and that it "is not imposed unless there is some conduct by the supporting spouse indicating deliberate behavior designed to avoid his financial responsibilities to his children." The trial court had rejected Karolyn's contention that James and Christine had quit their jobs and moved to avoid his parental responsibilities, instead believing James's testimony that the motives were more innocent; that they had moved to Reno for a simpler life.

The appeals court strenuously disagreed with Karolyn's argument that the trial judge should have considered Christine's earning potential.

We recognize in a motion to modify child support the court should consider the second spouse's income, if any, as available to reduce the paying spouse's personal expenses. When a second marriage reduces these expenses money is available for continued child support payments to the first spouse.

. . . However, a second wife's *ability to earn,* as distinguished from her *actual* earnings, has never been considered the appropriate measure for determining the amount of income available to a husband for making support payments to his former wife. If we were to use the ability to earn standard as the measure for assessing the amount available for child support, the result would be imposing an affirmative obligation to work on the second wife in order to increase the money available to support a first wife's children.

2. Supporting spouse's remarriage (D)

As we have just seen, the *actual* income of a new wife can make a difference. It may properly constitute substantial changed circumstances, which, coupled with increased need, can result in an upward modification, particularly with respect to child support, an area where courts are more likely to grant increases.

The opposite side of the coin is the possible expense of a new wife and, perhaps, family, and whether this can operate as changed circumstances for a downward reduction. It cannot. Courts refuse to take into account the additional expenses relating to a new spouse or family where the supporting spouse's income remains essentially the same. The universal view is that he was well aware of what his financial responsibilities were to his first family when he tied the new knot. In other words, you knew what you were getting yourself in for.

3. Dependent spouse's increased earnings (D)

There is no question that the dependent spouse's increased earnings are relevant changed circumstances, which in some cases may allow a downward modification, especially of maintenance payments. Her new income can also be considered as properly attributable to child support, which can cut both ways depending upon the particular facts. For example, Sally Case started working as a paralegal 2 years after the divorce. She was making about $17,000 when Timothy brought a petition for a downward modification, seeking to reduce the weekly $100 maintenance and $150 child support payments. After several days of hearing testimony, the Family Court judge permitted the downward reduction of maintenance because Sally had become self-sufficient. However, child support was actually *increased* by another $35 per week! The judge found that while Sally was now able to contribute to the support of the two children, which was her legal obligation, her child-related expenses had grown considerably. Because she was working full time, it was necessary for her to incur day care, housekeeping and extracurricular expenses. Furthermore, the needs of the children had increased since the divorce, and an upward modification was warranted.

If you are contemplating a downward modification motion, you will have to be careful to check that there are no signs that your ex's becoming employable and self-sufficient were contemplated in the original divorce or agreement. Gerald Swartz discovered this rule the hard way. When he and Esther signed a separation agreement some 10 years earlier, Gerald, an ophthalmologist, was earning $73,000; she was unemployed. The agreement provided that Gerald pay $1,217 monthly for alimony and $100 a month for each child. Following the divorce, Esther received a masters degree in English and began teaching in a local university at a salary of $13,000. Gerald petitioned the family court for a downward modification due to his former wife's earnings. His application was denied, and he appealed.

In a published opinion, the Appellate Division of the New York Supreme

Court reiterated the rule that determination of whether such changed circumstances require a modification involves a fine, realistic balancing of the wife's needs and her independent means for meeting them against the former husband's ability to pay. The scales of justice came down in Esther's favor. The Court noted that the wife's earnings are a relevant, but not controlling, factor to guide a modification determination. In this case, Esther's $13,000 salary was not considered a substantial change of circumstances sufficient to warrant a downward reduction in light of Gerald's current earnings of $92,000 and the parties' pre-separation standard of living. Significantly, the court interpreted a provision in their separation agreement whereby Gerald had agreed to pay "one-half of all reasonable tuition expense incurred by the wife for the purpose of training and preparing herself for gainful occupation or employment" as an indication that the parties contemplated that Esther would one day become gainfully employed. Therefore her going to work could not be used as changed circumstances.

4. Cohabitation (D)

What effect does living with another man have on the former wife's right to receive support? A good deal, as it turns out.

Courts examine the economic, and not moral, consequences of the arrangement. If it is evident that the dependent spouse is deriving monetary benefits from her live-in lover, a court may regard the cohabitation as substantial changed circumstances and permit a downward modification. Essentially the test is whether the cohabitants are maintaining a marriagelike relationship, with the dependent spouse's live-in partner contributing all or a good deal of the living expenses. A downward modification is appropriate if either a woman is supporting her lover or her lover is supporting her. In the latter case her expenses, and thus financial needs, may be legitimately reduced, and her former husband may be entitled to a downward modification.

In a reported case, *Gayet v. Gayet,* New Jersey's highest court was called upon to determine whether a divorced wife's cohabitation equals changed circumstances that can affect a prior maintenance award. The Supreme Court, following the majority rule, answered that the test is whether the relationship reduces the financial needs of the dependent spouse. Judge O'Hern wrote that, while courts must be careful to protect an individual's privacy, autonomy and freedom to develop personal relationships, there is a statutory requirement that maintenance terminates upon remarriage, signifying a policy to eliminate support when the financially dependent spouse forms a new bond that eliminates the dependency. He reviewed the laws in other states, and concluded that the majority of states have adopted an economic needs test that "permits modification for changed circumstances resulting from cohabitation only if one cohabitant supports or subsidizes the other under circumstances sufficient to entitle the supporting spouse to relief."

You may have noticed from the quotation from the *Gayet* opinion that there is an interesting twist to this topic. If a court finds that the dependent spouse is supporting or to any extent subsidizing her lover, the ax will swiftly fall and take a nice chunk out of her support. Again, this is not for espoused moral or religious reasons, but rather for the compelling argument that if the woman has enough money to spend on her living companion, obviously she no longer needs so much from her ex. Nor should a former husband be made to support her lover. The exact thing happened to Norma Jean Schneider last year in Florida. John Schneider had petitioned the circuit court for a downward modification order to eliminate or reduce his former wife's permanent alimony award. The trial court denied his application, because it found that there had not been a substantial change in the economic circumstances to justify a modification. The District Court of Appeal disagreed and returned the case for reconsideration. The reported opinion states:

> [The trial court's] finding is not supported by the undisputed evidence presented at the hearing. The former wife conceded that for approximately three years prior to the hearing she had been living as man and wife with Rex Springer whom she hoped to marry. They lived in a house which had been the marital residence of the parties here, but which had been awarded to the wife. Springer contributed little or nothing to the expenses of the household, because his income was sporadic and he had many obligations. Although the evidence supports a finding that Springer does not contribute to [Norma Jean's] support, the evidence is susceptible of a finding that to some extent, [she] contributes to Springer's support.

The appeals court sent John and Norma Jean back to the trial court, with instructions to give due consideration to how much of John's alimony was in effect supporting Rex, which would be the extent of the reduction. We do not know what eventually happened. The trial court's ruling was never published, and it is conceivable that the case may have been settled out of court. What we can safely guess, given the instructions of the Court of Appeal, is that whatever happened, Norma Jean took a cut in alimony, or made Rex move out.

As a word of advice, if you are receiving support and contemplating living with someone, you should be very careful to keep your and your companion's finances completely separate. Stay away from joint accounts, loans, purchases and credit cards. You may, however, set up a joint "household account," in which you *both* contribute money to pay household expenses. More than that is flirting with danger. If your economic affairs become so entwined that they begin to resemble a marriagelike relationship, your ex may indeed succeed in reducing the amount he has to pay you.

5. Serious illness or disability (U/D)

It should come as no surprise to discover that a serious illness or disability is a substantial change of circumstances, *provided it has an economic effect.* This means that if there is sufficient insurance or other benefits that essentially cover the monetary loss attributable to the illness or disability, there are no changed circumstances to allow either an upward or downward modification.

For example, a financially dependent wife requires extensive hospitalization and specialized nursing care on account of a sudden illness. Insurance will cover nearly all the costs, except for a small deductible and a percentage of the physicians' fees. Unless the deductible and the non-reimbursed doctor bills are large—several thousand dollars—there is no substantial change of circumstances. In another case, an ex-husband goes to play tennis, ends up in traction and stops working for 6 months. His company continues to pay him full salary for 30 days, after which he is picked up by the company's disability insurance carrier. The disability benefits are only 60 percent of his gross pay, *but* they are nontaxable. He thus is receiving approximately the same amount as his regular take-home pay. Result: no changed circumstances to qualify him for a downward modification.

6. Failed expectations (U/D)

Welcome to the land of broken dreams, hopes and promises. Nearly all divorce settlements and decrees today contemplate that at some point the financially dependent spouse will become partly or fully economically self-sufficient, except in cases of very long-term marriages where one party has been away from the job market for too long and is too old to reenter it. This situation used to be the rule, but nowadays it is quickly becoming the exception with the advent of many two-income families. The size of the maintenance or alimony payments is based at the time of the divorce upon a reasonable projection of how much a financially dependent spouse will require for support and for how long. The latter involves an estimation of the time it will probably take for that spouse to become employable at a level that can produce a significant contribution to her own support. The trouble is that no one—the husband, wife, the lawyers or the judge—knows for sure what is going to happen, and the best laid plans of mice, men and divorced couples often go astray within a few years.

Very often these failed expectations or assumptions take center stage in a modification proceeding. The wife may be looking for more money because she can no longer make ends meet, while the husband is cross-petitioning for a downward modification because he claims that she should have been gainfully employed by now. This very thing happened in a reported case in Florida a few years back.

Three years after her divorce, Helene Weinstein petitioned the Florida circuit court for an upward modification of alimony and child support, properly alleging the tandem changed circumstances—her increased needs and her former husband's increased ability to pay. Pierce Weinstein cross-petitioned for a downward modification. He contended that her expenses had been reduced by the emancipation (majority) of their eldest child and that the former marital home should be sold, which would provide his ex-wife with more than enough money for a comfortable existence.

The divorce judgment, ending their 16-year marriage, had granted Helene, then 47, custody of the two children and exclusive possession of the marital home until their eldest child was emancipated. Pierce, a licensed physician, was ordered to pay Helene child support of $100 weekly for each child and rehabilitative alimony of $500 weekly for 6 years, after which time it would be reduced to $200 per week.

Helene testified during the hearing that since the divorce she had borrowed over $11,000 from family and friends to cover expenses that included an 80-percent increase in the property taxes on their Palm Beach home. Recently she had received a real estate sales's license, and she earned about $800 from her first month of employment. Meanwhile, Pierce's annual income had risen to $160,000, and his net worth had materially increased. The trial court issued its decision after an extensive hearing. It found that while Pierce's income and assets had "increased significantly," Helene's circumstances had changed only to the extent of normal inflation and higher costs of living. The judge also found it significant that Helene had filed a false financial affidavit during the original divorce trial, exaggerating her expenses, and concluded that whatever increased expenses she now faced would be offset by approximately the same amount of overstated expenses in her first affidavit. (See how these things can come back and haunt you!) The court also found that Helene was free under the divorce judgment to vacate the former marital residence and reside anywhere she chooses, thereby reducing her monthly expenses. Finally, and to the point of this discussion, the judge determined that Helene had "made little or no effort to rehabilitate herself as was anticipated by the previous Order of this Court dated July 5, 1979, and in fact, still is not gainfully employed despite the fact that more than three years have elapsed out of the six years of rehabilitative alimony previously granted by the Court." For these reasons, both Helene's petition and Pierce's cross-petition were denied.

Helene appealed the denial of her upward modification petition. The appeals court was puzzled over the judge's failure to find changed circumstances. It was clear under Florida law that the markedly improved income of her ex-husband and worsening financial circumstances of Mrs. Weinstein due to inflation were normally proper grounds for an upward modification. Turning to the heart of the lower court's decision, the appellate court agreed with the observation that Helene had acted only minimally toward "rehabilitating" herself. However, it said that the divorce trial judge could not have been expected to predict just at what point the wife could "pick up the financial slack." The court, noting that Helene still had a minor child at home, who could have been a deterrent to efforts to find work, went on to decide:

True, the wife probably has not been as conscientious about becoming employed as she might have been. However, judicial decisions should not reflect flint and steel, but a realistic humanistic perception that may require firmness or otherwise, depending upon the proper application of the law to the facts. To be specific in this case, life deals each of us a succession of hands as our lives progress. Here, a 47-year-old woman who had been a housewife in an affluent home for 16 years has now been dealt losing cards—dissolution and a judicial determination which contemplates traumatic economic adjustment in mid-life by "rehabilitation." In sum, the trial court here may have properly admonished the wife for halfheartedness about locating a permanent position . . . but in light of all of the other facts should not have denied her an increase of alimony because of it. It is one thing for us to theorize about the purposes of rehabilitation; it is quite another to consider the wife's options in 1982 when the home mortgage payment cannot be met —one does not lightly disregard the howl of the wolf at the door.

The court concluded that the trial court's denial of the upward modification was wrong, and it sent the case back down for proper determination.

Before anyone gets the idea that a wife need not economically rehabilitate herself within the period reserved in the original decree or agreement, we would be remiss if we did not tell you that one year earlier a California appeals court upheld a denial of a former wife's petition to extend her maintenance beyond the 5 years ordered by the divorce court. Joyce Sheridan had been awarded $1,200 maintenance per month for 5 years, in addition to child support. During the 5 years, she studied for a real estate sales license, attempted to sell real estate with little success, began a polyester and silk flower business that failed, and for a few months tried selling business equipment with little success.

The court found that, indeed, there was a change of circumstances. Due to the expiration of the 5-year maintenance period, Joyce's monthly income went from $1,200 to zero. The judge who granted the divorce assumed she would be self-sufficient within 5 years, when in fact she was not. This readily constituted changed circumstances to support a modification, provided—and here is the catch—the "failure of the court's expectations to materialize" did *not* result from the former wife's own conduct.

Allan Sheridan had argued that Joyce did not diligently pursue employment opportunities. The trial judge had obviously agreed. He wrote, "And I can only conclude, based on the evidence in front of me, that after five years, the last two years of which were spent working at a job that paid zero money, going to school for enjoyment and not for education and being involved in the creative endeavors that sometimes cost her more than she reaped in terms of income, that she thought that something was going to happen at the end of five years that I am not aware of. And part of that possibility may be that the [former husband] was going to go on supporting her."

Joyce appealed, but she was unable to overturn the decision of the lower court. The appeals court was convinced that the major reason the trial judge had refused to extend her maintenance payments was because he felt that Joyce had done little to prepare herself for gainful employment. This was a proper reason to deny an application for upward modification.

The best way to reconcile these decisions, which at first glance may seem conflicting except for the fact that Helene Weinstein's six year "rehabilitation" period had not yet expired, is to recognize the rule that our courts apply in these situations. Essentially, a judge must look at the delay in seeking employment and determine if it is consistent with the person's ability. A 37-year-old woman with a bachelor's degree in accounting would be expected to find a good paying job a lot faster than a 49-year-old who never finished high school.

If you find yourself in this situation and plan on seeking an upward modification to extend your maintenance payments, you best be prepared to document real and good faith efforts to find gainful employment. Otherwise, you may find yourself in the same quickly sinking boat that Joyce Sheridan did.

7. Bankruptcy (U/D)

Under section 523(a)(5) of the United States Bankruptcy Act, bankruptcy cannot release a supporting spouse from debts or obligations due a spouse, a former spouse or child, for alimony, maintenance or support. Thus there is no such thing as a former spouse declaring bankruptcy to obtain in effect an indirect downward modification, if not elimination, of his obligations to his former wife and children. Maintenance and child support cannot be affected by the bankruptcy, and the wife is free to employ any of the enforcement devices discussed in Chapter 5 should her ex try to use it as an excuse. This is not to say that either spouse's bankruptcy cannot have an effect and result in a change of circumstances that can allow either an upward or downward modification. Let us take an example of an upward modification first.

Lea Teller had been receiving each month $80 child support and $50 maintenance—not great but at least something. Steven was heavily in debt when the divorce was granted, and he simply did not have sufficient income to provide for his family after he made all the installment payments on his outstanding loans, credit card charges and department store credit accounts. Lea never felt cheated, because Steven seemed even worse off than she and the children. He lived in a fleabag rooming house, drove a battered and rusty 1969 Ford pickup and never seemed to be dressed in any decent clothes. Then one day she ran into him in the middle of town. He had never looked so good.

"What the hell happened to you, Steve," Lea teased. "Get a new job or win the Irish sweepstakes?"

"Nah, nothing so good. I just got smart, that's all."

"What did you do?"

"I scraped together five hundred bucks and hired me this bankruptcy lawyer, who put me through the whole procedure one, two, three. All my debts were wiped out." He snapped his fingers. "Just like that."

"What do you mean . . ."

"Don't fret, honey. I still gotta pay you and the kids support. Bankruptcy doesn't get me off the hook."

"So, you don't have to pay all those people back? Is that what bankruptcy does?"

"Yes siree, babe. I'm a free man, and I can finally start to live like somebody."

Lea was amazed. "Why that's fantastic, Steve. We should have thought of it when we were married."

"Yeah, I know." He leaned over and pecked her forehead with a light kiss. "Anyway, I got to run. Nice seeing you, and tell the kids I'll pick them up Friday after dinner."

Lea watched him walk cross the street and climb into a fairly new-looking Toyota. When she got home, she could not help but marvel how easy it had been for her ex to lift the burden of indebtedness from his shoulders and get a new start. She was happy for him. It was not until she was making dinner that the thought hit her. If he doesn't have to pay all those creditors, why can't he pay me and the kids more money now? Several months later, she got to ask the same question again, this time in court and in the form of a petition for an upward modification.

The court ordered both Steve and Lea to file sworn financial declarations prior to the hearing. After it was all over, the judge granted Lea's petition and increased her monthly maintenance to $200 and child support to $375. "It appears that the respondent-husband has been relieved by operation of the bankruptcy laws from approximately $600 in monthly debt service obligations," wrote Judge Carson. "The petitioner-wife has satisfied this court of greater needs over the amount she is presently receiving, which was apparently fixed relatively low because of the respondent's then disadvantageous financial condition. Therefore this court finds the results of the bankruptcy as substantial changed circumstances to base an upward modification of both child and spousal support."

A bankruptcy can also result in a downward modification, if it is the dependent spouse who is the one going through it. As the procedure eliminates her debts, it may thereby reduce her monetary needs. However, a court will only find changed circumstances if the payment of the debts was taken into account at the time the needs were determined. If the debts were subsequent to the divorce and thus not part of the court's calculation, it is unlikely that a downward modification would result.

There have been some unusual ways by which bankruptcy has brought about a downward modification. In one reported case, the *Marriage of Clements*, the court permitted one when the ex-husband showed that his former wife's bankruptcy had *increased* his indebtedness. The California divorce court had divided the community assets and debts, as well as ordering maintenance and child support. Marlene Clements was directed to assume sole liability for two marital debts, $10,400 to C.I.T. Financial and $2,700 to Bank of America, and hold William free and harmless (indemnify him) from these obligations.

Marlene soon fell behind on her payments and eventually defaulted on both loans. Beset by financial woes she filed a petition for bankruptcy, which was granted. Thus all her debts were extinguished. C.I.T. and Bank of America were not. They still had William as a co-maker and were free to pursue their rights against him, which they did faster than you can say collection lawyer. William went to Family Court seeking a downward modification of the maintenance payments to offset his restored indebtedness, which was granted. The proceedings became quite entangled at this point, for Marlene claimed that the offset violated the relief granted her by the federal bankruptcy court in making her in effect repay those discharged obligations. Further, she argued that the divorce court's division of debts was a property settlement, which is dischargeable in a bankruptcy proceeding. A serious conflict between state family law and federal bankruptcy law seemed to be brewing. Ultimately, the California Court of Appeal resolved this Hobson's choice.

The court recognized that it faced two conflicting policy considerations, the bankruptcy court's "new start" and the Family Court's sense of responsibility for marital obligations. However, the test for modification remains the same. If the applicant can show that the economic situation of the parties has materially changed, a court may properly grant an application for a downward modification. Marlene's fortunes had substantially improved, as William's worsened. She reduced her indebtedness through bankruptcy; his obligations increased, because as a joint debtor he was still liable to C.I.T. and Bank of America no matter what. The court concluded that these facts amounted to substantial changed circumstances to permit a downward modification to offset William's assumption of Marlene's original indebtedness.

8. Inheritance (U/D)

An inheritance can be a sufficient change of circumstances that can be the basis of either an upward or downward modification, depending upon which former spouse receives it. Inherited money or income earning property is treated no differently than any other form of income, and it can be used in the same manner as a substantial salary increase or winning the state lottery. If you are looking for an upward modification because Uncle Edgar left your ex a million dollars, remember that you must still first demonstrate increased need before the Family Court will even bother to read Edgar's last will and testament. Similarly, if your ex-wife's parents finally left her that fortune they so begrudgingly sat on when you were married, you will have to satisfy the court that it was enough to reduce or eliminate her need for spousal support and, maybe, also enough to allow her to start sharing her financial responsibilities for the children.

9. Dependent spouse becoming a public charge (U)

"Becoming a public charge" means going on welfare. All states make sure that before they have to support someone, if there is still a financially able spouse or former spouse lying around he is going to be stuck with the bill. If your ex is about to receive public assistance, do not be startled when the state's social services agency, or equivalent, commences a support proceeding against you, either for more maintenance or an extension of the original support period. This is a built-in safety net that all jurisdictions have and do not hesitate to use. Unless you are flat broke, be prepared to pay something. The only good news is that the court is usually limited to providing your ex with bare necessities, and a "needs" test, instead of a "means" test, is ordinarily used as the dollar yardstick.

In other words the support level is determined solely by your ex's needs; the fact of whether you have the means to provide her with more is entirely irrelevant.

* * *

Having reviewed the major examples of changed circumstances throughout the country, we do not mean to imply for a second that the list is all-inclusive. There are many unique facts that in certain cases have been found to be a substantial change of circumstances for upward or downward modification, but it would be unfair to list each and every one since there is no consensus of judicial opinions upon which we may offer them as general examples. In the final analysis, the results of each case turn sharply on the facts of the case and the way they are presented, which is the subject of the next chapter. However, after reading our list of representative examples, you should come away with a very good idea of how the courts handle these modification requests. Never does the new event alone control the outcome. Rather, it is the totality of the facts present at the time the original decree was made and when the modification proceeding is commenced. You may also have realized how just a slightly different picture may have altered the outcome in some of the cases. Had Joyce Sheridan been more serious in her pursuit of a career, or more convincing to the trial judge, it is likely that her maintenance would have been extended. Then again, maybe she would have also found a good job.

Your task is to realize what facts you need to show the court and the best way to go about doing it. This goes for both prosecuting and defending a modification motion. The court's task is to try to achieve parity with the terms of the original divorce, to preserve as best as possible the post-divorce status quo despite the advent of the changed circumstances. If you think this is a juggling act, you are getting closer to the truth.

This chapter will conclude with a discussion of those changes of circumstance that specifically involve children, which usually make it easier to obtain a modification. But before we get into that, let's look at several factors that commonly never work.

FACTORS THAT DO NOT EQUAL CHANGED CIRCUMSTANCES

Although we have fairly exhausted the list of those situations that are commonly found to constitute changed circumstances for support modification orders, it may save you time if we also listed those that usually do *not* qualify:

1. Inflation

If we had a dollar for every published case that stated, "Inflation alone is not a substantial change of circumstances," we could have retired in comfort by now. There are two reasons for this universal view. First, a showing of inflation or the increased cost of living does not equal a demonstration of financial need. If today's higher prices can be reflected in your sworn financial statement that shows you no longer make ends meet, then you have a chance. But going into court and telling the judge that the inflation rate has gone up 10 percentage points is about as useful as explaining to him that the sky is blue.

The second reason that courts are disinclined to grant modifications solely because of inflation is because it affects both sides. A former wife may be having a tougher time because of it, but so is her ex-husband who may have to struggle to meet his court-imposed obligations and his regular bills. Of course, if the wife can show that his financial situation has markedly improved, it is a different ball game, which we already played in the preceding section.

2. Comparative standard of living

This is a variation of the theme that two people can live more cheaply than one. Although courts are ordained to maintain the pre-separation standard of living, the fact is that they frequently cannot. There is just not enough money to go around. As Judge Orfinger observed in *Schneider v. Schneider:*

> While two may or may not be able to live as cheaply as one, two living separately most likely cannot live as cheaply as two living together. Thus, depending on the financial circumstances of the parties, the provisions of a final judgment of dissolution may very well leave the parties in a financial posture not as good as the standard they enjoyed during the marriage. This often is one of the consequences of divorce.

3. Deliberate acts to reduce income

Anything a financially supporting spouse purposefully does to depress his income is never going to result in a downward modification. This can include everything from quitting a good-paying job to remarrying. Gambling debts can also be included in this category. The idea remains that he knew what his financial obligations were before he made his move or rolled the dice.

4. Good faith employment changes

As we have already seen, no one is going to be penalized for a good faith change of employment. Being divorced will not ordinarily affect one's right to choose an occupation. If a spouse leaves a high-paying job and enters a different field that pays less, a court will first have to be convinced that the career shift was purposefully done to depress his income so as to avoid paying his fair share of the family's costs, before it grants an upward modification on the basis of his potential, as opposed to actual, earning capacity. On the other hand, it is unlikely, but not impossible, for a supporting spouse to achieve a downward modification on this basis. We have come across a few cases where it was permitted, but the job changes were supported by reliable medical or persuasive business reasons. An example of the latter was a case in the Midwest where the husband had quit his job and purchased a small business. After taking into account the installment payments he had to make on the price of the business, his income was cut down by more than half. Nevertheless, the court found that he acted in good faith, since the evidence revealed that he was about to be laid off from his 20-year-plus job and that at the age of 57 he had no other earning alternatives open to him.

5. Temporary fluctuations

Little blips on the radar screens of life are never grounds for a modification. Temporary ups and downs in fortune cannot be used as changed circumstances in a modification proceeding. Courts look for changes that are relatively long lasting, if not permanent. This is not to say, however, that some extraordinary one-time expense cannot be recovered. Seeking payment or a financial contribution for an unexpected situation is different from looking for a change in maintenance or child support payments because of some brief interlude of new circumstances.

6. Comparatively lower standard of living

Often a former wife looks at the better way her ex is living since the divorce and feels entitled to an upward modification. Nearly as often her application is denied by the court. The rule is that a subsequent improvement in the supporting spouse's standard of living does not necessarily entail changed circumstances for an upward modification as long as the dependent spouse's needs are being met. The idea in divorce is to maintain the pre-separation standard of living. As long as that goal is being met, it matters little if one spouse's situation has improved since the dissolution of the marriage.

7. Voluntary payments

Nothing else works as poorly as trying to use a former spouse's voluntary payments as grounds for an upward modification. The judicial attitude is that a party who freely takes on extra responsibilities should be encouraged, rather than penalized by facing an upward modification. Courts find it somewhat incongruous, if not distasteful, for one spouse in essence to ask for guaranteed payments from a volunteering spouse who has proven so faithful over a number of years. Of course, should the voluntary payments stop, that may be a sufficient change of circumstances to permit modification.

CHILD SUPPORT—THE BEST INTERESTS TEST

Modifying child support payments upward is generally easier than changing maintenance or alimony because of the universal application of the "best interests" standard. The *best interests* of the children is exactly what it sounds like. Whatever a judge is convinced is for the good of the children and affordable by one or both parents is a best interest that may lead to an increase.

The obligation to provide reasonable child support is considerably wide, and it falls on both parents in proportion to their means. In making a child support award, a court determines the following factors:

1. The financial resources of each parent, and those of the child
2. The physical and emotional health of the child, and his educational or vocational needs and aptitudes
3. The standard of living that the child would have enjoyed had the family remained intact
4. The non-monetary contributions that either parent will make toward the care and well-being of the child

The same factors come into play at the time a modification application is being considered. It is evident that they give the court fairly extensive latitude in fashioning an appropriate award. Courts are empowered to include in a child support order provisions that pertain to shelter, food, clothing, care, medical and dental attention, education and any other "proper and reasonable" expenses. The last is a wildcard that in the proper circumstances may result in some unusual awards.

Belinda Thompkins was a beautiful child the day she was born. Friends and family constantly told her mother that she should encourage her to do commercials, but Stacey was uncertain whether it was the right thing for a young child to be doing. Besides, she was busy trying to get her freelance graphic design business off the ground, and she had little time to devote to researching the world of advertising. Belinda was five when a classmate was chosen to do a print advertisement for a well-known cereal. Stacey felt that maybe her daughter did stand a good chance. She began to do a little legwork, and she quickly discovered that the first thing her daughter needed was a slick, professional portfolio. Several photographers were recommended by the model agencies that she had visited. Stacey checked their prices and was startled that each one of them wanted several thousand dollars.

Stacey visited Jeffrey in his office to tell him about this project for Belinda and how much it would cost. Jeffrey was not opposed to the idea of his daughter modeling, but he felt that the expense of the photographs was ridiculous. He said that it was foolish to throw money away on such a long shot. Stacey countered that the odds really were not that bad. Two of the agencies had told her that there was no question they could get good assignments for Belinda, who they thought was perfect for television, but they needed a portfolio to show to various advertising agencies. Jeffrey asked why the agency did not pick up the tab if they were so sure of success. Stacey told him that it just was not done that way. She had tried to get them to go for it, but they would not.

Stacey was depressed. She did not have the $1,750 that one photographer, whose work she liked the best, had requested. Nor did it seem likely that she would be able to accumulate it from her meager earnings and the support that Jeffrey was sending her. Although the support payments were fairly generous, Stacey's living expenses were rather high. She and Jeffrey had a very comfortable standard of living before the breakup, and with a salary of over $150,000, he was able to maintain it. The money for the photographer would be nothing for him, she thought, but she knew he was not going to budge. Once he made up his mind, that was it.

One day she happened to call us on an unrelated matter. She mentioned in the course of the conversation her problem of getting Jeffrey to advance—by this time, she had offered to pay him back from any fees Belinda received—the money for the portfolio. She lamented that there did not seem like there was anything more she could do. We told her that she was wrong. If she could substantiate that this expense was legitimate and reasonably calculated to enhance the welfare of her child, there was a chance, and just that—a chance—that a court would compel Jeffrey to make the one-time payment.

Stacey was able to procure affidavits from two top people in different modeling agencies, plus an affidavit from the mother of Belinda's classmate who had done the cornflakes advertisement and an affidavit from the principal at Belinda's school saying that she did not feel that limited commercial work would detrimentally interfere with the child's education. We prepared the motion papers, using all of the affidavits. The court ruled that the matter required a hearing and referred it to a special referee. Neither side wanted to get involved with the cost of conducting a hearing, which easily would exceed the amount in controversy. Reason prevailed at the end. Jeffrey's lawyer, who was highly experienced and reputable in the field of matrimonial law, recommended to his client that he throw in the towel and pay the photographer's fees, as well as a portion of our fees. He counseled that given Jeffrey's very high income and the affluent lifestyle of the parties, it was not unlikely that the referee could decide that the portfolio expense was "reasonable and necessary."

The case was quickly settled, and Belinda got her portfolio. Almost 2 years have gone by. The other night one of us happened to catch the ending of a highly rated network sitcom. Who should be appearing as a guest star? You guessed it.

There is little dispute over the basic elements of child support. For example, no one can argue that shelter is not an essential need. Frequently, a non-custodial spouse—the one who does not have the children—is made to pay all or part of the custodial spouse's rent, mortgage, real estate taxes, household repairs and home insurance. There have even been cases where the cost of a summer home has been deemed an appropriate child support obligation because of the parties' affluent pre-divorce lifestyle. The same goes with such items as medical and dental care and the cost of education.

The determination of what is "reasonable and necessary" naturally varies with the circumstances of each case, as Belinda's mother happily discovered a short while ago. What may be a luxury for one family is a necessity for another. Moreover, the definition of what is necessary marches right along with our country's technology and lifestyles. A judge recently ruled that a father was responsible for the cost of an Apple computer, accessories and all educationally related software.

The following is a summary of those facts that are most often involved in a motion or petition for modifying child support awards. Once again, the initials—U for upward, D for downward—will be used to indicate the type of application.

1. Emancipation (D/U)

Children become "emancipated" when they become economically independent of their parents, or are old enough to be. Emancipation is a change of circumstances that immediately terminates child support obligations. Indeed, it is virtually automatic: one rarely needs a court order to confirm it. However, there are instances in which it is safer to modify the original order when it is not so clear that the child has become emancipated.

The following are so-called emancipation events:

1. Reaching the age of majority (18 or 21, depending upon the jurisdiction)
2. Marriage
3. Entering the military
4. Full-time employment
5. Incarceration (going to jail)
6. Death
7. Circumstances whereby the child *without cause* withdraws from parental control and guidance

It is obvious that the last item typically requires some judicial interpretation. What exactly does it mean? Surely it means more than the child is a brat, and it also means less than the child ran away from home and has never been heard from. It is the gray area in between that requires judicial definition if the parents themselves cannot agree on one. Further, there are issues of whether the child had good cause to leave the home, such as neglect or child abuse.

Of course, it is always possible for an emancipated child to "unemancipate" himself. A runaway or a child who had enlisted in the military may later return home to parental control and support before having reached the age of majority. If the supporting spouse does not agree to resume contributing to the support of the child, it will be necessary for the financially dependent spouse to seek an order from the court compelling such payments.

2. Termination of parental duty (D)

There are four situations whereby a parent's duty to support his child is terminated:

1. The parent's *death* ends his obligation. His estate cannot be held responsible for the child's support.
2. The *emancipation* of the child, which we already discussed.

3. The financial or mental *incapacity* of a parent can suspend his support obligations for as long as it exists, and terminate them if the incapacity is permanent.

4. The *adoption* of the child eliminates the natural parent's obligation to support the child, which is then assumed by the adoptive parent; or any court order that terminates parental rights, in which case the state assumes the obligation to support the child.

Any of these situations constitute substantially changed circumstances that can suspend or finish child support payments.

3. Change of custody (D/U)

At the risk of stating the obvious, a change of custody is a substantial change of circumstances that can result in a modification. The custodial change must be permanent in nature. Having the children for 2 weeks in the summer is not a change of custody. It is readily apparent that the formerly non-custodial parent no longer has to pay child support once custody is changed. However, it sometimes becomes necessary for this parent to turn around and look for child support from the parent who relinquished or lost custody.

Thomas Walker was amazed that Cheryl agreed that the boys could live with him. She explained that she wanted to move out of state anyway, but Thomas was convinced that she had just grown weary of being a parent and wanted to look for new horizons. Cheryl told him that of course she would not be looking for child support anymore. Six months later, Thomas realized that he no longer could make ends meet. He was going increasingly into debt, despite having cut expenses down to the bare bone. Meanwhile, Cheryl had moved to Las Vegas, where after going to school for a few months she had received a dealer's license and had gotten a job at Caesar's Palace. Several times he asked her for a small contribution, but each time she rebuffed him with insults to his virility. Finally he commenced a support proceeding under URESA, alleging that the change of custody was a substantially changed circumstance entitling him to support from his card-dealing ex. The family court in Nevada agreed. It ordered Cheryl to begin sending $50 a week.

4. Private school and college costs (U)

This area has become very fertile ground for litigation in the past several years. Increasingly courts are coming down on the side of the parent seeking the upward modification, as private school and a college education are viewed today as a necessity, especially the latter, depending on the circumstances of the parties. A direction to pay college expenses usually encompasses an *extension* of the obligation to support a child, which in some states normally ends by age 18. Nevertheless, courts are permitted to order such support.

Although the determination of whether a parent should be made to pay for private school or college education is done on a case-by-case basis, there are several factors that the court will focus upon:

change is practical and positively impacts on the child. When it comes to the kids, you don't necessarily have to look for obscure or creative reasons to petition the court.

8. Father's higher standard of living (U)

If the supporting spouse's standard of living improves after the divorce, the children—but not the ex-wife—are entitled to share in his good fortune and ability to pay. However, the mother better be careful that the father is not already taking care of the children's needs voluntarily.

Bonnie Young sought to increase the $300 weekly support for her 11- and 18-year-old daughters. She contended that the children had increased needs and that her ex had acknowledged this fact in the most persuasive way possible—by paying them. The record showed, for example, that Harvey Young had given the oldest daughter an automobile, along with paying for gasoline, insurance and maintenance, and a $30 weekly allowance, and that he paid for the youngest child's tuition and transportation for private school. The trial court denied any increase, and Bonnie lost again when she appealed the decision. The appeals court refused to mandate the voluntary payments, recognizing that a court order might jeopardize the excellent father–child relationship that had evolved since the divorce.

In our opinion, this result exemplifies a proper application of judicial restraint. Were courts to rule otherwise, voluntary efforts by supporting spouses would effectively be discouraged.

* * *

You should now have a good idea of how the legal system responds to the constantly changing needs of a family. It does so primarily by retaining flexibility and by applying well-documented general principles— changed circumstances and the best interests of the children. If you can demonstrate them, you can modify a prior child support order. The way to go about doing so is our next topic.

CHAPTER EIGHT

Modifying Maintenance and Child Support

In THE LAST chapter, we reviewed those factors that will (and will not) lead to a modification of maintenance and child support payments. Hopefully you have come across one that applies to your situation. Now you must take this changed circumstance and translate it into effective action.

There are two ways to modify an existing support order: (1) by consent of the parties, or (2) by direction of the court. The first is generally easier; the second ordinarily more common. There is an adage that no one likes change, and this seems ever so more the case when it comes to modifying spousal and child support payments. A father has been paying $125 per week for the last 4 years, and the last thing he wants to consider is increasing the payments by another $25. A mother has been barely scraping by on the $700 monthly support from her former husband and recently has taken a part-time job at McDonalds; she is not overly receptive to his recent requests that he be allowed to cut back a little on his payments. If change does come, it is usually prompted by some form of court action. This is not to say, though, that many former spouses are not able to negotiate and agree upon an appropriate modification, and we will soon be looking at approaches and tactics that have proved helpful. However, the fact remains that most modifications only come about after one party has initiated a post-divorce proceeding.

Since the ultimate success of a modification proceeding rests upon the grounds underlying it, we strongly urge you to review carefully the preceding chapter so that you are fully familiar with the right facts that you will need to emphasize in making your request. Keep in mind that there must always be a cause and effect relationship. Changed circumstances are not enough. They must be accompanied by a dollar impact.

Upon completing your review, you will be left with one of three possible conclusions. The first is that you are convinced that your situation warrants a change, either up or down. You don't yet know how to go about doing it, which is why you are reading this chapter. The second possibility is that you are disappointed because there have been no substantially changed circumstances on which to base your request. If this is so, you may as well stop reading right now, unless you think that you can persuade your ex otherwise, hoping that he or she has not already read this book. Finally, you may be uncertain. Your situation seems to fall in the grey area between those places where modifications have been permitted and those where they have not. Do not feel alone. We anticipate that a vast number of our readers will find that there is no clear-cut answer. The courts grant or deny modifications on a case-by-case basis. For every case we could show you where support was modified, we could show you another with essentially the same facts where it wasn't. However, we firmly believe that the difference was not so much the facts but the presentation of the case.

If you have ever played cards, even once in a while, you know that in each hand you get some good cards and some bad ones. Many trial lawyers are fond of saying that you can only play the cards you are dealt. The trick is to play the good cards and not the bad ones. This is particularly true in modification proceedings, where it becomes very important to emphasize those facts that can trigger modification and downplay the others that may lead to a denial of your application. We are not suggesting for a moment that you lie or cover up. That is not only unnecessary, it is illegal. We want you to present your case in the best way possible, to play your best cards. Even in those situations where the chances seem slim that you are entitled to a modification, if you do it properly the odds increase.

Before we go any further, let's do a simple exercise that should help to clarify where you stand. Take out a clean sheet of paper and divide it in half. One side should be labeled "+" and the other "−." Next, list in the appropriate columns those facts that are good and bad for your case. Let us assume for the moment that you are looking for more child support. You should be able to list on the plus side those increased costs and special expenses that you have incurred for your children, or soon expect to. You can also put on the plus side whether your income has diminished or otherwise stayed the same over the last several years. You can also list your ex's higher salary and other fringe benefits. Turning to the negative column, you should list those things that go against you. Maybe your ex's income has not increased, or worse yet, has gone down. Maybe his expenses have legitimately increased, or you are now able to contribute more to the support of your children. After you have completed this little exercise, you now have a nice schematic plan to use for Phase I.

PHASE I—NEGOTIATING A MODIFICATION

Before you take that car, bus or subway ride to your nearest courthouse, you should first go to the telephone and call your ex. We suggest arranging a face-to-face meeting, but you know how you and your ex get along better than we do, and you may have to deal with one another on the phone. In either case, the purpose of the call is the same—to begin negotiating a consensual modification.

Ordinarily the atmosphere for discussing a possible change of support is a lot calmer than the turbulent conditions that usually surround something like nonpayment or custodial interference. Plus there is no reason to begin a hurricane of court papers before you and your ex have an opportunity to calmly discuss your proposed change. In those other situations, commencing a court proceeding galvanizes the other side into action; here it may galvanize him or her into unnecessary rigidity. So first talk, don't fight.

If child support is the only thing that you are looking to change, your task is somewhat easier, for you can focus the discussion on the children. The trick is to talk about what they, and not you, need. If you can shift the emphasis of the conversation from your receiving money to the children's receiving certain necessities or even enhancements, you will have gone a long way toward creating an environment where your ex's consent is more likely. Yet even here you must let the facts speak, not your amorphous ideas or unsubstantiated needs. Keep in mind the scorecard we had you make. Stress the pluses, and don't volunteer the minuses.

The nice thing about dollars and cents is that they add up. If you can satisfy your ex that your expenses are so much, and that even with his assistance you still fall short, there may be a chance of settling the matter even before it starts. On the other side of the fence, if you can persuade your former wife that the payments have imposed an impossible burden upon you and that she really does not need the money—after all, why should she already have $5,000 in the bank when you have already tapped out all of your credit card advances—there may be a chance (and it is just that, a chance) that she may agree to a temporary or permanent reduction. Of course, the likelihood of reaching an agreement depends upon who you and your ex are, and the circumstances that you are using to justify the change. You are in a better position to judge this than we, yet we suggest dropping your dime, or nowadays a quarter, and making the call.

We can tell you how to change a support award, but no one can tell you how to persuade your ex, so we will leave that alone. Still, we can help you make the case that you are about to present to him or her more compelling. Later in this chapter you will come across a budget presentation form, which must accompany your post-judgment motion or application for the modification. Nevertheless, even at this initial stage you should prepare a rough version to show your ex and to assist your discussions. Give him or her the opportunity to dispute the expenses that you list. Explain why it is necessary to pay over $100 per month for babysitters, or why you had to get a new car. Many times reasons and justifications can dispel jealousies, and the further you can lead the discussion away from irrational emotions and to the consideration of hard reality, the better your chances of reaching a fair agreement.

Of course, the very best you can hope to achieve is a settlement that you both feel is fair and appropriate. "Settlement" implies just that. It is unlikely that either side will be completely overjoyed; each gives, and each takes. Hopefully what results is something that you both can live with.

Here are some specific points to keep in mind when you begin discussing your proposed change with your former spouse:

1. Isolate and define the changed circumstances that are the basis for your request.
2. Be prepared to show your former spouse the dollar effect of this change, how much it impacts upon your budget.

3. Satisfy your ex that there is no financial room for you to maneuver, by showing him or her a detailed monthly budget.
4. Outline to your ex those factors that you feel will enable him or her to withstand the change, which in most cases will be making more money or having less expenses.
5. When dealing with child support, move the discussion from yourself to the children and appeal to the other parent's love, duty and affection for the children.
6. Explain that circumstances as you have described them usually result in some court-ordered modification and that it would be in everyone's interest to avoid the unnecessary expense and hardship of a court proceeding.
7. Finally, make sure that he or she realizes that you are fully prepared to initiate court action should the discussions prove unsatisfactory.

As you can see, for all our talk of playing cards, we are not gamblers. We are telling you to put your cards on the table. Hold back nothing. Show your ex why you need the change and why you think you can get it. But please, do not go as far as volunteering the weaknesses of your case, although candid and fruitful discussions may force you every now and then to concede that there are certain weaknesses. We prefer a straightforward approach; bluffing and bravado rarely get you anywhere.

Ted Perry had been divorced from Ellen for 5 years. He never missed a single maintenance or child support payment. It was never easy, but he managed. One time, while waiting for a haircut, he read with a contemptuous grin a magazine article that claimed that the standard of living of the average divorced wife was substantially less than that of the average former husband. Well for once I'm not Joe Average, he thought as he turned to something else to read.

Ted still had 5 more years to go on the $85 weekly maintenance payments. He never could believe that he got stuck for a 10-year stretch, but at the time Ellen was a housewife and completely dependent on him. In a way, the judge's decision made some sense, yet they were only married for 12 years. Ted remembered when the decision came down. His shock was only matched by his lawyer's embarrassment. Prior to the trial he and his lawyer had turned down an offer from the other side calling for 6 years of maintenance payments. Ted's lawyer had assured him that there was no way in hell the judge was going to give Ellen more than 5. Well she found one who did.

Two years ago, as soon as Cindy began the first grade, Ellen found a job. It really did not amount to much at first. She was hardly making anything over her job-added expenses. But Ted always said the one thing about Ellen was that she stuck things out and worked hard at whatever she was doing, whether it was organizing a birthday party for the kids or taking a few courses at the community college. Therefore he was hardly surprised when she was quickly promoted all the way to district sales manager. Her salary was up to $18,000, excluding the perks. Ted was sure that his ex really no longer *needed* the weekly maintenance, although there was no question that she had become nicely accustomed to it. He had no beef with the child support payments. The girls were as much his daughters as Ellen's, and he was determined to stay a loving and providing father.

Ted's lawyer had told him on that eventful day when the decision came down that he could always make a motion later on for a downward modification as soon as Ellen's situation improved. Every now and then he mulled such a move over in his mind, yet he knew he could not do it. He was the first to admit it—he was gun shy. One ride through the judicial wheel of fortune was enough for him. Moreover, it was not as if his income had not improved since the divorce. He was making almost twice as much gross salary, although the after-tax piece was not as great. On the other hand, his expenses were higher. Ellen still lived in their house, and aside from an occasional property tax increase, her monthly carrying charges were fairly constant. He had to rent an apartment, and no one had ever heard of rent stabilization where he lived. Every year his rent went up. He did not even bother arguing with his landlord. Apartments were scarce, and each annual increase was announced on a take it or leave it basis. Ted could not wait until he could scrape together a down payment on a small condo. If only he did not have to pay Ellen $85 every week, he could do it in no time.

Actually Ted can thank his landlord for what eventually happened. Old man Stevens wanted another $150 a month for a new 1-year lease. Ted was fed up and wanted to tell him to go to hell, but he knew that wouldn't solve anything. Anticipating the latest gouge, he had been carefully checking the classified ads, but he never saw an apartment for less than what he was paying. Resigned to forking over the extra $150 to Stevens, Ted took out a pad and pencil and tried to figure how he would manage. He couldn't. No matter where he cut back, there still was not enough. No matter how he tried to avoid it, his eye kept coming back to the line "Ellen —$85/wk." It was almost midnight and he had no answer. He decided to call his ex the following morning.

Ted sat nervously at a small corner table in the cocktail lounge at the Ramada Inn off the Interstate. It was close to Ellen's office, and she had told him she would try to break away around 6 and meet him there. He nursed a gin and tonic to the hardly suppressed annoyance of the waitress, who gave up on him eventually. Although he would have liked nothing better than to tie one on, he knew he had to keep alert for his planned encounter. Ellen always criticized him for drinking too much, and he did not want the discussion to divert to an exercise in old wound openings.

She arrived at around 6:30, peering through the dimly lit room for him. When they were married she always wore glasses. Now she either has contacts in, he mused, or she will never find me. Ellen was impeccably dressed in a tailored grey herringbone suit. Her expression shifted to sudden recognition, and she walked over to him. Ted stood up to greet her. She held out her hand, but he pecked her on the cheek. After several minutes of pleasant small talk and ordering a round of drinks, Ted took a gulp of air and rushed right into what he wanted to talk about.

"Ellen, the reason I asked you to meet me tonight is because I need your help."

"Help? What kind of help do you need, Ted?" She sipped her bourbon.

Obviously she is going to enjoy this, he thought, but he repressed a sudden impulse to get up and leave.

"I'll get to the point. I need some money help."

"Money? Do you need a loan or something? You're not in over your head or something, are you?"

He hesitated. "Well, yeah, I am in sort of a way. I just can't make ends meet anymore. That bastard Stevens has hit me up for another $150 and . . ."

"Ted, if you want to talk about cutting back on my payments, you can stop right there. I'll say thanks for the drink and go. The girls and I have a hard enough time ourselves, and I don't need to be hearing about your troubles."

"But Ellen, just hear me out."

She stood up. "No, I won't. I have my own problems, kiddo."

"Look, I don't want to start a fight with you. All I'm asking is that you sit here for a few minutes and listen to what I gotta say. You haven't even finished your drink yet. After I'm done, you can tell me I'm full of shit and leave. Okay?"

"All right, go ahead. I'll listen." Her voice sounded like that would be the last thing she would do. She sat down and took another sip.

"Thanks," Ted smiled. "Okay, now let me try to explain this so it makes sense. Ever since the divorce . . ."

"Which you wanted."

". . . yes, which I wanted, my expenses have been going up. Mainly rent, although my car and insurance payments are a lot higher too."

"Yeah, but your income has gone way up also. Hasn't it?"

"Sure it has, but I'll show you in a minute that it hasn't been enough."

"Go ahead. I've still got half a glass left."

"Anyhow, I believe that your expenses, at least I'm talking about mortgage and taxes for now, have pretty much stayed the same."

"Yes, but I have a lot more expenses now. Like this little meeting is costing me time and a half overtime for the babysitter."

"I realize that, but I'll get to it in a second." Ellen said nothing and waited for him to continue. "Now, getting back to the time we split up. You weren't working."

"And now I am, so you don't want to pay me alimony anymore. Right˜"

"Ellen, please!" Ted pleaded. "Let me finish first."

"Sure, go right ahead. I already know what's coming."

Ellen really did not. She was not prepared for the detailed budget that Ted took from his briefcase, which showed to the virtual penny his expenses and disposable income. There was really nothing in it that Ellen could question. It did not look like he was living high on the hog. Even the car he drove was fairly modest by his old extravagant standards. He argued convincingly that there was nothing he could juggle to meet his financial obligations. They both agreed that getting further into debt was not an answer. Ellen was also amazed at how close he had come to her actual income and expenses. He explained that he had asked an accountant friend of his to estimate Ellen's take-home pay, and she conceded that it was right on the dime. His estimates for the girls' and the babysitter expenses were also rather accurate; he said he had asked a few of his friends' wives who had small children what their costs were. Obviously, Ted had done his homework.

Finally Ted showed Ellen that after adding together her salary and the support he was providing, she was left with a decent surplus each month. To the contrary, his monthly budget showed a substantial deficit.

"So, if you accept these figures," he concluded, "the only answer is that something has to give, and I think that something is your maintenance."

"Are you proposing to eliminate it entirely?" Ellen's tone had noticeably changed. Maybe there is a chance after all, Ted thought.

"No, not at all. What I think would be fair is some sort of graduated reduction."

"Such as?"

"Okay, I'm paying $85 a week now, right?" She nodded. "If I could cut you back to—say $45—that would give me enough slack to pay Stevens his rent increase. We could do that for a year."

"Then the following year?" Ellen shot a knowing look at her former husband. This time she knew for sure what was coming.

"Well, I think it would be fair to cut out the maintenance altogether." Ted squirmed slightly. To Ellen this was worth the price of admission. "You see that's why I want to do it this way. You know, I don't expect you to cold turkey."

"Darling, maintenance is not an addiction." She looked him in the eye. Then she smiled. "However, I have been working hard to get the old monkey off my back. I can't tell you how much I hated you when you left. Then I hated you because I still needed you—at least your money, anyway. I found the whole process demeaning, having to testify before that judge how much I needed your support. Poor old helpless housewife me. Well, I can thank you, Ted, for getting me off my ass. I've never been happier in my life, and I'm delighted that I'm earning my own keep. But I'm not all there yet. As much as I hate saying it, I still need your help."

"Does that mean you won't consider what I'm saying?"

"No, I'm not saying that at all. I'll think about it. Give me a few days, and I'll call you with a counter-proposal. Do you have extra copies of those budgets?"

Ted's face lit up. "Yeah, sure. Take these."

Ellen stood up and again held out her hand. This time Ted took it. "Been a pleasure, Mr. Perry. I'll touch base with you in a few days."

She started to walk away. "Ellen," Ted called after her. She turned around. "Thank you."

Formalizing Modification Agreements

If you are able to convince your ex that a change is indicated, the next thing you must convince him or her is of the necessity of putting it into a formal writing. Although an informal or verbal modification can be as effective as one imposed by the court, assuming both parties live up to it, such an arrangement does little to protect either side. What good does it do an ex-husband to get his former wife's consent to an alimony reduction, only to find 3 years later that she is suing him for the unpaid arrears and he has no way of effectively proving that the parties had previously agreed to reduce the payments? Similarly, a mother who is looking to get a payroll deduction order for the higher child support that her ex promised may find that she is limited to the original amount that appeared in the divorce decree. In either case, the change must be memorialized in a legal document.

Regardless of whether your child support or maintenance awards are set forth in a settlement agreement or in the divorce judgment, we suggest that the latter be amended to reflect the newly agreed-upon payments. This is accomplished in a three-step process:

1. Obtain your ex's agreement for the change.
2. Prepare and sign a written stipulation, which should then also be notarized.
3. Submit the stipulation along with a short affidavit to the court clerk with the request that the divorce judgment be modified.

Some courts require that you yourself prepare the amended judgment, but in most cases they will offer you sufficient assistance. In any event, the task is not as difficult as it may seem, since all you will be doing is copying the original judgment verbatim and changing those portions wherever appropriate that apply to maintenance and child support. For example, if your divorce decree requires that the husband pay $100 per week as child support and $50 per week as maintenance, and you and your ex have agreed upon a 25 percent increase, then only these numbers have to be changed by that amount to reflect the modification. Once the amended judgment is signed by a judge, it becomes as effective and enforceable as the original judgment.

As you will likely need more help for the preparation of the stipulation and the accompanying affidavit, we will give you those forms right here.

Your stipulation should look something like this:

- X

[COPY THE NAME OF THE COURT   Docket or
AND THE CAPTION OF YOUR ACTION   Index No.:
EXACTLY AS IT APPEARS
ON THE ORIGINAL JUDGMENT]   **STIPULATION OF**
       MODIFICATION

- X

WHEREAS, the parties were formerly husband and wife, having been divorced by this Court by judgment entered on or about ———, 19—;

WHEREAS, there are two children of the marriage, namely, ———, born on ———, 19—, and ———, born on ———, 19—;

WHEREAS, the judgment of divorce provided for the payment of child support in the amounts of $100.00 per week, and maintenance in the amount of $50.00 per week; and

WHEREAS, the parties have voluntarily agreed upon a modification of the aforesaid amounts as set forth herein.

IT IS HEREBY AGREED by the parties as follows:

1. The applicable portion of the aforesaid judgment is modified to provide for the payment of maintenance by defendant to plaintiff in the amount of $62.50 per week commencing on October 1, 1986, and the payment of child support in the amount of $125 per week commencing on the same date. Said payments to continue as provided in the original judgment.

2. There are no other changes to the divorce judgment, and the parties specifically ratify and confirm all the other terms and provisions therein.

3. This is the entire agreement between the parties, and there are no other writings or representations made between one another in this regard.

_____
MARY SMITH

_____
JOHN SMITH

STATE OF   )
COUNTY OF   ) ss.:

On the   day of   , 19__, before me personally came   , to me known to be the individual described herein and who executed the foregoing instrument and she acknowledged to me that she executed the same.

_____
NOTARY PUBLIC

STATE OF   )
COUNTY OF   ) ss.:

On the   day of   , 19__, before me personally came   , to me known to be the individual described herein and who executed the foregoing instrument and he acknowledged to me that he executed the same.

_____
NOTARY PUBLIC

The accompanying affidavit should read as follows:

-------------------------X

[COPY THE NAME OF THE COURT   Docket or
AND THE CAPTION OF YOUR ACTION   Index No.:
EXACTLY AS IT APPEARS
ON THE ORIGINAL JUDGMENT]   **AFFIDAVIT IN
                                     SUPPORT OF
                                     AMENDMENT OF
                                     JUDGMENT**

-------------------------X

STATE OF   )
COUNTY OF   ) ss.:

_____, being duly sworn, deposes and says:

1. I am the plaintiff (or defendant) in the above entitled action, and I submit this affidavit in connection with my application to amend the divorce judgment previously entered herein.

2. The parties were formerly divorced by this Court by judgment, entered on or about _____, 19__, signed by the Hon. _____, a copy of which is attached as Exhibit A.

3. Said judgment provided for the payment by defendant (or plaintiff) to plaintiff (or defendant) of maintenance in the amount of $50 per week and child support in the amount of $100 per week. The maintenance payments were to continue for ten (10) years, or until plaintiff (or defendant) died or remarried. The child support payments were to continue until the emancipation of the parties' two children.

4. Subsequently, the parties have entered into the written stipulation, modifying the maintenance and child support provisions of the judgment. Said stipulation increased the maintenance payments to $62.50 per week and the child support payments to $125.00 per week. A copy of the stipulation is attached as Exhibit B.

5. Plaintiff (or defendant) respectfully requests that this Court sign an amended judgment to reflect fully the above mentioned terms of the stipulation between the parties.

_____
YOUR   NAME

Sworn to before me this
    day of   , 19___.

_____
NOTARY PUBLIC

Once you have prepared these documents and obtained the signatures of your ex and the Notary Public, you should go to the Court that issued your divorce judgment and ask the clerk the proper method to submit the proposed amended judgment for the judge's signature. In most instances, he or she will be very cooperative, since your recent success means one less modification proceeding for the court to handle.

PHASE II—STARTING A MODIFICATION PROCEEDING

Starting a modification proceeding is no different from beginning any post-divorce court action. Although the specific requirements vary from one jurisdiction to another, all modification proceedings are based upon a sworn affidavit or petition in which the moving party, that is, the one seeking the change, sets forth all of the elements that constitute the substantial changed circumstances on account of which the modification is being sought. A complete set of the papers are delivered to the other party, who has an opportunity to prepare and submit opposition papers on or before the return date. The *return date* is the date set by the court for the hearing on the modification application. In all likelihood, it is just the date that the papers will be submitted to the court, which will then decide whether a hearing is necessary and, if so, the date for the hearing. Before we get into the specifics, it must be understood that beginning a post-divorce modification proceeding involves more than walking up to a counter in your local courthouse and asking for more money.

The degree of difficulty that you will encounter in commencing a post-divorce modification proceeding depends on where you live. Many Family Courts have preprinted, fill-in-the-blank forms that make it very easy for you to begin the proceeding. Others are not so cooperative and require that you draft your own set of papers. While it would be impossible for us to provide our readers with a specific set of forms for each courthouse throughout the country, we can supply enough information so that it is possible to draft your own set of papers, should the local court not be able to furnish the necessary forms.

A modification proceeding, in its simplest form, is nothing other than a post-divorce motion (or application) to modify the existing divorce judgment. Such applications are made by *order* or *rule to show cause,* and are accompanied by a supporting affidavit and copies of important documents (exhibits). There are slight differences in the specific language from one state to the other; however, these account mainly for form and do not reach the substance of the application itself. You can safely ignore these slight variations and instead concentrate on the essence of your application, which should include the following information:

- The financial terms of the original divorce decree or settlement
- A brief description of the financial and surrounding circumstances at the time of divorce
- The substantially changed circumstances, or in those few states with a stricter standard, the unexpected or extraordinary change of circumstances, upon which the application is based
- The resulting financial effect of the change, and the specific manner it impacts upon your situation
- A statement that no other, similar application has been made by you and is pending in this court or any other court

We will use as an example a recent application brought by Janet Spencer in the local Family Court against her former husband, where she sought increased child support payments due to the fact that she was laid off from her job and has been unable to find suitable employment since that time.

Janet had originally attempted to work out an informal settlement with Gerald, but he refused to consider her request for additional money for the children. Thus she was left with no other alternative than to begin Phase II, the modification proceeding. Janet's order to show cause looked like this:

> At a Motion Term of the Family Division of the Superior Court in the State of *(State),* held in the County of _____, at the Courthouse at Central Avenue, *(Town/City), (State)* on October 10, 1985.

P R E S E N T: *HON. LESTER WALKER,*
                                    JUSTICE

- X

JANET SPENCER,
                                    PLAINTIFF,   Docket or
                                                                                 Index No.: 1130/84

                    -against-   *ORDER TO SHOW CAUSE*
GERALD SPENCER,
                                    DEFENDANT.

- X

Upon the sworn affidavit of JANET SPENCER, dated October 8, 1985, together with the exhibits thereto, including the sworn financial declaration, and upon the judgment of divorce previously entered herein and all other papers and proceedings in connection herewith,

LET the defendant, GERALD SPENCER, show cause before a motion term of the Family Division of this Court, at 9:30 A.M. or as soon thereafter as the parties may be heard, on October 15, 1985, at the courthouse at Central Avenue, Portland, Oregon, why an order should not be made and entered against him modifying the judgment of divorce herein, by increasing the amount defendant is required to pay for child support from $300 per month to $450 per month for the reasons set forth in the accompanying affidavit, and for such other and further relief that is just and proper.

SUFFICIENT CAUSE appearing, let the service of a copy of this order and the papers upon which it is made be made personally upon the defendant, GERALD SPENCER, on or before October 12, 1985, be deemed good and sufficient service.

E N T E R,

_____

LESTER WALKER, JUSTICE

The order to show cause works something like a summons or citation. It directs the recipient to be prepared to appear in court and to submit papers in opposition to the post-divorce modification motion. It must be accompanied by an affidavit, or in some cases, a petition that specifically sets forth the grounds upon which the modification proceeding is based. Thus Janet's affidavit looked something like this:

------------------------X

JANET SPENCER,

                    PLAINTIFF,   Docket or
                                                  Index No.: 1130/84

            -against-   **AFFIDAVIT**

GERALD SPENCER,

                    DEFENDANT.

------------------------X

STATE OF _____)
COUNTY OF _____) ss.:

JANET SPENCER, being duly sworn, deposes and says:

1. I am the plaintiff in the above entitled action, and I submit this affidavit in support of my post-judgment motion to modify the prior divorce decree to provide for additional child support.

2. The parties were previously divorced by this Court by judgment entered on or about February 2, 1983, a copy of which is attached as Exhibit A. According to the judgment, the defendant was required to pay me monthly child support of $300 for our two children, David, age 12, and Kelly, age 8.

3. At the time of the divorce, defendant was employed as a systems analyst and was earning approximately $26,000 annually. I was also working full time as an assistant manager in a local department store, and my salary was approximately $11,000. Our children did not have any extraordinary needs or requirements, and based upon these facts, the court directed defendant to pay me $300

monthly as child support. Defendant did not have to pay me any spousal maintenance, because of the fact that I was employed.

4. Approximately two months ago, the company for which I was working filed for bankruptcy, and my position was eliminated. I have since been unable to obtain new and suitable employment, although I have constantly been in search of a new position and have made serious efforts to find a new job.

5. I am presently receiving unemployment benefits of $105 weekly, which is far below the take-home pay that I used to receive from my job. I attach as Exhibit B copies of a recent unemployment benefit check in the amount of $105, as well as a copy of my latest paycheck stub, which shows a take-home pay of $169.12, a reduction of more than $60 each week.

6. Throughout this period, defendant has continued to pay me $300 monthly for the support of our two children. He has refused my request to provide additional support through the time that I remain unemployed.

7. Upon information and belief, defendant is now earning in excess of $35,000, and I further believe that he has the means to pay me additional support until I can find a new position. While I realize that it is also my responsibility to support our children, I am doing everything possible at this time and require further assistance from the defendant.

8. The termination of my employment has been a substantial changed circumstance that has resulted in increased financial hardship for my family and me. I attach as Exhibit C a sworn financial statement in which this Court can readily see that I am unable to meet my and the children's monthly expenses with the combined unemployment benefits and defendant's monetary contribuions.

9. Although I have been doing everything possible to alleviate this situation by looking for a new job and by paring my expenses down to the bare minimum, my monthly budget still falls approximately $150–$200 short each month, and there is no other way that I can make up for this deficit without the active assistance of the defendant.

10. It is respectfully submitted that it would be proper for this Court to grant this motion and increase the amount of child support presently being paid by the defendant, so that I can receive the amount of $450 each month from him.

11. While I hope that I will be able someday to find a new job, I have discovered that my prospects are not very good. Because of my child rearing responsibilities, it is necessary for me to arrange my work schedule around that of our children. So far, I have been unable to find a prospective employer who would be willing to cooperate with me in this manner, as had my former, now bankrupt, employer. Without being able to work during the hours when my children are in school or by otherwise arranging for inexpensive day care supervision for them, I will be forced to incur further expenses for their care and supervision, which would in fact result in a greater expense to me, and ultimately, the defendant.

12. I have made no previous application for the modification sought herein.

WHEREFORE, plaintiff respectfully requests that this Court grant in her favor an order against the defendant modifying the divorce judgment herein to provide that defendant pay monthly child support in the amount of $450, and such other and further relief that is just and proper.

_____
JANET SPENCER

Sworn to before me this
October 8, 1985.

_____
NOTARY PUBLIC

The specific form for the sworn *financial statement* or *financial declaration* is different in each state, but with the purpose of summarizing your expenses and income, it will look something like the one that appears on the following pages.

When completing the financial statement, it is important that all your expenses be accurate and not overstated. In the course of a hearing, you may be compelled to substantiate them by producing written, corroborating proof. The worst thing you can do is to be caught in a lie or two and have the judge or hearing examiner begin to believe that there is no true basis for your application. In many respects, this financial statement is the most important part of your application because it will readily reveal whether there is a financial need, one way or the other, to warrant an upward or downward modification. We know for a fact that many judges quickly cut to the heart of the matter by carefully scrutinizing the figures contained in the statement; if they are not convincing, it is unlikely that the modification application will be granted.

You should not worry that your supporting affidavit and financial statement does not reveal the entire story, for it is extremely rare for a court to grant a modification without first having conducted a formal hearing. Nevertheless, it is still important for your affidavit to contain all the necessary elements, because if you fail to allege a substantial change of circumstances and the corresponding financial impact, it is possible that the judge may dismiss your application just on that basis alone. As long as there appears that there is a genuine dispute to resolve, however, the judge will direct that a hearing take place, so that each party has a full opportunity to present his or her side.

PHASE III—THE HEARING

At this stage, we suggest that you review carefully Chapter 4, which dealt with the way you go about conducting a support enforcement proceeding. The advice found there on how to conduct a hearing applies to this situation as well. If you skipped chapter 4, it is essential that you go back now and read it. A modification hearing likewise requires thorough preparation, and it is conducted in essentially the same manner as an enforcement hearing.

Since you are the one petitioning for a modification, you not only get to go first, but you have the burden of proof when it comes to persuading the judge that a modification is necessary. It is up to you to prove that there has been a substantial change of circumstances. If you do not, the hearing may not even get as far as inquiring into your ex's current financial affairs. Thus, like in an enforcement proceeding, your advance preparation will be the key to victory.

Preparing for a Modification Hearing

There are two things that you must prepare for your hearing—your documents and your witnesses. Like Elizabeth Hartley in Chapter 4, you will

```
                COURT OF THE STATE OF
COUNTY OF
------------------------------------------X


                        Plaintiff,            Index  No.:

              -against-                       STATEMENT OF
                                              NET WORTH


                        Defendant.

------------------------------------------X

STATE OF              COUNTY OF              ss.:
```

, the plaintiff/defendant herein, being duly sworn, deposes and says that the following is an accurate statement as of (date) , of my net worth, statement of income from all sources and statement of assets transferred of whatsoever kind and nature and wherever situated.

1.*FAMILY DATA:*

(a) Husband's age:.......
(b) Wife's age: ....
(c) Date married: ....
(d) Date separated: ....
(e) Number of dependent children
     under 21 years: ......
(f) Names and ages of children
     ....
     ....
     ....
     ....
(g) Custody of children:.........
(h) Minor children of prior marriage:.....
(i) Husband paying $......... as
     maintenance and/or $.....child support
     in connection with prior marriage
(j) Custody of children of prior marriage
     Name...............................
     ....
     Address............................
     ....
     Name...............................
     ....
     Address............................
(k) Marital residence occupied by: ....

(l) Husband's present address......
     ....
     ....
     Wife's present address........
     ....
     ....
(m) Occupation of Husband: ....
     Occupation of Wife: ....
(n) Husband's employer ....
     ....
     ....
(o) Wife's employer: ....:.....
     ....
     ....
(p) Husband's education, training
     and skills: ....
     ....
(q) Wife's education, training
     ....
     ....
(r) Husband's health: ....
(s) Wife's health: ....
(t) Children's health: ....
     ....

II. *EXPENSES:*

Expenses listed Monthly/Weekly

(a) Housing:
  1. Rent: ....   2. Condominium charges..........
  3. Cooperative apartment maintenance...........   Total ....
(b) Mortgage and Amortization............................   ....
(c) Taxes and charges:
  1. Realty Taxes.........   2. Water Charges: ....
(d) Utilities:
  1. Fuel: ....   3. Electricity: ....
  2. Gas: ....   4. Telephone: ....
                  5. Other: ....   Total ....
(e) Food (number of dependents, including self: ....
(f) Clothing (number of dependents, including self ....
(g) Laundry (number of dependents, including self ....
(h) Dry Cleaning (number of dependents, including self ....
(i) Insurance:
  1. Life............   3. Fire, Theft & Liability: ....
  2. Personal & Real Property: ....   4. Other ....   Total ....
(j) Medical..   ....
(k) Dental...   ....
(l) Optical..   ....
(m) Pharmaceutical...   ....
(n) Surgical, Nursing, Hospital.................................   ....
(o) Blue Cross, Blue Shield.....................................   ....
(p) Major Medical...   ....
(q) Other: ....
(r) Household Maintenance:
  1. Repairs: ....   4. Appliances: ......
  2. Furniture, Linens,   5. Painting: ......
       Furnishings: ......   6. Gardening: ......
  3. Cleaning Supplies: ......   7. Other.........   Total ....
(s) Household Help:
  1. Nurse...............   3. Other (cook, etc.).......
  2. Maid: ......   4. Baby Sitter.............   Total ....
(t) Automobile:
  Year: .....   Make: ....   Personal/Business

  1. Payments...........   3. Repairs: ....
  2. Gas and Oil: ....   4. Insurance: ....
                  5. Other.........   Total ....
(u) Education:
  1. Primary and Secondary: ....
     ....
  2. College (Name).................................
     ....
  3. Other(Name)....................................
     ....
(v) Summer Camp (Number of dependents.....)....................   ....
(w) Recreation:
  1. Vacation: ....   3. Theatre: ....
  2. Movie: ......   4. Dining Out: ......
                 5. Other...........   Total ....
(x) Income Tax ....
(y) Beauty Parlor(Barber).........................   ....

(z) Miscellaneous:
    1. Books, Magazines,
      Newspapers ....
    2. Cigarettes ....
    3. Music, dancing
      lessons ....
    4. Children's allowance .....
    5. School transportation ......
    6. School supplies
      and lunches ....
    7. Diaper service..........
    8. Gifts ....
    9. Charitable
      contributions ....
   10. Church or temple
      dues ....
   11. Sunday School ....

   12. Union & organization dues
      and assessments ....
   13a. Payments for child
      support ....
   13b. Payments for alimony or
      maintenance ....
   14. Payments on outstanding
      loans ....
   15. Commutation and
      transportation ....
   16. Lunches at work .....
   17. Sporting goods and
      hobbies ....
   18. Other ....

Total ....
TOTAL EXPENSES:.........

III. *GROSS INCOME* (State source of income and annual amount.)

(a) Salary or Wages:
    ....
    ....
    ....
    ....
    ....

(b) Weekly deductions:
    1. Social Security................................ ....
    2. New York State Tax............................. ....
    3. Federal Tax................................. ....
    4. Other payroll deductions: ....

(c) Social Security Number: ....
(d) Number and Names of dependents claimed: ....
    ....

(e) Bonus, commissions, fringe benefits ....
(f) Partnership, royalties, sale of assets....................... ....
(g) Dividends and interest..................................... ....
(h) Real Estate (Income only).................................. ....
(i) Trust, profit sharing and annuities......................... ....
(j) Pension... ....
(k) Awards, prizes, grants.................................... ....
(l) Income from bequests, legacies and gifts..................... ....
(m) Income from all other sources............................. ....
(n) Tax preference items:
    1. Long term capital gain deduction..................... ....
    2. Depreciation, amortization or depletion................. ....
    3. Stock options - excess of fair market value
      over amount paid.. ....
(o) If any child or other member of your household is employed,
    set forth name and that person's annual income.............. ....
(p) Social Security... ....
(q) Disability benefits.. ....
(r) Public Assistance... ....
(s) Other... ....

IV. ASSETS

Item No. Description of Asset	Location (Financial Inst. Address, Acct.#)	Title Owner	Date of Acquisition	Original Price or value	Source of funds to Acquire	Est. Fair market value	Amount of mortgage/ Lien Unpaid	Current Equity	Other Relevant Information
A. Cash Accounts									
1. Cash									
2. Checking									
3. Savings									
4. Security deposits earnest money, etc.									
5. Other									
B. Securities									
1. Bonds, Notes, mortgages									
2. Stocks, options and commodity contracts									
3. Other									
C. Brokers Margin Accounts									

IV. ASSETS

Item No. Description of Asset	Location (Financial Inst. Address, Acct.#)	Title Owner	Date of Acquisition	Original Price or value	Source of funds to Acquire	Est. Fair market value	Amount of mortgage/ Lien Unpaid	Current Equity	Other Relevant Information
D. Loans to others and Accounts Receivable from others									
E. Value of interest in any business									
F. Cash surrender value life insurance									
G. Vehicles									
H. Real Estate									
I. Vested interests in trusts									

IV. ASSETS

Item No. Description of Asset	Location (Financial Inst. Address, Acct.#)	Title Owner	Date of Acquisition	Original Price or value	Source of funds to Acquire	Est. Fair market value	Amount of mortgage/ Lien Unpaid	Current Equity	Other Relevant Information
J. Contingent Interests									
K. Household furnishings									
L. Jewelry, art, antiques, precious objects, gold and precious metals - total market value									
M. Other Assets									
TOTAL ASSETS									

IV. DEBTS AND LIABILITIES

Item No. Description of Debt	Purpose	Date of Incurring Debt	Debtor	Creditor	Amount of Original Debt	Amount of Current Debt	Required monthly or Periodic Payment	Other Relevant Information
A. Accounts Payable								
B. Notes Payable								
C. Installment Accounts Payable								
D. Brokers Margin Accounts								
E. Mortgages Payable on Real Estate								
F. Interest Payable								
G. Taxes Payable								
H. Loans on life insurance policies								
I. Other liabilities								

NET WORTH .... $................

VI. *ASSETS TRANSFERRED*

Description of Property	To Whom Transferred and Relationship to Transferee	Date of Transfer	Value
....	....	....	....
....	....	....	....

SUPPORT REQUIREMENTS:
(a) Deponent is at present paying   receiving $ per week   month and prior to separation paid   received $ per week   month to cover expense for..
These payments are being made voluntarily   pursuant to court order or judgment pursuant to separation agreement, and there are no arrears   outstanding to date.
(b) Deponent requests for support of each child $ per week   month. Total for child(ren) $
(c) Deponent requests for support of self $ per week   month.
(d) The day of the week   month on which payment should be made is.............

VIII. *COUNSEL FEES*
(a) Deponent requests for counsel fee and disbursements the sum of $
(b) Deponent has paid counsel the sum of $ and has agreed with counsel concerning fees as follows:
....
(c) *There is   not a retainer agreement relating to payment of legal fees.*

IX. *ACCOUNTANT AND APPRAISAL REQUIREMENTS*
(a) Deponent requests for accountants' fees and disbursements the sum of $.......
Total amount requested for license appraisal; real estate appraisal and pension actuary - $
(b) Deponent requests for appraisal fees and disbursements the sum of $.........
....
(c) Deponent requires the services of an accountant for the following reasons:
....
(d) Deponent requires the services of an appraiser for the following reasons:
....

X. Other data concerning the financial circumstances of the parties that should be brought to the attention of the Court are:

....
....
....

The foregoing statements *and a rider consisting of ...... page(s) annexed hereto and made part hereof* have been carefully read by the undersigned who states that they are true and correct.

_____

Sworn to before me this   Plaintiff   Defendant
day of   , 19__

_____
NOTARY PUBLIC

be your own star witness, and most of the documents that you will produce in connection with the hearing will be the documents that you have or should have in your possession. Therefore this part of the preparation is easier, but this does not mean that you should for a second skimp in this area. Your anticipated testimony should be thorough and to the point. The documents you intend to introduce to corroborate your statements should be organized and pre-marked to facilitate their introduction as exhibits during the hearing.

You should obtain beforehand any documents that you do not have by using a *subpoena duces tecum* that is directed to the appropriate person or entity (business, such as a bank) that is in possession of them. You will certainly want to be armed with certain financial information concerning your ex. A complete financial statement should be part of his or her opposition papers. However, that is only the beginning, and you should attempt to obtain documents that may possibly refute or cast into some doubt the figures contained in his or her financial statement. Thus we recommend that you subpoena your spouse's banking and payroll records for the last several years, as well as for the year of the divorce or the time the maintenance and child support provisions you are seeking to modify were originally made. As there is no such thing as too much preparation, we suggest that you try to obtain the following documents:

- Income tax returns for the time of the divorce and present
- Checking, savings and money market account bank records for the time of the divorce and the 3 years preceding the motion
- Payroll checks or stubs showing both your and your ex's income at the time of the divorce and the 3 years preceding the modification motion
- Any loan or credit card applications for the preceding years
- Any records of substantial purchases by your ex for the preceding 3 years, such as homes, automobiles, boats, etc.

Do not be too disappointed that the records you acquire reveal that your ex's financial situation is not as good as you anticipated. It may very well be that since the divorce, he or she is struggling as hard as you to make ends meet. Better you should know it sooner than later. Since you have to carry the burden of proof in your proceeding, you will have to show that there is possibly excessive income; he does not have to prove that he does not have any more money. Therefore your record request should be as thorough as you can make it, for you never know what little golden nugget of information your efforts may dig up.

If you anticipate calling any witnesses other than yourself and your ex, you should prepare them thoroughly before the hearing. Once again, you should refer to Chapter 4 for the way to go about preparing yourself and your witnesses for the hearing.

Conducting the Hearing

In your review of Chapter 4, you should once again become familiar with the basic evidentiary rules and the concept of burden of proof, especially the latter. Never lose sight of the fact that you must prove your case. You have to *prove* that there has been a substantial change of circumstances. You have to *prove* that this change has resulted in a dollar impact. And you have to *prove* that your ex has the financial wherewithal to alleviate this impact, either by contributing or receiving less money.

If you are looking only to modify child support, your burden is somewhat diminished by a general judicial perception that children's needs increase as they grow older. This very fact alone constitutes substantial changed circumstances in many states, and thus essentially satisfies your first threshold of proof, leaving it for you only to show the amount of such increase and that your ex can readily contribute towards it.

No matter what the issues are in your case, the following principles must always be kept in mind:

1. Do not forget that it is your burden of proving that the change occurred sometime between your divorce and the modification hearing. It is not enough to show that something has gotten worse; you must show how much worse it has gotten since the time of the divorce.
2. Introduce the original divorce decree or settlement agreement into evidence, along with any subsequent written modifications.
3. Show that the change has been SUBSTANTIAL. Give the court sufficient facts to measure the extent of the change. In other words, show how things were before and how they are now. Otherwise, you will have failed to sustain an important part of your burden of proof.
4. Prove the resulting dollar effect of the changed circumstances. *Remember, you must prove either need or effect; change alone is insufficient.* There is no better way to do this than by being able to produce documentary evidence: bills, receipts, statements, canceled checks and the like, all of which show the expenses to which you are testifying. No judge will sit and listen to general statements about increased expenses without having a chance to see documentary proof of it.
5. Satisfy the court that the changed circumstances are relatively permanent, and that their effects are not likely to subside in the near future.
6. Demonstrate those facts that indicate that your ex can financially withstand the change. If you are looking for a reduction, be prepared to prove that your ex no longer needs so much money from you. On the flip side, if you want more money, show that your ex can afford to pay it.

Your ability to prove your case will to a great extent depend on the documentary evidence that you can introduce at the hearing. In essence, your preparation is more important than your testimony, although you will still have to make sure that you remember to introduce all of the necessary evidence. Really, all you are doing is telling a story, but telling it in a structured way that touches all the bases.

Although you have the burden of proof, you also have on your side a judicial awareness that no divorce judgment or settlement is perfect, nor does it fully anticipate all possible future developments. Thus there is a general willingness to grant a modification, provided you provide the necessary ingredients—change, effect and ability. Once you have satisfied this triad of proof, your chances of success are highly likely.

You may recall from Chapter 4 that Peter Hartley lost his bid for a downward modification, although we did not fully explain why. Putting aside for the moment the fact that he put himself at a tremendous initial disadvantage by waiting until Elizabeth started her enforcement proceeding before he cross-petitioned for the reduction—automatically casting a shadow of artificiality upon his claim—we can show you precisely where he went wrong.

Peter wanted a downward modification because he claimed that he was not making as much money as before. His lawyer, Allan Cramwell, was able to introduce all of Peter's payroll records that substantiated his testimony. However, the reduction was sporadic and never amounted to that much over the course of a year. Most damaging, Elizabeth testified about Peter making some money off the books by doing weekend carpentry. She was never able to prove how much he made, but she did subpoena one of his customers, Terrence Bates, who testified that he had paid Peter

$550 in cash in December for some finished shelving. This likely created a reasonable doubt in Referee Lewis's mind. Since Peter had the burden of proof on his cross-petition for the downward modification, the rules of evidence required any doubts be resolved in favor of the party opposing the modification, in this case Elizabeth.

It was incumbent upon Peter and his lawyer to prove that there had been a substantial change of circumstances. They failed to introduce any convincing evidence. We really do not know what Peter's income was because of the extra cash he was apparently earning. Nevertheless, it did not seem that his financial circumstances changed significantly from the time of the divorce. Thus it would be fair to conclude that his cross-petition lacked merit and that it was designed to cow Elizabeth into accepting a settlement. Good for her that she didn't.

Another less obvious place where Peter and Cramwell went wrong is that they focused entirely upon Peter's alleged lower income, and never once tried to show that Elizabeth could afford to pick up any resulting slack from a court-ordered reduction. In all fairness, they probably could not have, but we will never know since they did not bother to carefully examine her financial records, nor did Cramwell really question Elizabeth about the monthly expenses she listed in her sworn financial affidavit. Many times a judge or hearing officer, even if there does not seem to be substantial changed circumstances, will permit a small reduction if he finds that the financially dependent spouse now has the means to contribute to her own or the children's support.

Referee Lewis found that Peter failed to demonstrate substantial changed circumstances to allow a downward modification. Simply put, nothing had really changed from the time of the divorce some 4 years before. Peter and Elizabeth had grown slightly older, and because of Peter's shenanigans, more bitter toward one another. But nowhere in our legal system will you find a case that holds that these amount to changed circumstances.

CHAPTER NINE

Do I Need a Lawyer?

THE ANSWER TO the question, do you need a lawyer, is: no, yes and maybe. In other words, it depends on the situation.

Let's start with the support collection agency system. We have already seen in Chapter 2 how you may take advantage of two extremely effective enforcement devices without hiring an attorney. You simply meet with the caseworker, and he or she assists you each step of the way. The entire system is geared *away* from lawyers; the idea is to provide the general public with a truly self-help mechanism.

The support agency system, however, is not the only available means of obtaining relief. As discussed, each state has a superimposed judicial system that focuses on post-divorce remedies. It may be that you had no children during your marriage; the support provision in your divorce judgment deals only with your absolute right to receive spousal mainte-nance for the next 5 years. In such a case, an enforcement agency is unavailable. We have emphasized that the support collection unit pro-vides its enforcement services only to those people with child support related problems.

But don't despair. Even if you find yourself prosecuting your claim in your county's Family Court, an attorney may still be totally unnecessary. This is particularly so when you are trying to collect outstanding arrears, as opposed to modifying—either upward or downward—an existing sup-port order. Indeed, many Family Courts have adopted a shortcut proce-dure, known as an administrative hearing, when the person is only seeking to enforce that which was already ordered by previous judicial fiat. This administrative hearing is usually a most informal affair; the purpose is to provide the public with a simplified procedure to receive support which has not yet been paid. This is another way of saying, "attorneys need not apply."

There are some situations, however, that warrant the retention of coun-sel. In Part II of this book, we discuss custody and visitation issues. Much of the time the questions presented are quite complex, as is the proof required to win your case. But even when the issues revolve around money only, there are times when you will need your own lawyer. Remem-ber, there is no hard and fast rule. We have met tough-minded corporate executives who tremble at the thought of court; they are willing to pay for a lawyer as a form of psychological hand-holding. Conversely, we know many people with little formal schooling and a minimum of financial experience who have been extremely successful with their claims in Fam-ily Court, without legal representation.

The purpose of this chapter is to briefly review those situations where

183

an attorney is most likely to be needed. We will also point you in the right direction if you feel that it will be difficult for you to find one. Many lawyers are hesitant to involve themselves in post-divorce issues. These professionals believe that their job is done when they hand you the divorce judgment. One lawyer we know is fond of saying: "I was the obstetrician. I delivered the baby. You need a pediatrician now!" Actually, this comment is not quite as insensitive as it may first appear. Post-divorce issues, particularly with the enactment of so much recent legislation, has become a virtual sub-specialty in the matrimonial law area. Many attorneys are naturally insecure about providing proper representation in situations that require so much new knowledge.

There is also something else at work here. It has been our experience that post-divorce collection and modification issues are among the most frustrating and troublesome that a lawyer must face, and many simply shy away from the fray. Very often the whereabouts of the other spouse is not even known. As the following horror story illustrates, sometimes even a lawyer will be unable to offer any practical help.

Dan wanted out of his marriage at all costs. His reasons for breaking up his 23-year marriage were complex but basically irrelevant for purposes of our discussion. His wife Robin was taken totally off guard. Even now, 2 years after the divorce, she would be hard-pressed to put her finger on any particular reason for the disintegration of the marriage.

The divorce was obtained quickly. Dan's attitude was almost too good to be true. Sometimes it appeared to Robin that her husband's own lawyer was under instructions to cave in whenever a sticking point arose during the negotiation process. A fair agreement was soon reached; Dan obligated himself to give 50 percent of his take-home pay to support his wife and child. His job seemed secure, and although Dan had never exhibited any real ambition, his place in middle management suited him well.

However, as soon as the divorce, which specifically incorporated the agreement, was finalized Dan simply walked off the job. A psychiatrist might characterize his actions as a mid-life crisis or an idealized return to the simplicity of childhood. Robin doesn't much care what they call it. She only knows that while Dan is apparently happy doing sporadic, odd jobs in the neighboring community, she won't be able to pay the mortgage without renting the basement to a stranger or taking a second job on the weekends.

When contacted by her lawyer, Dan merely replies that he has worked all his life and that he is now entitled to a rest. "Let them sell the house. I don't care."

This book is filled with answers. Yet we don't pretend to have a solution for every situation. In our society, individuals are still allowed to self-destruct. No authority exists to force a person to find work or to live a productive life. Although a judge has the flexibility to issue a judgment of arrears, the possibility of enforcing such judgment and changing the court document to legal tender remains virtually nil in situations like Robin's. And while you might find a judge willing to throw Dan in jail for his open violation of an existing support order, it probably wouldn't faze this particular guy anyway.

These kinds of situations turn lawyers' hair gray. Even those of us who not only want to help, but know how to help, occasionally find ourselves up against an unyielding brick wall. No matter how effective an enforcement device, the system has limitations, and a lawyer cannot do the impossible. At bottom line, attorneys prefer to get involved with situations that produce results. Is it any wonder that many of our colleagues simply shy away from the post-divorce arena? What if their next client turned out to be Robin? How do you tell someone who desperately needs support that her former husband has metamorphosed into a deadbeat, the better to slip through the system's cracks. Better not to get involved in any post-divorce problems at all.

While we obviously do not share this particular view, we understand that some cases cannot be solved. No matter how creative or hardworking the lawyer, Robin will get very little relief, if any. But in our experience, this kind of situation is relatively rare. Much more common is the former spouse who remains in a well-paying job, but refuses to recognize the court ordered support obligation. More often than not, a former spouse has property to attach. If every father simply stopped working in order to get out of paying child support, our unemployment rate would be a hell of a lot higher. As it is, most violations are rooted in emotional responses. "Why pay if I don't have to?" is the most frequent reason given. These individuals live by the credo "Out of sight, out of mind." Very often the saying is changed to "Out of *state,* out of mind." But as we have previously seen, state boundaries do not offer much protection when it comes to enforcement of support orders.

At any rate, let's get back to our primary focus: lawyer versus me, myself and I.

THE AGENCY SYSTEM

You do not need a lawyer when you are using the local child support collection office. So long as you have properly prepared yourself, having made use of the information in Chapter 2, you will do just fine.

In essence, the caseworker becomes your attorney. He or she has been trained to answer your questions and trigger the appropriate collection device, whether it be the wage deduction order or the tax intercept. Like any attorney–client relationship, you will need to cooperate with one another. This simply means that you must have the necessary information and documentation at your fingertips. Your caseworker is a busy person with literally hundreds of clients at any given time. So take care to make good use of your time spent with the caseworker. Having read this book, you are in the perfect position to be the sterling client all lawyers dream about. Your caseworker is no different. Help them and they will help you.

That is not to say that we are naive. Problems do crop up—problems that may be no one's fault, problems that may result from miscommunication or personality conflicts.

Mrs. Caroline Endive had enjoyed a childhood that most would call privileged. As expected, she had married well. Mr. Endive was a financial consultant to an old and established investment firm. It has only been 2 years since the divorce, and her former husband has unilaterally reduced the child support by 50 percent.

As we have seen, the violation of child support orders remains a national problem that cuts across economic and financial lines. In Mrs. Endive's case, her monthly child support is just as important to her as it is to the next person. And regardless of her particular family background, she has always enjoyed a bargain. "Why spend good money for expensive lawyers when I don't have to," she figures. "A wage deduction should work just as well for me as it does for anyone else."

She is totally correct. But things immediately go wrong.

Mrs. Endive walks into the agency office as if she owns it. She looks around for a few minutes, wrinkles her nose and pushes to the head of a small line. She interrupts a caseworker in mid-sentence, who tells her, "Madam, please fill out the form on the table over there and get in line like the rest of these people, please."

With an arched eyebrow, Mrs. Endive is about ready to deliver a speech that the entire office will long remember, but the caseworker has already turned her full attention back to the person in front of her, and Mrs. Endive's demonstration would be a waste of her time. She gets the form, begins filling it out but quickly loses interest in what she perceives to be a futile exercise.

And so it goes. When the caseworker finally calls her up to the front, battle lines have already been drawn. Mrs. Endive is everything the caseworker is not. Rather than minimizing their cultural differences, Mrs. Endive has done everything to emphasize them. The interview is a bust; the caseworker has already handled sixteen cases, and she is thinking about lunch. Mrs. Endive succeeds only in alienating the caseworker further when she insists on seeing a supervisor because "my case is so special."

While Mrs. Endive may eventually get her wage deduction order, her experience will be a negative one all down the line. She has broken the cardinal rule, forgetting that a caseworker in the support collection office has, for all intents and purposes, taken over the role that an attorney used to play. Along with the territory goes a lot of responsibility and enforcement power. If the caseworker is going to be putting that power behind you, the least that can be expected is a little understanding and respect.

If you remember to treat the caseworker as your own attorney, you will have no problem. And we do not believe that we ask so much in this regard. If our executive and judiciary branches were able to cooperate in the creation of a system that does not require you to hire a lawyer, then we do not think it is too much to ask that you cooperate with your caseworker to insure successful collection and enforcement.

FAMILY COURT

As we have seen, your situation may not make you eligible to use the agency system. In some cases you may opt for court because of the larger array of enforcement devices to which you are entitled. It should be emphasized that the support collection offices are set up to effectuate wage deduction orders and tax intercepts only. Restraining notices, money judgments, attachments and contempt orders are to be found only in your Family Court or Domestic Relations Division, depending on where you live. And if you are seeking either an upward or downward modification of an existing support order, it will be necessary to proceed with your case in Family Court as well.

We start with the basic premise that each state has attempted to make their respective Family Courts easily accessible to the general public. Oftentimes an attorney is simply not needed. For example, if your ex is obligated to pay you monthly maintenance, and he has not done so for several months, the Family Court is well-equipped to handle the situation without your being forced to hire a lawyer.

In such a case you will, of course, be required to prove the arrears. But that sounds like a taller order than it actually is. As we've seen, the "trial" usually occurs in front of a hearing officer. There are no black robes or courtrooms. The hearing officer is usually an attorney who will see to it that you get as much practical assistance as possible. Formal rules of evidence will not necessarily conspire to rob you of your right to receive support.

In nine out of ten cases, an individual does not need a lawyer to prove that support arrears are owed. By reviewing the information contained in Chapter 4, you will be in a position to present your case in a manner that virtually assures victory. A lawyer would do the exact same thing.

Nor should you be thrown for a loop if your ex has hired a lawyer to defend him. You will calmly provide the hearing officer or judge with the necessary elements that prove your claim. We don't care if your former spouse has retained a reincarnation of Clarence Darrow; facts are facts. Your ex has either paid the money that is owed or he has not. No amount of legal maneuvering can change that simple fact. Indeed, in our experience, your ex will actually be hurting his own case if on the one hand he hasn't seen fit to pay support, yet on the other is somehow able to have high-priced legal talent accompany him to court.

Marsha Mead felt faint when the court clerk called her support collection case and a well-dressed woman stood up on behalf of her former husband, saying she represented him.

"Would you like a short postponement to find your own lawyer, Mrs. Mead?" asked the clerk.

Marsha almost said yes, but she instinctively knew that any time delay would work to her ex's advantage. She bit the inside of her cheek and said that an adjournment wasn't needed and that she was ready to go forward.

After waiting an interminable 45 minutes for one of the side rooms to become available, Marsha heard her case called again. The attorney walked confidently forward, briefcase in hand. Marsha felt another stab of fear course through her body and she almost called the whole thing off. But she had waited too long for this opportunity; her former husband was in court and she needed some enforcement relief as soon as possible.

The actual hearing took only 20 minutes. Looking back on it later, it was pretty obvious to Marsha that the attorney had been hired only as a means of buying more time. It was clear that her ex had hoped that the mere appearance of an attorney would put the matter off track for a while.

At the hearing, Marsha did not allow herself to become distracted by the lawyer's objections which were consistently overruled by the hearing officer. Soon the lawyer even stopped objecting. She sensed that it was doing no good anyway. When it came time for her ex to defend his nonpayment, his lawyer simply stated that her client had nothing further to say. The attorney then went into a 5-minute summation that begged the entire issue of her client's open violation of an existing court order. The hearing officer then asked Marsha whether she had any questions to ask her former husband. Knowing enough to quit while she was ahead, Marsha started to say no, but then inspiration struck.

"Thank you, your Honor. I do have one question to ask if the Court pleases."

"Please go right ahead, Mrs. Mead."

Looking her husband right in the eye, she asked: "How much have you paid your lawyer to be here today?"

"Objection," the lawyer almost screamed.

"Objection overruled," said the hearing officer. "Your client's ability to pay counsel while refusing to honor his support obligation is a relevant inquiry. I will hear his answer."

"Fifteen hundred dollars, Judge," said Mr. Mead with downcast eyes.

The point had been made. The hearing officer did not even reserve decision. Instead, he decided right on the spot that the amount in question was truly owed to Marsha and that she was entitled to a money judgment for the entire amount. Knowing that it was only a matter of time before the money judgment would form the basis for other enforcement mechanisms, such as an attachment on his property and a possible restraint of his bank accounts, Mr. Mead wrote out a check for all the arrears, plus interest, a few days later. It hurt—he hadn't been aware of how fast the maintenance could accumulate—but it was the earlier check to his lawyer that really pained him. Fifteen hundred dollars for nothing, he fumed.

When it comes to enforcing your right to receive post-divorce support, you can count on the court system to help you. This help includes a simplified procedure that, for the most part, does away with the need to hire counsel. So long as you have adequately prepared and rehearsed your approach, an attorney becomes almost superfluous.

MODIFICATION PROCEEDINGS

An effort to change an existing support order is a more complicated matter than merely enforcing that same order. We have previously discussed the process involved in modification proceedings. And while many people have been successful in prosecuting their modification claims without the help of a lawyer, the proof required to be successful is sometimes quite involved. This is particularly so when the other side is vigorously contesting your right to amend the original order to reflect present circumstances.

Do you need an attorney to represent you when seeking to modify a prior court order? Our response is an unequivocal *maybe.*

It depends on the complexity of your case and the issues that give rise to your contention that a modification is warranted. If you answer yes to any of these questions, you probably need a lawyer:

- Is the modification based upon a change in your ex's circumstances, as opposed to a change in your own?
- Will you require documents and records that are in your ex's possession or control in order to prove the changed circumstance necessitating the commencement of your proceeding to modify?
- Has your former spouse hired a lawyer to defend him or her in connection with the proceeding?
- Will you need to avail yourself of any expert testimony, such as a child psychiatrist, physician, pension actuary or accountant?

These broad and basic questions highlight the elements which will go into the making of your decision to hire a lawyer. If you have answered yes to any of them, then your case is probably just a bit too complex for you to go it alone. A lawyer may be the difference between success or failure.

On the other hand, many modification proceedings are relatively simple. If you have lost your job and are receiving unemployment insurance as your only income, then you should not have much difficulty in convincing the court that you deserve a downward modification, at least temporarily until you get yourself back on your feet. In such a situation, an attorney is *probably* unnecessary.

We emphasize the word "probably" because it raises another important point. Any decision to hire a lawyer must be in tune with your own psychological makeup. No matter how factually simple your particular case may be, a lawyer will be necessary if you cannot imagine yourself doing it on your own. That's why we say at the beginning of this chapter that there is no hard and fast rule when it comes to retaining counsel. Not only does it depend on the complexities of your case; equally as important are such intangibles as the amount of time you can devote, your overall confidence and your ability to communicate in a rather formalized manner. We know an artist who has won several major national and international painting awards. It is obvious that he is a successful communicator in his area of expertise. Yet he will be the first to admit that it is extremely difficult for him to communicate his thoughts through everyday spoken conversation.

Actually, this type of paradox is not so uncommon. Many lawyers are eloquent speakers but cannot write two coherent sentences to save their lives. Many performers must overcome serious stage fright. And no matter how much education you might have, it doesn't necessarily mean that you will be able to assimilate some of the more archaic procedures that are still found within the judicial system. As we've seen in our case histories, many people with a limited educational background have been successful in trying their own cases. But a lawyer remains a viable option if you are unable to overcome your anxiety about approaching your case without legal backup.

In many instances, your anxiety and confusion may be amply alleviated by testing the waters a bit through an initial consultation with an attorney. At the outset, make it clear that the purpose of your conference is to obtain information that will make it easier for you to proceed on your own. Most lawyers will be pleased to offer any advice concerning the local procedures appropriate to your particular enforcement case. As a rule, attorneys charge between $75 and $250 for an initial consultation. When trying to decide whether to prosecute your case on your own, such investment is money well spent. The consultation process often is all you will need to fill in some of the gaps and questions that have made the idea of going it alone seem impossible.

ATTORNEYS' FEES

Another element that you must obviously consider before deciding whether or not to hire an attorney is the cost involved. After having spent thousands in lawyers' fees to get your divorce just a few years ago, the thought of invading your savings to enforce the judgment is probably enough to cause a major anxiety attack.

Your economic horizon may not be as bleak as it first appears. Virtually every state has created a neat little procedure for those former spouses who openly violate existing court orders of support, which permits a judge to impose attorneys' fees on the violating party.

Here's how it works. Let's assume that your ex is supposed to be paying you $150 per week in maintenance and child support. Not only are the payments chronically late but at least every 2 or 3 months, your former spouse unilaterally reduces the amount he gives you. Sometimes it is $75, other times a little more or less. This conduct has gone on for a year, and you decide to take him to Family Court to obtain a money judgment for the actual amount owed. It comes out to be close to $1,000.

You telephone the lawyer who represented you in a slip and fall case about 2 years ago. He seemed pretty competent: your case was settled out of court for about $3,500. But when you call about your most recent problem, his reaction is somewhat puzzling.

He tells you that the time it would take to draw up the necessary petition and accompany you to court would cost you about $500 in legal fees. "Even if I were willing to wait for my fees until you collected on your judgment, you would be paying me $500 to collect $1,000. That's not much of a return on your investment," he says.

But you have read this book, and you remain undaunted. "Doesn't my ex have to pay your legal fee?"

"You know, you may have something there. It's been a while since I got involved in post-divorce enforcement. Let me check the law and I'll get back to you later in the day."

Sure enough, your state, as do most, permits payment of attorneys fees when you sue for support enforcement on the basis of an obvious non-compliance with a support order. When your papers are drawn, your lawyer will also include a demand that his fees be paid over and above the amount of arrears owed at the time that enforcement is sought. In this particular case, your lawyer would demand $1,000 plus an additional sum as a fee to compensate him for the time that it took to successfully prosecute your collection case.

Some points to be made about this procedure:

- Your former spouse must pay the fee directly to your lawyer, not to you. The imposition of an attorney's fee does not represent a form of reimbursement to the client.
- The amount awarded is purely within the court's discretion. Your lawyer may have asked for $500; the judge may direct your ex to pay him $350.
- The court order to pay attorneys' fees has the same effect as a judge's directive that your ex must pay the arrears owed. Just like you, he hopes that your former spouse will comply with such directive and pay his fee without further enforcement efforts.
- A money judgment, even for attorneys' fees, does not guarantee payment by the other side. Remember, this is an individual whose nonpayment of child support forced you to hire a lawyer to get a money judgment against him. His attitude about compliance has already been demonstrated, and it has been our experience that a money judgment may be only the first step in obtaining actual collection.

Keeping these points in mind, you should immediately see both the pros and cons of the imposition of attorneys' fees. The benefit is obvious: it will save you money and might interest an attorney in representing you who otherwise might not want to get involved. An attorney fee award acts as a sort of incentive; the idea is to make the breaching party pay for the legal effects of the violation.

However, it should also be emphasized that in our experience, judges are quite conservative in the amounts that they order the other spouse to pay to your lawyer. He or she may have actually spent over 20 hours preparing your case and representing you through the hearing, but the court will award an amount that does not necessarily reflect such time expenditure. In other words, while your lawyer may have the right to collect his fees from your ex, it is usually not wholly sufficient.

Because of this conservative trend, many lawyers will continue to request some initial payment from you before they agree to formally represent you. These same attorneys are often much more willing to accept a reduced amount in expectation of a future payment from your former spouse. At the same time, however, the lawyer will make it absolutely clear that you are still ultimately responsible for his or her legal fees. It works something like this.

Your ex owes you $7500 in support payments. The lawyer explains that his rate is $100 per hour and that an advance payment of the first 10 hours is required. However, because your state permits a judge to impose attorneys' fees against your ex, your lawyer is willing to accept $500, looking to collect the balance from your former spouse after the case is successfully prosecuted. At the end of the case, your lawyer will petition the court for the balance of his fees. He or she might advise the judge that 11 hours of time have been expended; that $600 is owed taking into account your being credited with the amount you paid in advance as an initial retainer.

The judge may arbitrarily award your attorney $500, for a total of $1,000 received for the time devoted to your case. In such a situation, an attorney has the absolute right to look to you for another $100. Remember, you agreed to be *ultimately* responsible for his legal fee. While he is happy to get the contribution from your former spouse, such payment may not necessarily compensate him for all of his time.

Our example leaves a shortfall of only $100. In such a situation, most lawyers that we know would "call it square" and let you off the hook for the additional payment. But in many situations, the attorney's fee awarded remains far below the amount actually owed to the lawyer for time expended.

Although the imposition of attorneys' fees is an effective device which usually saves you money, it is not the perfect solution. That is why so many lawyers continue to require some advance payment for their anticipated time, as well as an acknowledgement and understanding that the *client* (as opposed to the former spouse) take final responsibility for payment of the legal fees. Leaving it all to a judge's discretion is a bit too chancy for most. By the same token, the imposition of an attorney's fee award to be paid by your ex often results in your being able to retain a lawyer who might otherwise be out of your economic reach.

ASSIGNMENT OF COUNSEL

In some situations a lawyer may be assigned to you. For example, all states maintain Legal Aid or Public Defender Units for individuals who cannot afford a lawyer. While the focus of Legal Aid is mostly on assigning counsel to indigent defendants in criminal cases, most bureaus have a civil/matrimonial division as well. If your income and net worth fall below a given level, you may be eligible for free legal representation.

Even for indigent families, however, the system is often inappropriate. First of all, in many instances the waiting period is torturously slow. The attorneys are immensely overworked and are forced to carry a caseload that staggers the imagination. But if you believe that the Public Defender's Office may be suitable to your needs, you owe it to yourself to telephone. Find out the eligibility requirements, and follow up with the information they require. Even a sometimes overworked lawyer is better than no attorney in situations that warrant such presence.

We have also discussed the Uniform Reciprocal Enforcement Support Act (URESA). We have seen that when your former spouse resides out of state, all is not lost. You may go into your Family Court and have the entire enforcement file forwarded directly to the state where your ex lives. Your enforcement and collection is then prosecuted through that state, called the "responding state." City or county attorneys within the responding state are then charged with the duty to act as your representative. For example, if you live in Ann Arbor and your ex resides in Manhattan, your file will be forwarded from Michigan directly to the Family Court located in New York City. The file and your case will then be processed by an attorney called an Assistant Corporation Counsel. In other jurisdictions, city attorneys are referred to by other names. Whatever the name used, you will have a legal representative to prosecute your collection efforts in another city in another state, without even the necessity of your having to speak with your "lawyer."

When using URESA the decision to hire a lawyer is made for you. Not a bad way to obtain legal counsel, is it? And because this attorney will be communicating with the Family Court in your locale, you are afforded periodic updates and status reports. At times the procedure gets a bit unwieldy, but every state has adopted URESA, and it is an extremely effective bit of legislation when it comes to enforcing support orders against out-of-state residents.

WHAT DO I LOOK FOR?

No discussion on lawyers would be complete without a few comments on what to look for when choosing an attorney to represent you, assuming that you are not entitled to an automatic assignment of counsel through URESA or the Public Defender's office. Nowhere is it more important to shop—not necessarily for price, but for competency and compassion. Because you will be working closely together, you must have confidence and trust in his or her abilities, and you should be able to confide in one another and get along. Remember, even your original divorce lawyer may not be particularly suited to post-divorce problems. As we indicated, this area of the law is becoming increasingly more specialized.

To begin with, you will need a matrimonial specialist. Actually, the term *specialist* is somewhat misleading. There are very few recognized specialties in the legal field. Most states will only certify an attorney as a specialist in such areas as patents and admiralty. However, there are attorneys who tend to confine their practice to a particular area of the law, such as divorce and domestic relations. Just because you are happy with the lawyer who handled your house closing does not necessarily make him an appropriate choice in the post-divorce area.

You will need a lawyer who combines sensitivity with aggressive tactics. You must believe that the attorney understands your plight and that the most effective, affirmative steps will be taken immediately. Knowledge of the various enforcement devices is absolutely necessary. But knowledge, itself, is not enough if a healthy working atmosphere cannot be established and maintained. Your lawyer should be accessible, but this does not mean that you have a right to bombard him or her with telephone calls at every hour of the day, either. It does mean that you should have confidence that he will be available to talk if a true emergency arises.

When you are involved in post-divorce enforcement, we recognize that an attorney often signifies a last-resort approach. The agency system may have failed, or your attempts to go it alone in Family Court might have been stopped cold for a variety of reasons. Calling a lawyer may be the last thing that you want to do. Therefore, you should choose a lawyer with whom you can communicate. We are talking about trust. When he or she telephones to say that a certain unexpected delay has materialized, you must believe your lawyer's statement. For example, as we will be discussing in Part II, post-divorce custody issues are frought with inherent complexities. The case never goes as expected, and if you doubt your lawyer's word that a wrench has been thrown into the works then you are in for big trouble.

We repeat our first statement: shop around. Do not be hesitant to interview several lawyers. Usually conference fees are relatively small. During these consultations, you must approach the hiring decision as if you were also interviewing the lawyer. Don't be afraid to ask those hard questions. Find out the specific procedure that the lawyer advises taking in order to solve your enforcement or custody problem.

Here are some guidelines to assist you in the interview process:

- Ask how much experience the lawyer has in handling problems such as yours.
- Is the attorney a member of any professional associations, such as the City or State Bar Association, and in particular any matrimonial or domestic relations divisions or committees within such associations?
- Has he or she ever lectured or published within the matrimonial field?
- How many actual trials has the lawyer completed within the last year or so? While it is true that you do not want to hire an attorney who is "trigger happy," it is equally true that he or she should not be afraid to litigate your controversy to completion if an acceptable settlement is not in the offing.
- If the post-divorce problem that you face is custody oriented, you must be particularly careful to hire a lawyer with specific experience in this area. Custody cases require a "special breed of cat." Invariably the lawyer must be able to combine compassion with practicality.
- Be suspicious of any professional who speaks of "winning" a custody case. When a child is in the middle of the competing wishes of his parents, the issue and focus should not be on winning; rather the legal and practical approach must remain on the "best interests" of the child. A matrimonial lawyer with proper experience knows enough to view a custody controversy as a mutual search for the proper environment in which to place your child. This doesn't mean that your lawyer cannot aggressively pursue your rights. However, an attorney who personalizes any post-divorce custody controversy to the point of discussing it in terms of winning or losing is probably setting you up for a fall.
- Do not forget to request specific information regarding the anticipated legal fee. While most attorneys charge an hourly rate, a lawyer with experience will be able to provide you with a reasonably accurate estimate of what it will take to resolve your particular controversy. Do not accept a comment such as "Who knows? Your final fee could be anywhere between

$1,000 and $25,000." This type of response indicates inexperience, a lack of professional sensitivity or even a basic dishonesty.

- Remember, many attorneys make a great first appearance. It is not until you are down in the lobby that you realize that not one question has been answered. At bottom line, choose someone with whom you can talk. Communication is the key that forms the bedrock of any decent attorney-client relationship.

Where To Go

Now that you have an idea of the type of lawyer you want, you may not have the slightest notion where to look. You are hardly alone. Lawyers may exist by the thousands, yet finding the right one can be an arduous task. It is relatively easy to define the attributes that characterize an effective lawyer; finding the real thing poses a more difficult problem.

The best way of finding a lawyer is through a referral. Once it becomes apparent that you are looking for legal assistance, all kinds of referrals will result. But be careful. Make sure that the person referring has had direct dealings with the recommended lawyer. Determine if the individual's legal practice is devoted primarily to matrimonial law. An emphasis in post-divorce related problems is, of course, even better. And do not blindly rely on well-meaning, but overzealous friends.

This is exactly what happened to James. He knew his situation was right for an attorney. He was sure that his former wife was making a lot of money off the books as a sales representative for a major sporting goods outfit, but he understood that in order to obtain documented proof he would need the touch of an expert. While he continued to pay the court-ordered maintenance and child support, it galled him that his ex's income had apparently tripled since the divorce while his had remained at the same level.

On a deeper level, he understood that his sudden interest in his legal obligation was the result of a relatively new relationship with a female co-worker. Nancy and he had grown quite close during the last several months. She was staying over at his place almost 2 nights a week and was beginning to press him for a major commitment. When James complained that his present financial obligation was too precarious on account of the prior support order, she countered with the strong suggestion that he seek modification.

Nancy said that her family lawyer was the person to see. She made it quite clear that if some definite action was not taken soon, the relationship would end.

"What kind of law does he practice?" asked James.

"How do I know? He's a lawyer, isn't he? It can't be too difficult to get this situation cleaned up," Nancy curtly responded.

"I'll make an appointment tomorrow."

"How about right now? I have his home telephone number."

Before James knew it, he was explaining his situation to a Mr. Adams. The lawyer seemed knowledgeable enough, but James was a little concerned about retaining such a large law firm. It turned out that Nancy's family lawyer was a partner in a sixty-person firm and had been handling her father's corporate business for several years.

It also turned out that the firm never handled matrimonial matters, let alone post-divorce issues. Mr. Adams took the case as a courtesy to Nancy's father. He figured that he would put one of the summer associates on the case; how difficult could a modification proceeding be when compared to corporate mergers?

Fortunately, James saw that his case was getting nowhere before too much damage had been done. It wasn't a question of incompetency or even legal neglect. It had only to do with the firm's experience and priorities. While Nancy certainly had good intentions in referring her boyfriend to Mr. Adams, James should have taken some initiative and pressed the search a bit further. In his mind, he did not want to hurt Nancy's feelings or cause any unnecessary tension in their relationship.

The point here is to recognize that referrals are an extremely important means of finding a lawyer, but that it is not an infallible method by any stretch of the imagination. You must not accept a referral out of some vague feeling of obligation to the referring party. Investigate the source of the referral as thoroughly as you would the attorney. While a criminal lawyer may be extremely effective in a post-divorce setting, it is more likely that someone with matrimonial experience will do you better.

In addition to referrals, you can contact your local Bar Association. Many of them have a public referral service at little or no charge that maintains lists of lawyers grouped according to stated expertise. Although the rules for every Bar Association vary, generally each requires a minimum period for a lawyer to be practicing before he or she can be placed on the list.

An attorney who is interested in being listed simply volunteers to fill out a detailed application that lists various information, including areas of legal emphasis. Often a face-to-face interview follows, after which time the lawyer's name is placed on the list. Most Bar Associations either rotate the list or select a name at random when an individual requests a lawyer for a particular purpose.

In order to use the Bar Association approach, you simply telephone your local Association and request that you be referred to a lawyer who has experience in handling post-divorce cases. During this telephone call, you will be interviewed by someone, often a retired lawyer, who will ascertain the exact nature of your problem, after which the matrimonial list will be consulted and you will be given the names and telephone numbers of several lawyers in your geographical area.

The next step is up to you. You must telephone any of the attorneys, advising him or her that you have been referred by the local Bar Association. This will result in your being charged a reduced initial consultation fee; attorneys who are on the list agree to this arrangement as part of their right to receive public referrals. The fee should be in the range of $15–$25, depending on your state's policy.

The referral and Bar Association methods are the two most effective and best means of finding an attorney to represent you. Other methods include contacting lawyers through their advertisements. While many in our profession disdain such lawyer advertising, we have found that many of these lawyers offer a valid option to those of you who cannot afford to pay expensive legal fees. Please be aware, however, that most of the attorneys who do advertise operate a rather large-volume business. We have found that some post-divorce enforcement is tailor made for high-volume processing, such as collection of support arrears or preparation and delivery of information subpoenas and bank account restraining notices. Other problems, such as modifications of support, custody or visitation require more personalized handling; a legal clinic or high-volume office may be ill-suited to your needs if you find yourself in such a situation.

If you want to find a lawyer, you will be able to do so. It may take several consultations and cost you a few bucks, but in the end, you will find an ally. Don't give up if your first choice turns out to be a wrong one. In every state, an individual may discharge his or her lawyer with or without cause. You have an absolute right to terminate your relationship and go elsewhere if you are unhappy. While much in this book can be accomplished without counsel, the times that you do need a lawyer require someone with compassion, aggressiveness and knowledge of the law governing your particular problem. This "someone" is out there. With some basic initiative on your part he or she can be found.

PART II

YOUR CHILDREN

CHAPTER TEN

Child Custody and Visitation

IN PART I of our book we dealt with post-divorce money problems. We now turn to the emotionally charged issues of custody and visitation. If there is anything that continues to bind numerous divorced couples together—like two scorpions locked in the fatal mating dance—it is the children.

Most parents agree to a custody/visitation arrangement at the time of their divorce. This understanding is then incorporated within the divorce decree. Sometimes the parties cannot come to terms with having to make a final decision about the children or are unwilling to compromise. The result is a full-blown custody battle that forces a judge to make the fateful determination: who gets the kids?

Whether the court has made the decision for you, or the two of you were able to reach an amicable accommodation, your divorce judgment will contain two basic elements. The first element necessarily specifies the children's primary residence: which parent will the children live with? This parent is said to have *custody* of the children. The second element describes and establishes the so-called *visitation rights* of the *non-custodial* parent; how much time does he or she get with them? Many fathers prefer the term *parenting time,* the thought being that the divorce hasn't somehow turned them into distant relatives. You don't "visit" your own kids, these fathers will tell you. While we appreciate and agree with this sentiment, we will generally continue to use the more familiar term "visitation."

A relatively recent trend is the *joint custody* arrangement where parents devise all kinds of creative means to share their children on an equal basis. Actually, the term "joint custody" is misunderstood by many. There is joint *physical* custody and there is joint *legal* custody. In the first situation, the parents are physically with their children an equal amount of the time. Joint *legal* custody has nothing to do with the physical whereabouts of the children or with whom they reside. The concept envisions a sharing of all major childrearing decisions, regardless of which parent has technical, physical custody. Joint legal custody permits the non-custodial parent to continue to offer parental input even though he or she is out of the house. Any major educational, health, religious, cultural or other significant childrearing decision must be agreed upon by *both* parents.

This brings us to another important concept: the "best interests" doctrine. In the following chapters, we will discuss a variety of custody and visitation-related problems. We will show you how to enforce or modify your visitation and custody rights, and we will provide many examples with both successful and not-so-successful conclusions. But whatever the issue or ultimate outcome, a common thread that you will see is the

201

judicial effort to solve the particular problem with an eye towards the children's best interests.

This phrase is intentionally broad and nebulous. The idea is to keep the children at center stage; your particular needs and desires are secondary. Let us say that you are the non-custodial parent, and you truly believe that you can offer more luxuries to your children. You are thinking about petitioning for a change of custody. The thought of having the children move in with you on a full-time basis sends chills of excitement and expectation down your spine. It would be so great to have the kids around. You know you could offer them so much. But in your self-centered approach, you forget a great many other important details. The children have now lived with their mother for the last 5 years. Actually, it is closer to 6 if you take into consideration your having moved out of the house approximately 8 months before the divorce was actually finalized. You live in a different school district; the children would have to adjust to an entirely new educational environment. Although your job permits you ever-increasing flexibility, there are still nights when you don't get out of the office until 9 or 10 o'clock. In short, the life that your children have made for themselves does not really need to be disturbed. In their best interests, the custody and visitation arrangement in effect for the last 5 years should continue. We are talking about the best interests of your *children.* Not *your* interests.

The best interests doctrine is particularly relevant when attempting to modify existing visitation or custody orders. While it is not always articulated, it is this doctrine that controls and forms the basis of virtually every court determination to either permit or reject a change or modification affecting the children. Post-divorce custody disputes consistently test a judge's resources. While a judge may order psychiatric examinations and listen to other experts hypothesize about which parent is the better one, the ultimate decision rests with the court. It has been our experience that the judicial robes are never worn with more seriousness than when the judge is called upon to decide a post-divorce issue affecting custody or visitation. In every state, the overriding concern and weightiest factor remains the best interests of the child.

ENFORCING YOUR VISITATION RIGHTS

In the next chapter, we will discuss the remedies available to you when your visitation rights are being improperly thwarted and frustrated. At the outset, we remind you that in 1985 only 10 percent of the 12 million children of divorced couples were in the custody of their fathers. While many states have done away with the legal presumption in favor of the mother, the fact remains that many judges still exhibit a maternal preference. For the most part, then, the father is the non-custodial parent and the visitation enforcement problem remains uniquely male-oriented. The examples in our book, based for the most part on true-life cases, do not reflect any gender orientation on our part. Rather, they reflect the societal reality that it is the father who must usually fight to remain a part of his child's life.

Many lawyers are of the opinion that it is often more difficult to enforce a father's visitation rights than it is to win sole custody for him at the divorce trial. But we see a definite trend in the father's favor when he finds himself having to enforce court-ordered visitation. The legal battle is still uphill, but things are definitely improving; some judges are actually arresting the defiant custodial parent. In our next chapter, we will highlight the enforcement devices available to the non-custodial parent who is being denied visitation. For now, we just want to illustrate some of the elements and issues that are present in a majority of post-divorce visitation-related problems.

Fred had compromised on the support issue so that his former spouse, Tina, would more readily agree to a liberal visitation schedule. The eventual divorce decree incorporated a provision that gave Fred a great deal of time with his 3-year-old son. But now that the divorce has been finalized, Tina has started to play games. While Fred has made every weekly child support and maintenance payment that he is supposed to, his ex has found one excuse after another to deny him access to his child.

One week he went over to the house only to discover that his ex had taken the child out of state to visit her mother. No one was home, but a neighbor was kind enough to inform Fred of his former wife's sudden travel arrangements. A few days later, Fred telephoned Tina to voice his anger and to make definite plans for the next weekend.

"But, Fred, the judge said every *other* weekend. This weekend is mine."

Fred tried to maintain his composure. "I know that. But on *my* weekend, you just up and left town. How did you expect me to exercise visitation in a deserted house?"

"Don't get snippy with me. You wanted the divorce; now you got it. We'll see you in two weeks." And with those words of wisdom, Tina hung up the phone.

Undaunted, Fred redialed. It was busy. And it stayed busy for the rest of the evening; she had obviously taken the telephone off the hook. When he called 3 days later, he got a recording that the "new" number was unlisted. Tina's games continued.

Suffice it to say that she found the most creative ways to keep father and son apart for the next 4 weeks. It wasn't until a month and a half later that Fred got to see his child, only to have the entire situation repeated for several weeks after that.

Fred's experience illustrates the most common problem that is encountered on the visitation enforcement battlefield. Although some of the details may change and the cast of characters differ, the same elements are generally present. First, there exists a prior court order that defines a parent's visitation arrangement, or legal rights as we often put it. Second, there is an evident and clear attempt by the non-custodial parent to exercise such rights pursuant to the judicial decree. Third, there is a denial of such visitation by the other parent. Although we consistently counsel individuals to attempt civilized discussion to arrive at a solution, if such negotiated stance proves unsuccessful, the fourth element arises; namely the commencement of a formal enforcement proceeding to secure rightful visitation.

As we will discuss more fully in the next chapter, courts do not look kindly upon former spouses who play the visitation denial game. Judges recognize that the real victims remain the children. Recent research indicates that a father's absence in his child's life often leads to major psychological difficulties. One associate clinical professor at a well-known medical school states unequivocally that children who lose touch with their fathers after a divorce are more likely to manifest serious depression and suffer severe loss of self-esteem. Another clinical psychologist associates father absence with a child's aggressive tendencies, difficulties in school and problems with gender identity. And courts are becoming increasingly more aware of the scope and disastrous consequences that trail in the wake of intentionally disrupted visitation.

Anything that tends to disturb healthy parent–child interaction is greatly discouraged. As mentioned, a court has the flexibility to impose sanctions on the violating party. These sanctions may include the imposition of a fine or award of attorneys' fees in your favor. As in the case with enforcement of child support and maintenance support orders, when it comes to simple enforcement of your visitation rights, virtually all family courts have simplified their procedures to insure expedited justice.

Before leaving this introductory discussion on visitation enforcement, we must also mention the other side of the coin. A quote attributed to Lillian Kozak, chairwoman of NOW's Domestic Relations Law Task Force, which appeared in a recent magazine article highlights the point. "I ran a NOW hotline for three years and got thousands of calls from divorced women," she said. "One of the most frequently asked questions was, 'How can I get my husband to live up to his visitation responsibilities?'"

While many fathers are involved in bitter fights to maintain parental contact with their children, others are involved in finding excuses to sever this all-important tie. A man who chooses not to exercise visitation creates a major and frustrating problem for the legal system to adequately resolve. We hope to provide some insight in our next chapter, but unfortunately the situation where a father decides to just fade away is fraught with difficulties.

MODIFICATION OF VISITATION RIGHTS

You may have been awarded certain visitation rights 7 years ago, but the court order no longer reflects present circumstances. Wednesday evenings and weekends were fine when Bobby was 6-years-old. But now you truly believe that he needs more time with you. It doesn't help any that Bobby's math tutor can only see your son on Wednesday night. The mid-week dinners have become a thing of the past. And what makes it even worse is your honest feeling that Bobby doesn't seem to mind that the two of you are seeing less of each other.

What is a sincere and caring father to do? In such a situation, he is heading directly into modification country. When circumstances warrant it and expanded visitation is really in your child's best interests, a prior visitation arrangement—even if court ordered—can be modified. So

Bobby's father has only to press the right legal button to obtain his desired goal, right? Wrong!

Before you turn to any legal artillery, you should take the practical step of discussing the matter with your former spouse. We are constantly amazed at the number of fathers who run to our office to modify visitation rights without having first explored a reasonable accommodation with the child's mother. It seems like such an obvious initial step, doesn't it? So why do so many fathers act so surprised when the first question that the lawyer asks is whether they have taken the time to work things out with their ex-spouses?

One colleague told us of the father who demanded a consultation immediately; he was calling from a pay telephone across the street. Fortunately, the lawyer's schedule permitted the requested conference a few minutes later.

CLIENT: You've got to help me. I just got assigned to the night shift. I'll only be able to see my daughter on weekends now.
LAWYER: What kind of visitation rights do you have?
CLIENT: Every other weekend and Tuesdays and Thursdays between 5:30 and 9:30 p.m. But don't you understand? I just told you; I'm supposed to be working nights. My shift starts at six.
LAWYER: What does your ex-wife say?
CLIENT: Haven't told her yet. I figured you could serve her with papers or something to stop her from denying me visitation.
LAWYER: I really don't see your point. It's not her fault that you will be working nights. There's been no denial of any rights at this point.
CLIENT: Hey, I thought you'd be on my side. I heard you're the best in the business. I'm willing to pay whatever it costs.
LAWYER: Pay for what? You don't have a case yet. Before I make another appointment with you, I urge you to try to work things out with your ex-wife.
CLIENT: She'll never understand. Let me tell you about the time . . .
LAWYER: Listen, I don't mean to be rude, but when you telephoned I was under the impression that this was a real emergency. Talk to your ex. You might be surprised.

Needless to say, our hapless father called back a day later to say that everything was fine. He and his former spouse had come up with a creative but obvious modification. Now their daughter gets picked up directly from school by her father at least 3 days a week. He drops her off back home about 3 hours later on his way to work. The obvious moral is don't be so trigger-happy when circumstances necessitate a change in your visitation schedule. The first approach should always be the direct one. Open communication remains the key.

Of course, we fully understand that good faith, civilized negotiations prove impossible in all too many situations. Rigid adherence to stale visitation awards are not in the children's best interests, but when it comes to the children many parents allow emotions to dictate irrational and often harmful actions. The courts will not usually involve themselves in the petty squabbles between parents who cannot see past their own motives. However, when a healthy parent–child relationship must be preserved through an expansion of visitation due to changed circumstances, a judge will take seriously your modification proceeding.

In Chapter 12 we explore the elements behind the legal procedures necessary to effect a modification of visitation rights. You will discover that no two cases are exactly the same. Often it is the intangible something that makes the difference between expansion or continuation of your visitation arrangement. If you are forced to actually testify at a modification hearing you will know what to expect when you attempt to rearrange your time with the children. Many times a lawyer will be necessary; the decisions often rest on shading the facts in a way that requires the experience of a trial attorney. However, you will be in a position to assist your lawyer by knowing the important factors to emphasize when presenting your case.

Throughout, we will repeatedly affirm our strong belief that most modification situations can be solved without resorting to lawyers and formal proceedings. It is not a question of *permitting* visitation, but rather recognizing that continued interaction between the non-custodial parent and the child should be openly encouraged. If all he wants is a little more quality time with his son, who are you to deny him the opportunity? You should consider yourself fortunate. As we observed earlier, there are some professionals who think that the major problem in the visitation area is with the parent who chooses not to exercise the right at all.

On the other hand, you should never lose sight of the best interests doctrine. While it may be your opinion that another 3 weeks during the summer would benefit Sally's relationship with you, don't close your eyes to other important facts. Your daughter has gone to camp every summer for the last 4 years. The extra 3 weeks translates to almost 2 full months because, as your visitation currently stands, she lives with you during the entire month of August. The extra time you want would mean no more camp for Sally. Are you quite sure that you want to press for modification in court?

Judges will strive to expand or sometimes even restrict visitation as the need arises. But the need that we are talking about remains the child's. That is the important point to remember when reading our more detailed discussion in the next chapters.

THE $ HYBRID

Sometimes a visitation enforcement or modification issue is complicated by another factor. Money. Michael has missed two child support payments, his ex retaliates by denying him visitation. Jeff asks for an expansion of his parenting time, only to be told by his former spouse that he will have to "buy it" for another $15 a week. In another situation, the father has always paid his court-ordered child support on time and in full. He brings a proceeding to enforce his visitation; his ex-wife counters by claiming that he is in arrears and files a cross-petition for an upward modification.

In each of these situations, the visitation question is muddied by a superimposed child support issue. It is almost like asking "what came first: the chicken or the egg?" In so many cases it is just plain impossible to determine what occurred first—the denial of visitation or the violation of a child support order. Can the custodial parent simply take it upon herself to refuse the father access to his children when no support has been forthcoming? Does denial of visitation warrant nonpayment of child support?

You will see in Chapter 11 that courts across our country are wrestling with this issue. At this juncture, we only mention it to underscore that visitation problems rarely arise or exist in a vacuum.

ENFORCING YOUR CUSTODY RIGHTS

You have been awarded custody; 2 years later your ex refuses to return Lisa after the summer visitation. Statistics are hard to come by, but one report indicates that 25,000 to 100,000 children are kidnapped by the non-custodial parent each year. Although states are increasingly cooperating with one another by recognizing and giving uniform effect to custody awards obtained in other states, you have no assurance that your ex's actions won't result in another major custody battle. Even when your ex remains within state boundaries, the enforcement of your original custody award can be a hellish legal experience. In such a situation, your former spouse will usually counter your enforcement proceeding with a demand for a change of custody in his or her favor. And the whole thing can be extremely expensive; it is not uncommon to spend over $15,000 in legal fees to enforce your original custody decree.

But this is a self-help book. We recognize some of the problems that you will face, but at the same time we intend to offer some practical advice in the upcoming chapters. First of all, an original custody award pulls some weight. The fact that your child has resided with you for the last several years remains an important factor when you are forced to commence a custody enforcement proceeding. No court wants to start all over again. If one judge has already spoken, you will have a subtle but nonetheless important presumptive advantage if your ex attempts to violate your custodial rights by attempting a change of custody.

It started with a telephone call from Sarah's 12-year-old daughter, Lisa, who has been temporarily residing with her father for the last 4 weeks as part of his summer visitation arrangement. "We've decided that I'm not going to live with you any more, Mom."

"What do you mean, *we've* decided. Who is we?"

"Me and Daddy. He says I don't have to come home after the summer if I don't want to. We'll only be three hundred miles away; I can visit you on holidays."

"Get your father on the phone right away!" Sarah felt her control slipping with each passing second.

"He says he doesn't want to talk with you now. I have to go. Bye."

Sarah cannot believe this is the child who she has raised virtually by herself during the past 9 years. When Lisa's father walked out, their daughter wasn't even 3. During the intervening years, and particularly since the divorce was finalized 5 years ago, her ex has hardly been around. But during the last year or so, he has resurfaced with a vengeance. Telephone calls every night; long weekends at his farm upstate and the whole month of July this summer. And now, after Sarah has already sent Lisa bus tickets for the trip back home, her daughter coolly advises that "we've decided" that she won't return.

We will return to this vignette in Chapter 13, using it to illustrate the effect that a child's stated preference may have on the issue of custody enforcement. We will also discuss the difference that exists between enforcing a support order as opposed to the enforcement of custodial rights. When the subject is money, a court will generally be interested only in whether it has been paid or not. As we saw in Part I, if the money is owed, the enforcement devices are let loose like a pack of wild dogs. When a child is in the middle of a custody visitation controversy, however, a judge remains more circumspect. Oftentimes it may seem that the custody issue is being litigated all over again when all you thought you were doing was enforcing a prior court award.

Judicial perceptions are changing, though. While not willing to automatically rubber-stamp an *original* custody award, a judge will not hesitate to strictly enforce it when circumstances warrant. Nor are child-snatching parents somehow protected by the imaginary lines that define our state boundaries. A father refuses to return the child after a visitation period and then compounds his wrong by taking the child out of state. It used to be that you could only hope to enforce your custodial rights by chasing the violating parent to the new state and then starting a proceeding in that state. For most, this was prohibitively time-consuming and expensive.

Enter: the Uniform Child Custody Jurisdiction Act (UCCJA). This law has been adopted by all fifty states, and its stated purpose is to avoid jurisdictional competition, deter abductions and other unilateral removals of children, as well as facilitate the enforcement of custody decrees on a uniform national basis. We will take you through the UCCJA later, but for now, we want only to emphasize that you no longer have to follow the fleeing parent. You are entitled to proceed in your home state, and the enforcement order you obtain is then given full force and effect in your ex's state. In other words, as the Act specifically recognizes, the physical presence of the child, "while desirable," is not a prerequisite to enforce your original custody award.

MODIFICATION OF CUSTODY RIGHTS

Actually, we understate ourselves when we refer to this next area of discussion as "modification" of custody. We are really talking about a change of custody from one parent to the other. Your ex-wife has had custody of the children for the last 3 and a half years. With increasing alarm, you realize that her prior alcohol problem is apparently out of control again. One evening you bring the children back to the house only to find your ex sprawled out drunk on the living room couch. The electric stove is still on; the boiling water has already evaporated and the bottom of the pot is a blackened mess.

In another case, you agreed that Ralph would have primary custody of your 11- and 9-year-old sons. It seemed the most appropriate plan. Ralph worked out of the house as a freelance journalist, while your job took you out of the country for weeks at a time. You had so-called "broad and liberal" visitation; indeed, Ralph has never attempted to deny you the right to see your two sons whenever you wished. Tonight, Ralph telephones to say that his lover is moving in with him and the kids. The real difficulty, however, arises when he calmly informs you that his lover's name is Harry.

An attempt to modify custody after the divorce depends upon a myriad of circumstances. Parents change, as do the needs of the children. No two cases are ever alike. What results in a change of custody for one father will not assure a court-ordered change for another. Again, the best interests doctrine plays a major role. A father may originally have wanted no part of his infant son, but now that the boy is 8, he thinks it would be great to have him around. A mother finds it increasingly more difficult to say goodbye to her daughter at the end of every summer visitation. As genuine as such feelings may be, they may not be enough to get a change of custody. When we discuss in greater detail the trauma of a custody proceeding, it will become apparent that the parent who approaches the process cavalierly is doomed to disappointment and failure. Even more importantly, the commencement of a change of custody proceeding puts your child in the middle of major conflict. Can you be sure that your child can handle it?

Sometimes a parent wishes only to change the original custodial arrangement to permit joint legal custody. Ten years ago it was just assumed that the mother would get exclusive custody of the children and take care of all the day-to-day problems of raising a child. John never questioned the scheme of things way back then. But over the last few years, he has seen that many of his divorced co-workers have been afforded the legal right to share in all major child-rearing decisions with their former spouses. Whenever John attempts to offer a suggestion regarding his child's upbringing, his ex-wife Jean resists. "I'm the mother; I have custody; I make the decisions." She repeats this refrain so many times that it has become almost a freakish nursery rhyme.

John has had enough; he consults with a lawyer. His aim is to get joint legal custody so that he can discharge his duties as a parent in a more meaningful, practical way—a way that he truly believes can only inure to the child's benefit.

"I'm not looking for a major battle," he says. "I only want the right to share in my child's life, to help make some of the decisions that a parent is supposed to make."

His lawyer explains that approximately 30 states have already passed some form of joint custody legislation. In some, there is a legal presumption in favor of granting initial joint legal custody. In others, the state leaves it to the judge's discretion. Unfortunately, John's state does not have a formal statute of this type. "Even if we did have a joint custody law," explains his lawyer, "you would still be forced to make a formal application because these laws are relatively new and none that I know of affect a custody award obtained ten years ago, like yours."

"What do I do? I've been trying to get my ex to agree on this thing for over two years. She just refuses to be reasonable."

John is told that he must commence a change of custody proceeding. Although no joint custody statute has been enacted in his state, his lawyer advises him that the judge has the discretion to order his ex to permit him consultation and decision-making rights.

"The good news, John, is that there is a noticeable trend in this direction. Although an actual proceeding must be commenced, it seems to me that you can accumulate more than enough evidence to show that a joint legal custody arrangement is in the best interests of your child."

We emphasize that you are reading this book at the right time. Courts have become much more receptive to change of custody requests that are brought in good faith and remain in the best interests of the child. We have seen too many fathers attempt to change custody after the divorce because of some complicated ego-related reasons. Let's get something straight at the outset: this is not a popularity contest. With your children in the middle, an ill-advised and selfishly motivated custody fight can only wreak havoc in their lives.

Even in those relatively few cases where the change of custody poses no undue legal complexities and the ultimate result appears obvious to all, the children are often unintentionally victimized. We will show you how to properly present your argument if you find yourself in a situation that demands a post-divorce change of custody. No system is perfect, but if the best interests of your child remain of paramount concern, the probability of success is greatly increased.

CHAPTER ELEVEN

Enforcing Visitation Rights

LINDA PACE WAS watching *Miami Vice* when her doorbell rang. Although it was a bit late for someone to be dropping in unannounced, she immediately got up from the sofa to answer the door. "Who is it," she called out as she grasped the latch.

"Police," an anonymous male voice answered.

Linda's immediate reaction was to think that the person at the door was using the police routine as a ruse to gain entry. The neighborhood was changing, but she never thought that a burglar would be so brazen, or think her so stupid.

The person outside apparently sensed her hesitancy and called out again, "Mrs. Pace, it's the police. Please open up. We have a warrant for your arrest."

"A what?" She stifled a scream. Yet even as the words were being spoken, Linda was moving quickly to her left in order to look out the dining room window. What she saw made her blood run cold, and as she moved back to the closed door, it felt like she was walking in slow motion. Sure enough, two uniformed policemen stood outside her door. The squad car was clearly visible in the driveway.

"Open up. Now." This last demand from a huskier voice, obviously the second officer.

Linda unclasped the latch and swung the door open. Immediately, the two policemen were standing in the foyer. "This is a joke, right? You're going to sing me a telegram or something." Linda's voice had taken on a strange, singsong lilt.

"Sorry ma'am." Already the cop was pulling a yellow sheet of paper from his inside jacket pocket.

As she watched, the other man made sure of her identity. "You *are* Linda Pace. Correct?"

"Yes, yes I am. But what is this all about? Do you know I have an eight-year-old boy sleeping upstairs?"

The officer with the yellow paper began to read in bored, clipped sentences. "You, Linda Pace, are under arrest. You have the right to remain . . ."

Linda didn't hear the rest. She knew that she was being read her rights, and at one point she had to swallow back a hysterical giggle. It really *was* just like television. The policeman was finally winding down. "This warrant of arrest is being issued on account of your willful violation of a court order of visitation obtained by Martin Pace, your former husband. You will now accompany us to the stationhouse for processing."

"What about my son? What's . . ."

Before she could finish, the huskier voiced policeman responded. "Ma'am. Mr. Pace is sitting in our squad car. As soon as you get your things, we will call him into the house, and he will take your son home with him for the evening. Standard procedure, ma'am."

The rest of the evening was a continuation of the slow-motion nightmare that had begun with the doorbell. She was brought to the stationhouse and booked just like a common criminal. She was permitted to call her lawyer, but she was unable to reach him. She was told that in a few hours she would be taken to the criminal court to be officially arraigned on the charge of violating an existing visitation order. Throughout her ordeal, Linda Pace could think of only one thing: she had been arrested. Incarcerated. Jailed. Here she was a college graduate and mother, and her hands were dirty from the ink pad used to take her fingerprints. This couldn't be happening. She would wake up any minute.

* * *

Linda's arrest is not a dream sequence or an exaggerated, cautionary tale. It is real. And we could be talking about you if you take it upon yourself to deny your ex his proper and lawful visitation rights. Judicial enforcement of visitation rights has increased dramatically over the last few years. States are virtually unanimous in their avowed goal to see that noncustodial parents are able to interact freely with their children after the divorce if there is no valid reason why they should not. Indeed, the judicial emphasis being placed on the protection of visitation rights has caused a veritable revolution in the area of post-divorce enforcement.

Before discussing the panoply of judicial devices that are used to enforce a non-custodial parent's visitation rights—including the gradual increase in arrest warrants—we must start with the visitation right itself. How does it come about; how is it defined? The legal right to be with your child arises from your parental status. As we have consistently noted throughout this book, such status is not extinguished by virtue of the divorce decree. As a parent you have an absolute right to maintain contact with your child after the divorce. But it is not an unfettered right. The law recognizes that certain practical accommodations have to be made when the parents are living in two households. A child cannot be in two places at one time; hence, the concept of "visitation."

Visitation is not a perfect system. Not by a long shot. But besides those rather rare situations where the parents share equal physical contact with their child, a visitation plan provides the only viable alternative to bedlam. While all of the psychologists and judges agree that a child benefits from continued and consistent interaction with the non-custodial parent, these same people also recognize that the child's custodial environment must be kept as stable as possible. This means that no matter how much a father loves his son, he cannot drop by at 2 in the morning to see if the kid is having a good night's sleep. Most post-divorce situations call for some kind of organized arrangement—not because such necessary schedule is the *best* answer to parent-child development, but because for most it remains the only practical solution.

Competing interests are obvious. On the one hand, the custodial parent must be afforded the flexibility to make a post-divorce life for herself. On the other hand, the non-custodial parent must be permitted enough quantitative time to maintain meaningful contact with the child. These goals sometimes conflict. The custodial parent has started dating another man; she is looking forward to the weekend trip that has been planned for some time now. On Thursday evening, her ex telephones to say that something has come up, and he cannot take the child for the weekend. It is indeed a short trip from keen disappointment to bitter resentment. Conversely, the noncustodial parent is told at the last minute that the boy's grandparents are visiting from out of state. The weekend visitation is no longe practical, and his former spouse begs him to understand and forego his parenting time for another 7 days.

Nor are the parents the only players in situations of this sort. How do you deal with the daughter whose recent enrollment in dancing school conflicts with your treasured midweek visits? What good is scheduled visitation when the participants outgrow it? We are not talking about a modification of visitation issue. This topic will be discussed in the next chapter. At this juncture we wish only to underscore that inherent complexities exist regarding parenting time that have nothing whatsoever to do with enforcement-related problems. That is the underlying reason why most divorce decrees contain a formalized schedule defining visitation rights. It is not that a judge believes that the non-custodial parent's visitation must be automatically limited because the child does not live with him. Rather, such schedule results from the practical recognition that "a right that is defined is a right that is more capable of ready enforcement."

Some divorced couples find that they have no need for set visitation schedules. These couples rely on an understanding that one or the other will be afforded "broad and liberal visitation." It is then up to the parents to define the parameters of their particular arrangement. But we have found that even the most cooperative and flexible couples find that before too long they are following a set schedule. It might not be rigidly defined, but on the basis of pure practicalities a pattern soon emerges.

The majority of divorced couples, however, have a divorce decree that contains a specifically defined visitation arrangement. Typically, the visitation period envisions weekend visits by the non-custodial parent combined with weekday, holiday and summer parenting time with the child. In situations such as these, the post-divorce visitation right is apparent. So long as both parents abide by the schedule, no enforcement issues will arise. The problem, of course, rears its ugly head when the right of visitation is interrupted, restricted or hampered in some manner.

Sometimes a visitation violation is not as clear-cut as one might think. David and Marilyn have been divorced for 3 years. Their children, Judy and Mark, are 8 and 11, respectively. They reside with Marilyn, and David visits with the kids on alternate weekends and has 3 consecutive weeks during the summer. For the last year and a half, David has also visited with his older son on Wednesday nights.

One day Marilyn informs her ex that she has enrolled Mark in a community swimming program. You guessed it, the classes are held on Monday and Wednesday evenings. David becomes enraged; "She is attempting some kind of power play," he tells a receptive ear at the plant.

David vows that he will not let Marilyn get away with this "violation of visitation." He has recently read a magazine article that relates how violating mothers are now subject to arrest. The idea of his former wife in prison stripes makes him smile.

Have his rights been violated?

No way. All visitation enforcement issues start with the underlying divorce decree. It is this original court judgment that defines the particular visitation right at issue. It does not matter that the parties have "modified" the original parenting time through subsequent conduct. Self-modification is no modification. In David's case, he conveniently forgot that the original decree did not specify a midweek visit. While it is true that Marilyn accommodated him for a year and a half, such accommodation was based upon an informal understanding. It did not result in any actual change to the original visitation order. Therefore, Marilyn's conduct was not in violation of any formal visitation right.

Let us assume for the moment that David's original court order *did* give him the midweek visitation. With this factual change in our illustration, can it be said with certainty that Marilyn's enrollment of her son in a swimming program represents a clear visitation violation? Not necessarily. There are more than enough willful and intentional denials of visitation that need immediate court attention. The conflict between David and Marilyn is petty and insignificant when weighed against the thousands who are being systematically cut off from their children by vindictive custodial parents.

Therefore, even if we assumed that the divorce court had originally ordered a Wednesday evening visitation, Marilyn's conduct is not the type of violation that cries out for enforcement relief. Indeed, this illustration comes from an actual case. After the hearing, the judge had no difficulty in denying enforcement relief to David, noting:

- The father could still see his son during the swimming program if he wished.
- The father never attempted to obtain his ex's permission to see his son on another midweek evening.
- The child expressed a sincere desire to enroll in the swimming program, and many of his friends were likewise involved.
- The program itself was temporary in nature. The father's visitation would be adversely affected for a period of no more than 12 weeks—assuming that the parties could not reach a compromise regarding another interim midweek visitation.
- The mother was not willfully violating any order. In fact, she openly encouraged the father to visit with the child after swimming lessons were over for the evening.
- Significantly, the court made an independent evaluation that, all things considered, the community-run program was in the child's best interests even though it temporarily interfered with visitation.
- Finally, the court ruled that David's application was frivolous and unnecessary, and therefore ordered him to pay Marilyn's legal fees.

Ironically, by the time the judge rendered his decision, Mark's swimming program had concluded; the original visitation was back in effect.

In short, David's legal action was "much ado about nothing." Only in this case, David was playing craps with his son's psychological well-being. A visitation enforcement proceeding is not to be taken lightly. If you trigger the mechanism, you should be damn sure that your rights are actually being violated and that all other steps have been taken to keep the matter out of court.

So throughout the rest of this chapter, when we discuss the various enforcement devices available to a non-custodial parent who is being denied visitation we will be assuming that:

1. The visitation rights stem from the actual language contained in the original divorce decree or court stipulation.
2. The custodial parent's violation of the visitation rights is clear, without justification and maliciously motivated, and there is no possibility of the parties resolving the problem between themselves.

We have rarely seen a case where the custodial parent does not put forth some excuse, that is *affirmative defense*, when visitation enforcement is sought. Often these excuses are lame, to say the least. Recently we represented a father who was attempting to enforce his visitation rights. Our client's former spouse had defended her conduct by claiming that the boys were allowed to watch too much TV when they were with him. Score one for the non-custodial parent! In another case that we know of, the excuse was that the father always allowed the children to eat Hostess Twinkies for breakfast. The mother defended her visitation denial by affirmatively alleging that their "nutritional requirements are being ignored and violated."

The custodial parent is simply not permitted to use visitation as a weapon or a means of making a statement. Such conduct is simply not in anyone's best interests. Nor may the custodial parent use the children as vindictive ammunition or for emotional blackmail. For example, we know of many cases where the denial of visitation springs from the custodial parent's disapproval of the former spouse's new love interest. These parents often don't even realize that their jealousy has spawned an unnecessary legal battle.

In all of the illustrations that we have just used, the common thread remains an *unjustified* denial of parenting time. But sometimes justification itself is a difficult concept to define. The custodial parent may honestly think the interference is a legitimate response. Let us say that you have missed a few child support payments. Or perhaps your child has raised a question in your ex's mind that he is being left unsupervised or even neglected during his times with you. How about the situation where the child simply refuses to leave your ex-wife's side and grows hysterical at the thought of being with you during visitation? These examples serve to underscore several crucial points. First, a visitation enforcement issue rarely arises in a vacuum. Just when you think you have an airtight case, your ex affirmatively defends her conduct by claiming that you have not been paying child support. Many times, a proceeding to enforce visitation is met with a counter-petition to modify the very arrangement you seek to enforce. In short, the issues are often comingled and muddied by self-serving or even legitimate defenses and countercharges.

It is easy to advise custodial parents not to allow emotions to dictate their actions regarding visitation rights. However, our words may run right past a parent who has been forced to apply for food stamps because her ex has ignored his child support obligation for the last 4 months and then shows up on the doorstep to see the child. At the same time, judges must acknowledge that *both* parents may be emotionally involved. A father is 2 days late in paying child support, only to find that his ex refuses to let him see the child. In response, he misses the next child support payment entirely. Not too surprisingly, his parenting time is thwarted again. And the vicious cycle continues, with both parents testifying in court that it was the other's "fault" that matters have escalated the way that they have.

Because of all these grey areas and fuzzy definitions, the courts have created certain general rules when dealing with visitation enforcement claims.

1. Resorting to what lawyers refer to as "self-help," or taking matters into one's own hands, is greatly discouraged. In other words, the custodial parent cannot unilaterally decide to deny visitation, even when such individual feels entirely justified in doing so.
2. Similarly, the non-custodial parent cannot play the "money game" and refuse to pay child support in response to a visitation violation.
3. In either of the above situations, the parent is affirmatively charged with the duty to petition the court for visitation or child support enforcement, as the case may be. As we will see, courts have become more willing to *link* the obligations to pay child support with the right to exercise visitation—or vice-versa.
4. In true emergency situations, such as when physical or sexual abuse is evidenced, you are certainly not expected to blithely turn over your child to the non-custodial parent for further torment. However, it is imperative that any resort to self-help be combined with an *immediate* application to the court for an order suspending or restricting the visitation in issue.
5. Custodial parents are not only legally obligated to comply with the original visitation order, but they must openly *encourage* such parenting time.

This last point forms the foundation upon which virtually the entire visitation enforcement procedure is built. Judges are getting tough, not because they have discovered a new cause, but as a result of a gradual awareness that the child's post-divorce readjustment is quicker and healthier if contact is preserved between the child and the non-custodial parent. Just as importantly, the most recent studies point to the inescapable conclusion that the child's overall mental, psychological and even physical health are positively affected *for the long term* when the child maintains a pattern of consistent interaction with both parents after the breakup.

There may also be some judicial self-interest involved. Other studies have shown that non-custodial parents who regularly visit with their children are several times more likely to continue paying child support. Judges realize that such encouragement may very well eliminate the chances of seeing the same parties again in a support enforcement proceeding.

So if you are being denied visitation, you should not hesitate to enforce your rights. However, the direction you take should be toward the courthouse steps. The violation of your rights may be hard to take. We understand that you are angry, even thinking of revenge. But you must stifle those emotions. Whatever advantage you may have had in court will be lost if you resort to self-help, such as nonpayment of child support.

THE ENFORCEMENT ARSENAL

If you are being denied your rightful visitation, you may be entitled to all or some of the following enforcement relief:

1. An order of contempt against your ex
2. An order of protection requiring compliance with visitation
3. An order suspending the payment of child support until visitation is permitted
4. An order fining your former spouse in an amount that ranges anywhere from $500 to $5,000—and up
5. The civil arrest of your ex-spouse
6. A permanent or temporary change of physical custody in your favor

In most cases, the court deals with a visitation enforcement situation on a two-step basis. Assuming that enforcement is warranted, the court will initially direct immediate compliance with the underlying visitation order contained in the parties' divorce decree. The language utilized in such orders is generally provisional, anticipating the second step.

CIRCUIT COURT: STATE OF FLORIDA
FAMILY DIVISION: BROWARD COUNTY

. . . . X

FREDERICK LYONS,
                  PETITIONER,   Docket No.: 473/86
     -against-   **ORDER**

   SUZANNE LYONS,
                RESPONDENT.

. . . . X

WHEREAS, petitioner has petitioned this Court for enforcement of certain visitation rights contained in the parties' divorce decree dated September 15, 1982, and duly entered in the County Clerk's Office of this jurisdiction; and

WHEREAS, respondent has appeared and offered a defense in connection with this proceeding; and

WHEREAS, this Court after due deliberation finds in favor of the petitioner;

NOW, THEREFORE, respondent is hereby:

ORDERED to permit and provide visitation of the parties' child to petitioner, as set forth in the judgment of divorce dated September 15, 1982, commencing forthwith; and it is further

ORDERED, that respondent's failure to comply with this directive shall be deemed a contempt of court punishable by fine or imprisonment, or both; and it is finally

ORDERED, that this Court retains jurisdiction over this matter to make any other rulings, findings or determinations that may be in the child's best interest, and upon good cause shown, including without limitation modification of custody.

E N T E R:

S/ _____
Justice John E. H. Firestone

Dated: October 6, 1986

Fred Lyons has obtained what the courts often call a *provisional order.* This means that the court directive is self-triggering: that it provides the preliminary basis for later, and more drastic, enforcement relief which is said to have already been "provisionally" granted. If the non-custodial parent is forced back into court because of further interference with his visitation, the judge will not hesitate to trigger one of the six enforcement devices listed above.

Before showing you how these enforcement tools work, we should briefly describe the procedure which must first be completed before you are entitled to use them against your former spouse. We are, of course, talking about the visitation enforcement hearing. This may be a good time to review Chapter 4; we will assume that you now have a working knowledge of those basic elements that are common to all situations where an individual is seeking to enforce his or her rights in court.

When it comes to a violation of visitation, many of you will be able to enforce your parenting time without hiring an attorney. As we will see in a moment, the procedure is relatively simple, and your burden of proof is far from complex. However, a good many visitation proceedings may start out easily enough, but because of issues that are later raised by the violating spouse, the going can become a bit rough. You may find yourself in over your head, at which point you should not hesitate to ask for a postponement in order to find an attorney to represent you.

For example, you have just put in your case, having testified to your ex's unjustified refusal to let you see your son. The direct examination went well; you followed the instructions that we gave to Elizabeth in Chapter 4, and your preparation was superb. The lawyer representing your ex-spouse was unable to rattle you during cross-examination. You had anticipated some of the questions, and you were ready with succinct, responsive answers. The judge asks whether "petitioner rests." You answer affirmatively and settle back to see what your former spouse has to say about things.

She gets on the stand and readily admits that she has not allowed you to see your boy for the last 4 months running. But she explains that the only reason that the problem has arisen is because the child adamantly refuses to go anywhere near you. Her lawyer then makes an oral application that the child be interviewed by the judge immediately and intimates that visitation has become psychologically harmful to your son. The judge grants the application and orders that your 5-year-old child be brought to court that afternoon so that he may interview the boy alone in chambers.

The case has suddenly turned sour. When you first heard the lawyer's application you were absolutely confident that your son would not corroborate his mother's statements. Suddenly, your confidence wanes; you are forced to recognize that there has been absolutely no contact for the last 4 months. You think it is possible that your ex could have used this time to poison the child's mind, filling him with all kinds of hateful lies and distortions. Panic sets in; you don't know what to do.

Now is the time to request a short postponement of the proceeding to permit you the opportunity to seek legal counsel. In virtually all cases, the judge or hearing officer will be most amenable to this application. Even if after getting the postponement you decide that you have overreacted and continue to go it alone, the interruption will have allowed you time to make the decision free from courtroom anxieties and insecurities.

In our example, the judge immediately acquiesced to your request and adjourned the proceeding for one week. Obviously, the afternoon interview with your child was similarly adjourned until the proceeding was to be reconvened. In this particular case, you consulted with several lawyers. Although they stood ready to represent you, the consultations were all that you needed. On the next court date you are ready, and when the judge asks why you are not sitting with a lawyer, you are able to confidently respond.

"If it please the court, I appreciate the postponement and opportunity to retain my own lawyer. During this past week, I have consulted with several attorneys. On the basis of their advice, I am confident that I can continue to represent myself."

The judge scrutinizes you for a minute. You feel your renewed confidence oozing out of your body like melting butter from a brown bag. "Are you absolutely sure, sir? I will not be so permissive regarding any future requests for postponements for the reasons made last week. Do you understand?"

Taking a deep breath and telling yourself to remain calm, you reply. "I do, your Honor. And based upon my talking the matter over with other lawyers, I would ask the Court at this point in time to entertain an oral application."

"An application? If I recall, I advised that an interview with your son was warranted."

Your ex-wife's lawyer immediately chimes in. "That's right, Judge. And we have the child waiting outside with his aunt right now."

The judge turns impatiently to you. "Well, what is your application. I think we have wasted enough time here."

This last remark sets your teeth on edge. Have you worn out your welcome? Another deep breath and then you plunge. "My application is a request that this court assign a lawyer to represent my son. I believe that during the time when I have been unjustifiably refused access to my boy, the respondent may have been consciously or unconsciously manipulating the child." You hesitate for a moment to organize your thoughts.

"Please continue," the judge says with what you perceive to be renewed interest.

"Well, I just believe the child should have someone objective to talk to. If my son is being pressured to make statements against me or conduct himself in a certain way, then a person not connected to either parent will more likely get to the bottom of all this. Your Honor, I can't believe that my child would suddenly turn against me in only 4 months. I was advised during one of my consultations last week that this jurisdiction recognizes that, under appropriate circumstances, the child may have independent representation."

"You are entirely correct," the judge says.

Before your ex's attorney can get to his feet to make an objection, the judge explains that he will review a blind list of domestic relations lawyers that has been compiled for this very contingency and set up a meeting between child and lawyer the very next day. In the meantime, the judge will not conduct his interview with the child, choosing to wait until he is in receipt of the written report to be submitted by the child's attorney after your son and his appointed counsel meet with one another without interference from either parent.

Our illustration raises several important points. *First,* let's not forget our original emphasis: if you feel out of your depth at any point during the visitation enforcement proceeding, do not hesitate to retain counsel. While we believe that the information contained in this chapter will permit many of you to undertake the enforcement of your visitation rights on your own, we also recognize that unanticipated circumstances may arise that require professional assistance. *Second,* our illustration highlights our initial observation that enforcement issues rarely exist in a vacuum. Even though the custodial parent readily admitted her interference with her ex's parenting time, she had no trouble in confusing matters by raising the specter of the child's psychological welfare. *Third,* we saw the judge use an increasingly more common and favored post-divorce procedure. This occurred when he directed that an attorney be assigned to represent the child. This attorney is generally referred to as the legal *guardian* or *guardian ad litem* to the child.

RUNNING WITH THE BALL

Just like the situation where a person is owed child support and seeks enforcement of the monetary obligation, the parent attempting to enforce visitation must start with the underlying divorce decree or settlement agreement. In this document your visitation rights were specifically defined, and from this definition springs your ability to seek enforcement relief. Remember, there are two elements to your claim: (1) the visitation right and (2) the violation or interference with such right.

As in the case with money enforcement, the first element is easy to prove. At the hearing, you will merely submit, that is, *introduce,* a certified or authenticated copy of the prior court order or agreement as your first evidentiary exhibit. That part is easy; you have now established your visitation right. Your next step is to prove that the right has been violated. Generally, this will entail a narrative description during your direct testimony of how your attempts to see your child have been thwarted. Sometimes you may be lucky and be able to produce a witness or two to verify that your parenting time has been prevented. Far more frequently, a witness will be unavailable; the hearing comes down to her word against yours. That is why we recommend that you don't push the enforcement button prematurely, rushing into court after only one frustrating visitation experience. Instead, repress your impulse and let some time pass— time that we call the *period of preparation.* During these agonizing days you will:

- Immediately begin keeping a daily diary. Log the time and place of your attempted visits as well as the particular interference that was used against you.
- This diary should also include a record of any other contacts that you have attempted, such as telephone calls, postcards or other mailings.
- Give yourself a time limitation that anticipates that you will be forced to suffer for at least 6 weeks or 3 consecutive missed visits. Only when your ex's conduct can be said to be an obvious and consistent interference will a court take your petition for enforcement seriously. The key here is to give the custodial parent enough rope to hang herself.
- While you are attempting to maintain contact with your child, make sure to stay in touch with your ex, if possible. Again, we urge that the two of you try to accommodate each other before you seek formal legal enforcement. At the hearing, most judges will want to hear some evidence that you have first attempted to solve your visitation problems without resorting to courtroom drama.
- If practical, have a friend, relative or other trusted individual accompany you to the custodial home during your scheduled visitation. This person will be able to testify that your attempt to see your child was in fact frustrated. Your witness will be able to corroborate and describe the particular ploy that was used to deny you the rightful parenting time. Sometimes it is nothing more than a locked house and refusal to come to the door. Other parents are more "creative," hiding the children at a neighbor's while swearing that they are in their room recovering from some virulent childhood disease.
- As bad as your ex's conduct becomes during this "period of preparation," *your* actions must be beyond reproach. Remember, the courts discourage self-help, so make sure that you continue to fulfill your obligations to the letter. If child support is due on Monday of each week, see that it gets there. And not on Tuesday! In short, take away every possible excuse to which your ex may resort in defending her unjustified refusal to allow you to exercise your visitation.
- Closely tied to our advice that you continue to fulfill *your* court ordered obligations, is our equally strong recommendation that you maintain meticulous records of your actions in this regard. Keep all of your bank statements and canceled checks as proof positive that you've continued to pay child support on time. These records will be crucial if you are forced at trial to rebut any unfounded allegations of nonpayment.
- Lastly, write your ex a letter; something that looks like this and contains the following information:

May 13, 1986

Mrs. Eleanor Glass
215 Victoria Road
Freehold, North Dakota

RE: *DENIAL OF VISITATION*

Dear Eleanor,

It has now been three weeks since you have allowed me to see the children. Each time that I have sought to exercise visitation as per our original divorce judgment, I have met with interference and resistance. It has been one excuse after another.

You have offered no justifiable reason for denying me access to my son and daughter. While I have been fulfilling all of my monetary obligations to both you and the children, you have been violating my court ordered visitation rights.

The purpose of this letter is two-fold. First, I want to emphasize my desire to resolve this problem between us through civilized discussion. I will meet and talk with you at any time that is convenient for you.

Second, you should know that if you continue to interfere with my contact with the children, I will have no other choice but to seek judicial enforcement of my rights. I trust that this step will not be necessary, and I look forward to hearing from you immediately upon your receipt of this letter so that we may discuss this intolerable situation at greater length.

Of course, should you refuse my request and continue with your present conduct, I will petition the court for enforcement relief, without further notice to you.

Yours truly,

Joseph Glass

Before mailing your letter, don't overlook the obvious. Make sure that you have retained a copy for yourself. This copy should be either a xerox or a carbon; writing the letter over in longhand is not only a waste of time, but it will be subjected to too many questions when you seek to introduce it at the hearing.

Many of you will jump to the conclusion that the letter must be forwarded to your ex by registered or certified mail, return receipt requested. This is not necessary. And besides, your former spouse can still always claim that she never received the letter. All she has to do is refuse to sign for it. Instead, you should utilize a little known post office procedure which will result in your getting "proof of mailing." All you do is bring the letter to the post office and ask the clerk to give you a proof of mailing certificate. This is a small receipt which is postmarked at the same time that the letter is. The receipt verifies that you have mailed directly from the post office a letter addressed to your former spouse; it is then assumed that the United States Postal Service did its job and got the letter to her. Meanwhile, you retain the receipt, the cost of which is less than a dollar.

The purpose of the letter is to buttress your claim that the interference to your visitation has been unjustified. This correspondence will be introduced as an exhibit during your direct case. The scenario will go something like this:

YOU: . . . and when another week passed, I wrote a letter to my ex-wife, I mean the respondent, and told her that she was leaving me no alternative but to bring on this proceeding.

JUDGE: Did you keep a copy of this correspondence?

YOU: Yes, your Honor, and before asking that it be received into evidence, I would like to read into the record certain portions of my letter. [Reads the relevant portions].

JUDGE: Are you offering it as an exhibit, now?

YOU: Yes, your Honor.

JUDGE: Show it to Mr. Bramble [your ex's lawyer].

MR. BRAMBLE: [Reviews copy of letter with his client] Your Honor, I have been advised by my client that she never received this letter. I do note, for the record, that the petitioner has not indicated that it was forwarded by registered or certified mail.

JUDGE: How was it mailed, sir?

YOU: By ordinary mail, but—

MR. BRAMBLE: [Interrupting] I object to it being put into evidence. He could have manufactured a copy of this letter for this hearing. My client insists that she never received any correspondence from her former spouse during the period in question.

YOU: If I may, your Honor. At the time that I mailed the letter, I received this proof of mailing certificate from the post office. May I introduce it as my next exhibit, your Honor?

JUDGE: Certainly.

YOU: Thank you, sir. [Handing the certificate over to the court officer while trying to keep a straight face as you watch the judge glare at your adversary who attempts some muddled words of apology for the "confusion."]

Even if you don't get to spring the proof of mailing trap—which by the way has determined the outcome of more than one trial—the letter is still an important part of your burden of proof. A judge will correctly assume that a letter written before the commencement of an actual enforcement proceeding is to be given credible weight. Moreover, you will find that judges psychologically approve of tangible evidence. If you say that your visitation was being violated, and in addition you have correspondence dated prior to the proceeding which tends to verify your claims, the court will take you that much more seriously. In the battle of your word against hers, every little bit helps.

* * *

So far, so good. You have used the period of preparation to your advantage, and now the inevitable is upon you. You are ready to commence a visitation enforcement proceeding. Your first step is to contact the Family Division of your jurisdiction's court system. As we have discussed, each state has developed its own judicial hierarchy; the majority of states continue to deal with post-divorce related issues in the equivalent of their Family Court. Indeed, you will find that most states have a particular unit within the Family Court that is devoted exclusively to post-divorce visitation and custody issues. The clerks are trained to assist you in the drafting of the necessary petition which gives your ex notice of your enforcement claim.

A petition for visitation enforcement must contain the following information, so follow this checklist closely, making sure that you have all the data at your fingertips. As willing as court personnel may be to assist you in your endeavor, the majority remain overburdened with a multitude of duties and a staggering case load. Anticipating the questions that they will ask will not only make the going a lot easier, but it will virtually assure that your case is taken seriously from the get go. Your petition will contain, and you must provide, the following:

- Your full name, address and social security number
- The custodial parent's full name, address and social security number, if you know it
- Each child's full name and date of birth
- The date of your divorce, and the county and state where it was obtained
- An accurate description of your original visitation rights as either defined in your divorce decree or prior agreement that was incorporated in such judgment of divorce
- Information pertaining to any subsequent *court* or *written consensual* modifications to your original visitation schedule, including the date of such formal modification and the location of the court that handled the matter
- A description of the conduct giving rise to your petition, including the date and times of your ex's interference and the specific efforts you have made to exercise your visitation
- The custodial parent's place of employment, if any
- Copies (most states require certified or authenticated copies) of the divorce judgment and agreements pertaining to visitation, if applicable. Of course, you should also bring copies of any subsequent court orders that modified or amended your original visitation rights.

After the petition is drafted, sworn to and delivered, the custodial parent has the opportunity to submit her *answer,* or as it is sometimes called, a *responsive pleading.* In such document, your former spouse is obligated to either admit or deny allegations of visitation interference. The answer also provides the custodian with the procedural vehicle to explain, that is, defend, the conduct giving rise to the enforcement proceeding. This is done by way of an *affirmative defense.* The most common affirmative defenses are nonpayment of child support, physical or psychological neglect, or the child's alleged refusal to cooperate. Don't be daunted by frivolous defenses or even outright misrepresentations. Take solace from the fact that, as in the case of money enforcement, an affirmative defense must be proved by the person asserting it.

Upon receipt of the petition, the custodial parent also has the right to *cross-petition* for various relief, such as a modification of the existing visitation arrangement or, in extreme cases, a complete termination of parenting time. We will defer a discussion of visitation modification for the next chapter. However, in regard to a situation where complete termination of visitation is at issue, we offer the following observations:

- Total denial of visitation to a natural parent is the most drastic remedy that a court can fashion.

- Such termination occurs only when, by convincing evidence, it is substantially uncontroverted that the visitation at issue is "clearly detrimental" to the child's welfare.
- Stated another way, only in the most "extraordinary circumstances" will a non-custodial parent's visitation rights be terminated.
- Do not confuse the term *suspended* with *terminated.* In the first instance, a judge may believe that a temporary discontinuance is in the child's best interests. In the latter case, parenting time is vitiated entirely.
- Because every state "jealously protects" the visitation rights of a non-custodial parent, total termination of such rights will generally only surface when physical or sexual abuse is proved by convincing evidence, when the child has been neglected to such a degree that he or she has been placed in serious danger, or when the non-custodial parent has, in the first instance, attempted or succeeded in an extra-jurisdictional child snatching.
- And even in these three extreme situations, the courts will continually endeavor to arrive at a solution which anticipates renewal of visitation at some future time.

After the petition and answer or cross-petition have been exchanged between the parties, the matter is put on the hearing calendar. Visitation enforcement proceedings are given preference; the court will try its best to schedule the trial as quickly as possible. But the system is not perfect. In large urban areas, delay is unavoidable. Generally, you will be forced to grit your teeth and bear it.

However, in those cases where the hearing will not occur because of circumstances beyond your control, such as unavoidable court backlog, you may request a pre-hearing conference. The case *Warren Phillips v. Patricia Phillips* illustrates the point nicely.

Warren's petition claimed that he had been unjustifiably denied his visitation with the children for the last 8 months. While he had succeeded in maintaining intermittent contact with them during this time, the visits had been few and far between. Patricia had affirmatively defended by contending that the children were "traumatized" by visitation with their father.

On the petition, the clerk had set the hearing date for November 2nd. Both parents show up on that date, only to find that they are number 63 on the hearing calendar. It is obvious to Warren that most of the cases are being adjourned to dates well in the future. He watches several fathers whose cases are called before his merely hanging their heads in apathetic resignation when they are advised by the judge that their hearings must be postponed for another 4 to 6 weeks.

Warren, however, has taken our advice, and when his case is called he knows just what to do to cut through the logjam. As he and his former wife approach the bench, the judge is already looking down at his desk calendar, muttering to himself about the chronic shortage of judges and hearing officers. He looks at the parties. "I'm sorry. If you've been sitting here in this courtroom this morning, I guess you know our problem. It looks like this matter cannot be heard until the second week in January."

This is Warren's cue. "Judge, I have no objection to the postponement. I realize that the system is grossly overburdened. However, I do have an application to make, if the Court pleases."

The judge peers over his reading glasses, and Warren continues.

"I ask that a pre-hearing conference be scheduled immediately. My ex-wife's responsive pleading puts forward absolutely no justification or affirmative defense for her continued refusal to let me see my children. And her cross-petition to modify my present visitation is, in my respectful opinion, extremely weak. The longer this intolerable situation goes on, the harder it is for the children."

"Your application is granted. At the end of my second call of the calendar I will announce your case again, and we will speak in my chambers. Please make sure that you do not leave the courthouse, ma'am," he says to your ex.

Two interminable hours later, Warren gets his pre-hearing conference. The judge listens to both sides and agrees that Patricia hasn't been able to reveal any sound reasons for her consistent interference with visitation. About the best that she can say in her defense is that Warren has missed or been late with a couple of child support payments during the last year or so. Her cross-petition to limit Warren's parenting time to once a month is similarly without any apparent legal merit or practical basis. Under these circumstances, the judge will not permit Patricia to avoid the inevitable and avail herself of any advantage occasioned by the court backlog. The pre-hearing conference concludes with the judge signing a "short form" order that expressly directs immediate compliance with Warren's visitation rights pending final judicial determination.

As each parent gets a copy of the document, the judge warns Patricia that further noncompliance will not be tolerated. Of course, he is also constrained to remind Warren that such order is "without prejudice" to any findings that the trial judge may make at the hearing in connection with Patricia's cross-petition for visitation modification.

As is apparent, the focus of the pre-hearing conference is to maintain the status quo pending the trial. Even when the custodial parent has countered with a cross-petition of her own, you are generally entitled to have your original order recognized. Any change to the existing visitation arrangement will necessarily await the denial or granting of the relief requested in the cross-petition. Many lawyers also utilize the pre-hearing procedure to obtain temporary court directives that help them prepare for the trial, such as a directive that the parents and child undergo psychiatric evaluation, a directive that a legal guardian be appointed to represent the child, or some other like request.

So if you find yourself in a predicament like Warren's, do not curse the court system. Instead, request a pre-hearing conference. It may not occur on the same day, but it may get you to a receptive ear sooner than the court calendar can.

THE TRIAL

Your job at the hearing is simply to convince the judge that you have been denied visitation and therefore are entitled to enforcement relief. Again, the preparation advice contained in chapter 4 should be reviewed. The same rules will apply in the visitation enforcement arena.

In your situation, however, the credibility issue looms even larger. When it comes to child support, a judge can rightly expect that there will be documentary evidence such as bank records and canceled checks to rely upon in making the ultimate determination. With child visitation, documentary evidence is usually a much scarcer commodity. That is the purpose of the "period of preparation" discussed earlier in this chapter. The more tangible evidence that you can collect, the better.

Let's assume that you are in the middle of your direct testimony. As the issues have become more crystallized, it appears that your ex's defense is based almost entirely on her claim that no interference has occurred. She argues that you have been the one who has failed to come around during the scheduled visitation periods. On this basis, she has cross-petitioned for a modification seeking to limit your parenting time because "he doesn't even use the time he has, your Honor." You have just testified to the trials and tribulations that you endured in your futile attempt to see the children.

YOU/PETITIONER:	. . . And when it became clear that her interference was continuing, I began keeping a diary. I noted every time I tried telephoning and all the times that I came around the house to exercise my visitation. May I have it introduced as an exhibit, your Honor?
JUDGE:	You kept this record daily, you say?
YOU/PETITIONER:	Just about, sir. There were some days that I got home so late from work that no calls were made. And as you saw from my first exhibit, my visitation is supposed to be every weekend, as well as alternate Tuesdays and Thursdays. My diary will show that on my days, I always attempted to exercise visitation.
JUDGE:	Under the circumstances, I will accept this log-book as petitioner's next exhibit. Please continue with your testimony.
YOU/PETITIONER:	Your Honor, at this time I would also like to introduce my telephone bills for the months of April through and including the July statement. The respondent lives in the next county, so I am charged for a toll call every time I telephone to the house. I have underlined in red magic marker the applicable calls. On an average I telephoned no less than three or four times a week during these last several months. You will also see that most of my calls lasted less than twenty seconds. That is because the respondent usually hung up on me when I asked to speak to the children.
	[The telephone bills are offered and accepted as another exhibit.]
YOU/PETITIONER:	I also have a copy of two letters that I mailed to the respondent, with a certificate of proof of mailing attached to each copy. These letters describe the visitation problems that I was having at the time, as well as my continued readiness to reach some kind of compromise with my ex-wife.

Get the picture? Like the inexorable spring flooding of the banks of the Nile, the introduction of documentary evidence during your direct testimony has significantly buttressed your case. In so doing, your ex's credibility has been virtually washed up in the flotsam of her own vindictive lies.

During a visitation enforcement proceeding, as in all cases where the child remains the central issue, certain ancillary procedures often come into play. For example, the judge may use his or her discretion to interview the child alone, outside of the courtroom. Usually this occurs in the judge's chambers, although we know of situations where the child has been interviewed in the court library or cafeteria. The idea is to place the child in an atmosphere as free from anxiety and pressure as possible. You can count on the interview process occurring when the custodial parent has raised the issue that parenting time has traumatized the child in some way. Such a claim is usually made in support of a petition to modify visitation, but you will also see it asserted when the custodial parent is seeking to justify the visitation denial.

As mentioned earlier, another common procedure is to appoint a legal guardian to represent the child's interests during the proceeding. All states maintain a list of attorneys who are willing to serve in such capacity. Separate representation for the child is a definite trend in most states. Indeed, a handful of jurisdictions have already made such appointments mandatory in visitation and custody controversies. The idea behind the appointment of a legal guardian is to permit the child to speak with an objective individual. Most children find it extremely difficult to articulate their views to parents who are in the midst of battling for custody. Obviously the child does not want to alienate either of them; many children end up saying what they think their mother or father wants to hear. In addition, a legal guardian makes parental manipulation more difficult; such occurrences are more likely to be discovered if the child has his own lawyer with whom to discuss matters.

The child (and parents in many cases) may also be ordered to undergo psychiatric or other professional evaluation. Again, such procedure usually occurs only when the custodial parent has placed the child's welfare in issue in response to the other parent's attempt to enforce visitation. The point to remember is that these ancillary court services are becoming increasingly more familiar landmarks against the horizon of visitation enforcement proceedings. So don't think yourself unique or your case weak if the judge employs these various procedures. Their purpose is merely to assist the court in reaching its final determination and to help clarify the child's best interests.

A SHORT BUT IMPORTANT DETOUR: GRANDPARENTS' RIGHTS

One of the most heartening legal trends in the area of visitation enforcement is the recognition of grandparents' rights. As one enlightened judge said, "Visits with a grandparent are often a precious part of a child's experience, and there are benefits which devolve upon the grandchild which he cannot derive from any other relationship." This growing humanistic approach has resulted in the enactment of legislation in many states that expressly gives grandparents the right to visit with their grandchildren even after the divorce. The states that have not yet promulgated a specific grandparent visitation statute will, nevertheless, judicially recognize the right on an ever-increasing basis.

Simply stated, grandparents may enforce their visitation rights in the exact same manner as the non-custodial parent. Because the right in the vast majority of cases, however, has not been specifically defined by prior court order, the judge will first have to determine an appropriate visitation arrangement. This schedule will be based upon a variety of circumstances existing at the time application is made. Such factors as the age and health of the grandparents, as well as the child's availability and preference will be considered. This will necessarily entail either testimony taken from the grandchildren or a private judicial interview.

Usually, the custodial parent's interference with grandparent visitation is the result of overt sabotage. Needless to say, it is usually the parents of the non-custodial spouse whose rights are being thwarted, although there have been cases where estranged parents of the *custodial* spouse have sought court assistance.

Sometimes, the difficulty exists because of a complete lack of desire or interest on the part of the children to see their grandparents. In either case, the judge maintains absolute discretion to define and then enforce appropriate grandparent–grandchild visitation contact. While a child's wishes will be considered, it will not be wholly determinative of the visitation issue. We know of at least one case where the custodial parent truthfully stated that she had never stood between the children and their grandparents, advancing the claim that the teenage children were "too busy with their other activities to visit with their grandparents." In fact, at the hearing, the teenagers verified that they simply did not feel compelled to see their father's parents. Nevertheless, the court made an independent evaluation of what would be in the children's "best interests" and ordered once-a-month visitation.

So if you are a grandparent, you have as much legal standing as anyone to insist upon continued contact with your grandchildren. Indeed, some states have gone so far as to permit visitation even though the grandchildren have been formally adopted by the custodial parent's new spouse, as often occurs after the death of the natural parent. Our advice: Don't hesitate to seek judicial enforcement if you are being denied your right to continue to share in your grandchild's post-divorce life.

WINNER TAKES ALL

As we saw at the beginning of this chapter, a non-custodial parent who is being denied visitation without cause or justification has a potent arsenal of enforcement weapons. All post-divorce enforcement necessarily starts with the original court order, or divorce judgment. Because you already have such an order even before you trigger the visitation enforcement proceeding, the court must fashion some relief to insure compliance, while minimizing the possibility that you will be forced back into court in the future to litigate another visitation-related problem. Simply stated, judges are getting tougher.

By necessity, virtually all of the enforcement devices are punitive in nature. Some refer to it as a system of reward and punishment. At any rate, you cannot get what you don't ask for, so review the list of enforcement devices on page 207 of this chapter and be sure to request the appropriate sanctions at the beginning and close of your enforcement proceeding.

Monetary Fines

Monetary fines are generally given to you when it is clear that your visitation has been maliciously or vindictively thwarted. In other words, the judge will penalize custodial parents if there has been no viable excuse offered for the interference. The court figures that if you hurt them in their pocketbook, they may not be so quick to violate visitation in the future.

These monetary penalties are generally seen in two guises. Some judges will order the custodial parent to contribute to your attorneys' fees. Even when you have represented yourself, the judge recognizes that your legal efforts have been time consuming and may have possibly resulted in lost earnings. Hence, the court will enter an order such as this:

> ORDERED, that respondent shall pay unto the petitioner the sum of ONE THOUSAND ($1,000.00) DOLLARS as and for attorneys' fees; said sum to be paid within sixty (60) days from the date of entry of this Order.

Other judges will merely direct your ex to pay you a sum of money, characterizing such payment as a "monetary fine and penalty for willfully and intentionally interfering with petitioner's visitation rights." It obviously does not matter what the court calls your payment. A dollar in your wallet does not know whether it is an attorney's fee or a monetary fine! The point remains: Ask for the penalty and prove unjustifiable interference with visitation, and many judges will make it worth your financial while.

The Linkage Order

There is a growing body of case law that holds that the court may direct that support from a father be suspended if visitation is unreasonably withheld or denied. As is apparent, the concept *links* the support obligation with the freedom to exercise rightful visitation; thus the term *linkage order.* Some important observations and comments should be made:

- The linkage concept is not a signal that frustrated non-custodial parents can automatically withhold child support on their own when experiencing interference with visitation. In virtually all situations, you need the court's permission *before* this enforcement mechanism may be triggered. As one judge recently stated, "By not paying his child support, the father has in effect taken the law into his own hands, and such behavior is to be condemned, not condoned."

- Having just provided you with the general rule, we must tell you that a handful of judges have actually approved self-help by allowing the withholding of support even without a prior linkage order. The state of California seems to have taken the lead in this regard, but we still urge all of you on the West Coast to proceed with extreme caution. Play it safe, and get the order first.

- Although the trend is definitely toward greater acceptance of linkage orders, some judges do have difficulty with the entire concept. If you think about it, the withholding of child support because of the custodial parent's deprivation of visitation poses a cruel dilemma. Often the child has nothing whatsoever to do with the visitation violation. The interference is due solely to the caprices of the custodial parent. Meanwhile, the child's continued welfare may be tied indivisibly to the custodial parent's continued receipt of economic support. The linkage order may unintentionally result in another family slipping below the poverty line.

- Because of these competing interests, courts will grant linkage orders only on a case-by-case basis. While a judge may recognize his power to terminate support in response to visitation denial, he may be hesitant to utilize it when he feels that the only outcome will be to punish the child.

Civil Arrest

We now come full circle, returning to the saga of Linda Pace described at the beginning of this chapter. How did she get into such a predicament? How ready are judges to incarcerate mothers or fathers who frustrate the other parent's visitation rights?

The answer to the second question is that civil arrest for visitation violators represents the largest and fastest growing trend in this entire post-divorce enforcement area. In fact, there are at least two different procedural routes that result in the custodial parent's arrest. Specifically, incarceration may result from the violation of either a provisional *order of contempt* or an *order of protection.* Let's take both situations in turn, starting with the latter.

Order of Protection

We know; you thought that orders of protection were only given to battered wives. Indeed, the original purpose of such orders was to insure that the police would not hesitate to interfere with marital disputes when necessary, as in the case of physical assault. We say "hesitate" because without such a court order, police most often refuse to get involved in domestic free-for-alls. The order of protection device serves the needs of an abused or threatened spouse nicely. Generally, the spouse obtains a specific court directive that the offending party must abstain, refrain from and cease all forms of harassment, abuse, menacing or other threatening conduct—or face a fine or imprisonment.

No one knows for sure when the order of protection device was expanded to include visitation violations. But expand, it has. Typically, the order of protection will be given to a non-custodial parent at the end of the enforcement proceeding if the judge rules in his or her favor. Although the phraseology may vary from state to state, the following language is common and lies at the heart of virtually all orders of protection that are utilized to trigger the arrest of the offending party:

NOW, THEREFORE, upon all the papers and proceedings had herein, it is

ORDERED, that the respondent/custodial parent shall observe the following conditions of behavior:

1. Comply with all orders of visitation running in favor of petitioner;
2. Abstain from direct or indirect interference with said visitation;
3. Affirmatively permit petitioner's children, to wit: ANDREW CARVER and EVA CARVER, to be with and visit the petitioner on [dates supplied from original divorce decree];
4. Cease any and all forms of interference with petitioner's visitation as herein above defined and actively encourage the exercise of same;

And it is further

ORDERED, that the directions herein shall be and remain in force until subsequent order of this Court; and it is further

ORDERED, that the Clerk of the Court shall file a copy of this Order and any amendments thereto, with the appropriate police agency having jurisdiction in this matter.

The order of protection usually includes a warning in large boldface type, such as this one:

**A VIOLATION OF THIS ORDER MAY BE
PUNISHABLE BY A FINE OF AS MUCH
AS $2,000 OR BY CONFINEMENT IN
JAIL FOR AS LONG AS SIX (6) MONTHS OR BOTH**

Just like in the situation of an abused spouse, this order of protection is self-triggering. Upon continued violation of his visitation rights, a father (or mother, as the case may be) can telephone the police and press charges for the violation of an existing court order. As word gets around, more precincts are willing to arrest the custodial parent in situations where there has been willful, noncompliance with an order of protection affirmatively directing that visitation occur. And as you have probably guessed, this is exactly what happened to Linda Pace.

Order of Contempt

Technically, the disobedience of any court order results in a contempt of court. When you receive a notice demanding that you serve on jury duty, your failure to show up is as much a contempt as a custodial parent's withholding of visitation in violation of a court's previous directive. The difference is the degree to which the court will tolerate the figurative slap to its face and flouting of its authority. Obviously, our judicial system is more willing to punish violators in the second category! And this willingness is becoming increasingly more pervasive. Disobedience in the area of parenting time equals contempt that, in turn, equals possible arrest and imprisonment—the reality of it, not just the threat.

Basically, there is little difference between an order of protection and an order of contempt. However, in the latter case contempt is usually not as self-triggering or automatically enforceable. You cannot automatically summon the police to assist you in your efforts to see the children. You must go back into court and affirmatively move for what is known as a *warrant of confinement* that is then served on the local sheriff or police department to execute.

We must be honest, though. A warrant of confinement is the last judicial resort. On the other hand, with the increasing tendency to take a hard line against visitation violators, we believe that the contempt enforcement device remains an important weapon in your arsenal.

The Ultimate Sanction

Tabitha had found herself a named respondent in her ex's visitation enforcement proceeding no less than 4 times over the last 2 years. Stephen, her former husband, had won every case, but his experience had been bitter and frustrating. Each time, Tabitha had been unable to defend her conduct and each time, the judge had affirmatively directed that visitation be permitted as originally envisioned by the divorce decree. After the hearing Tabitha would permit visitation again, but within 2 or 3 months, the situation would revert to consistent interference once again.

Stephen would be forced to start the whole thing over; his ex seemed to flourish in a courtroom environment. At the conclusion of the last hearing, only 3 months ago, Stephen had been optimistic. The judge had given him a linkage order and suspended his child support obligation until he was permitted to see his kids. No luck. Interference continued; Tabitha didn't seem to care that the child was going without. After a few months, Stephen broke down and began sending child support despite the fact that he was still being denied visitation. He went back into court for the fifth time.

Now what? How far can the court go when faced with a totally recalcitrant parent?

The answer is a modification of custody. When the custodial parent's actions demonstrate such a callous disregard for both the court system and the child's welfare, the judge may deem such person unfit and change custody to the non-custodial parent. Indeed, interference with visitation is one of the more important factors that gives rise to custody modification proceedings. We discuss this topic fully in Chapter 14. In Stephen's case, the custody change was effectuated within one short week.

Alas, we know all too well that for many non-custodial parents a change of custody is simply out of the question. It remains impractical. You are working 9 hours a day; a modification of the existing custody arrangement is, unfortunately, wholly unworkable.

However, the ultimate sanction, as we call it, remains a viable solution to many. When you can demonstrate a pattern of long-term and consistent visitation interference, coupled with repeated violations of court orders by your former spouse, the court may order that physical custody of the child be turned over to you. Needless to say, such a ruling presupposes that you have the practical ability to offer custodial supervision to the child. Moreover, regardless of the extent of the visitation interference, the judge must still find that any modification of custody is in the child's best interests.

OUT-OF-STATE CONFLICTS

Disruption of visitation commonly arises when the custodial parent changes her residence and that of the child to an out-of-state location. Obviously, such conduct thwarts your right to visitation like no other. The flip side of the coin is, of course, when the non-custodial parent moves the child out of state, giving rise to a *custody* enforcement proceeding.

Because the procedure is basically the same when enforcing either visitation or custody across state lines, we will defer our discussion until Chapter 13. If an unwarranted move outside of the state has made a mockery of your original court-ordered visitation rights, you are then permitted to trigger the Uniform Child Custody Jurisdiction Act. This legislative enactment, which has been adopted by all fifty states, expressly includes the situation where a parent is seeking to enforce visitation. In other words, the Act does not apply only to *custody* enforcement situations.

Rather than repeat ourselves unnecessarily, we ask that you turn to the portion of Chapter 13 that explores this Act and all of its legal ramifications. You will find that your visitation rights may be enforced even though the child is halfway across the country. The system is far from perfect, but judges will bend over backwards to rearrange your visitation so that the move does not result in a loss of meaningful child contact.

We strongly recommend that if you learn that your former spouse is about to leave the jurisdiction, *and* if nothing practical can be worked out between you, an immediate enforcement proceeding be commenced in your state before she leaves. There have been such cases that have ultimately resulted in one of the following:

• Parent denied the right to leave and retain custody at the same time
• Child support obligation reduced to offset the anticipated cost of travel expenses for visitation
• Visitation restructured to provide the non-custodial parent with longer intervals
• Custody awarded to the non-custodial parent because the court determines the move is against the best interests of the children.

Normally, these proceedings are begun by an order to show cause that contains a *temporary restraining order* that forbids the custodial parent from moving until the dispute is determined by the court.

THE UNWANTED CHILD

With all the positive information contained in this chapter, we certainly do not want to burst the bubble. But there is an unfortunate situation that warrants some discussion. We are talking about the non-custodial parent who refuses to exercise his visitation rights. It must seem ironic to read about those fathers who are fighting so hard to maintain contact with their child, when your ex-spouse has taken the completely different route of turning his back on his family.

We wish we could provide you with a simple solution to your problem. The issue, however, is not really a legal one. Under our judicial system, a court cannot force a man to be a father against his will. This makes good sense. Even if a court were somehow able to force a non-custodial parent to exercise visitation (which it cannot), such a judicial ultimatum would have severely detrimental consequences for both adult and child. You may be quite able to enforce your child support and maintenance obligations, but you cannot make your ex magically appear during his scheduled visitation periods. The father who refuses to exercise parenting time while maintaining his financial obligations is, and remains, beyond the reach of the law. Pure and simple.

The only practical advice that we can provide is for you not to give up. Don't write the non-custodial parent off. Continue to exert efforts to get your ex to see the error of his ways. Occasionally a father will initially distance himself from his family after the divorce in order to lick his psychological wounds. A few months or even a year later this individual may be sufficiently stabilized to re-enter his child's life. By maintaining or attempting contact during this "distancing" period, as painful as it might be, you can maximize the chance of this occurring.

CHAPTER TWELVE

Modifying Visitation Rights

No CHILD VISITATION arrangement can possibly foresee every post-divorce circumstance or predicament that may arise. The needs of the parents and child change as time goes by. A schedule that was created when your daughter was an infant will not suffice when she is a teenager going to "Sweet Sixteen" parties. The rigid visitation plan of yesteryear must give way to a more flexible approach.

Or the parents may have started with a broad, play-it-by-ear visitation arrangement that worked extremely well during the years immediately following the divorce. Eight or nine years later, such pervasive flexibility must become more defined and regimented. The custodial parent has remarried; the kids are in school all day; and your just dropping in unannounced no longer works. So in your situation, the flexibility of yesteryear gives way to a more rigid and defined approach.

This chapter is about modifying your original visitation order so that it more properly reflects existing circumstances. Whether the circumstances be tangible, such as a relocation to a more distant residence, or intangible, such as the psychological needs of the child, a court is fully empowered to change the visitation that was first awarded or agreed upon at the time of the divorce. When it comes to modifying visitation, the "best interests" doctrine reigns supreme. If a judge believes that increased (or decreased) parenting time will positively impact on the child, the modification petition will be granted.

As a general rule, the court's analysis when faced with a visitation modification demand is four-fold:

1. The judge will review the existing visitation arrangement. This review will include all prior modifications that may have been ordered after the divorce.
2. Judges will familiarize themselves with and fully explore all of the factual circumstances which give rise to the claim that modification is warranted.
3. The court will ask itself whether the anticipated modification can be properly effectuated on a purely practical basis. Requesting the change and being able to accept the responsibilities that go along with it are two entirely different things.
4. The judge will make an independent evaluation regarding the best interests of the child. The non-custodial parent may present an excellent argument in support of the request for modification, and he or she may be in a position to put the new plan into effect immediately, but if the judge feels that such change is not in the best interests of the child, it will not be ordered.

In virtually every state, the parent seeking the change must prove two things. The first requirement mandates a significant showing of "substantial changed circumstances." The second prerequisite is that the modification remains in the child's best interests. Only when *both* factors are present will a judge be amenable to changing the existing arrangement. Again, we are dealing with a court's predisposition to maintain the status quo. As you will learn from reading Chapter 14, which is devoted to *custody* modifications, one of the hardest hurdles to overcome is the general reticence on the part of the judge to disturb the present arrangement, whether such arrangement relates to parenting time or physical custody.

However, when it comes to a modification of visitation—as opposed to a demand that custody be changed—the court is generally more willing to entertain the request. The reason for this view is based on the simple observation that changes to visitation are less disruptive than a change in custody. So all you have to do is seek and ye shall get. Right? Not quite.

There is another predisposition that must be taken into account, one which is uniquely peculiar to visitation modification issues and which represents another hurdle for petitioning parents to overcome. We are referring to an almost universal belief among judges that parents should be able to resolve post-divorce visitation questions on their own. Therefore, when formal modification proceedings are launched, the court has a natural hesitancy to entertain the application. They simply reason that there are a lot more important problems to be judicially resolved. Where an *enforcement* of visitation issue will be acted upon with all due dispatch, the *modification* of visitation is treated more like a distant cousin. We are certainly not implying that a judge will refuse to hear your case or deny your modification request merely because he or she does not enjoy presiding over visitation-related cases. On the other hand, this judicial resistance may surface in any number of ways. For example, the judge may put both parents under enormous pressure to settle the case prior to trial.

It has been 3 years since their divorce, and Bryan and Allison remain barely civil to one another. Why mince words? They hate each other with a passion. Amazingly, their 5-year-old daughter Dawn is happy and extremely well adjusted. At the time of the divorce, the parents agreed to a joint legal custody arrangement, with Dawn to reside primarily with her mother. Although desiring more time with his child, Bryan's work schedule allowed him only the typical alternate weekend visitation arrangement.

Approximately a year ago, Bryan changed careers. He became a local sales representative for a large carpeting concern. Although he must attend out-of-state sales conferences 3 times a year, his hours and employment schedule are a good deal more flexible than they were at the time of the divorce. Meanwhile, troubles with Allison are unabated. She has never gone so far as to openly interfere with his weekend visitation, but she hasn't actively cooperated either.

The stage is set. Six weeks ago, Bryan telephoned his ex-wife and asked her for an enlargement of his parenting time. He reminded her that the two of them shared equal responsibility in making child-rearing decisions and that he truly believed that Dawn would benefit from seeing him more often. Bryan particularly stressed his keen desire to visit with Dawn a couple of evenings during the week at her home. He told Allison that he didn't relish his role as weekend father "in charge of fun and games"; he wanted to be with Dawn in a different setting, help her with school assignments and generally be a larger presence in her life.

Allison turned him down cold. She said that she could not abide the thought of Bryan visiting their child in the former marital residence. She argued that she had a right to her own privacy; that the requested enlargement would throw the two of them together in an environment where he "no longer had a place." Allison told Bryan that, in her opinion, Dawn was too young to adapt to mid-week visitation and that their child's life would be unduly disrupted. The conversation ended on the usual note of unresolved bitterness and rancor.

The next day Bryan went to the Family Division of the Superior Court to file a visitation modification petition. Now 6 weeks later the parents are in court waiting to see the judge for the first time. Justice Marvin B. Stryker is known for his no-nonsense approach. He calls Bryan and Allison to the bench.

"I see that you both are representing yourselves. Am I correct?"

The parents both nod their heads in affirmance.

"Speak up, and show some respect. I don't understand sign language. My question calls for a verbal response so that the court reporter can obtain a clear record of these proceedings. Do I make myself clear?"

"Yes," both parents reply.

Justice Stryker turns to the court reporter. "Bob, don't bother with the rest of this. I am going to have an off the record discussion with these people." Then turning to Bryan and his ex-wife, the judge motions them closer to the bench so that his words are not overheard by the other litigants milling about in the courtroom waiting for their cases to be called.

"Look," he begins. "Before we get a hearing officer involved, I just want to know one thing. Have you discussed a possible settlement or compromise between yourselves?"

The parties then tell the judge the substance of their telephone conversation when Bryan first broached the subject. They are forced to admit that no other discussions have occurred. It doesn't take a mind reader to glean that Justice Stryker is fuming.

He turns to Bryan. "That's it? One conversation and you run into court like some little crybaby." Fixing his gaze on Allison, he says quickly, "Don't look so smug, young lady. It seems to me that his original request wasn't so unreasonable."

The judge then informs the chastened litigants that he is putting the case down for a "second call," and that he will summon them to the bench in approximately an hour. In the meantime, he directs them to put aside their pettiness and come up with a solution that is in their child's best interests. He emphasizes that should no settlement be reached on this "trivial question," he will personally see to it that he is appointed the presiding judge at the trial. It is fairly obvious that Bryan and Allison are more afraid of the judge's wrath than they are of each other. They walk out of the courtroom in agreement for the first time in years: "That Judge Stryker is one mean bastard."

Needless to say, the parties do succeed in reaching an accommodation. While Bryan wanted two evenings per week, he settles for one night. The parents agree that they will reevaluate the visitation plan again in 6 months in order to determine how it has affected their daughter. They reenter the courtroom; the case is called again and they report their progress to the judge. He is delighted and flashes them both a smile that more than hints that his earlier demeanor may have been an act designed to frighten them into affirmative action. And as they leave the courtroom, Bryan and Allison both acknowledge that they momentarily lost sight of the bottom line: their 5-year-old daughter's best interests.

The lesson to be learned from this illustration is that divorced couples must strive to keep a modification of visitation issue out of court. Your goal should be to create a visitation arrangement that promotes meaningful contact with the child by *both* parents. In an effort to assist couples to achieve this all-important goal, we have devised a three-phase plan that has been most successful in providing the foundation upon which a suitable settlement can be built. We call it the "Stretch Program" because it forces the parents to widen their approach to the issue. In this way, the combatants are forced to jettison their self-limiting arguments in favor of a more elastic stance.

THE STRETCH PROGRAM

We will assume for the following discussion that you are the non-custodial parent wishing to enlarge your post-divorce parenting time. As we will see later in this chapter, the custodial parent sometimes requests that the visitation schedule be decreased or restricted. At any rate, the Stretch Program is suited to either contingency. We choose only to focus on the enlargement issue because it is seen far more often in visitation modification proceedings than a demand for some type of limitation. With these preliminary comments in mind, we turn to our three-pronged approach:

Phase I. *Maneuver for a face to face meeting.*
Phase II. *Agree that you are talking about the child, not yourselves.*
Phase III. *Talk child contact, not visitation schedule.*

Let's take each of the three elements in turn. Phase I has been forged from our professional experience that the telephone encourages a multitude of sins. It is easy for your ex to take an unreasonable position when he or she does not have to look you in the eye, when there are miles of telephone wires separating you and when your respective arguments are being made by disembodied voices. Demand a personal meeting to discuss the problem at hand. We think that you should be ready to go to great lengths to ensure that such a meeting actually comes off. If it entails a bus or plane ticket, think of it as an investment in your child's well-being.

No matter how bitter the divorce process, a personal conference emphasizes the one thing that the court could not take away from either of you: your status as parents. It is not the divorce nor the visitation problem that you have in common. Rather, it is parenthood that firmly establishes your commonality of purpose. Having reaffirmed your joint status as parents through personal interaction, you are now ready to enter Phase II.

This second level represents the nerve center of our three-phase program. Because our premise is so simple and basic, it is often overlooked. Unless you focus your discussions on the proper subject, *the child,* you run the risk of your meeting deteriorating into name calling and useless recriminations. At the outset, it must be absolutely clear that you are meeting to discuss the child. If you keep your eye on this "ball" you will minimize the chance of being drawn into a rehash of old disputes and irrelevant digressions. The purpose of your conference is not to reopen psychic wounds. You are there to work out a compromise regarding your good faith desire to see more of your child.

Having subtly shifted the emphasis from a talk that is focused on each other's motives to that which is properly centered upon the child's best interests, you are now ready to tackle the nuts and bolts of your particular problem. This is where you trigger Phase III of the Stretch Program. Let's say that you are requesting another 2 weeks of consecutive parenting time to be exercised during the child's summer vacation. Your approach must be positive, not negative. What do we mean? Well, the easiest way to demonstrate our point is for you to listen in on two conferences. In both, the issue remains the same: an extra 2 weeks during the summer with 8-year-old Paul. However, our first father argues negatively, while the second father takes a different tack.

FATHER NO. 1: What about me? Aren't I entitled to see my son a little bit more? Summertime is perfect. I get two whole weeks off. Is it too much to ask for another fourteen days with Paul when I have a chance to be with him full time? A judge would see it my way.

Father No. 1 is discussing the issue from an entirely self-centered approach. With each sentence, his negativism becomes more apparent. Not only does he subtly attempt to make his ex feel guilty, but his argument leaves absolutely no room for further negotiation. And his last comment implicitly threatens legal action. Now let's see Father No. 2 in action.

FATHER NO. 2: I think that we can agree that our son is at the age where a male influence is important. Weekend visits are fine, but they don't really give Paul enough time to be himself. We try to pack so much into each weekend that at the end of the day we're both too tired to get into any serious discussions—well, you know, about things that boys and fathers talk about. I think the summertime would be perfect for the two of us to get to know each other a little bit better.

The second father never argued a schedule. Instead, he emphasized parent–child contact. Nor did he put himself at the center of the universe.

It was his son who would benefit from an enlargement of parenting time. Finally, he did not offer his ex an ultimatum or threaten to take her to court. He made it easy for her to "save face" by "agreeing" to only 1 week, not 2. This enables Paul's father to perhaps negotiate for 10 days or an arrangement where visitation enlargement could proceed on a gradual basis, 1 week this summer, 2 weeks the next and maybe even 3 within a short time after that.

Our Stretch Program has worked for many of our clients who initially stormed into our office with war drums beating. By positively focusing on the child, you expand the possibilities of settlement. The same enlargement process occurs when you emphasize the benefits of increased contact, as opposed to an increase that is measured in days or weeks. It is easy to say no to a calendar. It is harder to deny a non-custodial parent more contact with his child. Finally, don't underestimate the importance of a face-to-face meeting. Voices are one thing; parents attempting to resolve a problem together are quite another.

* * *

Not all visitation modification problems are amenable to negotiated settlement. Sometimes it is the inherent complexities to be found in the controversy itself; other times it is the inability of the parents to shed the defensive armor of their past. Whatever the cause, a failure to reach a compromise results in either one of two things happening: (1) the parent requesting the modification simply gives up or (2) the parent commences a formal post-divorce proceeding.

The rest of this chapter will discuss the latter situation. At the outset, however, it is crucial for you to understand the factors that result in a modification of visitation being ordered by the court. No use going forward with a legal hearing if you have absolutely no basis or chance of success. In other words, we wish more parents would "give up" before triggering the court system. Of course, we are talking about those of you who want visitation changed for no valid reason. You know who you are. We have no tolerance for parents who are willing to put their children in the middle of a court battle that did not really have to be waged.

Using the four-prong approach discussed at the beginning of this chapter, a judge will determine whether the visitation modification should be ordered. Any number of legitimate factors may arise after the divorce, which warrant some fine tuning of your existing arrangement. Many of the same factual elements that determine whether a change of custody should occur will also apply when a court is faced with a demand that visitation be modified. As we will explore in Chapter 14, some factors are more important than others. Generally, the same priority system that is detailed in Chapter 14 applies with equal validity to visitation cases.

Some additional observations and comments are in order. To begin with, the child's stated preference that visitation be enlarged will carry a great deal of weight. While such preference is never determinative of a change of *custody* petition, the child's wishes can be more easily accommodated when it comes to a request that *parenting time* be increased. The child's preference factor, therefore, is sometimes determinative of the modification problem. Of course, the "best interests" doctrine is never lurking far behind; if the court believes that despite the child's desires there will be no benefit to modifying the original visitation award, the judge will not be controlled by the child's stated preference.

It is also important to reemphasize that a visitation modification rarely arises in a pure form. Most often, it is coupled with countercharges and affirmative defenses asserted by the other parent. For example, the custodial parent may be moving to another part of the state—200 miles away from your house. You seek enforcement of the existing visitation arrangement. Your ex counters with a petition for modification. This is a very typical, factual scenario. Indeed, the change of residence syndrome affects the visitation modification question so greatly that it must be given its own sub-heading.

CHANGING THE RESIDENCE

If the custodial parent moves away with the child, visitation is thrown into disarray. You will learn in Chapter 14 that an unnecessary change of residence by your ex-spouse gives you a legal basis to petition for a change of custody. The theory is that a parent who unilaterally disrupts visitation in such a callous fashion is signaling a general incapacity and unfitness to carry on in his or her supervisory role. But let's assume that you are in no position to accept primary physical custody of your child. Similarly, let us say for the sake of argument that your ex has legitimate and well-meaning reasons for leaving the present locale. What happens to your parenting time in these situations?

Obviously, some modification to the existing arrangement must occur. Do we have to say it again? The first step that you take is to attempt to reach a negotiated compromise with the custodial parent. When it comes time to propose an out-of-court solution, these possibilities may work for you:

- Request extended and consecutive periods of time during the child's school or summer vacations. We know many fathers who are able to arrange for their children to be with them the entire summer. This extended parenting time allows the non-custodial parent to reestablish meaningful contact and permits the kids to visit with grandparents and old friends who they haven't seen for a while.
- A possible reduction in child support or maintenance may permit you to save enough funds to buy plane tickets, pay hotel bills and meet other expenses that may be necessary to maintain reasonable child contact. Tell your ex that you will still be paying the support, except that it will be going into a bank account to be used for the reasons just mentioned.
- As a corollary to the above point, you may ask your ex to contribute to the out-of-pocket expenses that will necessarily be incurred for travel, hotels and even long distance telephone calls.
- Make sure that your ex provides your name and address to the child's new school so that all progress reports, report cards and the like may be forwarded directly to you.
- You will also ask for the custodial parent's agreement to disclose any future moves at least 60 days before it is to occur. In this way, you will have

the opportunity to negotiate further changes to the visitation schedule should circumstances dictate.

- Request greater overall flexibility in any modified schedule that the two of you come up with. For example, if you unexpectedly find yourself with a 4-day weekend or a business trip to the child's new residence, there should be no question that, upon reasonable prior notice, you get a chance to take advantage of your good luck, availing yourself of this unexpected opportunity to exercise visitation.

This checklist is not meant to be exhaustive. It merely offers some typical alternatives that you may overlook when fighting to maintain contact with your child. Assuming that you and your ex are able to reach an understanding, your work is not yet done. In order to fully protect your rights and ensure that the modified visitation will be legally enforceable, you should see to it that the original divorce judgment is amended; that the present visitation schedule is replaced by the new one. The procedure is simple, just follow these steps:

1. Reduce your understanding to a formal writing, or *stipulation*. This document acknowledges the agreement, and it provides the court with the basis for amending the visitation schedule. The changed visitation arrangement described in your stipulation is then incorporated within a new, "amended" divorce judgment. We provide you with a sample stipulation on page 236.

2. You and your ex will sign three or four copies of this stipulation. One is for your ex, one is for you, and the others are for court filing. You will take the document to the court clerk where either you or your spouse reside. Preferably the stipulation should be delivered to the court that originally issued your divorce decree, which is called the "originating court."

3. If your divorce was obtained out of state, then you must get a copy of such decree authenticated from the originating court directly. This only takes a letter of request and appropriate court fee, usually no more than $20. Be sure to enclose with your request a self-addressed stamped envelope. Upon your receipt of the authenticated copy, you file it in the county clerk's office where either you or your ex reside, just like in Step 2. Your court will treat the authenticated copy of the divorce as if it were a judgment originally obtained from a judge sitting in one of the courtrooms upstairs as opposed to an out-of-state jurisdiction.

4. You will show the stipulation to the clerk, and ask him or her to submit the document directly to the appropriate judge so that an amended decree may be issued. Some jurisdictions may require that *you* prepare the amended decree for the judge's signature; other courts will do the necessary drafting on your behalf. If you will be required to submit the proposed amended decree, you should ask the clerk for the "official form" in this regard.

5. Some courts do not have such official form for you to copy. In such a situation, you will have to improvise. Perhaps you can ask the clerk to provide you with a *redacted copy* of a divorce judgment that has been successfully amended by someone else. The term "redacted" refers to a process where a copy of the judgment is made for your review but only after the names, addresses and other identifying characterizations have been deleted.

6. Assuming your paperwork has been properly completed and accepted by the clerk, you will hand him or her a self-addressed stamped enve-

lope. This will insure that once your modified visitation stipulation has been incorporated within an amended divorce decree, you will thereafter receive a copy of the judgment signed by the judge. Don't despair if it isn't comfortably nestled in your mailbox after only a few days; the process often takes 6 weeks, depending upon the county in which you file.

THE STIPULATION

The basic purpose of the stipulation is to minimize confusion. What better statement of intent than a formal writing? In addition, you officially acknowledge that both parents have consented that the modified visitation stipulation be incorporated within the original judgment of divorce. Upon such incorporation, you now have an *amended* divorce judgment. It is this mutual consent that is the key to your being able to obtain the court order of modification without going through a formal hearing. However, one crucial point must be emphasized. The court always retains the discretion to call the parents into court so that an independent evaluation may be made regarding the proposed modification of visitation and how it impacts on the child's best interests. Although this is rather rare when the parents have submitted a signed stipulation, you should not be rattled if you receive a postcard summoning you to court to explain the new visitation arrangement in greater detail. The reason may be most innocuous.

Raymond had been initially taken aback when his ex-wife, Sheila, had informed him that she and the kids were moving out of state. It seemed that Sheila had been offered a position as vice president in her company's home office, about five-hundred miles across state lines. As she explained it, such relocation was the only way that she could continue to move up the "corporate ladder," and she just could not afford to give up this once-in-a-career opportunity.

After his initial surprise and anxiety had abated, Raymond was able to work out a new visitation schedule that called for extended vacation periods with the children, as well as a reduction in his child support. Indeed, with Sheila's increased earnings, she agreed to pay for 50 percent of the travel expenses to be incurred by the children when they visited their father. Raymond and Sheila signed a written stipulation memorializing their agreement and filed the necessary papers with the court, requesting that their original divorce decree be modified to reflect the new visitation arrangement. The clerk had accepted the papers and assured Raymond that he should expect no problem and would probably receive a copy of the amended decree within "a few weeks."

Instead, about 10 days later, Raymond received a notice in the mail requesting that he appear in court the following week at a "Special Term Part 9-A; Room 372, in connection with a hearing to amend a divorce decree, dated and entered February 16, 1982." He immediately telephoned his ex, and she informed him that she had also received such notice to appear in court.

On the designated day, they arrived a few minutes apart and found themselves directed to a small courtroom where a trial actually seemed to be in progress. They both took seats in the back. Both were obviously confused and frightened, and they were just about to call everything off when the judge interrupted the trial and called them to the bench. As they approached, they heard the judge tell one of the lawyers that "this next matter won't take more than 5 minutes; we will reconvene at 10:40."

Raymond didn't know whether such news was encouraging or not. Did it mean that they would be given short shrift and told that they had overstepped some unknown legal boundary?

The judge began. "The court takes notice of an application before it to modify an existing divorce decree to include a changed visitation schedule. Do I state the case correctly?"

"That is correct, your Honor," Raymond replied.

"The purpose of my issuing a notice for your personal appearance is to satisfy myself of one thing. Has the non-custodial parent's consent to the modified visitation been freely given?" He looked directly at Raymond.

"Yes it has, Sir."

"Fine. I will sign the proposed amended decree, and you may pick up your respective copies directly from the clerk's office in about a week. Thank you for coming; as you can see I am in the middle of a trial so I only have time to wish both of you the best of luck and offer the court's personal appreciation for your having reached an agreement."

Raymond and Sheila couldn't believe it. It was so easy. They had both feared that they had set some monstrous procedure into motion that would result in frustrating their cordial relationship. Instead, they had learned that the judge had only wanted to make sure that their stipulation had been voluntarily signed. Raymond could only think of getting back to his apartment to catch up on the sleep he had missed because of his unfounded concern regarding today's "hearing."

The experience of Raymond and Sheila is fairly typical in those relatively rare cases when the parties are summoned into court despite the filing of a written stipulation consenting to the terms of a modified visitation schedule. In such cases the court is usually only interested in protecting the legal "integrity" of the amended judgment by ascertaining that the understanding has been voluntarily and knowingly reached.

As is apparent, the important element in all this remains the written stipulation. Of course, we do not mean to imply that parents necessarily require a writing to insure that they will abide by the new visitation schedule. However, should enforcement of your visitation rights be required, the only real protection is to claim that your ex's conduct violates an existing order. So let's look a bit closer at this sample stipulation so that you and your ex will be able to draft your own without necessarily incurring the expense of a lawyer, although you may want a lawyer to review your draft. He or she may have some small additions to make that incorporate the local rules of your jurisdiction. Because you are not asking the lawyer to draft the agreement or negotiate it for you, you will, in most instances, only be charged a small fee.

STIPULATION OF AMENDMENT

THIS STIPULATION dated February 9, 1986 between RAYMOND DOWNEY ("Father"), residing at 7004 Boulevard East, Charing, Massachusetts, and SHEILA DOWNEY ("Mother"), residing at 37 Fairview Avenue, Redhook, Massachusetts.

W I T N E S S E T H:

WHEREAS, the parties obtained a judgment of divorce entered in the County of Suffolk, State of Massachusetts on March 8, 1985; and

WHEREAS, such divorce judgment incorporated a certain visitation schedule regarding the parties' two children, namely: ROBERT, born on August 3, 1978 and JENNIFER, born on December 20, 1980; and

WHEREAS, the Father and Mother wish to amend their original divorce decree by including a modified visitation schedule on account of the Mother's anticipated change of residence to Connecticut;

NOW, THEREFORE, in consideration of the mutual promises set forth below, and in order to accomplish the ends sought, the parties do fully, knowingly and voluntarily agree as follows:

1. Paragraph "7" of the divorce decree shall henceforth be amended as follows:

[describe the modified arrangement in detail]

2. Except as specifically described above, the parties' original divorce decree shall not be amended, modified or in any way changed.

3. It is hereby agreed that either the Father or the Mother may submit an amended judgment of divorce which specifically incorporates the terms of this agreement. Such proposed, modified decree may be submitted to the court without further notice to either party, and the Father and Mother affirmatively consent to the entry of such decree as soon as practicable, so long as it properly and accurately incorporates the modification to visitation as set forth in paragraph "1" above.

4. Both Father and Mother wish to acknowledge that the agreement to modify existing visitation has been made after full discussion and open disclosure. The parties believe the modification to be in the children's best interests, and this agreement is being signed voluntarily, knowingly and without coercion or duress exercised by either party against the other.

5. There are no other promises or understandings between the parties relating to any matters contained in this agreement.

_____
RAYMOND DOWNEY

_____
SHEILA DOWNEY

[It is best to have your signatures notarized and acknowledged before a Notary Public.]

PARENTAL CONFLICTS

Oftentimes, a modification to visitation is necessitated by the parents themselves, as opposed to unanticipated outside influences. For example, we represented a father who was seeking a modification in his parenting time after only 3 months from the date of the divorce. His son was a 4-month-old infant. The judge had awarded the father liberal visitation to be exercised at his ex-wife's home. This type of arrangement is quite common when the child is an infant; judges believe that it is often impractical to take the child away from the home for extended periods of time. Emergencies may arise; feeding schedules will be unnecessarily interrupted, and in general the visit is likely to create a major disruption. Therefore, our client was directed to exercise his visitation at the child's home until his son had reached his first birthday.

From the outset, it became apparent that our client's former spouse was unable to control the bitterness that had unfortunately surfaced once the breakup had been formalized. She had grown increasingly more vindictive, and when our client attempted to exercise his rights, he was beleaguered by temper tantrums, verbal abuse and threats of physical violence. His ex refused to leave the baby's room when our client entered it to see his child, and in all respects she made the exercise of visitation extremely disruptive.

Technically, our client was not being denied visitation. He was always permitted into the house and always allowed access to his son. But it was clear that this father was being frustrated to such an extent that he was seriously thinking about absenting himself for the next 8 months, waiting until the child was old enough to be taken from the home.

Under these circumstances, the court modified the visitation to permit out-of-the-home parenting time despite his son's age. The judge viewed the mother's conduct as "detrimental" to the child's best interests, stating: "When a parent's actions demonstrate an inability to foster or encourage reasonable visitation, the circumstance giving rise to such action must be changed in some manner." In this case, the judge believed that the only way to preserve parent–child contact was to allow the father to have visitation outside of the mother's home.

The obvious lesson to be learned from this case is that parents should not permit their own emotions to interfere with proper and reasonable parent–child contact. If the custodian's belligerence or other emotional mind set is so troublesome and pervasive that it creates an atmosphere where visitation is stunted, disturbed or hindered, you have a right to seek modification. All things being equal, you will obtain it.

THE OTHER SIDE OF THE COIN

There are times when the petitioning parent is the *custodial* parent. This occurs when the modification requested is a restriction or a limitation to the existing visitation arrangement. For example, the non-custodial parent may be putting the child in a dangerous situation during visitation periods. Sometimes it is a claim that the child is not being properly supervised, other times the allegation may raise more complex issues, as in the case where the custodial parent complains that her former husband's girlfriend sleeps over at the house when the child is present.

When a judge's personal definition of morality collides with the non-custodial parent's visitation rights, watch out! There is absolutely no way in which the outcome can be predicted. As we point out in our chapter on custody modification proceedings, the legal result is tied inextricably to the judge's personal views and conscious or unconscious prejudices. One hearing officer may see nothing wrong with the situation where the non-custodial father is cohabiting with a female friend. Another may view it quite differently, believing that a child should not be exposed to such "immoral conduct." In the latter situation, the court will be more inclined to rule in the petitioning parent's favor. In other words, you may find yourself looking at a modified visitation order that states:

> ORDERED, that respondent/father shall refrain from having female visitors stay overnight at his residence when the child is visiting with him.

Restrictive visitation orders are fairly common when the non-custodial parent is involved in a homosexual relationship. In such situations, many judges believe that the non-custodial parent's sexual preference may act as a negative influence upon the child. Such parent will be directed to limit contact with his or her lover when in the child's presence. Again, the "best interests" doctrine is supposed to control. In our experience, a claim of homosexuality almost always results in some modification to the existing visitation arrangement if—and this is a large *if*— the *child* articulates any discomfiture whatsoever. Conversely, if the child is unaware of or does not register any anxiety about the parent's homosexual relationship, the non-custodial parent's case for modification based solely on such relationship is weakened.

Similarly, a restriction in the existing visitation arrangement is sometimes the result of an initial demand that parenting time be terminated altogether. As we discussed in the last chapter, a termination of visitation is the most drastic remedy available to the court; it will rarely trigger such an event unless there is clear evidence that the child is truly endangered. However, while the judge may refuse to terminate visitation entirely, he or she may feel that circumstances warrant a temporary restriction. For example, we know of a case where the non-custodial father's girlfriend was a drug abuser. While refusing to "visit the sins" of the girlfriend upon the father by terminating his visitation time, the court ordered that future visitation could not occur in this female's presence and had to be exercised at the mother's home, under her direct supervision.

* * *

When circumstances are present that call for a change to the existing visitation plan, the petitioning parent has a high likelihood of success. The key is that virtually all judges agree that consistent, meaningful interaction with the child by *both* parents is to be encouraged because it positively impacts on the child's best interests. A custodial parent who opposes your request for enlargement out of spite, particularly when you can demonstrate that you have attempted to reach a compromise before triggering the court mechanism, will be viewed most unfavorably. The bottom line: Try to work it out first. If that fails, start the modification ball rolling. Increased visitation time remains a laudable goal, but only when you can truthfully say that you can accept the responsibilities that go along with the visitation enlargement *and* the child can handle the change.

If communication does break down and no settlement or compromise can be reached, do not resort to self-help. If your parenting time requires modification, ask the court to direct the change; do not simply take the child. And if such fine-tuning is in the offing, take the necessary legal steps in the first instance without procrastination. As strong as your case may be, it becomes diluted if it is approached by way of a counter-petition. For the most part, judges intuitively believe that if the modification was really needed, you would not have waited to assert it *after* your ex went into court to request, for example, child support enforcement. Something as important as your visitation rights should be acted upon without delay.

CHAPTER THIRTEEN

Enforcing Custody Rights

WE HAVE SPOKEN with scores of parents throughout the country who have found themselves in the unenviable position of having to enforce their child custody rights. Virtually all of them agree that the experience is a living hell, that the initial feeling of losing custodial control is as heart-rending as an actual death in the family. Although the facts in each case are a bit different, the custody crisis most commonly arises when the non-custodial parent refuses to relinquish the child after exercising his or her rightful visitation. The child is supposed to be returned by Sunday morning; it is now 10 P.M. and you *don't* know where your child is. In rarer situations, the non-custodial parent doesn't even bother using visitation as an excuse. The child is simply snatched from the school, playground or some other common area.

As attorneys, this is perhaps the most emotionally painful chapter to write. We deplore individuals who view their parental status as a license to steal. And "steal" is the only appropriate word that can be used to describe such misguided, self-centered and often illegal conduct. Not only does such conduct provide ample evidence that the snatching parent is generally unfit to properly care for the child, but it places the child in such a confusing and frightening position that serious psychological damage is often the result.

Fortunately, the custodial parent is not totally helpless. Legal procedures exist, the purpose of which is the preservation of parent–child contact; the courts have become increasingly more vigilant in seeing to it that such rights are recognized and enforced.

Whatever subterfuge your ex has used to interfere with your custody, the result is the same: you no longer have physical control of your child. For the moment, we will assume that you know where your child has been taken. Either it is somewhere else within your state or the child has been removed to an out-of-state location. The location of your child, intrastate or interstate, will determine what legal enforcement procedure you will use. We will turn to each situation in a few moments, but two other possibilities must first be explored.

Specifically, you may know that your child has been unlawfully abducted yet, at the same time, have no idea where he or she is. Perhaps you are not even sure that the non-custodial parent is responsible. The second possibility is that the child has been taken to a foreign country. In either case, the hell that you are experiencing on account of the child snatching will be compounded and magnified. But you are not without recourse.

WHERE IS MY CHILD?

Before we provide any additional information, you should first turn back to Chapter 6 and review our discussion on parent locator services. Although we discuss such services in the context of an attempt to enforce a money judgment, the tips we give you are applicable to custody cases as well. However, the parent locator services available to help parents obtain a payroll deduction order or tax intercept will generally not be available when the custodial parent is looking for the *child.* On the other hand, our experience shows that the non-custodial parent is rarely successful in destroying all traces of your son or daughter. The child has probably been taken to your ex's hometown, a place close to where he works or some other locale with which he has significant contact. If you don't panic, you can probably come up with some very good clues as to your ex's whereabouts—and that means that your child may not be far away. Such things as telephone and social security numbers, old addresses, prior places of employment and the like are excellent starting points.

While you are searching your memory and home for information that can be used to help locate your ex, you must follow up your own efforts with a call for outside assistance—be it the police or some other organization, as we will discuss in this chapter. And you should do so within the first 24 hours after the alleged child snatching has occurred. This time period remains the most crucial; after a day the trail begins to run cold and the possibility of successful location may grow dimmer.

As indicated, in a child snatching situation the perpetrator is either the non-custodial parent or a stranger having nothing to do with the custodial arrangement. For our purposes, we will assume that the non-custodial parent has created the crisis. We will further assume that your ex's actions have been motivated by a desire to utilize self-help to effectuate a change in the physical custody arrangement originally awarded at the time of the divorce. Enough of the assumptions. What do you do if your ex has taken the child to who knows where?

First, call the police. It is simply an old wive's tale that the police will refuse to respond if less than 24 hours have elapsed since the abduction. This "just to make sure" police theory has fallen into almost complete disfavor within the last few years as a direct result of the alarmingly high number of child abductions within this country. When you telephone, be sure to have this information handy:

- Full name of ex-spouse
- Your ex's present or last known home residence
- Your ex's present or last known telephone number
- Your ex's present or last known place of employment and work address
- Your ex's office or workplace telephone number
- Full name of child, taken from birth certificate
- Pet or nicknames of the child
- Child's age and birthdate
- An accurate description of the child

- Date and place of original court that entered the divorce decree awarding you physical custody of the child
- Any other helpful information such as former spouse's social security number, military service record and the like
- The location from where the child was abducted

Obviously, the first concern of the police will be whether the child has been taken by a parent or if the child's absence is the result of a kidnapping by a stranger. The latter situation is basically beyond the scope of this book. You don't need us to remind you of the national tragedy that results in thousands of missing children each year—children that are suspected of being victims of this decade's version of "white slavery." However, we do pause for a moment to provide the names and addresses of several organizations that are devoted to finding missing children and assisting parents in dealing with the emotional agony that results.

CHILD FIND, INC.
P.O. Box 277
New Paltz, New York 12561
Hotline: 800-IAM-LOST

NATIONAL CENTER FOR MISSING AND EXPLOITED CHILDREN
1835 K Street, N.W.
Suite 700
Washington, D.C. 20006
Hotline: 800-THE-LOST

SEARCH, INC.
560 Sylvan Avenue
Englewood Cliffs, New Jersey 07632
201-567-4040

THE LOST CHILD NETWORK
8900 State Line Road
Suite 351
Leawood, Kansas 66206
913-649-6723

THE NATIONAL CHILD SAFETY COUNCIL
P.O. Box 1368
Jackson, Michigan 49204
517-764-6070

Most of the above organizations are nonprofit agencies dedicated to controlling the epidemic of missing and possibly exploited children. They provide direct assistance, offer practical suggestions to the parents, and most have initiated various photo campaigns aimed at maximizing the possibility of locating your child.

Turning, now, to your particular problem—presumably a child snatching by the non-custodial parent—a few preliminary remarks are in order. Perhaps most importantly, the majority of parental child-snatching cases do not involve the difficult issue of finding the child. Rather, it is more than likely that your ex will simply telephone, tell you where he and the child have surfaced, and then either implicitly or expressly dare you to "come and get them." Well, after reading this chapter, you will have the ability to do just that. And successfully, too. However, we understand that it is indeed a small consolation to read about the *majority* of parents when *you* are faced with the rarer situation when the non-custodial parent takes the child without disclosing their final destination. What do you do? You get help from the Federal Bureau of Investigation!

In order to get the FBI's attention in a parental kidnapping case, you must follow a particular and somewhat tedious procedure, without deviation. You may rightly ask, why go to all the trouble? What can the Feds do? Actually, your question is a good one and if you were asking it in 1981 we would be forced to admit that the FBI could not really do all that much. But in 1982, President Reagan signed federal legislation that goes under the colloquial name of the "Missing Children's Act." This legislation required that, from 1982 on, the FBI had to accept the records of missing children in the National Information Center computer. Most law enforcement officials agree that this computer network represents the most sophisticated tool of its kind. Who are we to argue? The FBI represents your best shot when attempting to locate your child.

Understandably, the FBI is reluctant to involve itself in every parental child snatching case. As one Special Agent told us, the Bureau simply does not have the manpower to investigate and prosecute every missing child case. Therefore, the FBI has set down certain guidelines and limitations, which we will first list and then explore in detail:

1. The complaining parent must document legal custody.
2. A local *felony arrest warrant* must be outstanding.
3. A letter requesting the FBI's assistance from your local prosecutor's office must be forwarded.

Once the FBI has the requisite information, a warrant is obtained from a federal judge or magistrate. It is this warrant that provides the Bureau with the authority to pursue a missing child investigation. Unlike the perception that we have from television, the reality is that the FBI has no authority to bring the child back to the home state once he or she is found. It works this way: When the FBI locates the missing child, he or she is turned over to the local child care center and the child's home state is then notified. When the non-custodial parent is located, he or she will be arrested as a result of the federal warrant and then turned over to the local authorities for processing. The local authorities then contact the child's home state and begin the procedure that will result in a return of the child to the custodial parent, as well as the extradition of the guilty parent. It is important to emphasize that the FBI will generally not launch a missing *parent* investigation when the issue is child support delinquency. As we saw in Chapter 6, this remains primarily an issue that is handled through the support collection unit in cooperation with the local authorities.

The first prerequisite to FBI involvement poses no difficulty. The Bureau will merely be provided with an authenticated or certified copy of the divorce decree or judicial order that gave you physical or primary custody of your child. The second prerequisite, however, envisions an initial step that must be taken prior to your contacting the FBI and results in your obtaining a *local felony* arrest warrant that gives the FBI the legal "excuse" to involve themselves in your case.

Notice the word *felony*. Surprisingly, a parent who violates a custody order and refuses to turn over the child is not necessarily committing a felony. Parental kidnapping in some states remains a misdemeanor, a less serious crime than a felony. And without a local, *state* felony charge, the Bureau will have no authority to investigate your case. Your initial step, then, should be to telephone your local prosecutor's office in order to determine whether parental kidnapping in your jurisdiction is automatically a felony crime. But don't lose hope if you are told that your state *usually* considers parental kidnapping a "mere" misdemeanor. Many "misdemeanor" states will "upgrade" parental child snatching from a misdemeanor to a felony if certain circumstances are present.

For example, New York has a typical approach. While stating that your ex's conduct will generally be a misdemeanor, parental kidnapping becomes a felony when:

1. there is an intent to permanently remove the child from the state,
2. the child is actually removed from the state, or
3. the non-custodial parent has placed or is placing the child in a situation that endangers the child's safety or materially impairs his or her health.

In other words, if you fear that the child is in danger or has actually been taken across the state border, a felony warrant will be issued even in those states that usually look at the crime as a misdemeanor. Fortunately, most states make parental child snatching an automatic felony without requiring a separate showing of an out-of-state removal or serious endangerment to the child's welfare. While we cannot in good conscience tell you to misrepresent your situation to the local authorities solely because you want the FBI to get involved, we do point out that most of the misdemeanor jurisdictions provide sufficient flexibility to characterize the snatching as a felony if circumstances warrant. We emphasize this point because we have found some prosecutors' offices to be much too eager to advise panic-stricken parents that their former spouse's conduct is only a misdemeanor so "please stop babbling about the FBI, we are fully capable of investigating this matter locally." The only reason that we can come up with for such evasion is that interaction and cooperation with the FBI increases the paperwork within the prosecutor's office. Therefore, do not be denied your right to obtain a felony warrant even when you experience some initial prosecutorial resistance. Enough said.

Assuming that the prosecutor's office issues the local felony warrant for the apprehension of the non-custodial parent, you are still not assured that the FBI will take your case. You will need further cooperation from the local prosecutor's office. This third prerequisite requires that a letter be signed by the prosecutor's office and forwarded to the Bureau. It must contain these elements:

• That the complaining parent has legal custody of the child
• That the requisite local felony warrant has been issued and remains outstanding

- That if, and when, the non-custodial parent is apprehended, your local prosecutor's office will fund and arrange for the return of both the violating parent and missing child
- That there is a reasonable belief that the child has been taken out of state, including the reasons upon which you base such belief
- Although not required, any information concerning possible locations, such as your ex's last known address; a postmark from recent correspondence; or any other information of this type

This is what a typical letter looks like:

April 7, 1986

Mr. William Brandon
FEDERAL BUREAU OF INVESTIGATION
1712 West Broadway
New York, New York 10005

RE: REQUEST FOR BUREAU ASSISTANCE
Complaining Parent: Dorothy Brown
Missing Child: Jennifer Brown

Dear Sir:

The purpose of this letter is to request your assistance in investigating a parental kidnapping that occurred on or about April 2, 1986. The complaining parent, Mrs. Dorothy Brown, has legal custody of her two-year-old child, Jennifer Brown, born on March 14, 1984. I enclose in this regard an authenticated copy of the divorce decree which specifically awards primary custody to Mrs. Brown.

Because we have good reason to suspect that the subject child has been taken out of state, we have charged Mr. Robert Brown, the custodial parent's former spouse, with one felony count of parental kidnapping. Our office was successful in obtaining a felony warrant based upon the sworn allegations of Mrs. Brown, a copy of which we enclose for the Bureau's review.

Because of the nature of this particular crime, we affirmatively state that this Office stands ready to offer whatever assistance the Federal Bureau of Investigation may need when the violating parent and innocent child are apprehended. We are willing to fund the costs of extradition and arrange for the swift return of both Mr. Brown and Jennifer when circumstances warrant. We intend to work closely with any jurisdiction wherein either the child or her father, or both, are found so that the custodial rights of Mrs. Brown are amply protected.

While it is true that, at this juncture, we do not have any positive indication of the child's whereabouts, we believe that it may reasonably be inferred that Jennifer has been taken out of state. Mr. Brown's last known residence is in Denver, Colorado, and his parents continue to reside within such state. In addition, Mr. Brown was employed by Whitten Products Co., a subsidiary of Dayton Enterprises, which has a manufacturing firm within the city limits of Denver.

Finally, Mrs. Brown received a telephone call from her former husband approximately two days after the child's abduction whereby Mr. Brown acknowledged that he had the child but refused to return her to Mrs. Brown's residence. During such conversation, Mr. Brown acknowledged that he was at Kennedy International Airport and that he was taking the child to "parts unknown."

We ask that you contact this office upon review of this correspondence and its enclosures, and we thank you in advance for your immediate cooperation and attention. Please direct your inquiry to case number 7784/86 so that we may have ready access to our file in this matter should you need further assistance or require additional information.

> Very truly yours,
>
> Daniel White,
> Assistant District Attorney

DW:grm
encs.

Obtaining Cooperation From Foreign Countries

Parents who are involved in foreign country child custody disputes must look to the Department of State and American embassies and consulates for assistance. That is the good news. The bad news is that such assistance is quite restricted.

When your child has been taken to another country or is being kept abroad by the non-custodial parent in violation of your custody rights, the Department of State, through its Foreign Service posts, can help to locate the child, monitor the child's welfare, provide general information about the country's custody laws and procedures, and furnish you with a list of attorneys in that country who have experience in this area. If it appears that your child is being abused or neglected, State Department officers can alert the foreign authorities or Social Service agencies in that country.

If you need help in ascertaining the welfare or whereabouts of your child, you must send the following information to the Office of Citizens Consular Services, Department of State, Washington D.C. 20520, or to the U.S. Embassy or Consulate nearest the child's foreign residence:

- The full name of the child
- The child's date and place of birth
- Passport data, if known
- Any available information about the child's departure from the United States or destination
- The names and, if possible, addresses and telephone numbers of persons with whom the child traveled or is believed to be staying
- Your own telephone number, should the Department or Foreign Service post need further details

If your child has been abducted to a foreign country, your only recourse, alas, is to start a court action in the country where your child is located. We understand that this is economically prohibitive for most; we only wish we had a better solution to this horrendous dilemma. However, things may gradually be changing for the better. The concept of an international treaty that gives legal recognition and enforcement to a prior awarded foreign custody decree is gaining favor. Let us all hope for the best.

The Local Child Snatching

Although no hard statistics are available, most attorneys agree that the majority of custody enforcement cases involve intrastate abductions; the child is not taken outside of the state's borders. Becky's former husband,

Herbert, resides two counties over. He visits their son Alex every weekend, picking the child up early Friday evening and returning him by 1 or 2 in the afternoon on Sunday. The arrangement has worked well for the 3 years since the divorce; 6-year-old Alex appears to be well adjusted.

A few months ago, Becky formally announced her plans to remarry. Something inside her ex snapped. He just couldn't see his son living with a "strange" man. Last Sunday, Alex was simply not returned to his mother.

By 10 P.M. it was obvious that Alex was not coming home. Had there been a tragedy? A car accident? With shaking fingers, Becky dialed her ex's home number. In a rather cheerful voice, her ex got on the telephone almost immediately. Becky's fear turned to anger at what appeared to be a complete lack of responsibility on her ex's part. The worst, however, was to come.

After listening patiently to Becky's outrage over his lack of concern and foolish behavior, Herbert merely answered with the five dreaded words that no custodial parent wants to hear: "Alex is not coming home."

"What are you saying? Are you mad? It's almost 10:30 already. Alex has school tomorrow morning."

"That's right, dear. Alex *does* have school tomorrow. Except I have enrolled him in the Cheshire Academy. We signed all the papers on Saturday."

Becky is now thoroughly confused. She hasn't quite accepted the obvious, but her sense of crisis is growing by the second. "Stop joking, Herb, will you. If you get in the car now, you can be here before 11:30."

"Get the cotton out of your ears, Becky. Alex is staying with me from now on. I've always wanted cust—"

Becky interrupts in a voice that vaguely resembles a growl. "Put him on, you bastard. I want to talk to my son."

The click of the telephone being placed back on the receiver sounds as loud as dynamite to Becky. She sits there staring at the wall for about 20 seconds, redials her ex's number and is greeted with the harsh drone of a busy signal. To borrow a well-known phrase, and with apologies to the memory of Rod Serling, Becky has just crossed over into the "Custody Enforcement Zone."

* * *

All interstate custody enforcement proceedings begin with the delivery of a writ or petition to the non-custodial parent. Many states call such initiating document a "writ of habeas corpus," which roughly translates to "we demand the return of the body." Of course the "body" is the child. It is the writ that starts the enforcement ball rolling.

Having read this far in our book, you probably have a good idea about what information must be contained in the writ. Specifically, you must allege that you were awarded legal custody of the child and that the non-custodial parent is violating such rights by refusing to return the child to your control and custody. As we have continuously seen, the commencement of an enforcement action is relatively easy. Whether you are enforcing visitation, monetary, or custody rights, the proceeding is initiated by delivering a formal notice to the violating parent. However, when it comes to custody enforcement, the individual who receives a copy of your writ better heed its demand that on a certain date (usually within a week from its delivery) *both* the non-custodial parent and the child must appear in court. Most states require that the writ be *personally* delivered to the non-custodial parent. Sometimes this can pose some practical problems.

A few years ago we represented a mother whose ex had refused to return their daughter after a weekend visitation. Our client's former husband was a relatively well-known performer, and it always seemed that he had dozens of "assistants" running interference for him. Our process server was having difficulty delivering the writ to this man, and time was running out. It appeared that the father would be leaving the country on an extended musical tour within the very near future, and if the writ was not delivered to him prior to his leaving, our client's enforcement rights might be delayed indefinitely.

Following closely our target's touring schedule, we ascertained that he would be performing at a local country and western bar. Our process server purchased a couple of advance tickets, and on the specified evening he found himself seated close to the stage. There was a shaky moment or two when a rumor swept the place that the band had canceled their appearance for that evening. Did our recalcitrant father know that he was being set up for an enforcement proceeding? Fortunately, the rumor proved unfounded; the lights dimmed and the band was announced. And with that, our process server leaped onto the stage and handed the writ to our client's ex in full view of approximately two hundred people. And so the proceeding was launched.

* * *

We will return to this case momentarily to illustrate another point that we made earlier: that courts deal harshly with non-custodial parents who ignore the return date of the writ. "Return date" is a term used to describe the day when the child must be produced in court. Generally, the return date is distinct from the hearing date. It merely gives the court an initial opportunity to reinstate the status quo and reunite the custodial parent with his or her child. A trial date will then be scheduled, and the judge will make any other interim decisions that may be appropriate, such as the appointment of a law guardian to represent the child, the request that both parents submit to psychiatric evaluation and other such collateral services that we spoke about in Chapter 11.

Sometimes the judge will refuse to simply rubber stamp the original custody award on the writ's return date. For example, we were involved in a case where the 11-year-old son informed the judge when he came into court that he had "run away" from home because his mother was abusing drugs. When the court tried to reunite the child with his mother, he became visibly distraught and almost hysterical. After interviewing the child alone in his chambers for approximately an hour, the judge decided that he would press for a trial within 10 days but that during this time the child could remain with the non-custodial father. Of course, he permitted open and liberal visitation to the mother.

As you might have concluded, custody enforcement cases represent another post-divorce situation that rarely arises in a nice neat package. Many custodial parents find their enforcement efforts countered with a cross-petition for a change of custody or for some other substantial modification to the existing visitation arrangement. In our last example, the judge largely based his decision to allow the father to maintain temporary custodial rights pending trial because such parent had answered the writ with a demand of his own that custody be changed to his favor. The factual elements that determine custody modification requests are discussed in the next chapter. For now, we wish only to highlight that enforcement of your custody rights may ironically result in a situation where you are forced to litigate the question of custody all over again.

However, don't lose heart if your ex appears to be acting as if he or she has just graduated from the school where the students are taught that the best defense is a good offense. Just because your former spouse attempts to defend his violation of your custodial rights by counter-petitioning for a change of custody, you will have these important factors in your favor:

- Any request for modification that is put forward *after* the other parent has been forced to seek formal enforcement is viewed less favorably than modification efforts that are affirmatively commenced in the first instance.
- As we discuss in the next chapter, courts are generally reluctant to disturb the continuity that has naturally resulted from the original custody award; the fact that you have been the supervising parent since the divorce will hold a great deal of weight when your ex attempts to modify the original award.
- The very fact that your ex has resorted to self-help by refusing to return your child is entirely inconsistent with his claim that custody should be changed to him. Courts believe that parental child snatchers—no matter how well-meaning—are actually exhibiting traits that militate against any such modification.

Some non-custodial parents believe that they are simply beyond the reach of the law. You go to all the trouble of commencing a formal proceeding to enforce your custodial rights, which often means having to hire an attorney, and when delivery of the writ occurs, your ex ignores it completely. On the return date you sit in court waiting for your child to be produced. Waiting. Waiting. Five o'clock and time to go home. He never showed.

Indeed, this is what our semi-famous performer did after receiving the writ in front of an entire audience. He was supposed to be in court 10 days later and we sat with our client almost all day waiting for him or the child to walk through the door. While the mother sank deeper and deeper into depression, we were planning our next move—a move that is quite common in custody enforcement cases where the violating parent ignores the court summons. After convincing the judge that delivery had, in fact, been properly made, we asked that the judge immediately issue a warrant for the arrest of the father for willful disobedience of the writ.

This arrest warrant goes by several names, depending on which state issues it. Some jurisdictions refer to it as a *warrant of attachment;* others call it a *civil precept.* Many just characterize it as a *civil bench warrant.* Whatever term is used, the purpose and effect remains the same: your former spouse will be picked up and arrested anywhere that he or she may be found within the state.

In our situation, the warrant was issued the next morning and we were able to track our client's ex to a northern city where the band was performing for a few nights. In a virtual replay, the father was approached on stage at the beginning of the show. Only this time, he was surrounded by three sheriffs who unceremoniously escorted him off the stage to the waiting squad car for processing. He was held overnight at the local precinct and the next morning he was arraigned before a criminal magistrate. After being made to post $2,000 cash bail, he was told to report to the court which issued the warrant within 2 days. Our court contacted us and advised that the father would be appearing before the judge within the next 48 hours. Needless to say, we were there to meet him.

Sometimes the non-custodial parent actually shows up on the return date of the writ but without the child. Now what? Most judges when faced with this situation will act decisively and without hesitation. The judge will simply order the non-custodial parent to arrange for the child to be brought into court immediately. Oh, and one other thing. The judge will also refuse to allow such parent to leave the courtroom until the order is actually carried out. If by the end of the day the child has still not been produced, the court has absolute authority to have the violating parent confined. And not in court. The local jail will do just fine, thank you. When faced with such a proposition, most parents will see to it that the child is duly delivered to the courthouse.

Now that all of the participants have finally been brought together, you are ready to prosecute your custody enforcement proceeding. Remember, your ex will probably be defending the custodial interference with a demand for custody modification. Even if your former spouse has virtually no chance of succeeding, he or she will probably figure that the unlawful conduct giving rise to the enforcement proceeding will be "camouflaged" within the legal battle that you are waging. Most states, however, permit a custodial parent to collect attorneys' fees directly from the violating parent, even when there exists a cross-petition for custody modification. A judge will consider these factors when determining whether your ex will be ordered to contribute towards your legal expenses:

- Did you prevail in your enforcement claim?
- Is it clear that there is no reasonable excuse or defense for the interruption of your custodial rights?
- Has your ex interposed a counter-petition that is without any real legal merit?
- Did your ex cooperate with the court during all of the stages of the proceeding, or did he obstruct the process so that your expenses were unnecessarily increased?
- Does your ex have sufficient assets or earnings to pay the court awarded attorneys' fees if ordered to do so?

If you can answer yes to any of these questions, then it is likely that your winning custody enforcement will be accompanied by a judicial decree that your ex must help finance your litigation expenses occasioned by his conduct.

Because the best interests doctrine remains superimposed on any enforcement proceeding, judges are under an obligation to explore all allegations that are made regarding the welfare of the child. This means the possible appointment of legal guardians, psychiatric evaluations, private interviews with the parties and any other procedures that will assist the judge in making his or her decision. But it doesn't take long for a judge to determine that the non-custodial parent's assertions are usually frivolous and without any merit. In such a case you can be sure that the court will come down hard on your ex by not only reaffirming the original custody order but awarding you a sizable chunk of money, as well.

ENFORCEMENT FACTORS

We have already underscored that a custody enforcement proceeding is rarely fought in a one-sided manner. It is indeed a unique case that requires a judge to merely look at the custody award, determine that it has been violated, order the return of the child to the custodial parent and punish the violating parent by assessing attorneys' fees. Because you can expect some affirmative defense, we will explore those factors that determine the likelihood of success and how they may affect your case. If the custody modification demand is made in the context of an enforcement proceeding, the factual elements discussed in the next chapter take on a different "texture."

For example, custody enforcement is made more complex when your child articulates a desire to stay with the non-custodial parent. If you will recall Sarah's telephone call from her daughter Lisa described in Chapter 10, you will begin to understand what we are talking about. In fact, in Sarah's case, her ex never actually asserted a formal cross-petition for a change of custody. He merely went into court and told the judge that his daughter simply refused to return home to her mother. What was he supposed to do, he queried. Certainly, the court could not punish him for listening to his 12-year-old daughter, could it?

The issue here concerns the weight to be given to the child's preference when it causes a disruption of the existing custody arrangement. The corresponding issue is whether the child's stated preference provides the non-custodial parent with a valid excuse to unilaterally refuse to return the child. It can be safely said that most courts recognize that the child's wishes are to be considered, but that the preference standing alone will not be determinative of the enforcement proceeding. This is especially so when the non-custodial parent has not interposed an affirmative request for custody modification. When the court is faced only with a demand that the original custody award be enforced, the child's wishes will certainly not thwart the enforcement efforts. The judge may order counseling for the parties or some other remedial relief, but the custody award will be recognized and the non-custodial parent will be ordered to comply with it in all respects. In short, then, your child's articulated wish to be with you does not give you the right to unilaterally interrupt the original custody arrangement.

Even when your ex affirmatively demands custody modification on the basis of the child's stated preference to be with him, you need not fear that the child's desires will control and be absolutely determinative. You will see in the next chapter that the preference of the child is only one of many factual elements that go into the court's ultimate determination regarding a modification of custody request. Just because your ex demands a custodial change does not mean that he will succeed—even when he has the child "on his side." Your ex still has the burden of proving that such change is in the child's best interests. And again it is worth repeating that a judge will take less seriously a claim for custody modification when it is asserted only *after* the enforcement proceeding has been commenced.

You will also have the continuity element on your side, another factor that is important in custody proceedings. Simply stated, the court will always hesitate to modify the status quo. If you have been providing a stable and safe home for your child, the mere fact that your ex counters with a modification proceeding should not cause you to lose any sleep. Remember, you are seeking to enforce a right that has already been awarded. On the other hand, your ex is attempting to modify the existing arrangement only after having been served with your writ of habeas corpus. Not only does the continuity factor assist you in prosecuting your custody rights, but it offers a solid defense to any attempt to modify the existing arrangement.

The last (but not least) factor that is generally discussed in custody *enforcement* cases is "the best interests doctrine." You have the original custody award. And your child's stated preference to be with your ex is not controlling. However, the courts approach a post-divorce issue that affects children a lot differently than they approach a parent's problem in collecting child support or maintenance. In Part I of this book you saw the readiness of the court system to automatically trigger enforcement devices when it came to collecting monetary awards. This "automatic" mind set is not present in custody enforcement cases, simply because our courts are ever-vigilant in seeing to it that the living environment created by the parent continues to promote the child's welfare.

We emphasize this point to help you understand the motives of the judge when it appears that your fitness as a parent is being questioned. You might have thought that it was simply a matter of submitting an authenticated copy of your original custody order and that after a few minutes of testimony the judge would strike his gavel and direct your ex to comply with the custody award. You would walk out that afternoon with your child, and that would be that. Unfortunately, you may find that the proceeding is more complex. For example, the judge may want to interview the child and hear other relevant testimony.

Such judicial analysis is the rule, not the exception. It is not that the judge is getting ready to decide against you. Instead, this analysis represents the court's crucial judicial duty to insure that the child's best interests are always paramount, no matter what the issue and no matter how righteous you may feel. Of course, we now come full circle and remind you that you wouldn't be in court seeking enforcement of your custody rights if your ex had not resorted to self-help or child snatching in the first instance. The judge also recognizes this uncontroverted fact. And this usually means that the child's best interests will correspond with *your* interests in enforcing your custody rights!

COOPERATION BETWEEN STATES

You may find yourself in a situation where you must enforce your custody rights after your ex has spirited the child out of state. Prior to 1980, such action on the part of the non-custodial parent would have posed insurmountable problems. Many states just ignored a prior custody award rendered in another jurisdiction, litigating the entire issue all over again on the sole basis that the child was now within its boundaries. For example, it was not uncommon for a father to have custody in Texas and the mother to have a separate custody order in her favor in Florida.

Interestingly, the legal "culprit" in this area was the "best interests" doctrine. Courts believed that custody was always freely modifiable so long as the analysis focused on the child's best interests. If the child was within any particular state, the judge believed it his or her duty to review the custodial arrangement anew. However, the judicial clamor to protect the welfare of the child created the anomalous situation of "forum shopping." That is, non-custodial parents quickly discovered that the custody award decided in, for example, New York, did not mean that Delaware would give it automatic effect. In essence, the best interests doctrine was unexpectedly encouraging parents to snatch children across state lines in order to try their luck in another jurisdiction.

By late 1970 most states were awakening to this chaotic situation that seemingly resulted in the constant shifting of children from state to state, competition and conflict between jurisdictions and a general weakening of the legal effectiveness of custody decisions. In response, the federal government and the states themselves got their respective acts together. Actually, two Acts: the Uniform Child Custody Jurisdiction Act (UCCJA) and the Parental Kidnapping Prevention Act (PKPA). Some enlightened states had enacted the UCCJA as early as 1975, but it wasn't until this decade that all fifty states had finally come into line. The PKPA was the federal response and it became law in 1980.

When the courts are dealing with out-of-state child snatching cases, they must now follow the policy enunciated by these two legislative enactments. Indeed, because the PKPA is a federal statute, it must be afforded priority even before the UCCJA, but the two statutes are so similar that very few conflicts ever arise. In actuality, the federal statute provides general guidelines to be followed, and the UCCJA gives the details and specific procedures that are used in custody enforcement between states. Because it is now recognized that the adoption of the UCCJA is "consistent" with the federal legislation, our discussion will focus on the former legislation, which, as we have said, has been effectuated in all fifty states, plus the District of Columbia.

The Uniform Child Custody Jurisdiction Act

At the outset, we must emphasize that the UCCJA may also be used to enforce your visitation rights when the custodial parent has departed from the state. Therefore, what we discuss in this section is equally applicable to situations where you are attempting to protect and enforce your parenting time.

Although the UCCJA has several salutory purposes, the most important aspect is its express recognition that you no longer have to follow your child to another jurisdiction to enforce your rights. Prior to the enactment of this legislation and its federal counterpart, a parent was forced to travel to the state where the non-custodial parent had taken the child. If you tried to enforce your custodial rights in your home state, the judge would invariably ask where your child was. Without the child, the court would advise you that it had no power to enforce your post-divorce custody rights.

No more. The UCCJA stops the advantages of forum shopping by allowing the custodial parent to seek enforcement of his or her rights without traveling to the state where the child has been unlawfully taken. In addition, the non-custodial parent is no longer allowed to petition for a change in the existing arrangement merely because the child "happens to be with him" at the time that the modification application is made. The Act accomplishes these goals by giving jurisdictional priority to the child's "home state." This is defined as the place where the child has resided with the custodial parent for at least 6 consecutive months.

Let us take this scenario. You have had custody of your daughter for the last 3 years. You live in New Mexico and your ex resides in Nevada. Whether it be an actual child snatching or a refusal to return your daughter after a visitation, the bottom line remains that your custodial rights have been violated. To make matters worse, your ex petitions the Nevada court for a change of custody to his favor. Do you:

1. Jump out the nearest window?
2. Sell your personal belongings to finance a two month trip to Nevada so that you can defend your custodial rights?
3. Petition *your* local court for custody enforcement?

While the second option is, of course, available (and until recently was your only chance to get enforcement), the last choice is what the UCCJA is all about.

First of all, the Nevada court would probably dismiss your ex's modification petition immediately. Because the UCCJA controls in every state, the judge sitting in Nevada would determine that the child had not been within its state's borders for more than 6 months. Hence, the court would inform your ex-husband that it had no power to entertain the demand that custody be changed to his favor. Just as importantly, you would have the right to file an enforcement petition in your home state. So long as your original custody decree was in conformance with your state's rules or, even better, obtained in the state where you currently reside, it will be "binding upon all parties" and "conclusive as to all issues of law and fact decided . . . until that determination is modified pursuant to the UCCJA." This language comes directly from the Act.

In your situation, Nevada has no power to modify the existing custody award. Consequently, your custody decree will be given full "force and effect" and be entitled to recognition in Nevada. Indeed, that state will have no choice in the matter. It will have to issue an order dismissing the modification proceeding and directing that the child be turned over to you. If your ex refuses to obey, Nevada will assure compliance through whatever devices it has in its enforcement arsenal, including the possibility of a contempt order leading to your ex husband's arrest.

There is one major exception to the 6-month rule. This occurs when a court believes that a true emergency exists: that the child is actually in danger should the judge refuse to hear the case. For example, we know of a case where the non-custodial mother picked her son up at the airport to begin a 1-month summer visitation period. Her son was strangely withdrawn, and when she got him home she discovered to her horror that the child's body was covered with lice. It didn't take her too long to determine that during the intervening 7 months from her last extended visit with her son, his father had "fallen off the wagon" in a big way. It appeared that her ex's drinking had become excessive to the point where her son was being left completely unsupervised for days at a time. Indeed, it was obvious that the lack of supervision had risen to the level of outright neglect. After a few days, her son corroborated the situation, begging to stay with his mother. In this case, the court heard her petition for a change of custody even though the child had been within the jurisdiction for less than 6 months. The court simply triggered that portion of the UCCJA that allows a non-custodial parent to refuse to return the child to his home state when the child has been abandoned or an emergency exists that requires prompt legal action to protect the child's safety and welfare.

We emphasize that this situation remains the exception. Because the Act requires that priority be given to the home state, non-custodial parents who snatch their kids are finding that they cannot take refuge in another jurisdiction. Not only will these parents discover that they are the target of an FBI investigation where the possibility of criminal arrest looms large, but any self-serving gesture by way of a petition to change the existing custody arrangement will fail and be unceremoniously thrown out of court.

The Injunction: What to Do if the Non-Custodial Parent Threatens to Keep Your Child

A writ of habeas corpus, the UCCJA, or even the Federal Bureau of Investigation are effective tools when it comes to protecting your custodial rights. Yet you won't have to rely on them if the child snatching is successfully prevented. Let's say that your ex announces his intent to take the child away with him. Actually, such advance knowledge is more common than many people realize. In a great many cases, your ex either expressly or implicitly demonstrates a definite intent to interrupt your custody rights. And the number of custodial parents who become paralyzed and offer no resistance remains legion. You do not have to join their ranks.

If you have advance knowledge of your ex's attempt to spirit your child from the state, you are entitled to seek judicial intervention. This is accomplished by requesting that the court issue an order or injunction directing your ex to stay within your state's borders until the matter can be reviewed at a hearing. If you are afraid that your ex-spouse is thinking of snatching your child, you must act swiftly and follow this advice:

- Contact the police. Remember, in most states a child snatching is an automatic felony; the possibility that such crime is about to be committed will galvanize police action.
- If the child remains under your custodial control, do not relinquish him or her to your ex even if you will be in technical violation of your ex's visitation rights. But follow up your action immediately with our next bit of important advice.
- Get into court immediately. Usually this will require the assistance of an attorney; you cannot afford the time that it may take for you to learn your court's procedures.
- File an application that requires your ex to immediately "show cause" why a judge should not suspend the existing visitation rights or direct supervised visitation until the true intent of your former spouse may be determined at a hearing.
- If your ex already has control or possession of your child, then your petition will demand that your former spouse appear in court within a short time to explain his or her conduct. Pending such appearance, the court will issue a temporary *injunction* or *restraint notice* directing your ex to remain within the jurisdiction.
- If you believe that your child will be taken out of the country, then your petition should also request a court order directing your ex to turn over his and the child's passport, assuming, of course, that the passports are in his possession.
- If no passport has yet been issued to your child or it is in your drawer at home, your goal is to restrict your ex's ability to get a new passport issued. This means a telephone call to the Department of State in Washington, D.C. Based on your telephone call and the assurance that you will be forwarding the applicable court order to their attention, the State Department will try their best to insure that no passport is issued to your child.

No advice that we give you is foolproof; we cannot guarantee that your ex will not violate the restraint notice and surreptitiously leave the state. However, if you hesitate or don't take any action, you will have *no* chance to thwart your ex's plans. The steps described above give you a good chance of stopping your ex from accomplishing his improper goals.

* * *

Enforcing your custody rights can be a frustrating and painful experience. While the law remains on your side, the procedures are still imperfect. However, with increasing interstate cooperation and a greater willingness to deal harshly with child-snatching parents, the odds of success are definitely in your favor. The watchword remains *speed.* If you are attempting to locate your child after an abduction, the first 24 hours are crucial. If you wait more than 6 months to trigger the UCCJA, you are in jeopardy of losing the Act's home state advantage; your ex will claim that a new one has been created. And if you fear that a child snatching is about to occur, the faster you petition the court for the appropriate restraint orders, the better. In short, get moving!

CHAPTER FOURTEEN

Modifying Custody Rights

You believe that the present custody arrangement needs modification. You are thinking about attempting to change the custody of your children to your favor. Without question, you are facing one of the most important and far-reaching post-divorce decisions that any parent can make. If you act precipitously you are in jeopardy of not only failing in your attempt but of putting your children in a situation that creates a major disruption to their lives. By blindly pressing the custody modification trigger, you are virtually assured that your child will be the true victim.

The purpose of this chapter is to provide you with enough information so that an intelligent and reasoned decision can be made regarding any anticipated legal effort to modify custody. We will discuss the factors—both pro and con—that generally warrant a legal change. Our goal is to separate and distinguish ego-related motivation from external circumstances that actually affect the best interests of your child. In so doing, it is our fervent hope that a parent with good cause will feel more confident and not hesitate to commence a child custody modification proceeding if circumstances warrant.

As importantly, we wish to discourage those of you who are contemplating a change for frivolous or ill-conceived reasons from going through with the attempt. For those parents who find that their present custodial rights are being formally challenged or implicitly threatened, we intend to provide the necessary information that should either quell your anxieties or demonstrate your former spouse's likelihood of success. Finally, for those of you who are not yet faced with a change of custody dilemma, we believe that the illustrations contained in this chapter will help you to avoid those situations that generally give rise to a demand that custody be modified.

At the outset, it is important to emphasize that our discussion in this chapter generally relates to the post-divorce *legal and physical* custody arrangement presently in effect. While some modification proceedings are commenced in order to permit *joint legal* custody, the major thrust here will be modification petitions that demand custody and that the child's physical residence be changed from one parent to the other. In this chapter, when we talk about the custodial parent we mean the parent with whom the children live, either on a full-time or primary basis. The non-custodial parent is the one who has visitation rights or has the children less frequently than the other parent.

THE LEGAL STANDARDS

Not too surprisingly, a different legal standard is applied when the courts are dealing with a post-divorce effort to change custody, as opposed to the original custody issue that arose during the divorce process. In the latter case, a judge will have utilized an almost pure "best interests" approach. That means that the judge would have listened to all of the evidence regarding the relative fitness of both parents and then made a custody determination that placed the primary focus on the child's best interests.

While it is true that in the post-divorce arena the best interests doctrine is never far behind, the court will generally not modify the original award of custody unless there has been a *"substantial and material"* change of circumstance. Take note. When the courts speak about a change of circumstance, they are invariably focusing on a change in the *custodial* parent's situation. It is simply not enough that the non-custodial parent's circumstances have improved. Two and a half years after the divorce, Larry's economic situation has changed drastically. His company was bought out by a Fortune 500 conglomerate, and he was made vice president in change of merchandising. His salary has tripled, and let's not forget about his leased Mercedes and generous expense account. Having moved from his small apartment to a three-bedroom house, he has set his sights on the kids moving in with him.

"Look at all I can give them, now," he says to Janet, his ex-wife. "The boys will have their own bedrooms, a yard to play in and they'd still be pretty close to you. Come on, Janet. Why should they still be cooped up in that apartment of yours?"

"They like it where they are, Larry. Hey, we're all happy about your new position. But the kids have been in one place for the last three years . . ."

"Two and a half, to be precise."

"No, Larry. Three. You forget that you were out of the apartment for at least six months before we got the divorce," Janet corrects.

"Okay, okay. The point is . . . I mean . . . well, I just think they'd be better off with me. Have I ever missed a child support payment? Haven't I always given you a little extra when you asked? Can't you do something for me for a change?"

"Larry, you haven't stopped talking about yourself. How about the children? Do you really think they're going to be overjoyed about changing schools and having to make new friends?"

Larry started to say something else, but he sensed that he was beginning to whine. After his ex left, he sat down and poured himself a brandy. "Ah, what the hell. Let me see if Phil is in."

Phil and Larry had recently met at the local golf club. With Larry's new position, he figured that it wouldn't hurt to expand his social network a bit. Phil was a lawyer, and they'd had a couple of drinks together during the last month or so. They weren't yet friends, but Larry felt that he could trust Phil's judgment.

"Look. I'm not an expert in matrimonial law," began Phil. "But unless you can show some significant change in your kids' living environment, I don't think you have much of a chance. You might be getting in over your head."

"But what about the change in *my* living environment?"

"All things being equal, Larry, I'm pretty sure that your improved economic position won't mean too much. In my opinion, you are going to need a lot more proof."

Somewhat chastened, Larry began to put two and two together. Although a little late, he came to the realization that his own self-interests had been his primary motivating force. Did he really think that the children would be better off with him? Or was it really his own gratification that was unconsciously coming to the surface?

Larry was fortunate. Without anything to go on but a short conversation with an attorney and his instincts as a caring parent, he was able to determine for himself that a modification proceeding was not really necessary. For our purposes, it is also important to underscore that if such proceeding had been commenced, it would have been doomed to failure. Not only would Larry have been unable to show a substantial or material change in the *children's* post-divorce circumstances, but he would have learned to his horror that his trigger-happy approach would have surely traumatized the kids by forcing them into the middle of a totally unnecessary custody battle. So remember, the substantial change doctrine almost always begins and ends with an analysis of the *custodial parent's* situation. Conversely, if such change is only a "substantial" improvement in the non-custodial parent's circumstances, a post-divorce change of custody is extremely unlikely.

Instead of starting a legal proceeding, you can do some other practical things if you find that your lifestyle has significantly improved. If you have more money to spend, then why not offer to pay more child support? Obviously, the children will benefit from your generosity, and, in our experience, we have seen that such conduct generally creates a healthier parent–child relationship. We are not talking about bribing your child. We are suggesting that your good fortune should be shared in a reasonable manner—a manner calculated to provide your child with a more quality filled life.

Have you moved into larger living quarters? Then why not make the most of it. When your children visit, create an environment that provides them with the security and privacy that they need. If your two boys must share a bedroom in their mother's home, think how pleased they will be to have a room of their own when they visit your house. Again, we are not talking about bribery or popularity contests. We are merely making some practical suggestions that can only benefit your children. And if the quality of their lives is made better, then we can almost assure you that your post-divorce relationship will be more satisfying and successful.

If the non-custodial parent's circumstances change for the better, and such parent is willing to share his good fortune with the child, then often times the custodial parent will openly encourage and promote ever-expanding contact. You will find that you are seeing your child more often. Before you know it, you may have obtained indirectly what you could never have obtained directly: a virtual change in the custody arrangement. However, this change will have been the result of a gradual and natural process. No judges. No court. No victimized child in the middle of a battle, the genesis of which was in fact an egocentric power play.

Again, we emphasize that we are not encouraging the non-custodial parent to bribe his child with the fruits of his improved economic position. Rather, we are advising that you use your good fortune to proper and reasonable advantage. We do not mean *your* advantage. We mean, instead, an advantage to be experienced by your child. Your good fortune should result not only in an improvement in your lifestyle, but it should also be used to create fertile ground for an overall improvement in the relationship between you and your child. Think about our advice before you jump into the tricky and unpredictable current we call custody modification proceedings.

In a few moments, we will explore the "substantial and material change" doctrine. But first we should emphasize that although this doctrine is the legal standard used by the majority of states in determining post-divorce custody modifications, some jurisdictions use different legal approaches. Several states, for example, utilize a stricter, two-level system of determination. These states say that, except for emergencies, they won't even consider a modification request if 2 years have not elapsed from the date of the divorce. Within this time period, a change of custody proceeding will only be entertained if there is a *clear showing* that the child's existing environment *seriously endangers* the physical, mental, moral or emotional health of the child.

After 2 years have elapsed, the courts that have adopted this approach become a little more flexible—and we emphasize the phrase "a little more." If more than 2 years have passed, these states will modify either upon the consent of the custodial parent or if "the child's present environment seriously endangers his physical, mental, moral or emotional health, and the harm likely to be caused by a change of environment is outweighed by its advantages to the child."

As is apparent, the legal standard is not much different from that applied in cases where the change is sought before 2 years have elapsed from the divorce or original custody award. In our opinion, this stricter legal standard is gradually losing favor even in those states that pay it lip service. While it is true that all states will carefully scrutinize a post-divorce custody modification demand in order to insure and encourage family stability, and so that children don't find themselves bounced back and forth between parents like Mexican jumping beans, it is equally true that these same courts recognize that a change may be necessary even though the factual context is devoid of evidence that the child's mental or physical health is "seriously endangered." Indeed, we see a definite trend where states are not only rejecting the serious endangerment standard, but adopting an even more liberal approach than the substantial change doctrine.

For example, Michigan has adopted a standard whereby post-divorce change in custody will occur if there exists "clear and convincing evidence" that such modification is in the "child's best interests." And in New York, the courts recently shed their old standard which had required an *extraordinary* change of circumstance, adopting, instead, an approach that considers "the totality of circumstances." While a court will never change custody because of a parent's or child's whims, fantasies or transient emotions, it appears that more and more judges are recognizing that different situations require a more fluid approach. Only by accepting a flexible legal standard will the child's best interests remain at the forefront of any modification proceeding.

ANATOMY OF A MODIFICATION PROCEEDING

So what do courts look for when a post-divorce demand for a change in custody is made? The answer is simple to express, a lot more difficult to apply. Succinctly put, the courts look for the existence of those *factual elements* that warrant a change. A basic statement, isn't it? But stop reading for a moment and give yourself time to think about it. Seriously, no cheating. Take 2 minutes and allow the concept to sink in.

If you actually conducted this experiment, we are willing to bet that your mind approached it on two levels. The first level was an immediate curiosity regarding the meaning of "factual elements." Like most, your second level of approach was to think of certain situations that you believed a judge would consider to be relevant to a custody modification issue. In other words, you would have defined the concept by yourself—a definition born out of your own background and unique life experiences.

This is exactly what a court will do. A judge cannot help but bring to the modification proceeding his or her own personal beliefs, prejudices and predilections. Whenever we ask our clients to tell us the three most important "factual elements" that they think a judge will consider in making a custody modification determination, we hardly ever get the same answer twice. Each one of us carries our own priority system. So do judges. We may all share a deep concern for the welfare of our children, yet our religious, moral and cultural beliefs may be entirely dissimilar. While it is definitely true that these differences are "what make the world go 'round," it also makes a custody modification proceeding entirely unpredictable and downright complex.

You must also add to this inherent complexity another element: change. Couples who remain married change, as do their divorced counterparts. The reckless attitudes of youth are gradually replaced by play-it-safe conservativism. Or just the opposite may occur. The middle-aged banker may suddenly quit his job and change his entire lifestyle. And these changes affect the way a parent will approach the subject of child-rearing.

Now, add another ingredient: the divorce. After the divorce, parenting difficulties are magnified. Visitation is unfortunately a poor solution to an even worse problem. Communication is essential to successful parenting.

Yet the divorce process all too often results in just the opposite. We need not remind you that wounded people find it difficult to speak civilly to one another. And throughout it all, the children are caught in the middle

We believe that many child custody modification proceedings are entirely unnecessary. And so do many judges. That is why some states, such as California, require the parents to mediate their differences before permitting one or the other to commence a formal court proceeding. More times than not, a demand for custodial change is the result of frustration and an overall inability to work the problem out through open discussion between the parents. It just seems that the divorce has left too many scars. While it cannot be denied that your ex remains your son's father, you also can't deny your bitterness. You will never forgive him for putting down all those lies on the divorce petition, and you simply cannot forget his look of righteous indignation when you asked him for $10 per week more in child support.

And there is this common situation: Rick never came to terms with his divorce. It seemed that his wife of 12 years just walked in one day and said it was all over. After a lot of indirect discussion, he discovered that his ex was romantically involved with another man. Rick would not give his wife the satisfaction of seeing him hurt or in pain; he gave her everything she wanted, including the divorce.

But Rick remains an angry and bitter man. Three years after the divorce his social life is still totally unfulfilling. He just cannot seem to interact with another female. When he is honest with himself, he admits that his buddies at work are a poor substitute for the companionship he is seemingly unable to find.

His boys are now 5 and 7. Unknown to even Rick, he has unconsciously transferred the residual fallout from the divorce to the children. To have them live with him has become an overriding obsession. He believes that it is the only way to regain his self-worth. Another part of him also recognizes that a change of custody would be a satisfying way to get back at his ex for the pain that she has caused him.

Forget for a moment that the children know nothing of their father's desire. If they were told, both boys wouldn't know quite what to say. They love their father and like to see him as much as possible. But their home remains with their mother. Rick, however, has psyched himself up to a point where he doesn't give a damn.

The die is cast. He doesn't even know that he is waiting for an excuse to "attack." You can finish the rest of this illustration yourself, because it could be anything—literally anything—that will "force" Rick to commence a formal proceeding. Is his ex dating a man he doesn't like? Does she get home just a bit late for his taste? Are the children doing poorly in school?

In the hands of a man like Rick, these types of situations take on sinister overtones. In his mind, his ex-wife's choice of boyfriend brands her a slut. Her coming home late a few times means that she is an unfit mother who doesn't know how to supervise the children. And of course, it is obviously her fault that the boys are having trouble in school; according to Rick, she is just not providing them with a suitable intellectual environment.

So the modification proceeding is launched. Rick loses. The children are victimized. His ex-wife's bank account is depleted from being forced to defend the case. And our society has another father who is always eager to tell you how the system doesn't work because it favors the mother.

We have no illusions. We can urge divorced parents to continue to maintain open communication until we are blue in the face, but many parents are unable to get over the negative effects of the divorce process. The only thing that we can say is that in our experience many post-divorce custody fights can be avoided without resorting to formal proceedings and hired legal guns if the parents are willing to subvert their hostility toward one another in the name of their children's best interests. We leave you with these two important pieces of advice:

1. Remember that the divorce only terminates the marriage, not your status as parents. If more people kept this in mind, there would be fewer custody modification proceedings after the divorce. The parties would be able to approach their perceived difficulties without residual bitterness and rancor.
2. Once divorced, never cut the lines of communication with your former spouse. So long as you remain parents, it is of paramount importance that you are able to put aside your personal animosity in order to promote a healthier parent-child relationship. It is high time that divorced couples woke up to the fact that their personal feelings for one another are less important than their willingness to work together to raise a reasonably well-adjusted child.

THE FACTUAL ELEMENTS

If you have a custody-related problem and you are not reaching for the telephone to talk it over with your former spouse at this very moment, then one of two things must have happened. Either you have already attempted to reach a compromise with your ex and such efforts have failed, or you still remain unsure about whether your situation warrants modification. If you *are* sure but do not know how to go about effectuating the necessary legal apparatus, be patient. We will get to you in a little while.

But first, we must discuss in greater detail the most important factors, that is, the factual elements that usually determine whether a post-divorce change of custody will occur or whether the effort is doomed to ignominious and harmful failure. While at least one of the following factual elements will be present in a majority of custody modification proceedings, we emphasize that no hard and fast rule exists. What one judge considers to be serious endangerment, another judge considers trivial. A substantial and material change of circumstance often means something different to each judge—even when those judges are sitting in courts within the same state. Inconsistent decisions are rampant. There is no certainty in the area of post-divorce custody litigation. But several general rules and trends are clear.

Here is a list of the eight most important and common factual elements that tend to predetermine a court's decision to either modify or retain the post-divorce custody arrangement. In order of importance:

1. The continuity factor
2. The sexual relationship factor
3. The child's preference factor
4. The interference with visitation factor
5. The step parent/new family factor
6. The drug and alcohol factor
7. The quantitative time factor
8. The maternal preference/primary caretaker factor

The Continuity Factor

Even when a legitimate request has been made to change an initial custody determination, the courts will bend over backward to insure minimal disruption to the child's life. A review of the legal standards that are generally used to determine whether custody will be modified reveals that there exists a general predisposition to maintain the status quo. Why else require that there be a substantial change in circumstances before permitting the custody change? The idea is to promote stability in the child's life by discouraging frequent modification proceedings.

Let's say that your child has been residing with your ex-wife for the 4 years since the divorce was finalized. During this time you have maintained close contact with your child, visiting often and sharing in all major child-rearing decisions. Through the years, you have used your parenting time to help your child get over the initial confusion and disorientation that resulted from the termination of your marriage. From the ashes of a bitter divorce, a healthy parent–child relationship has developed.

Is this the continuity factor to which we refer? From your point of view, especially if you are contemplating a change of custody request, the answer is unfortunately an unequivocal *no*.

When the judge talks about the stability and continuity factor, he is always referring to the child's life with the *custodial* parent. Your visitation may be a model of healthy parent–child interaction. You may never have missed even one weekend with your son. Whenever your ex needed a last minute stand-in for the babysitter, you were there. Yet throughout this time period your child has continued to reside primarily with his mother. He has gone to the same school, played with the same neighbors and taken the same bus from the same corner to the same Sunday school for the past 4 years.

No matter how solid your relationship with your boy, no judge in any jurisdiction we know will change custody if the child's life with his mother has been continuous and stable. Stated another way, the continuity factor is most often used to *deny* post-divorce custody modifications. When all things are equal between the competing parents, the one with whom the child has resided on a continual and stable basis will win. Don't even think about changing custody if the *only* factual element that you can point to is your own improved relationship with your child. So long as the child's environment with the custodial parent has been consistent and continuous, the court will not entertain your application to modify unless other factual elements warrant. Again, we emphasize that the purpose behind this general rule remains the desire to promote stability in the child's life, minimize further trauma and avoid the disruption that is always present when a change of custody is actually put into effect.

When a court writes a decision that denies a request to change custody, it will invariably make reference to the continuity factor. A judge rightly figures that if the child has made a reasonably healthy adjustment to the divorce, there is no reason why another adjustment should be forced upon him. It just makes sense to deny modification when the child has become used to his post-divorce environment.

Of course, a custody modification proceeding is never black and white. This is as good a time as any to emphasize that it is an extremely rare case that presents only one factual element to be resolved. Most times the factors that we will be discussing interrelate and overlap. A custodial parent may have the continuity factor on his or her side, but there may be evidence that such custodial parent is abusing alcohol or drugs. Or your daughter may have lived with your ex for the last 6 years, but she is now vociferously voicing a keen desire to move in with you. The point is that the continuity factor—and all of the other factual elements that we will explore—rarely arise in a singular context. The issues are almost always more subtle and complex. As we discuss the remaining factors, you must remember that, except in the most unique circumstances, the existence of any one factor is rarely determinative of a custody modification.

Getting back to the issue of continuity, we have already seen that this factual element remains a difficult burden to overcome when seeking a change in the original custody award. However, a judge sometimes talks about this factual element against a slightly different backdrop. This occurs when the custodial parent has made frequent changes of residence during the post-divorce period.

Rita was awarded custody of her two children approximately two and one half years ago. There is no question that during this time she has been the primary custodial parent; her two children have remained with her on a continuous basis since the divorce. Her ex has recently petitioned the court for a change of custody. No sweat, you say? The continuity factor controls; her ex will most definitely lose. To which we reply: not so fast. You haven't let us finish describing the factual setting.

As it turns out, since the initial custody determination, Rita has moved five times. The children have attended schools in three different districts, and their mother has switched jobs seven times. On the other hand, her ex-husband has remained in the same home since the divorce, and except for the time that he was laid off because of a back injury, John has been employed at the same manufacturing firm.

In Rita's case, the judge changed custody, finding that the continuity of the children's residence with the custodial parent had been nullified by so many moves within such a short time period. The judge took particular note that Rita's frequent moves had made it impossible for the children to form any lasting friendships with children their own age. It was particularly important to this judge that the children had been forced to attend three different schools and that one of the children was already manifesting signs of disorientation by poor academic performance. John was given custody, and his ex was granted liberal and broad visitation rights.

But don't get too comfortable with your new-found knowledge. As we said at the beginning of this chapter, there is no hard and fast rule when it comes to custody modification proceedings. More than one judge has refused to change custody solely on the basis of the custodial parent's frequent changes of residence. Many courts do not buy the argument that the location of a child's home necessarily impacts on environmental stability. These judges believe that stability remains a function of a parent's attitude and child-rearing approach. It is how well a parent copes with his or her moves that determines the child's best interests, as well as the child's adaption. In other cases, the judge will look behind the moves to determine the reasons why they have occurred. For example, we represented a custodial mother who had enlisted in the United States Air Force. As a part of her job, she was forced to relocate quite a bit, particularly in the early years of her commission. In this situation, the judge refused to modify the custody arrangement and specifically noted that the children had shown no ill effects from their required moves. This judge went so far as to actually observe that many of our most esteemed Americans had grown up as "army brats."

Hence, the continuity factor may be characterized as both a positive or negative element when seeking to modify the initial determination of child custody. All things being equal, and so long as the children appear reasonably well adjusted, the continuity factor will act as a major foil to your modification demand. No judge will want to disrupt the custodial pattern that has been created since the divorce—even when you can show that your own relationship with the child has vastly improved. The general rule, then, is that where there exists no indication that a change in custody will significantly enhance a child's welfare, it is considered to be in the child's best interests not to disrupt his or her life. Conversely, continuity means relatively little when the custodial parent has made frequent and disruptive moves during the interim period. But even then, a non-custodial parent cannot be assured of winning a modification of custody. As one judge recently said, "Stability is a function of parental attitude and not of geography."

The Sexual Relationship Factor

In this day and age, couples who live together outside of marriage hardly warrant a raised eyebrow. "Palimony" is a word we find in most dictionaries. And even with a return to more traditional values, resulting in an increase in marriage and decrease in cohabitation, millions of people openly live with a member of the opposite sex without the benefit of a marriage license. Of course we must mention homosexual relationships as well. Cohabitation is not necessarily defined by the particular couple's sexual orientation or preference.

We are about to attempt to navigate some of the murkiest waters to be found in the seas of custody modifications. The going will be treacherous. The currents are constantly changing. It really doesn't matter that we have the most recent navigational chart. The weather continues to be unpredictable and the sandbar we avoided last week may pop up without warning in an entirely different location.

Our metaphor is, indeed, apt. When a parent engages in nonmarital sex after the divorce, the legal repercussions upon the original custody award may be quite surprising. States differ in their approach, and it is not uncommon to have two different decisions in the same state arising from extremely similar facts, the only distinction being the identity of the judge who rendered the custody opinion. General rules are hard to come by; even major trends are difficult to discern. But one thing remains clear: if a custodial parent decides to have an open, nonmarital sexual affair, he or she is inviting a demand for custody modification.

Let's start with the rule enunciated by a majority of states These jurisdictions say that a nonmarital sexual relationship, standing alone, should not automatically result in a change of custody. Pretty open-minded, you might initially conclude. But let's look a bit closer and analyze the language that these very same courts often utilize in defining this general rule:

> A parent's *infidelity* or sexual *indiscretions* should be a consideration in a custody modification dispute only if it can be shown that such factor may adversely affect the child's welfare.

Note the words *infidelity* and *indiscretions*. Are you getting the picture? And you must remember that these are the more liberal jurisdictions.

Other states have developed a presumptive negative bias against a custodial parent who engages in nonmarital sexual relations. Although most courts remain willing to look beyond the mere existence of the sexual relationship to see if the conduct is actually having a negative effect on the children, some judges will automatically assume that the relationship itself is determinative of the change of custody demand. For example, the Illinois Supreme Court permitted modification of custody to the father on the basis that the children's mother had lived with another man in "open and public" adultery. Since 1979, the date of this notorious decision, the courts in Illinois have attempted to back away somewhat from this automatic presumptive approach. But the decision remains the law in that state, and indeed, is entirely reflective of approaches used in many other courts. These judges will just assume that nonmarital cohabitation makes the parent unfit to retain custody.

Remember, we are still dealing with heterosexual relationships. It is also important to emphasize that a distinction must be drawn between a relatively monogamous nonmarital relationship and sexual conduct that a court may determine is promiscuous. The former situation will more likely be tolerated in change of custody disputes. The thrust of this chapter is to offer practical advice to the parent either contemplating or defending a post-divorce custody proceeding. It is beyond our scope to discuss the all too common chauvinistic value system that, unfortunately, continues to permeate entire sectors of our legal system. A father with several sexual partners may be viewed quite differently than his former wife who has also taken several lovers since the divorce. Of course, we disagree with sexual chauvinism in any of its guises. As we will be discussing shortly, we therefore oppose those states that have retained an automatic preference in favor of the mother when child custody is at issue.

At any rate, the more general view continues to be that a nonmarital sexual relationship or open cohabitation will not be presumed to have an automatic negative effect upon the children. If you choose to petition the court for a change of custody based upon your ex's sexual conduct, then you will have the burden of proving that such relationship negatively impacts upon the psychological or emotional welfare of your children. Before pressing the modification button, however, you should ask yourself these basic questions:

- Has your ex's lover moved into the house with your child on a full or majority time basis?
- Is the pursuit of your former spouse's recent love interest taking so much time and energy that your child is not being properly cared for?
- Has your child recently complained about his or her relationship with your ex's companion?
- What is the physical layout of your former spouse's home as it pertains to the all-important privacy factor? Is your child sufficiently distanced from the bedroom to avoid embarrassment and anxiety-ridden confusion?
- What kind of relationship has developed between your child and the other individual? Does he or she openly display affection, help with homework, discipline your child and take a role in child rearing decisions?
- Has your child complained about being pressured to call the individual "mommy" or "daddy" as the case may be?
- Has your child manifested sudden shyness, nervousness, anger or other similar emotional responses? Has your child's academic performance fallen off to any significant degree?
- Has your child been put under pressure by your former spouse and/or his or her companion to keep the relationship a "secret" from you?

These questions are designed only as a guide. Their purpose is to help you focus on those issues that are most important—at least in post-divorce custody modification proceedings. Obviously, if your ex's love interest has caused him or her to lose all perspective so that the children are being left unsupervised or suddenly neglected, a change in custody is warranted. Similarly, the relationship that your child has with the custodial parent's "partner" remains of paramount importance. The quality of nonmarital relationships differs as widely as the quality of marriages. The individual may be a positive factor in your child's growth period.

On the other hand, your spouse may be involved with an individual who is abusive, has a drinking problem or in some other way creates a negative or even dangerous atmosphere. Sometimes your former spouse's cohabitation partner may unintentionally cause your child to experience anxiety, such as when there is pressure to refer to him or her as "daddy" or "mommy." Most psychologists that we have interviewed, as well as judges, do not take kindly to any premature popularity contests, even when the motives are well-meaning.

The bottom line remains the effect that the relationship has on your child. Many 14-year-old boys have no trouble integrating their mother's live-in companion with the healthy parenting time spent with their natural father. On the other hand, an 11-year-old girl just approaching puberty may be confused and overtly disturbed by her father's female friend who she cannot help but see as a rival for her father's affections. This child may suddenly verbalize a desire to live with her mother, thereby forcing the issue and creating a situation ripe for post-divorce legal maneuvering.

Each case must be judged on its own merits. While you may find a judge who will change custody on the basis of cohabitation alone, more and more are looking to the totality of circumstances in an effort to determine the actual impact upon the child. If the child remains happy and well-adjusted, you can bet that custody will not be changed. While the judge may feel constrained to discuss traditional moral values, the continuity factor will still prevail. But let any evidence of even the slightest negative consequence creep into the modification proceeding, and no matter how untraditional or liberal a judge's personal views may be, he will undoubtedly decide in favor of the petitioning parent. Indeed, in 1982, approximately twice as many custody arrangements were modified on account of cohabitation, as were retained for the same reason.

* * *

Homosexuality, as you can guess, is even more problematic in the post-divorce arena.

Robert and Ann had been married for 7 years before irreconcilable differences drove them apart. At the time of their divorce, their daughter Becky was 6 years old. Husband and wife had no desire to drag the process out, so they signed a separation agreement that became the basis for their divorce. The divorce decree specifically incorporated that portion of the separation agreement which gave custody of Becky to her mother.

Six years later, Robert is petitioning the court for a change of custody. During the time from the divorce to the commencement of the modification proceeding, Robert had visitation rights with Becky, which he exercised every Sunday when he picked his child up from his former wife's apartment and brought her to his home where he resides with his present wife who he married almost a year ago. Robert's petition states that approximately 2 years ago, a woman named Shana moved into the apartment with his former wife and daughter. The petition further documents that while Becky has a separate bedroom, his ex-wife and Shana sleep together in the other bedroom.

Before the trial, and based on Robert's sworn petition, the judge appoints another lawyer, known as a *legal guardian,* to represent the child's interests. As we will see later in this chapter, such an appointment is very common in custody modification situations. The judge further orders that the legal guardian visit the mother's apartment immediately in order to verify some of the allegations that are being made. A few days later, the lawyer reports that he found the premises to be "very clean and modern"; and that he met Shana on his visit, and she readily admitted that she and Ann shared a bedroom and that they were involved in a "healthy" lesbian relationship.

Armed with this independent data, the judge next appoints a psychiatrist to interview the child and both parents, as well as Shana. The psychiatrist advises the court that Ann and Shana freely admitted their homosexual relationship. He is quick to add, however, that they told him that they never discuss homosexuality in front of Becky, nor demonstrate any overt or open affection toward one another in the presence of the child.

At the actual hearing, all of the testimony of the parties was in keeping with the findings of both the legal guardian and court-appointed psychiatrist. In addition, the father called another psychiatrist as a witness, who testified that a child can emulate the conduct of one parent and that, in his opinion, the present living environment would be harmful to Becky. Not to be outdone, Ann called a psychiatrist of her own as a supporting witness. Not too surprisingly, this psychiatrist sharply disagreed with the former, stating that it was "highly unlikely" that a child would become a homosexual on the basis of a mother's conduct in the privacy of her own bedroom.

In the privacy of *his* chambers—another procedure that you will find is common in custody hearings—the judge interviews Becky. She tells him that she loves both parents equally but that she wants to continue living with her mother. She advises the judge that she really doesn't get along with her paternal grandmother who lives with her father, although his new wife and she are becoming "great friends." The judge observes Becky to be clean, well dressed, and normal in her appearances and responses to the questions posed by him. In his discretion, the judge decides not to question Becky at all on the issue of any "alleged" homosexuality, believing instead that the indirect approach will give him a better reading about the child's emotional and psychological stability.

The hearing continues. The school psychologist testifies that Becky is doing well in her classes, although she apparently is not working "to her full intellectual capacity." Although he finds Becky to be well motivated, he is surprised at her average grades in light of her performance on a standardized IQ test which indicated a "superior" score.

Now to the decision. The judge ruled in favor of the father. Although stating that a homosexual mother, "by virtue of that fact alone," is not necessarily an unfit mother, the court decided that Becky's home environment was not a proper atmosphere in which to be brought up, nor was the "lesbian relationship" in the child's best interests. The decision emphasized that the mother was free to establish her own lifestyle, but added that in the court's opinion, this particular lifestyle was jeopardizing Becky's emotional health and welfare. But it didn't stop there. Not only did the judge change custody to Robert, but he ordered that Ann's visitation be restricted and subject to these absolute conditions:

1. That the child will not remain overnight at the mother's residence, nor is she to be taken there to visit while Shana or other homosexuals are present

2. That Ann will not take Becky to any place where known homosexuals are present
3. That Ann will not "involve this child in any homosexual activities or publicity"

We would like to say that we have made our point. But as you have probably guessed, we are about to tell you again that things are never quite as they appear. In the same year in another state, a strikingly similar custody modification case went forward. There, the court permitted a homosexual mother to retain custody of her two daughters, ages 7 and 11. The judge refused to allow the non-custodial parent to modify custody, observing that the children were being raised in a stable, loving home and could obviously overcome any societal pressure or prejudice that they might encounter.

And in another situation with similar facts, the judge also refused to take custody away from a homosexual mother. But the court surprised everyone by reinstating an order that the mother's "lesbian friend" could not continue to reside with her and the children anymore. As should be obvious, no set pattern exists in these types of situations. We can only offer this practical advice:

- If your ex has custody of your child and is engaged in a homosexual relationship, don't jump the gun prematurely. Take a few steps back and attempt to overcome your initial outrage and anxiety. Even mental health professionals are divided over the question of homosexual parenting. Most rely on a belief—as opposed to hard data and facts—that children will either emulate the parent and become homosexual or will develop their own sexual preference through a natural and internally motivated value system.
- Keep your eye on the ball. That is, maintain a focus on the actual affect that the relationship is having on your child. If your review points to a negative affect, then do not hesitate. On the other hand, the trauma caused by a formal legal proceeding may be more injurious to your child than your former spouse's homosexual relationship.
- Remember, the majority of judges will still view the homosexual issue as only one factual element to be analyzed. If you are thinking about petitioning for a change, get your own act together. Make sure that a change of custody to your favor is actually practical. Do you have enough space? Are your hours flexible? Can you offer proper supervision and security? You may as well ask yourself these questions before you petition because the court most certainly will. And if you don't have the right answers, then you shouldn't be wasting your time as well as the court's. Your petition for modification will be viewed as a vindictive and knee-jerk reaction.

For those custodial parents who are either involved in or contemplating a homosexual relationship, please heed these words:

- Be discreet, but not unduly secretive.
- Never attempt to thrust your views upon the child.
- Never display overt, sexual affection except in the privacy of your bedroom.
- And never permit your relationship to cloud the responsibility you owe to your child to maintain a clean, safe and healthy home environment.

The Child's Preference Factor

The child's preference regarding who he or she wants to live with is roughly twice as important a factual element in post-divorce situations as compared to initial custody determinations. Basically, the reason for this noticeable shift in emphasis results from a court's willingness to give more weight to a child's preference after a custodial arrangement is actually in effect for a while. At the divorce level, the custody question is filled with hypotheticals and necessary projections. However, once the decision has been made, the child's living environment can more readily be analyzed.

It is rather like an architect's drawing. Without some experience or formal training, most of us look at these plans with only a prayer to guide us in our final decision. Once the walls are up, however, it becomes a lot easier to see what the architect is actually doing. At this point you may recognize aspects that were never obvious or apparent when you were looking at the two-dimensional diagrams. You may discover certain possibilities that could only have occurred to you while walking through a three-dimensional structure.

This is the way it is after the divorce. All things having been equal at the divorce stage, a judge might have decided custody on nothing but instinct. But now, after 2 years, the custody arrangement has a real form and shape. Mid-course corrections may be necessary, and who is best to assist us than the child himself?

Let us also keep in mind the obvious factor of change. After 4 years, your child has developed in new ways and directions. His or her child-rearing requirements may be entirely different. The non-custodial parent may really be in the better position to meet those new requirements and needs. And it is only time that defines and refines what is in the child's continued best interest.

There may be a more prosaic reason why a child's preference is taken more seriously in post-divorce custody cases. Many divorces occur when the children are still too young to voice any opinion regarding custody arrangements. With the passage of time, children tend to find their voices.

So how is the child's preference factor applied? As one judge recently told us, "If all I had to do was automatically heed a child's wishes, there would be no such thing as a custody modification trial." This brings us to the majority rule as it is applied by most courts throughout our nation. Simply stated, this principle holds that the child's preference regarding custody must be considered as an important factual element but not the determinative factor. It comes down to a question of weight. The more mature and articulate the child, the more weight his preference will be given. The younger and less mature child will not be taken as seriously.

Judges will interview the child—either on or off the record—in the privacy of court chambers, without attorneys present. The purpose of this interview is to ascertain not only the child's desire but, more importantly, the underlying reasons for the stated preference. Michael was a case in point. Throughout the proceedings he had consistently held that he wanted a change of custody to his father's residence. It appeared that his father had some legitimate reasons for the demanded modification, but

Justice Oberline continued to have misgivings. It made sense that 13-year-old Michael might want to become closer to his father, but the court couldn't shake its feeling that something was being overlooked.

During his first interview with the child, Justice Oberline knew that the child was holding something back. He decided on an indirect approach, terminating the interview after only 5 minutes but reserving the right to call Michael back into chambers when he saw fit. Meanwhile, the hearing proceeded; the father put in evidence of his increased assets, and the mother was forced to admit that her son was having trouble in school.

Actually, the judge almost missed it. Cognizant of the general rule that an improvement in the non-custodial parent's financial position is generally not relevant, he was daydreaming somewhat when the evidence of the father's increased spending powers was introduced. In fact, he was just about to cut the lawyer off at the knees, having heard enough about dinners in expensive restaurants and season tickets at the stadium when fate intervened.

As the father continued to testify, Justice Oberline distractedly looked over the financial information that had just been introduced and marked as evidence. He saw it immediately and called a brief recess to interview Michael a second time.

In chambers, Michael was a little more guarded. Justice Oberline got right to the point.

"How do you like your new minibike?" asked the judge.

"What minibike, your Honor?"

"Enough of this nonsense, Michael. You're thirteen years old. If you want me to take you seriously, then let's not bull one another around. I just saw a receipt for the minibike outside. Your dad bought it for you, didn't he?"

"I guess so," replied the boy.

It took a little more time to get the rest of it out of Michael, but before 20 minutes had elapsed Justice Oberline had what he needed. His subsequent decision, denying the father's demand for a custody change, reflected his discovery. In part, it read:

> I found the child to be a mature and articulate thirteen-year-old boy who expressed a burning desire to live with his father. I conducted an interview with the child, off the record. It appeared to me that the child had been prepared to maintain a conspiracy of silence in respect to certain occurrences, which, because of the holiday season, I must say reminded me of "The Twelve Days of Christmas."
>
> The child's stated preference is entirely understandable in light of the father's presentation of expensive gifts immediately preceding his petition to modify custody. These gifts, all given to his son within a two-week period, included a horse, two color-television sets, a shotgun, a minibike, a motorcycle and a private telephone. Under such circumstances, the court shall deal with the child's preference with due dispatch, and finds . . .

This case illustrates some of the inherent problems in giving too much weight to a child's preference. It underscores the scrutiny and caution with which judges approach the issue. If you are basing your request for a custody modification solely on your child's statements that he wants to live with you, then you are flirting with disappointment. Of all the factual elements that a court will consider, the child's preference is closest to a "wild card." While this factor may act as a tie breaker in appropriate situations, it is often nullified by the existence of other factual elements such as the continuity and stability factor.

The Interference With Visitation Factor

As you saw from the chapter on enforcement of visitation rights, the courts have become extremely serious in their efforts to protect the non-custodial parent's contact with the child. While enforcement devices such as fines and even imprisonment of the violating parent remain persuasive legal tools, the ultimate sanction is a change of custody. From the custodial parent's point of view, the interference with or denial of visitation is, perhaps, the most harmful factual element to continued custody except for actual physical abuse of the child. In short, the interference with the non-custodial parent's visitation may be a *determinative* factor when a court is called upon to decide a modification demand.

Our advice is simple: don't do it. Under appropriate circumstances, you are handing custody to your ex on a silver platter. It can no longer be denied that children of divorced couples need the psychological anchor of consistent contact with *both* parents. A custodial parent who maliciously or intentionally places barriers in the path of a child's time with his other parent is exhibiting a callous disregard for the child's welfare. And judges are increasingly less tolerant of such behavior—a trend that will no doubt continue.

How good are your instincts?

1. Your 10-year-old son says that he doesn't like his father's new girlfriend. The last time that your ex dropped him off after a weekend visitation, the child cried for 2 hours.

   Question: Do you refuse to allow your ex his parenting time next scheduled visit?

2. Your ex has missed three child support payments in a row. He had the nerve to come around this morning to see his daughter. You told him to get off your property and refused to permit Jennifer to be with him.

   Question: Was your decision correct?

3. Your 12-year-old has suddenly begun demanding that she be allowed to live with your ex, that she would like to "visit you and live with Mom." You fear that your former spouse has been resorting to brainwashing. You figure that if your daughter is kept away from her mother for a month or so, you may have won a major battle in the war of manipulation and possibly avoided a legal custody fight.

   Question: Should you begin to work on your strategy?

4. Your son has just failed another arithmetic test. When you tell him that you are banishing him to his room for the weekend to study, he reminds you that this is "father's weekend with me." To make matters worse, it appears that your ex has already paid for two tickets to a local recital. You get on the telephone and demand that your ex-husband cancel his plans for the weekend. "He's got to study and I don't give a damn about this weekend's plans," you tell him.

Question: Have you properly discharged your custodial responsibilities?

If you answered "no" to all of these questions, there is little chance that your present custody arrangement will become vulnerable to a modification attack based upon a claim that visitation is being denied. The lesson here is to resist resorting to "self-help." In other words, do not take matters into your own hands.

Of course, we recognize that true emergencies may arise. There may be those times where you have received verifiable evidence that your child's physical or emotional welfare is seriously endangered by a continuation of the existing visitation arrangement. We recently represented a father who had custody of his 6-year old daughter. Our client told us that he feared that his child had been sexually molested by the mother's boyfriend. We immediately arranged for a doctor to examine the child. By the end of the day, the physician reported that there was "some physical evidence" of sexual contact. Almost simultaneously, the father reported that his daughter had anxiously admitted that the boyfriend had "touched me where he's not allowed."

Armed with this information, we petitioned the court for an immediate suspension of outside-the-home visitation with the mother, pending fuller investigation and fact-finding. The judge signed the order, but upon our client's consent, the non-custodial parent's visitation continued in the father's home without, obviously, the presence of the boyfriend. Several points need be made: most importantly, we did not advise our client to deny visitation. Instead, we sought court intervention so that it could never be claimed that the custodial parent had intentionally interfered with visitation. Similarly, the court itself refused to entirely terminate parenting time. Rather, the judge ordered that the mother continue to have visitation under supervised conditions until the controversy could be more fully explored. Hence, even in an unquestionable emergency, the court refused to sever parental ties completely.

We should also mention that many "emergencies" turn out to be false alarms. Even doctors can make mistakes. And many a professional will tell you that a child sometimes has difficulty distinguishing between reality and the imaginary world which is often superimposed. Finally, there have been a recent rash of cases where custodial parents have, unfortunately, "cried wolf" regarding the existence of sexual or physical abuse. These parents have merely discovered another excuse to vindictively deny visitation. The courts, in most cases, are onto this scam. That is why a judge will hardly ever encourage or countenance self-help. If you act on your own in denying visitation—even when you are motivated by laudable intent—you almost always lose points.

In each of our four examples, a decision to suspend or interfere with visitation would have been wrong. If no child support is forthcoming, you cannot simply suspend visitation as a reflex action. When it comes to visitation, turnabout is *not* fair play. As we discussed in the chapter on visitation enforcement, many courts are willing to *link* the payment of child support with the right to see your child. But only by court order; you are not allowed to do it on your own. What about the brainwashing example? First of all, we should mention that studies indicate that true brainwashing is relatively rare. Perhaps only one in ten children are manipulated to the point of losing their own free will. Again, we are not talking about simple parental bribery that results in only a transitory switch of allegiance. In both the second and third illustrations, your response should have been a court petition to modify the existing visitation arrangement. Only after obtaining the court's permission would it have been safe for you to "fine tune" your ex's visitation rights.

In the last example your first step should have been to discuss the matter with your ex-husband. Your goal is to persuade him that, under the circumstances, a better grade in math is more important than a recital. Allow him room to reach his own conclusion. Make sure he understands that he must share in this child-rearing decision with you. Finally, alleviate any anxiety on his part by encouraging your ex to forsake this one weekend in exchange for an "unscheduled" visit during the week or on one of "your" weekends. An ultimatum or unilateral denial of visitation to prove a point is definitely not in your child's best interests.

We cannot emphasize too much that the custodial parent does not have the automatic legal right to interfere with visitation even when there appears to be a good reason to do so. In order to fully protect your own custodial rights, virtually all states require that you first ask the court, by way of formal petition, for permission to do so. As we saw in Chapter 12, modification of visitation is not necessarily an insurmountable legal obstacle. If circumstances warrant, a judge will be entirely receptive to a change in the visitation arrangement, so long as such modification remains in the children's best interests.

Three cardinal rules:

1. DON'T interfere with visitation for base reasons grounded in emotion and vindictiveness.
2. DON'T resort to self-help in modifying or suspending visitation, even when you believe that you have good reasons to do so.
3. DO petition the court for a formal modification in visitation if circumstances warrant and so that no claim can ever be made that you have intentionally built barriers between your child and the non-custodial parent.

Before turning to the next factual element, we must discuss another common post-divorce occurrence which results in a technical interference with the visitation rights of the non-custodial parent. This occurs when the parent with custody decides to move to another locale. Obviously, a move out of state or a far distance away from the non-custodial parent's residence threatens the existing visitation arrangement. Court-ordered or agreed-upon mid-week parenting time is impossible if your child lives 600 miles away. If such a move does not represent an "interference" with visitation, what does?

In keeping with the tougher stance regarding the protection of visitation rights that we explained in Chapter 11, an ever-increasing number of judges are permitting relocation only where there exist *compelling* financial, educational, employment or health considerations. In addition, even when such compelling reasons exist, the court must be *clearly* satisfied that the move is in the child's best interests. Although legal decisions remain inconsistent when dealing with this issue, a judge will look to the following factors in deciding whether custody should be changed to the non-moving parent:

- What does the child have to say about the anticipated relocation?
- Can visitation be modified so that the non-custodial parent ends up with a visitation schedule that is roughly equivalent to the original arrangement?
- What are the true motives of the parent seeking to change his or her residence?
- Can the needs of the moving parent be met without uprooting the child's residence?
- What ties have developed between the child and the home community?

Certain other factors may be determinative as well. For example, did the custodial parent ever discuss the anticipated move with his or her ex? If the parent began to effectuate the change in residence without disclosing her intentions, then the court will look less favorably on the move. It is also important that the moving parent evidence a legitimate desire to cooperate with the court in preserving as much parent–child contact as possible.

Like most post-divorce custody issues, a judge will look to the best interests of the child. Will the change of residence actually enhance the quality of the child's life? This is the overriding question that a court must answer. So long as a judge believes that the reasons for the move are legitimate and that meaningful visitation can continue in some modified form, the non-custodial parent probably will not succeed in getting actual custody on the basis of the child's accepted change of residence. But let the motives behind the custodial parent's move be even remotely questionable or frivolous, and you will find courts increasingly more willing to modify custody to the petitioning parent. And should you attempt to sneak out of town, you have just about sealed your child's fate. You may be allowed to move, but without your child.

The Stepparent/New Family Factor

Statistics show that the vast majority of people remarry after their divorce. Approximately one out of four households are now headed by single parents. It doesn't take too much imagination to figure that second marriages, therefore, often result in a commingling of children from prior relationships. These children are then faced with the issues that necessarily result from living or interrelating with a stepparent or stepbrother/sister.

When Victor first heard of his ex-wife's remarriage he experienced certain misgivings. He became increasingly more anxious about how his 10-year-old son Dan would adjust to his stepfather. Immediately after the marriage, Victor's fears crystallized.

After only 2 weeks of living with his ex's new husband, Dan was bitterly complaining to his father. These complaints were varied but consistent. It appeared that the new man in Dan's life was "too strict," "eats too much," "yells at Mom" and that he was sending Dan to bed half an hour earlier than his son had become accustomed to. By the third week Dan was complaining even more vociferously, and Victor was sharing the child's anxiety. He loved his son, and he couldn't stand that the boy was so unhappy.

Without exploring the matter further, he pressed the modification trigger. The judge refused to change custody, and we quote from portions of the written opinion because the points made are generally applicable to the majority of situations where a child's adjustment to a stepparent or stepsibling is at issue.

> The fact that the custodial parent remarries and necessarily creates a readjustment period on the part of the child is rarely determinative of a change of custody request in this jurisdiction. This is particularly the case when, as here, the stepparent has testified that he has already begun counseling to assist him in his relationship with the parties' child.
>
> This Court is well aware that Daniel is unhappy with his present living situation. However, we are of the firm opinion that insufficient time has elapsed to properly appraise the situation. In these circumstances, the court is well advised to refrain from ordering a change of custody which, under the circumstances, can only cause further disruption in the child's life.
>
> Under the facts existing herein, we deny the petitioner's request for custody modification. This denial is without prejudice to petitioner's right to commence another proceeding after the parties have attempted readjustment for a period of time to be no less than one year from the date hereof.

Obviously, if the child is being abused at the hands of the stepparent, then immediate modification is entirely warranted. More often than not, however, the child's initial resistance is based more on petty emotions than on real endangerment. New relationships are never easy to form. A child may feel jealous or insecure. He may not get along with his stepbrother or stepsister because they are better athletes or get better grades.

Our advice is simple: Do not jump the gun when your child's complaints signal normal confusion and disorientation, as opposed to victimized physical or mental trauma. Allow enough time to pass to truly determine whether your child's readjustment problems are transitory or more complex. We also urge you not to automatically take your child's side when he begins to complain. The natural tendency may be to feel that you are being "replaced." This emotional response is extremely detrimental to your child's readjustment and well-being. Instead, you should view the remarriage as a natural process, one that can have practical benefits for all involved.

In short, monitor the situation for a while. Encourage your child to be patient. At your end, this is the time where you should redouble your efforts to maintain meaningful contact with your child. If your son or daughter realizes that you are not particularly concerned or upset with the marriage and corresponding change in living environment, the child's anxiety will be alleviated somewhat. And this can only make the readjustment period easier. Do not use the remarriage as an excuse to initiate a popularity contest.

Remember that your child's problem in adjusting to his or her step-family is rarely a determinative factor in custody modification proceedings. When this factual element is discussed, it can be both a negative or positive factor. It all depends on whether the child's relationship with the parent's new spouse is good or bad. But sufficient time must elapse before anyone can properly evaluate such relationship. Therefore, we strongly urge that you permit a "cooling off" period to transpire before talking to a lawyer.

The Drug and Alcohol Factor

This is a relatively easy one. You don't need any illustrations or examples to emphasize what you already know: an abusive parent is unfit to discharge custodial responsibilities. You might ask why this factor is not listed as number one on our list of eight factual elements. You might be surprised to learn that although obvious drug and alcohol abuse is always a determinative factor, it does not come up very often in custody modification proceedings. Most times, the evidence of abuse is clear at the time of the initial custody determination. In only a handful of cases does the custodial parent manifest drug or alcohol related problems after custody has already been awarded.

But if you have evidence that your child is in danger, then do not hesitate to petition for a change of custody. And don't wait for disaster to strike. We know of one situation when custody was changed to the father because the mother had been convicted of driving while intoxicated. The judge believed it was better to be safe than sorry. In another case, the father lost custody when his roommate was arrested for possession of drugs and a search of the apartment turned up drug paraphernalia. The judge reasoned that the child was living in an environment that was "detrimental to her health."

We should also include in this category the mental instability factor. A situation may exist where the custodial parent has been hospitalized for depression or, in extreme cases, has actually attempted suicide. When faced with a claim of emotional instability, the court will invariably rely on psychiatric reports that have been ordered as part of the modification proceeding. The parent who is being subjected to the claim will always have the opportunity to have his or her own psychiatric testimony introduced at the hearing. Again, we are dealing with a rather subjective judicial approach. One lawyer we know claims that his client was denied a change of custody to his favor even though the custodial parent had been hospitalized for severe depression on no less than eight different occasions. Another judge might have modified custody on this basis. It all depends on the variety of factual elements that are present at any given time.

The question of the custodial parent's psychological health rarely exists as the only factual element to be decided in a modification proceeding.

For example, the parent's hospitalization may have been for relatively short periods of time, during which time the child was always supervised and well cared for. Indeed, the child may want to continue to reside with such parent, and the court may give much weight to such wish depending on existing circumstances.

The claim that a custodial parent's ability to care for the child has become impaired may not necessarily be based on a psychological or drug/alcohol related basis, as the following case makes clear. In 1982, Stephanie and George were divorced. Just prior to their trial, they worked out an agreement which the judge accepted and incorporated in their divorce judgment. Regarding their 5-year-old daughter, Carrie, they agreed to a joint legal custody arrangement, with the mother having primary physical custody of the child.

Seventeen months after the divorce, Stephanie was involved in a car accident in which she sustained permanent injuries resulting in paraplegia. During the approximately 6 months in which the mother was hospitalized, Carrie resided with her father. After Stephanie returned home, Carrie resumed living with her, at which point George commenced a custody modification proceeding. His petition was premised on the concept that by reason of his ex's paraplegia, a substantial change in circumstances had occurred and, hence, he should now be awarded primary physical custody of his daughter.

Using the totality of circumstances approach, the judge refused to order the requested custody change. He noted that, among other things, Stephanie was adjusting well to her handicap from both a psychological and physical standpoint. The court noted that one of our most famous presidents had also been confined to a wheelchair and, accordingly, saw no reason to change custody on this basis alone.

We leave this discussion with several observations:

- If there exists a drug or alcohol abuse problem on the part of the custodial parent, then the issue is almost always determinative in favor of the modification.
- A claim of psychological impairment creates more complex issues. If the instability is transient, then a non-custodial parent should think twice before starting formal proceedings. In other words, your focus should remain on the actual effect that the impairment has upon your child. Obviously, if extensive psychiatric hospitalization is required, your custody change will occur virtually by default; no real issue will need to be resolved.
- In cases of actual abuse or neglect, the court is not really faced with a custody question. The path is crystal clear, and the judge will not hesitate to effectuate an immediate change so as to protect the child's physical or psychological health.
- When your modification demand is based on either abuse or neglect—in any of its numerous manifestations—the burden of proof remains on you. If all you have to go on are the statements made by your 8-year old, you are asking for trouble. We suggest that you launch an independent investigation of your own in order to determine for yourself whether your child is living in a dangerous situation. Only then should you press the custody modification button.

The Quantitative Time Factor

Whatever the changes that may have occurred in a parent's life after the divorce, the natural question that is asked concerns *time.* Does the change give you more time to be with your child? When custody was originally awarded to your ex-wife, you were working 8-hour shifts and going to night school. Four years later you work part time and have an adjunct professorship at the local community college.

Or the flipside: you only worked on weekends when the initial custody determination was made. Now you work full time in a retail store where you usually put in 10 hours, 6 days a week. As it is, you get home just in time to pay the housekeeper and kiss your daughter goodnight.

Do these changes auger well for a modification of the existing custody arrangement? Maybe yes; maybe no. While it is true that this factor arises fairly often in post-divorce custody cases, it is equally true that it is *never* a determinative factor. It is merely weighed against all of the other factual elements. But some general comments are in order. First, the child's custody will not be disturbed if you cannot demonstrate that the time you can spend with your child is *significantly* greater than the time that the custodial parent can devote. Your argument for a modification will also be made much stronger if your ex's available time to spend with the child has decreased during the same period that your available time has increased. Finally, under no circumstances should you depend on the mere fact that you have more time to be with your child as your ace in the hole or trump card.

When we listed the factual elements at the beginning of this chapter, this factor was number seven. There is good reason for this. Courts recognize the difference between quantitative time and qualitative time. That is, a judge will focus on what occurs during the period the child is with each parent as opposed to the length of time itself. We shouldn't have to remind you that, when it comes to children, the *quality* of time is more crucial than the quantity. So long as the custodial parent can offer proper supervision, a court will ordinarily not be persuaded by your new-found flexibility. In other words, the quantitative time factor becomes relevant only in those cases when you can show that more time equals better care and supervision for your child.

The Maternal Preference/Primary Caretaker Factor

The last factor relates to certain presumptions that a court may make in custody modification proceedings. Most states have rescinded the old statute that used to give mothers an automatic preference over fathers in custody battles. However, a handful of jurisdictions still retain some vestige of this outdated approach. We say outdated because statistics show that in the last 20 years the percentage of mothers who work outside of the home has doubled. In the 1980's, approximately 60 percent of mothers who have children under 18 and 45 percent of mothers of preschoolers work outside of the home. In addition, most professionals readily agree that parenting has nothing to do with gender.

But despite these uncontroverted facts and statistics, many judges are unfortunately still enrolled in the "old school." These individuals have either a conscious or unconscious bias in favor of the so-called maternal instinct. We mention this factual element only in the interests of telling you the whole story. Although unlikely, you may come before a judge who disregards all of your relevant proof because of his unshakable belief that children must live with their mother. Thankfully, this approach is gradually being replaced by more enlightened thinking.

In fact, such enlightenment has produced an "up and coming" preference. Many states now look to award custody to the *primary caretaker*. As is apparent, such characterization is gender-neutral. Interestingly, this last factual element dovetails quite nicely with the first item on our list, the continuity factor. In essence, these two factors are basically the same; they reward stability while discouraging frequent changes in custody. Regardless of whether you are a male or female, you are the primary caretaker if

1. you prepare and plan the child's meals;
2. your tasks include bathing, grooming and dressing the child;
3. you purchase, clean and care for the child's clothes;
4. you provide the primary medical care, including nursing or arranging needed visits to physicians;
5. you arrange alternative care, *i.e.,* babysitting, day-care, and the like;
6. you put the child to bed at night, attending to him or her in the middle of the night and upon waking in the morning;
7. you are involved in disciplining your child, that is, teaching general manners and toilet training;
8. your child looks to you for religious, cultural and social education; and
9. you are involved in teaching the child such elementary and basic skills as reading, writing and arithmetic.

The primary caretaker factor is really just another way of defining a "fit" parent. Rarely will such parent lose custody after the divorce. The idea is to keep the child in the custody of the parent who is involved in the nitty-gritty of child rearing. Obviously, this factor is less important in joint custody situations where both parents are with the child on a roughly equivalent basis. The courts generally recognize that some post-divorce relationships do not have a "primary" caretaker, that each parent shares the necessary tasks that go into raising the child. Again, we emphasize that this last factor is, in actuality, only a more technical application of the all-important continuity factor.

* * *

You would be sadly mistakened if you thought that our list of eight factual elements represents the entire picture. Other facts may be present in your situation which determine how a modification proceeding will turn out. It would be foolish of us to imply that we have revealed every type of post-divorce custody issue. Just the opposite is true.

The only absolute is that there are no absolutes when dealing with custody questions. There are just too many variables. However, we have attempted to provide you with an overview of the types of issues that usually arise when custody modification proceedings are started. Your particular controversy may be entirely different, but the judicial analysis will be extremely similar. As a petitioning parent, you will be forced to overcome inertia, that is, the court's natural inclination to maintain the status quo. Post-divorce custody changes are viewed as a major disruption in a child's life. Consequently, modifications are discouraged except for good cause and when the change appears to be in the child's best interests.

BEGINNING THE PROCESS

Let us say that you have attempted to reach an accommodation with your ex-spouse. It hasn't done any good. Next, you have carefully and unemotionally reviewed the pros and cons of petitioning for a modification of custody. You have considered the effect that such action will have on your child and have balanced all of the competing issues that exist in your particular situation. In your mind, there is no question that modification of custody is indicated. STOP!

If you are truly honest with yourself, then there should always be a doubt before waging custody warfare. Every factual element may be on your side, but you can never predict how the case will turn out. Most importantly, court proceedings—especially those dealing with custody issues—often have severely negative repercussions upon your child's emotional and psychological welfare. For example, in virtually every instance, the judge will be speaking with your child, and if the child is sufficiently mature, formal sworn testimony will be taken. The vast majority of judges report that the interview process is a frightening experience for the child and that most children exhibit some form of overt anxiety during the interview. Formal testimony is even worse. Many a child has been reduced to tears during cross-examination when opposing counsel is given the opportunity to fully explore the child's stated custodial preference. In general, the child loses all sense of control during a custody battle. He or she is forced to discuss intimate details with the judge, your ex's lawyer and court-appointed psychiatrists. All this formalized procedure can seem quite scary to a child.

Moreover, you can never be sure that your child actually shares *your* belief that custody should be changed to your favor. Many children just don't know what is in their best interests. They may resist the change when it is for their own good, and even when a judge actually orders it. In short, even when modification is warranted, you should never feel too good about it. A self-righteous parent is a shortsighted one.

So you say that you have made the difficult decision to seek judicial intervention regarding the existing custody arrangement. What do you do now? Where do you go?

First stop: your lawyer's office. Throughout this book we have often said that lawyers will not necessarily be needed to accomplish your goal. Enforcement of child support, registering with a collection unit, even visitation enforcement can often be done without hiring an attorney. Alas, the same thing cannot ordinarily be said when it comes to a post-divorce petition to modify custody; an attorney with experience in custody matters is often needed. This is not to say that some individuals do not succeed in roughing it out on their own. The vast majority, however, will require professional legal assistance.

But a knowledgeable client is a successful client. The more you know about the legal area, the more you can assist your own lawyer. That is why we have detailed the various elements that determine modification cases. In discussing your case with your lawyer you will naturally be in a better position to emphasize those factors that can help your argument. Of course, it is certainly not wise to ignore the negative factual elements that may exist, either. You must disclose every relevant factor to your attorney. Otherwise he will be ambushed at the proceeding, and you will have wasted a lot of time, money and emotional energy.

Before your first consultation prepare a written list that succinctly places each of the factors in proper context. This list should reveal both the pros and cons of your given situation. We have found that when individuals are forced to take pencil in hand, they tend to focus better on the issue. It goes without saying that you should keep this list with you, jotting down new ideas as they may occur.

Let's assume that your attorney agrees that you have a case for modification. First of all, be prepared to pay a fee. Most lawyers will not take a post-divorce custody case without a rather large initial retainer that is paid in advance. The range can be anywhere from $1,500 to $25,000. You are now off and running. What can you expect?

The Preliminaries

All modification proceedings start with the petition. Indeed, the actual preliminary legal procedure is not so different from the one utilized when attempting to modify visitation rights. Take a moment to review our discussion in Chapter 12.

As with visitation, the petition will have to be verified. You must swear to the allegations concerning the circumstances that give rise to your demand that the existing custody arrangement be changed to your favor. Usually the petition provides just a general description of the factual elements that are relevant to your situation. However, sufficient detail must be present to indicate that an issue exists regarding your claim that modification is warranted. Your lawyer will obviously assist you with this document, but he or she will need sufficient data that demonstrates why you claim that a substantial or material change has occurred since the divorce. As discussed earlier, some states will require initial evidence that the child's actual physical or psychological health is seriously endangered.

The petition is then delivered to your ex. She will also retain a lawyer to protect the status quo. In rare instances, the custodial parent will cave in at this point, consenting to the change without putting up a fight. But even in those unique cases, the judge remains the final arbiter. It doesn't matter what the parents agree to; the inquiry is always focused on the best interests of the child.

Here is a case in point. Ralph petitioned for a change of custody in 1982. Upon receipt of the formal modification demand, Ralph's former spouse, Lena, immediately arranged to meet with her ex-husband.

After beating around the bush for a while, Lena didn't mince words. "I know that I haven't been around much lately. I had no idea that nursing school would take so much time. Maybe the children should live with you for a while."

"Are you saying that you agree to the change?" asked an incredulous Ralph.

"I guess so—at least temporarily. I don't really have much of a choice. No way do I want the children in the middle of all this, and Lord knows, I could use more time to study."

In his elation, Ralph chose not to hear the major thrust of Lena's decision. What she was saying was that she was in accord with a *temporary* modification. She never really came out and said that she thought the children should live with her ex permanently. In her mind, modification neatly solved the problem of her completing nursing school. It was a means to an end. Nothing more.

The next day, Ralph told his lawyer to withdraw the petition. By week's end, the children had moved into his residence. And approximately 2 years after that, Lena graduated nursing school with honors. She arranged another meeting with her ex. However, during this meeting, she advised her former husband that she was now ready to have the kids move back with her, that her new job at the hospital gave her plenty of time to supervise and see to their needs. Ralph refused and started the whole thing over again, serving Lena with legal papers for custody modification shortly thereafter.

Any guesses as to how this one turned out? I bet that we surprise many of you when we inform you that Ralph's modification demand was denied. His lawyer based almost the entire case on the parents' agreement. The judge had no trouble with disposing of this argument. At the outset, Justice Hortense Wagner stated that she did not agree that the parties had ever actually reached an understanding. She noted that Lena had specified that the custodial modification was to be only temporary. Justice Wagner further held that even had an agreement been reached, it was not controlling upon the court. The sole inquiry remained the children's best interests.

The lesson: when it comes to parental custody contracts, they are about as secure as chains made out of spaghetti. Even when parents consent to a change, a court may disregard such understanding when it believes that the changed custody arrangement does not serve the child's best interests. After all, the child was never a signatory to the "agreement" reached between his parents.

The Players

We will not tread on old ground. A custody modification proceeding does not differ substantially from a hearing involving visitation, or for that matter, any post-divorce proceeding. Evidence is introduced; burdens of proof are discharged. Arguments are made by opposing counsel; objections are either sustained or overruled.

However, it does bear repeating that in custody situations, there are more players on the field. Invariably, the court appoints a social worker or psychiatrist to interview the parents and the child. With increasing frequency, the court will also appoint a lawyer to represent the child's interests. It is believed that the child will be more willing to open up to an individual who is not connected with either of the parents. The use of outside professional experts is known as forensic investigation. Virtually all judges will attempt to obtain as much expert input as possible when it comes to determining how various factual elements affect the child's emotional, mental, psychological or physical well-being.

Some specific advice is in order:

- Never attempt to influence either directly or indirectly the court-appointed lawyer representing your child. This individual reports directly to the judge, and you can be sure that he or she will advise the court of any shenanigans on your part.
- Recognize from the outset that a custody modification hearing is emotionally debilitating. You must be prepared for anything. While the focus is supposed to be on the child, many lawyers attempt to break the other parent down by personal attack and innuendo.
- Understand that the judge will be interviewing your child in private. This approach is, by far, the most frequent procedure utilized by judges in custody modification proceedings. The prevailing view is that a child will speak more honestly if taken outside of the courtroom, away from the sight, sound and possible influence of the competing parents.
- Although you should expect the child to undergo the private interview process, do not attempt to prep your child or influence him or her in any way. We have spoken to many judges who tell us that in the privacy of their chambers a child who has been overly prepared is quite easy to spot. Within a few minutes, their answers get confused and unresponsive. The only result is that you will lose points for attempting to manipulate the proceeding.
- Never—but never—make a false statement under oath. As far as many judges are concerned, a deliberate misrepresentation of facts indicates that you are probably an unsuitable custodian for the child. In at least one case that we know of, the court based its decision to permit custody modification *solely* because the mother had lied about her relationship with another man. Don't take a chance; play it straight.

Concluding Remarks

We end this chapter by reemphasizing one of our first points. Do yourself a big favor and avoid custody modification proceedings. If at all possible, reach some kind of compromise with the custodial parent. No one really wins a custody battle. You may achieve your goal, but your child may be scarred for life. And your ex may be so emotionally battered that he or she gradually turns off to both of you; the child may end up actually losing a parent.

But if no other alternative remains, take the plunge. The waters will be cold; the undertow fierce. But the information contained in this chapter will be your lifeboat.

APPENDIX

STATE CHILD SUPPORT ENFORCEMENT OFFICES

ALABAMA

Director
Division of Child Support Activities
Bureau of Public Assistance
State Department of Pensions
and Security
64 North Union Street
Montgomery, Alabama 36130
(205) 261-2872

ALASKA

Administrator
Child Support Enforcement Agency
Department of Revenue
201 East 9th Avenue
Room 302
Anchorage, Alaska 99501
(907) 276-3441

ARIZONA

Program Administrator
Child Support Enforcement Administration
Department of Economic Security
P.O. Box 6123—Site Code 966C
Phoenix, Arizona 85005
(602) 255-3465

ARKANSAS

Director
Office of Child Support Enforcement
Arkansas Social Services
P.O. Box 3358
Little Rock, Arkansas 72203
(501) 371-2464

CALIFORNIA

Chief
Child Support Program
Management Branch
Department of Social Services
744 P Street
Sacramento, California 95814
(916) 323-8994

COLORADO

Director
Division of Child Support Enforcement
Department of Social Services
1575 Sherman Street—Room 423
Denver, Colorado 80203
(303) 866-2422

CONNECTICUT

Director
Child Support Division
Department of Human Resources
110 Bartholemew Avenue
Hartford, Connecticut 06115
(203) 566-3053

DELAWARE

Chief
Bureau of Child Support Enforcement
Department of Health & Social Services
P.O. Box 904
New Castle, Delaware 19720
(302) 571-3620

DISTRICT OF COLUMBIA

Chief
Office of Paternity & Child Support
Department of Human Services
425 "I" Street, N.W., 3rd Floor
Washington, D.C. 20001
(202) 724-5610

FLORIDA

Director
Office of Child Support Enforcement
Department of Health & Rehabilitative Services
1317 Winewood Boulevard
Tallahassee, Florida 32301
(904) 488-9900

GEORGIA

Director
Office of Child Support Recovery
State Department of Human Resources
P.O. Box 80000
Atlanta, Georgia 30357
(404) 894-5194

GUAM

Supervisor
Child Support Enforcement Unit
Department of Public Health & Social Services
Government of Guam
P.O. Box 2816
Agana, Guam 96910
(671) 734-2947

301

HAWAII

Director
Child Support Enforcement Agency
Suite 606
770 Kapiolani Boulevard
Honolulu, Hawaii 96813
(808) 548-5779

IDAHO

Chief
Bureau of Child Support Enforcement
Department of Health & Welfare
Statehouse Mail
Boise, Idaho 83720
(208) 334-4422

ILLINOIS

Chief
Bureau of Child Support
Department of Public Aid
316 South Second Street
Springfield, Illinois 62762
(217) 782-1366

INDIANA

Director
Child Support Enforcement Division
State Department of Public Welfare
141 S. Merridian Street, 4th Floor
Indianapolis, Indiana 46225
(317) 232-4894

IOWA

Director
Child Support Recovery Unit
Iowa Department of Social Services
Hoover Building—1st Floor
Des Moines, Iowa 50319
(515) 281-5580

KANSAS

Administrator
Child Support Enforcement Program
Department of Social Rehabilitation Services
2700 West Sixth
1st Floor, Perry Building
Topeka, Kansas 66606
(913) 296-3237

KENTUCKY

Director
Division of Child Support Enforcement
Department of Social Insurance
Cabinet for Human Resources
275 East Main Street
6th Floor East
Frankfort, Kentucky 40621
(502) 564-2285

LOUISIANA

Director
Support Enforcement Services
P. O. Box 44276
Baton Rouge, Louisiana 70804
(504) 342-4780

MAINE

Director
Support Enforcement and Location Unit
Bureau of Social Welfare
Department of Human Services
State House, Station 11
Augusta, Maine 04333
(207) 289-2886

MARYLAND

Executive Director
Child Support Enforcement Administration
Department of Human Resources
300 West Preston Street
5th Floor
Baltimore, Maryland 21201
(301) 383-4773

MASSACHUSETTS

Director
Child Support Enforcement Unit
Department of Public Welfare
600 Washington Street
Boston, Massachusetts 02111
(617) 727-7177

MICHIGAN

Director
Office of Child Support
Department of Social Services
300 South Capitol Avenue
Suite 621
Lansing, Michigan 48909
(517) 373-7570

MINNESOTA

Director
Office of Child Support
Department of Human Services
Space Center Building
444 Lafayette Road
St. Paul, Minnesota 55101
(612) 296-2499

MISSISSIPPI

Director
Child Support Division
State Department of Public Welfare
P.O. Box 352
515 East Amite Street
Jackson, Mississippi 39205
(601) 354-0341, ext. 503

MISSOURI

Administrator
Child Support Enforcement Unit
Division of Family Services
Department of Social Services
P.O. Box 88
Jefferson City, Missouri 65103
(314) 751-4301

MONTANA

Director
Investigation & Enforcement Bureau
Department of Revenue
Legal & Enforcement Division
Sam Mitchell Building
Room 465
Helena, Montana 59620
(406) 444-2846

NEBRASKA

Administrator
Child Support Enforcement Office
Department of Social Services
P.O. Box 95026
Lincoln, Nebraska 68509
(402) 471-3121, ext. 221

NEVADA

Chief
Child Support Enforcement
Nevada State Welfare Division
Department of Human Services
430 Jeanell Drive
Carson City, Nevada 89710
(702) 885-4744

NEW HAMPSHIRE

Administrator
Office of Child Support Enforcement Services
Division of Welfare
Health and Welfare Building
Hazen Drive
Concord, New Hampshire 03301
(603) 271-4426

NEW JERSEY

Director
Child Support and Paternity Unit
Department of Human Services
CN 716
Trenton, New Jersey 08625
(609) 633-6268

NEW MEXICO

Chief
Child Support Enforcement Bureau
Department of Human Services
P.O. Box 2348—PERA Building
Santa Fe, New Mexico 87503
(505) 827-4230

NEW YORK

Director
Office of Child Support Enforcement
New York State Department of Social Services
P.O. Box 14, 1 Commerce Plaza
Albany, New York 12260
(518) 474-9081

NORTH CAROLINA

Chief
Child Support Enforcement Section
Division of Social Services
Department of Human Resources
433 N. Harrington Street
Raleigh, North Carolina 27603-1393
(919) 733-4120

NORTH DAKOTA

Administrator
Child Support Enforcement Agency
North Dakota Department of Human Services
State Capitol
Bismarck, North Dakota 58505
(701) 224-3582

OHIO

Chief
Bureau of Child Support
Ohio Department of Human Services
State Office Tower
30 East Broad Street
Columbus, Ohio 43215
(614) 466-3233

OKLAHOMA

Administrator
Attention: Division of Child Support
Department of Human Services
P.O. Box 25352
Oklahoma City, Oklahoma 73125
(405) 424-5871

OREGON

Child Support Program
Department of Human Resources
Adult & Family Services Division
P.O. Box 14506
Salem, Oregon 97309
(503) 378-6093

PENNSYLVANIA

Director
Child Support Programs
Bureau of Claim Settlement
Department of Public Welfare
P.O. Box 8018
Harrisburg, Pennsylvania 17105
(717) 783-1779

PUERTO RICO

Director
Child Support Enforcement Program
Department of Social Services
P.O. Box 11398
Fernandez Juncos Station
Santurce, Puerto Rico 00910
(809) 722-2409

RHODE ISLAND

Chief Supervisor
Bureau of Family Support
Department of Social & Rehabilitative Services
77 Dorance Street
Providence, Rhode Island 02903
(401) 277-2409

SOUTH CAROLINA

Director
Division of Child Support
Public Assistance Division
Bureau of Public Assistance & Field Operations
Department of Social Services
P.O. Box 1520
Columbus, South Carolina 29202
(803) 758-8860

SOUTH DAKOTA

Program Administrator
Office of Child Support Enforcement
Department of Social Services
700 Illinois Street
Pierre, South Dakota 57501-2291
(605) 773-3641

TENNESSEE

Director
Child Support Services
Department of Human Services
111–19 7th Avenue North
5th Floor
Nashville, Tennessee 37203
(615) 741-1820

TEXAS

Director
Child Support Enforcement Branch
Texas Department of Human Resources
P.O. Box 2960
Austin, Texas 78769
(512) 450-3011

UTAH

Director
Office Recovery Services
Department of Social Services
P.O. Box 15400
3195 South Main Street
Salt Lake City, Utah 84115
(801) 486-1812

VERMONT

Director
Child Support Division
Department of Social Welfare
103 South Main Street
Waterbury, Vermont 05676
(802) 241-2868

VIRGIN ISLANDS

Director
Paternity & Child Support Program
Department of Law
P.O. Box 1074
Christiansted
St. Croix, Virgin Islands 00820
(809) 773-8240

VIRGINIA

Director
Division of Support Enforcement Program
Department of Social Services
8007 Discovery Drive
Richmond, Virginia 23288
(804) 281-9108

WASHINGTON

Chief
Office of Support Enforcement
Department of Social & Health Services
P.O. Box 9162-FU-11
Olympia, Washington 98504
(206) 459-6481

WEST VIRGINIA

Director
Office of Child Support Enforcement
Department of Human Services
1900 Washington Street, East
Charleston, West Virginia 25305
(304) 348-3780

WISCONSIN

Director
Bureau of Child Support
Division of Economic Assistance
18 South Thornton Avenue
Madison, Wisconsin 53708
(608) 266-0528

WYOMING

Director
Child Support Enforcement Section
Division of Public Assistance & Social Services
State Department of Health & Social Services
Hathaway Building
Cheyenne, Wyoming 82002
(307) 777-6083

REGIONAL OFFICES OF THE OFFICE OF CHILD SUPPORT ENFORCEMENT

REGION I— CONNECTICUT, MAINE, MASSACHUSETTS, NEW HAMPSHIRE, RHODE ISLAND, VERMONT

OCSE Regional Representative
150 Causeway Street
Room 1300
Boston, Massachusets 02114
(617) 223-1138

REGION II— NEW YORK, NEW JERSEY, PUERTO RICO, VIRGIN ISLANDS

OCSE Regional Representative
Federal Building, Room 4016
26 Federal Plaza
New York, New York 10278
(212) 596-4021

REGION III— DELAWARE, MARYLAND, PENNSYLVANIA, VIRGINIA, WEST VIRGINIA, DISTRICT OF COLUMBIA

OCSE Regional Representative
3535 Market Street
Philadelphia, Pennsylvania 19101
(215) 596-1396

REGION IV— ALABAMA, FLORIDA, GEORGIA, KENTUCKY, MISSISSIPPI, NORTH CAROLINA, SOUTH CAROLINA, TENNESSEE

OCSE Regional Representative
101 Marietta Tower—Suite 2102
Atlanta, Georgia 30323
(404) 221-2180

REGION V— ILLINOIS, INDIANA, MICHIGAN, MINNESOTA, OHIO, WISCONSIN

OCSE Regional Representative
10 West Jackson Boulevard, 4th Floor
Chicago, Illinois 60604
(312) 353-5415

REGION VI— ARKANSAS, LOUISIANA, NEW MEXICO, OKLAHOMA, TEXAS

OCSE Regional Representative
1100 Commerce Street—Room 8A20
Dallas, Texas 75242
(214) 767-3749

REGION VII— IOWA, KANSAS, MISSOURI, NEBRASKA

OCSE Regional Representative
601 East 12th Street—Room 515
Kansas City, Missouri 64106
(816) 374-3584

REGION VIII— COLORADO, MONTANA, NORTH DAKOTA, SOUTH DAKOTA, UTAH, WYOMING

OCSE Regional Representative
Federal Office Building, Room 1137
19th and Stout Streets
Denver, Colorado 80294
(303) 837-5661

REGION IX— ARIZONA, CALIFORNIA, HAWAII, NEVADA, GUAM

OCSE Regional Representative
50 United Nations Plaza, Room 338
San Francisco, California 94102
(415) 556-5176

REGION X— ALASKA, IDAHO, OREGON, WASHINGTON

OCSE Regional Representative
Third and Broad Building
2901 Third Avenue, Mail Stop 415
Seattle, Washington 98121
(206) 442-0943

STATE-BY-STATE LISTING OF COURTS FOR POST-DIVORCE PROCEDURES

State	Court Name	Comments
Alabama	Circuit Court	County Court may also be used
Alaska	Superior Court	
Arizona	Superior Court	
Arkansas	Circuit Court	Chancery Court may also be used
California	Superior Court	
Colorado	District Court	In Denver, the Juvenile Court has original jurisdiction of custody and child support hearings
Connecticut	Superior Court	
Delaware	Family Court	
Florida	Circuit Court	
Georgia	Superior Court	
Hawaii	Family Court	

Idaho	District Court	Magistrate Division has jurisdiction over all child-related proceedings
Illinois	Circuit Court	
Indiana	Superior Court	Circuit Court may also be used; BUT Juvenile Court must be used for all child custody and support proceedings
Iowa	District Court	
Kansas	District Court	
Kentucky	Circuit Court	
Louisiana	District Court	Juvenile Court and the Family Court of East Baton Rouge have exclusive jurisdiction over non-support cases
Maine	District Court	Probate Court may also be used
Maryland	Circuit Court	
Massachusetts	Superior Court	Probate Court may also be used
Michigan	Circuit Court	
Minnesota	District Court	Family Court division of the County Court may also be used
Mississippi	Circuit Court	Chancery Court may also be used
Missouri	Circuit Court	In Hannibal county, the Court of Common Pleas may also be used
Montana	District Court	
Nebraska	District Court	Juvenile Court has jurisdiction over children under 18 who lack proper support
Nevada	District Court	
New Hampshire	Superior Court	
New Jersey	Superior Court	County Court may also be used; Juvenile and Domestic Relations Court has jurisdiction over child welfare and custody matters
New Mexico	District Court	
New York	Supreme Court	Family Court also has jurisdiction over support and custody cases

North Carolina	Superior Court	District Court also has jurisdiction over child custody and support cases
North Dakota	District Court	
Ohio	Court of Common Pleas	
Oklahoma	District Court	
Oregon	Circuit Court	
Pennsylvania	Court of Common Pleas	
Rhode Island	Superior Court	Family Court may also be used
South Carolina	Circuit Court	Family, Juvenile and Domestic Relations Courts exist in larger counties; Probate Court has jurisdiction over custody and support cases in the other counties
South Dakota	Circuit Court	
Tennessee	Circuit Court	County Courts may be used in certain counties; Juvenile Court has jurisdiction over custody cases
Texas	District Court	Domestic Relations and Juvenile Courts may also be used
Utah	District Court	Juvenile Court has jurisdiction over custody cases
Vermont	Superior Court	
Virginia	Circuit Court	Juvenile and Domestic Relations Court has jurisdiction over custody and support cases
Washington	Superior Court	
West Virginia	Circuit Court	
Wisconsin	Circuit Court	County Court may also be used
Wyoming	District Court	